Symbolic Power, Politics, and Intellectuals

Symbolic Power, Politics, and Intellectuals

The Political Sociology of Pierre Bourdieu

DAVID L. SWARTZ

THE UNIVERSITY OF CHICAGO PRESS   CHICAGO AND LONDON

David L. Swartz is assistant professor of sociology at Boston University. He is the author of *Culture & Power: The Sociology of Pierre Bourdieu* and coeditor with Vera L. Zolberg of *After Bourdieu: Influence, Critique, Elaboration.*

The University of Chicago Press, Chicago 60637
The University of Chicago Press, Ltd., London
© 2013 by The University of Chicago
All rights reserved. Published 2013.
Printed in the United States of America

22 21 20 19 18 17 16 15 14 13   1 2 3 4 5

ISBN-13: 978-0-226-92500-4 (cloth)
ISBN-13: 978-0-226-92501-1 (paper)
ISBN-13: 978-0-226-92502-8 (e-book)
ISBN-10: 0-226-92500-5 (cloth)
ISBN-10: 0-226-92501-3 (paper)
ISBN-10: 0-226-92502-1 (e-book)

Library of Congress Cataloging-in-Publication Data

Swartz, David, 1945–
    Symbolic power, politics, and intellectuals : the political sociology of Pierre Bourdieu / David L. Swartz.
        pages. cm.
    Includes bibliographical references and index.
    ISBN 978-0-226-92500-4 (cloth : alk. paper) — ISBN 0-226-92500-5 (cloth : alk. paper) — ISBN 978-0-226-92501-1 (pbk. : alk. paper) — ISBN 0-226-92501-3 (pbk. : alk. paper) — ISBN 978-0-226-92502-8 (e-book) — ISBN 0-226-92502-1 (e-book)   1. Sociology. 2. Political sociology. 3. State, The. 4. Power (Social sciences). 5. Bourdieu, Pierre, 1930–2002—Political and social views.   I. Title.
    HM585.S93 2013
    301—dc23

                                                            2012023407

Contents

Preface and Acknowledgments

The multifaceted work of Pierre Bourdieu, clearly one of the greatest post–World War II sociologists, has inspired much research in a wide variety of areas, such as culture, taste, education, theory, and stratification. Largely neglected, however, are the underlying political analysis in Bourdieu's sociology, his political project for sociology, and his own political activism. Yet the analysis of power, particularly in its cultural forms, stands at the heart of Bourdieu's sociology. Bourdieu challenges the commonly held view that symbolic power is simply "symbolic." His sociology sensitizes us to the subtle and influential ways that cultural resources and symbolic categories and classifications interweave prevailing power arrangements into everyday life practices. Indeed, cultural resources and processes help constitute and maintain social hierarchies. And these form the bedrock of political life.

Moreover, Bourdieu offers not only a sociology of politics but also a politics of sociology. He assigns to sociology as science a critical debunking role of existing relations of domination. Sociology is not only science; it is also a form of political engagement, or, in his words, "scholarship with commitment" for a more just and democratic life.

This interconnected vision for sociology as science and sociology as political engagement is not well understood, nor is the way this vision found formulation, elaboration, and modification in Bourdieu's own life, work, and political engagements. I wrote this book to explain this vision and evaluate its potential for contributing to a better understanding and a more democratic ordering of political life.

That power stands at the core of Bourdieu's sociology became clear to me as a student in Paris in the early 1970s, when I first became acquainted with Bourdieu's work, followed his seminar, and met a number of colleagues and students affiliated with his Center for European Sociology. The theme of power guided the way I presented his work in *Culture and Power* (University of Chicago Press, 1997).

* * *

Power also stands at the heart of political sociology. It was in preparing a paper for the 2001 Nordic Governance Summit at the Center for Research in Public Organization and Management, Department of Political Science, University of Copenhagen, that I started to compare Bourdieu's thinking on power, politics, and the state to other political perspectives. Then I began to realize that Bourdieu could be read as a political sociologist. That conference presentation led to the publication of "Pierre Bourdieu's Political Sociology and Governance Perspectives" in *Governance as Social and Political Communication*, edited by Henrik P. Bang (Manchester: Manchester University Press, 2003). I wish to thank Henrik Bang for his invitation to participate in that conference, which in hindsight proved to be a starting point for this book.

The theme of Bourdieu's sociology of politics and his politics of sociology took shape in my thinking over several years through numerous conversations and presentations at a variety of professional gatherings. In May 2003 I gave a lecture titled "The Politics of Symbolic Power: On Pierre Bourdieu's Politics, His Analysis of Power, and His Own Political Activism" at the City University of New York Graduate Center. In November 2003 I helped convene the Paris group (Erik Neveu, Daniel Gaxie, Michel Offrelé, and Niilo Kauppi) for the Bourdieu Workshop, on Bourdieu as a political sociologist. That group planted the seeds for what would eventually become the Political Sociology Standing Group (http://www3.unil.ch/wpmu/ecpr-polsoc/) within the European Consortium for Political Research (ECPR). My presentation at the September 2005 Budapest meeting of the ECPR led to the publication of "Pierre Bourdieu and North American Sociology: Why He Doesn't Fit In but Should" (*French Politics* 4 [2006]: 84–99). I want to thank Elizabeth Silva and Alain Warde for their invitation to present a paper at the Cultural Analysis: The Legacy of Bourdieu symposium at the Open University, Milton Keynes, UK, July 11–12, 2007. This presentation led to the publication of "Pierre Bourdieu's Political Sociology and Public Sociology" in *Cultural Analysis and Bourdieu's Legacy: Settling Accounts and Developing Alternatives*, edited by Elizabeth Silva and Alain Warde (London: Routledge, 2010). My thanks to Jessé Souza for the invitation to present "How to Research with Bourdieu's Master Concepts" at the International Seminar of Contemporary Theory called "Social Conflict at the Heart and Periphery of Capitalism: Bourdieu as a Starting Point" (University of Juiz de Fora, Brazil, September 3–5, 2008). A special thanks to Uwe Bittlingmayer for inviting me to give the lecture "Bourdieu and the Sociology of Politics" at the "Was tun mit dem Erbe?" conference at the University of Bielefeld, Germany, October 2–3, 2009. My thanks also to Rebecca Adler-Nissen for the invitation to participate in the "Bourdieu in International Relations" workshop at the Center for Advanced Security Theory, Department of Political Science, University of Copenhagen (December 2010). Finally, special thanks to Stefan Bernhard and Christian Schmidt-Wellenburg for their invitation to present at the Research Program of Field Analysis Conference, University of Potsdam, Germany, May 26, 2011, which led to the publication of "Zu einer Bourdieu'schen Analyse der Politik" in *Feldanalyse als Forschungsprogramm 1: Der programmatische Kern*, edited by Stefan Bernhard and Christian Schmidt-Wellenburg (Wiesbaden: VS, 2012). Portions of these presentations and publications figure into some of the chapters in this book, though elaborated significantly.

On the topic of Bourdieu and politics, I have benefited from fruitful conversations and e-mail exchanges with many individuals and want to thank in particular the following: Afrânio Garcia, Virginie Guiraudon, Julian Go, David Karen, Gérard Mauger, Frank Poupeau, Gisèle Sapiro, Rhys Williams, and Vera Zolberg. Particular thanks go to Niilo Kauppi for numerous conversations and e-mail exchanges about Bourdieu over the last several years.

Several colleagues read portions of earlier drafts of chapters; I want to acknowledge the helpful comments of Steve Brint, Michael Burawoy, Kevin Dougherty, Niilo Kauppi, and David Karen. Ted Murphy kindly read an earlier version of the entire manuscript and offered numerous helpful suggestions. I am particularly indebted to Craig Calhoun and Tom Medvitz, who reviewed the manuscript for the University of Chicago Press. They carefully assessed each chapter and offered many helpful observations and some useful corrections. Therese Boyd skillfully copyedited the manuscript, and Ruth Goring managed the editorial process with great care. I thank both of them.

Without the support of that legendary social sciences editor Doug Mitchell, publishing this second book with the University of Chicago Press would not have been possible. I thank him. I also thank Tim McGovern, who always responded to my queries.

Finally, a big thanks to Lisa, my wife, and our children, Elena and Daniel, for their unwavering forbearance and love.

CHAPTER ONE

Reading Bourdieu as a Political Sociologist

Power is a central organizing feature of all social life. Power finds expression in many valued resources that become objects of struggle. Power also finds symbolic expression in cultural forms and practices that legitimate the unequal distribution of valued resources. And power concentrates in particular arenas of struggle for control of the social order. So contends Pierre Bourdieu, arguably one of the greatest post–World War II sociologists.

The multifaceted work of Pierre Bourdieu has been widely discussed, if not always understood, outside of France. All of his major books have received extensive attention and discussion. Many sociologists are by now familiar with most of his principal concepts and arguments. He has inspired much work in the sociology of culture, education, theory, taste, and stratification, but received very little attention in political sociology and practically none in political science. Neglected by most observers is the underlying political analysis in Bourdieu's work, both his sociology of politics and his underlying political project.[1] Bourdieu is often read as a theorist, a sociologist of culture or education, or an anthropologist, but only seldom as a political sociologist. This is particularly the case in the United States though generally true in Great Britain and Europe as well (Voutat

---

1. Alford and Friedland (1985), for example, situate Raymond Boudon in the pluralist camp but say nothing of Bourdieu. Some notable exceptions include Bon and Schemeil 1980; Calhoun 1993, 2005b; Caro 1980; Fritsch 2000; Grenfell 2005; Lee 1998; Pinto 1998; Robbins 1991; Steinmetz 1999a; Topper 2001. The work of Loïc Wacquant (1992b, 2004, 2005b) and Jeremy Lane (2000, 2006) in particular highlight the political significance of Bourdieu's work.

2002). Yet arguably Bourdieu was also a political sociologist.[2] Bourdieu was centrally concerned with power and saw his work as an expression of political struggle.[3] However, his work did not follow the usual categories or objects of investigation commonly found in political sociology and particularly in political science. Nevertheless, Bourdieu's life and work fundamentally concerned power and politics.

Bourdieu's work on politics has been neglected by political sociologists and political scientists alike because he did not write books or articles that fit directly within the disciplinary contours of the subfield of political sociology or the academic discipline of political science. Indeed, Bourdieu did not devote much attention to political parties, voting, lobbying, electoral campaigns, government administration, legislatures, or social movements. Except for the act of delegating political power, Bourdieu did not accord much attention to political processes, such as decisionmaking, coalition building, or leadership selection.[4] Bourdieu's sociology attempts a broader sweep of political issues than those delineated by the boundaries of these

2. Wacquant (2005c, 10) also observes that "Pierre Bourdieu has rarely been read as a political sociologist." Wacquant's (2005b) edited collection of papers fruitfully illustrates how Bourdieu can be read this way.

Of course not all observers share this view that there is a political sociology in Bourdieu. Take, for example, Lahouai Addi (2002), who argues that the strong anthropological emphasis beginning with Bourdieu's early work in Algeria, particularly the emphasis on symbolic violence, prevails to such an extent that it leaves Bourdieu without a sufficient appreciation of the public-private distinction and without a conceptual basis for treating politics nonreductively or the state as an autonomous institution—hence without a political sociology. I do not share Addi's assessment and find it to be a reductive reading of Bourdieu's later work. Bourdieu's view of fields and the state—research and conceptualization developed after his Algerian work—are much too beholden to Max Weber's thinking on spheres, the state, and the multidimensionality of power to reduce to just an anthropological concern with the symbolic. I examine Bourdieu's view of fields and the state in chapters 3 and 5.

3. Wacquant (2005a, 1) calls him "sociologically political" to capture the idea of an intensely political person, not in the conventional sense of one who runs for office, advises political leadership, or mobilizes within political organizations, but meaning someone who takes a critical, analytical, disenchanting stance toward politics as a sociologist.

4. In contrast to Alain Touraine (1968), Bourdieu devoted little attention to social movements, including the May 1968 student movement that was analyzed by virtually every French sociologist at the time (e.g., Boudon 1970). Bourdieu's (Bourdieu 1988c; Bourdieu, Boltanski, and Maldidier 1971) observations on May 1968 come later and stress the effects of academic professionalization and social stratification rather than the dynamics of a social movement. His analysis in *Homo Academicus* (1988b) is more of a structuralist mapping of the field of Parisian university professoriate than an examination of processes operative during the May '68 events.

academic disciplines. Indeed, I argue that Bourdieu's sociology makes no distinction between the sociological approach to the study of the social world and the study of political power. Bourdieu sees *all* of sociology as fundamentally dealing with power. He sees power as a central organizing dimension of all social life. Power is not an independent domain that can be separated from culture or economics but a force that pervades all human relations. Politics concern the structures and exercise of power; the sociology of politics must reveal that fundamental dimension of social relations regardless of level of analysis or substantive area. Bourdieu's sociology of symbolic power and violence highlights that political dimension of all social life. He therefore rejects the validity of a substantive area of investigation specialized in the study of only the power dimension of social life. He rejects the traditional academic division of labor between sociology, political sociology, and political science.[5]

This book aims to offer a richer understanding of Bourdieu's life and work to those who until now have focused on particular aspects of Bourdieu's sociology without considering the concern for power and politics that unifies his endeavors. In many instances, this deeper purpose of Bourdieu's concepts and sociological investigations has been lost as selective appropriations of his work have been fit into subfields and conceptual arguments of mainstream academic social science. This is particularly the case for his work on culture and education where elements of his approach, such as cultural capital, have been abstracted from the critical political perspective he invested in his work. One purpose of this book is to correct these shortcomings. Chapters 2 and 3 illuminate this deeper mission of Bourdieu's sociology.

Relatedly, there is an ongoing concern from his early work to his later writings with the relationship of sociology-as-science to politics and the role of the critical social scientist in the public arena. This concern is too frequently missed in the selective use of his concepts and arguments within conventional sociology. Yet this selective academic disciplinary appropriation from Bourdieu's work frequently misses another overriding concern for Bourdieu: what Robert Lynd (1986 [1939]) classically phrased as "knowledge for what?" Bourdieu thought and acted politically throughout

---

5. Indeed, as Bon and Schemeil (1980, 1203) point out, Bourdieu refuses to grant political science the status of a genuine social science. He considers it a form of practical knowledge designed to assist professional politicians in advancing their interests within the political field. He calls it a "false science" in that it legitimates this political practice as ostensibly scientific.

his life and work, and this is insufficiently appreciated by many who draw selectively from him. We see this concern present in his choice of research objects (he often picked topics to have a political impact), in his critical defense of the intellectual autonomy of sociology, and in his public interventions, particularly later in his life. As Bourdieu (1988c) himself puts it, "to think politics without thinking politically" represents the challenge he saw in offering a sociology that "intervened" not as advocacy but as a critical force in public life. Understanding Bourdieu's view of the relationship of social science to politics will appeal to those interested in recent debates over public sociology. Chapters 6 and 7 explore Bourdieu's vision and practice of the political vocation of sociology.

Perhaps most important, the book also aims to show the relevance of Bourdieu's thinking and work to readers with a particular interest in political sociology. Bourdieu has much to offer to political sociology, particularly in his analysis of symbolic power and his challenges to received views of state power. Chapters 1, 4, 5, and 8 identify his most salient contributions for the sociological analysis of politics. Finally, the book also offers critical evaluation of central tensions in Bourdieu's thought and work on the relationship between sociology and politics.

Though he is not known as a political sociologist, Bourdieu's analysis of power, particularly in the form of domination, stands at the heart of his sociology. He proposes a theory that centrally includes the concepts of *symbolic power*, *violence*, and *capital* that stress the active role that symbolic forms play as resources that both constitute and maintain social hierarchies. Bourdieu's perspective challenges the commonly held view that symbolic power is simply "symbolic." His sociology sensitizes us to the more subtle and influential forms of power that operate particularly through the cultural resources and symbolic categories and classifications that interweave prevailing institutional arrangements into everyday life practices. Moreover, he identifies a wide variety of valued resources beyond sheer economic interests that function as power resources and that he calls forms of *capital*, such as social capital and cultural capital. Furthermore, individuals and groups struggle over the very definition and distribution of these capitals in distinct power arenas that Bourdieu calls *fields*. He sees concentrations of various capitals in particular arenas of struggle, such as the *field of power*, the *political field*, and the *state*. Key to Bourdieu's understanding is how power resources (*capitals*) and field struggles over them become legitimated (*misrecognized*) as something other than power relations. The struggle for symbolic power in the political field for gaining access to state power is particularly salient. In addition, he examines critically how leadership representation and delegated authority "dispossess" individuals of their effective voice in political life. Finally, Bourdieu offers not only a sociology of politics but also a politics of sociology. Sociology as science can challenge a key foundation of power relations—their legitimation—and thereby open up the possibility for social transformation.

One finds in his work a vision for what he thinks the practice of social science can do for democratic life and a critical role he assigns to social scientists as intellectuals (Swartz 1997, 247–66; Wacquant 2004, 9–12). There is, therefore, a political project in his sociology that for the most part goes overlooked in its reception outside of France. At the time of his death in 2002 Bourdieu was the leading public intellectual and social scientist in France, and perhaps in Europe as well, of the antiglobalization movement (Swartz 2003a). But less well understood is how political concerns shaped his life and work from the very beginning in Algeria. This book highlights these political sociological aspects of Bourdieu's life and work. Readers interested in how Bourdieu's work can inspire specific types of political analysis will find later in this chapter a selected list of promising contributions.

This introductory chapter makes the argument that Bourdieu can be fruitfully read as a political sociologist. It offers a selective survey of this kind of reading of Bourdieu in other countries. It also suggests a number of reasons why American political sociology and political science have been slow in seeing the relevance of Bourdieu's work for understanding political life. And it identifies some new directions in North American political sociology that are more open to the promising insights of Bourdieu's thinking for political analysis. Chapter 2 gives an overview of the key conceptual tools Bourdieu uses in his thinking and research on power and domination. How does Bourdieu conceptualize power as domination? Forms of capital, power fields, symbolic power, violence, and capital will be briefly introduced and then explored more fully in later chapters. This chapter situates Bourdieu's thinking relative to dominant foci in political sociology and suggests some implications for the analysis of power and politics. Chapter 3 examines Bourdieu's key conceptual tools of capital and field to analyze power. Political practices, as all practices, occur using strategic resources (*capitals*) in structured arenas of conflict that Bourdieu calls *fields*. Particular attention is given to the field of power, political capital, and the political field.

Chapter 4 presents Bourdieu's thinking on symbolic power as a form of domination that elaborates and modifies Max Weber's emphasis on the legitimation of power. Bourdieu proposes a theory of symbolic power, violence, and capital that stresses the active role that symbolic forms play as resources that reflect, constitute, maintain, and change social hierarchies. While contested, symbolic power is also naturalized and misrecognized as taken-for-granted inequality so that it constitutes a form of violence. Symbolic power plays a central role in the political field particularly through the processes of representation, delegation, and dispossession that limit broad participation in democratic life. In chapter 4 Bourdieu's conceptual language of symbolic power, symbolic violence, and symbolic capital are distinguished, explored, and evaluated. In modern differentiated societies, Bourdieu argues that symbolic power tends to be centered in one key institution—the state.

Chapter 5 explores Bourdieu's view of the state as an extension of his sociology of culture, particularly his conceptualization of symbolic power, classification struggles, and his field analysis. It examines how Bourdieu understands the origins of the modern state, its leadership and ideology, and situates his view of the state relative to his concept of the field of power. His emphasis on the symbolic power of the state and its internal divisions as a field of struggle over statist capital marks out a distinctive position relative to the prevailing unitary, state-centric views in political sociology that stress the physically coercive character and material resources of state power. The chapter concludes with an evaluation of Bourdieu's thinking about the state, including comparisons to other leading theoretical perspectives on the state.

Bourdieu offers not only a sociology of politics but also a politics of sociology. He assigns to sociology as science a critical debunking role of symbolic power and violence. Because of its critical nature, sociology as science is also a form of political engagement. Doing sociology is doing politics in a different way. Chapter 6 examines Bourdieu's normative vision for the political vocation of the sociologist. His model for intellectual political activism is compared with several other views, notably Michael Burawoy's advocacy for a public sociology. Chapter 7 explores how Bourdieu implemented his vision in various public interventions during his career, beginning with his decisive experience in wartorn Algeria during the 1950s. It examines the process by which Bourdieu both produced a prodigious scholarly record and became near the end of his career the leading European public intellectual at the head of the antiglobalization movement that emerged in France and other Western European countries in the 1990s. It illustrates and evaluates how Bourdieu pursued his "scholarship with commitment" strategy. And chapter 8 identifies key features of Bourdieu's thinking about social change, revisits his understanding of the relationship between sociology and politics, and explores his normative vision for democratic politics.

Bourdieu in France and Europe

Bourdieu's work has been enormously influential in France. Many of his ideas have shaped the general sociological environment there so they are taught, referenced, criticized, or simply assumed as the way to think sociologically about issues. His influence on political sociology and particularly political science, however, has been more uneven. Philippe Corcuff (1998) refers to the "bourdieusian school" in French political science. I think the term *school* is too strong if that suggests a geographical location or close network of political analysts. Outside of the networks of scholars gravitating around *Actes de la Recherches en Sciences Sociales* and *Raisons d'Agir*, two very productive publications directly influenced by Bourdieu, his influence among French scholars of politics is broad but fragmented, and often more one of selective inspiration than faithful application of his full research program.[6]

Certainly lines of influence can be identified. Daniel Gaxie (1978, 1990), Erik Neveu (2005), and Michel Offerlé (1987), themselves students during the sixties and now university professors, in their own works offer notable illustrations of Bourdieu's impact on political analysis in that country.[7] Today many of their students continue to draw inspiration from Bourdieu. That influence takes the form often of challenging traditional academic compartmentalization of knowledge by opening up traditional political analytical concerns to sociological and historical considerations (Voutat 2002, 104). However, Bourdieu's influence in France has been highly segmented, largely ignored, or sharply opposed by many of Bourdieu's own generation of French political scientists, particularly among those

6. One can also see Bourdieu's influence in *Politix*.

7. Other influential books in France include Blondiaux 1998; Cohen, Lacroix, and Riutort 2009; Dobry 1986; Dulong 2010; Favre 1990; Garrigou 1992; Lacroix and Lagroye 1992; Lagroye 2002; Pudal 1989.

holding positions in the Institutes of Political Studies (Instituts d'études politiques). One can see the influence in the work of a few individuals in certain university departments and a few political studies institutes but no single academic program as a whole in France today would be considered strongly Bourdieusian. For example, some Bourdieusian influence can be found at the University of Paris I (Pantheon-Sorbonne), the University of Amiens and of Lille, and the political studies institutes in Strasbourg, Toulouse, and Rennes. While a Bourdieusian presence is more likely found in French university political sociology than in political science, there are anomalies. The University of Strasbourg sociology, for example, has little Bourdieusian presence whereas the Strasbourg Institute of Political Studies (particularly within the Groupe de sociologie politique européenne— European Political Sociology Group) has considerable.

In general, Bourdieu's influence on French political science has been strikingly less pronounced, indeed strongly resisted for the most part in the French institutes of political studies, particularly at the flagship Paris Institute of Political Studies. Traditionally, the political studies institutes focused on public administration offering little political sociology; however, some of that resistance was no doubt due to the fact that Bourdieu himself did not hold political science and the French institutes of political studies in high esteem. He called political science a "false science" and a "rationalization" project in which its practitioners offer rational tools for political professionals rather than engaging in genuine scientific analysis.[8] Bourdieu's antagonistic relationship with the Paris Institute of Political Studies was legendary, though in recent years that has been changing as some researchers from that institute draw inspiration from Bourdieu and take up beyond traditional electoral sociology a broader range of sociological considerations, such as racism, anti-Semitism, the media, and right-wing political movements.[9]

---

8. Bourdieu's sharp criticism of political science reflects in part his philosophical training in École Normale Supérieure and the traditional antagonism between that academically very selective institution and the less academically but socially more selective political studies institutes that train future state administrators and political leaders in France. However, Bourdieu is not alone among famous sociologists of his generation to take this kind of position. Tom Bottomore (1993), who wrote a widely regarded statement on the key concerns of political sociology, as well does not grant political science a particular theoretical vantage point.

9. Another sign of growing recognition of Bourdieu's work: in November 2010 the Paris Institute of Political Studies hosted an international conference in recognition of Bourdieu's landmark work *Distinction*, thirty years after its 1979 publication.

Bourdieu's influence beyond France in Europe is more diffuse but increasingly coming to represent an interesting critical alternative to mainstream scholarship in sociology, political sociology, international relations, administrative studies, and European studies. Governance perspectives, which stress the emergence of new local, regional, and more individualized expressions of self-government than found in centralized welfare states, have received considerable attention in political thought in recent years, particularly in Western Europe, and there are some points of convergence yet sharp differences between Bourdieu and governance thinking (Bang 2003; Swartz 2003b). While governance perspectives, as has been noted by numerous observers (Stoker 1998), remain an eclectic orientation designating a great variety of descriptive, analytical, and theoretical concerns, some general comparisons can be made. Bourdieu was *not* a governance theorist; he did not use the language of governance. Governance theorists, particularly those advocating for a cultural governance, are more likely to draw inspiration from the later writings of Foucault than from Bourdieu (e.g., Dean 2003). Bourdieu does not cast his work within disciplinary boundaries of political sociology, political science, or administrative science where the idea of governance is most widely discussed. Indeed, Bourdieu rejects much of what is advocated under a governance perspective, particularly where normative claims are made about how public policy should be implemented. He, for example, is sharply critical of privatizing public enterprises and services and decreasing the role of the state, policy preferences favored by many governance theorists (Merrien 1998, 59). In later years Bourdieu (1998d) became a sharp public critic of neoliberalism, decrying the increasing reliance on market mechanisms for social welfare provision. The focus of Bourdieu's work is on power and domination, particularly the more subtle forms of cultural power, and not on the concerns of efficiency in political decisionmaking that seem to drive the governance imagination.

Nonetheless, there are points of overlap. Bourdieu devoted considerable attention to the crisis of education and social service provision in France (e.g., Bourdieu 1998c). He therefore shares with many governance theorists the concern that modern welfare societies face a severe crisis. He was sharply critical of French state leadership for pursuing its own particular interests to the neglect of broader social interests, particularly where the lower social classes are concerned. He wanted, as do many governance theorists, to render public services more democratic. Bourdieu's approach to the study of power in terms of fields of conflict rather than focusing exclusive attention on particular institutions, such as the centralized state, gives a relational and multicentered analytical view of power that overlaps to some extent with concerns of governance thinkers.

The influence of Bourdieu's thinking on political sociology can be seen in various European countries, such as Germany where the impact is particularly strong even if his influence has been greater in cultural theory and stratification analysis (Bernhard 2011; Bernhard and Schmidt-Wellenburg 2012a, 2012b; Bittlingmayer et al. 2002; Gemperle 2009; Vester 2003; Vester et al. 1993, 2001). He visited several times, gave lectures, and participated in public political debates. All of his key works are translated into German in large part due to the remarkable efforts of the Swiss sociologist Franz Schultheis (2007).

A further indicator of growing influence of Bourdieu's work on political analysis beyond France can be seen in the European Consortium for Political Research conferences, which, beginning in Budapest in 2005, have regularly had paper presentations drawing from Bourdieu's work, particularly in sessions organized by the Standing Group for Political Sociology.[10] Through conferences and publications Bourdieu's influence can be seen as a growing critical alternative to mainstream international relations and European studies.[11] Bourdieu's concept of field is now a widely used conceptual tool in French and European political analysis though the exact terminology, theoretical significance, and empirical operalization vary considerably. A useful illustration of field analysis is the work on the European Union by Niilo Kauppi and colleagues at the European Political Sociology Group in Strasbourg.

In a 2004 paper Kauppi outlines a research program and offers illustrative uses of key concepts of Bourdieu, particularly political field and types of capital, to understand the European Union. He treats the European Union as a transnational political field in formation. Kauppi observes that at this stage of its development this new political entity is taking on some of functions of the nation-state but is slow to develop a European civil

10. See http://www.unil.ch/ecpr-polsoc.

11. To illustrate: a special issue on Bourdieu in the journal *International Political Sociology* 5 (3): 219–347 and the "Bourdieu in International Relations" workshop held December 7–8, 2010, at the Centre for Advanced Security Theory, Department of Political Science, University of Copenhagen. Bourdieu's growing influence on political analysis can be seen in the meetings and publication of several key scholarly associations such as the International Studies Association, including one of its flagship journals *International Political Sociology*.

society and effective democracy. The European Union constitutes a kind of institutional superfield that is composed of a variety of smaller, relatively autonomous fields of action such as national political fields (e.g., the French political field and the Finnish political field), institutional fields such as the European Commission and the European Parliament, and specialized sectors of public policies (e.g., defense, transport and social policy). Each field of political action is composed of individuals, groups, institutions, procedures, and policies. Kauppi constructs the European political field along two axes: European executive or legislative resources (or forms of power) and national executive or legislative resources. In the French political field for instance, political groups in executive positions utilize European posts as an extension of the domestic ministerial cabinet system, whereas other political groups use these posts as a means to enter national electoral politics through the back door provided by the European Parliament. One interesting finding is how the European Parliament elections in 1996 permitted in the case of France certain candidates with little political capital at home to transform their cultural capital into political capital at the European level through successful candidacies. Capital conversion strategies by candidates and the opportunity provided by European elections enabled certain individuals and groups to challenge traditional political careers at the national level and the dominant national political culture (Kauppi 2004, 326, 327).[12]

Kauppi's research program—informed by Bourdieu's view of fields and capitals—challenges traditional political institutional approaches that are state-centric or focus only on particular EU institutions. Kauppi's field analysis is not confined to one level of analysis or one particular institution but takes into account transnational (in this case European), national, and regional units that all intersect in various ways. He looks not at the structure of the EU per se but examines the interaction between individuals and the roles they occupy in the EU as a political field. Elaborated from Bourdieu's concepts of field and capital, this research program is

---

12. In the same paper Kauppi presents several key studies illustrating how aspects of Bourdieu's sociology of politics are being used to generate useful research on European integration. For example, Willy Beauvallet (2003), a colleague of Kauppi at the European Political Sociology Group in Strasbourg, applies the concept of field to the European Parliament by examining the kinds of capitals European parliamentarians bring to their field positions and how they strategically use the French political field for advantage in the European Parliament.

generating a significant body of work with a distinctive theoretical orientation in European studies. While a Bourdieusian field approach to understanding the EU is currently marginal to mainstream approaches, just as
are approaches drawing inspiration from Foucault (governmentality), and
Habermas (public sphere) (Zimmermann and Favell 2011), in the hands
of a younger generation of scholars it shows strong signs of an expanding
influence.

Bourdieu Globally

Beyond France and Europe Bourdieu has become a global sociologist and
intellectual, judging from the citations to his works and their translations
as well as the considerable number of secondary works presenting and
evaluating his conceptual framework. Since 1999 Bourdieu has become
the most internationally cited sociologist according to the US ISI Web
of sciences, surpassing other renowned figures such as Anthony Giddens,
Erving Goffman, and Jürgen Habermas (Santoro 2008a). By 2008, 347 of
Bourdieu's titles were in translation, published in thirty-four languages
and forty-two countries. Examining the 1958–2008 period, Sapiro and
Bustamante find that in the mid-1990s, particularly after the 1996 publication of *On Television* (Bourdieu 1998e), Bourdieu moved from a position
of an internationally recognized sociologist to a "global thinker" (Sapiro
and Bustamante 2009)

Today there is even a growing literature specialized in examining the
export of Bourdieu's ideas into other countries.[13] One notable expression
of this is the symposium of papers edited by Marco Santoro in the online
journal *Sociologica* (Santoro 2008b, 2009a, 2009b). Those papers clearly
illustrate that Bourdieu's reach is extensive and growing, particularly in
Latin America and Asia, including China. Much of that influence is in
areas of culture, education, stratification, and theory. Less well dissemi-
nated is Bourdieu's political sociology scholarship, such as *The State
Nobility*, with the important exception of his public intellectual writings
after 1996 when he became more engaged in antiglobalization struggles.[14]

13. Much of this research is prompted by Bourdieu's (1999c, 2002b) own interest in the
international circulation of ideas and has been carried out by those drawing inspiration from
Bourdieu in their own work.

14. Brazil would be one such example. See Baranger 2008; Garcia 1994, 2003, 2004; Leite
Lopes 1978, 2003.

Nonetheless, one can find growing influence and interest in drawing from his work for political analysis particularly in an interdisciplinary orientation. Santoro is not wrong in saying that Bourdieu entered the twentieth-first century as "the most influential single sociologist in the world." With the current status of a "global thinker" it is very likely that Bourdieu's work will gain increasing influence even in political analysis.

The Missing Bourdieu in American Political Sociology and Political Science

It is striking that few in American political sociology, and even fewer in political science, have seen Bourdieu as relevant to their fields. Bourdieu is seldom cited, let alone discussed, in American political sociology and particularly political science.[15] Alford and Friedland (1985), in their masterful summary and synthesis of political sociology by the mid-eighties, situate Raymond Boudon in the pluralist camp but say nothing of Bourdieu. There is very little mention of Bourdieu's work in the Research in Political Sociology series. Consider two 2001 volumes. The only reference in Dobratz, Waldner, and Buzzell 2001 is the Bloemraad 2001 paper that takes up collective identity and political mobilization in Quebec. (Canadian political sociology may be more open to Bourdieu's work [Fournier and Vécin 2009].) There is no significant influence of Bourdieu reflected in Dobratz, Waldner, and Buzzell (2003), Dobratz, Buzzell, and Waldner (2002), or Waldner, Buzzell, and Dobratz (2002) either. A survey (Checa et al. 2005) of 120 US PhD sociology program websites, of 106 individuals within academic departments, and an examination of 17 graduate syllabi identifies (in rank order) the following five authors most frequently assigned in graduate political science courses: Theda Skocpol, Seymour Martin Lipset, Charles Tilly, G. William Domhoff, and Juan Linz.[16] Examination of their writings reveals little acquaintance with the work of

15. This contrasts with the steadily growing influence of Bourdieu's work on American sociology over the last twenty years, an influence that moves well beyond faddish ceremonial citations to conceptual and methodological applications generating new and interesting empirical research (Sallaz and Zavisca 2007). However, as I document later in the chapter, interest in his political sociology is beginning to grow as well and holds promise for making noteworthy contributions in that substantive area.

16. This survey is not based on random selection and reflects a low response rate frequent in Internet surveys. Its findings, however, support our informal survey of a number of textbooks, literatures reviews, and key writings in the field.

Bourdieu. Skocpol has, in fact, been sharply critical of cultural approaches to the study of political power and state institutions.

Bourdieu's work has yet to find its place in any significant way in many contemporary textbooks in political sociology. An illustrative textbook from the late 1990s (Kourvetaris 1997) mentions Alain Touraine's work on social movements but nothing on Bourdieu. Another example from an even more recent textbook in political sociology (Neuman 2005, 347–48) illustrates the very limited way that Bourdieu's work is now coming to be acknowledged. Only his early work (Bourdieu and Passeron 1977) on education reproducing class inequalities through the unequal transmission of cultural capital is mentioned in a chapter on cultural institutions that build and reinforce societal assumptions, values, and beliefs that shape political life. In their introduction to *The Handbook of Political Sociology* Hicks, Janoski and Schwartz (2005) do reference Bourdieu as offering a cultural perspective approach to political sociology. However, the handbook contains few references to Bourdieu; only Van den Berg and Janoski (2005) note some of Bourdieu's key political writings and present briefly his field perspective. They consider that Bourdieu "may well be the most influential of the contemporary neo-Weberian conflict theorists" though Bourdieu himself resisted such intellectual classifications.

Bourdieu is hardly cited at all in American political science. An informal survey of the flagship *American Political Science Review* shows little familiarity with Bourdieu.[17] And when he is occasionally cited, it is not because of any direct contribution to our understanding of politics. Illustrative is Lisa Wedeen's 2002 paper arguing for the usefulness of introducing culture as "semiotic practices" to enhance understanding of political analyses. In an area where Bourdieu is particularly strong, Wedeen cites Bourdieu only as contributing to practice-oriented anthropology, which in turn has had some influence in political science, rather than contributing directly to political analyses.

The United States may not be unique in this regard for a relatively recent review of the situation of political sociology in Great Britain shows

17. According to the APSA journal articles website the most popular article downloads from the key APSA journals (*American Political Science Review*, *Perspectives in Politics*, and *PS: Political Science and Politics*) reveal the following major themes of interest: terrorism, war, US foreign policy, and governance in a globalized world (http://www.apsanet.org/section_604.cfm; accessed April 16, 2012). None of these themes receive any extensive treatment by Bourdieu. And Bourdieu is seldom cited in these publications.

no particular interest in Bourdieu and does not reference any of his work (Rootes 1996). The Kate Nash texts (2000, 2010), which capture the cultural turn in political sociology, make no reference to Bourdieu, although a few references to Bourdieu appear in her edited collection (Nash and Scott 2004). And another textbook by another scholar working in the British sphere (Faulks 2000, 112), but drawing significantly on American political sociology literature, offers but one reference to Bourdieu's concept of cultural capital and its unequal distribution to help explain why dominant political culture is not more frequently resisted. Bourdieu appears not to have been picked up much in political science in other countries as well (Voutat 2002).

Why has Bourdieu rarely been cited by political sociologists and political scientists in the United States? Two obvious reasons are that Bourdieu's work focuses on France and has been sometimes slow in translation. American political sociologists and political scientists tend to read American work with the notable exception of comparative historical sociology and the recent interest in globalization. In addition, Wacquant (1993a) points up the fragmented reception of Bourdieu in the United States, attributing it to both the character of Bourdieu's work and the nature of the intellectual field in the United States where strong academic disciplinary specialization selectively and narrowly channeled Bourdieu's work into the sociology of education and anthropology, or simply ignored it altogether. While this is true generally of Bourdieu's work, it is particularly the case of his analysis of politics. His intellectual project, his initial training in philosophy, and the less-bounded intellectual tradition of sociology in the French context have generated an intellectual project and method that clash with the sharply delimited academic disciplinary specializations in American universities.

One cannot say that North American students of politics have been resistant to Bourdieu's work simply because it is French. Consider the influence of Foucault. In Kate Nash's book that makes a case for the "postmodern turn" in political sociology, meaning the paradigm shift away from state-centered, class-based models of participation (or nonparticipation) to a "cultural politics, understood in the broadest possible sense as the contestation and transformation of social identities and structures," she argues that the single most important theoretical contributor to this shift has been Michel Foucault (Nash 2000, 3, 19). Indeed, the author claims that Foucault's work "on the new political sociology cannot be overestimated. His direct influence is widely acknowledged by those who work on issues in the politics of identity and difference" (26). Foucault's ideas on governmentality, discipline, and the interrelations of knowledge and power have been even more important in orienting attention toward the practices of power and the formation of identities across a broad range of domains. Foucault has been significant in shifting attention from conventional politics and dominant political institutions to other forms of political power in the organizations and institutions of civil society, in everyday life and interpersonal relations, and in global culture. Why Foucault's influence has been measurably greater in political sociology than Bourdieu's is an important topic in itself though not taken up here.[18] But it reinforces a central point of this book that Bourdieu's importation into American social science has been highly selective reflecting in part the disciplinary concerns and preoccupations rather than just the stylistic and national character of his work.

American Academic Specialization

The Case of Political Science

Bourdieu's broad socioanthropological approach to power and politics clashes with the academic specialization of American universities. The American academic discipline of political science has focused on how political institutions actually operate (one of the legacies of the behaviorist school), on the more visible aspects of governing operations (elections, laws, policies, parties, constitutions, judiciaries, executives, legislatures— the study of political institutions), and on the ideal forms of governing, such as normative political theory. By contrast, Bourdieu approached the topic of power as a sociologist and anthropologist stressing the social and cultural bases of politics at the micro as well as macro levels, often focusing on those less-visible aspects in the actual functioning of political institutions. Moreover, Bourdieu was decidedly interdisciplinary in his work, making it less attractive for import into academic disciplines with strong boundaries. And perhaps more important, Bourdieu approached the topic of power critically, as someone who challenges the fundamental assumptions of existing political institutions. Thus, Bourdieu showed little interest in studying how political institutions actually operate on a day-to-day basis but focused his attention on their fundamental presuppositions for operation. What kinds of social classifications and divisions, for example,

18. See Power 2011 for an analysis of Foucault's influence in sociology.

do political institutions simply assume? Bourdieu (1984a, 397–465; 1990d; 1993b; 1993g) sharply criticized political opinion polling for constructing forms of political understanding and knowledge that are dominated by professionals rather than focusing his attention on what the polls purportedly report about public opinion. Moreover, Bourdieu's work does not fit within any of the distinct schools of thought in political science on the actual working of the state in liberal democracies: pluralism, Marxism, rational choice, elite theory, or neopluralism (O'Leary 2003). And he is not frequently cited in widely used political science texts (e.g., Dye, Zeigler, and Schubert 2012).

Political scientists have tended to focus on the instrumentally rational calculations of class interests, party politics, and international security. This has been reinforced in recent years by the growth of "rational-choice" theory in the social sciences, particularly in political science. Indeed one estimate in the mid-1990s estimated that nearly 40 percent of the articles in the *American Political Science Review* had a "clear rational-choice orientation."[19] Bourdieu was a sharp critic of the rational-choice model of human action.

Since the 1995 publication of his landmark article "Bowling Alone: America's Declining Social Capital," Robert Putnam's (1995, 2000) notion of "social capital" as the key basis for civic virtue and good governance has experienced a veritable bull market in conceptual fortune, debate, and research in political science. Putnam (2000, 19) acknowledges the much earlier use of the term by Bourdieu but notes that it was James S. Coleman (1990) who put the term on the American intellectual agenda in the late 1980s. Bourdieu first treated the term in 1980 (Bourdieu 1980a), and the English translation of its subsequent formulation (Bourdieu 1986) did not receive much attention in the English-speaking world. But the introduction and rapidly expanding use of the term in American political science has not created an inroad for Bourdieu's work in the US literature because the intellectual agendas are quite different. Putnam thinks of social capital as a structural property of large aggregates (communities, cities, states) that provides the key cement for political unity and effective action. Bourdieu's concept focuses on the potential benefits accruing to individuals and social groups because of their ability to draw upon network resources and he stresses the stratifying effects of its unequal distribution.[20]

19. The estimate comes from Hedström 1996 and is cited in Steinmetz 1999a, 13.

20. Bourdieu (1986, 248) defines social capital as "the aggregate of the actual or potential resources which are linked to possession of a durable network of more or less institutionalized

The Case of Political Sociology

If not in political science, why has Bourdieu's influence not been greater in
political sociology where his distinctly more sociological concerns might
receive greater hearing? As Allardt (2001, 11701) insightfully points out,
political sociology emerged historically as a "border field between political science and sociology" and there has been "no stable consensus of
what counts as political sociology in contrast to sociology and political
science proper."[21] If the common theme of the social bases of politics can
be found in both the post–World War II history of political sociology and
in Bourdieu's work, two areas of concern have not been preoccupations of
Bourdieu: the study of electoral behavior as a central measure of citizens
participation in democratic life and the study of "master patterns of societal change" with increasing attention to the formation of states and nations, their problematic features, their globalization, and the breakdowns
of social and political orders.[22] While Bourdieu devoted some attention to
political participation, particularly opinion polling, and later in his career
to the symbolic dimension of modern states, his principal works did not
concern directly these overarching topics of political sociology.

A State-Centric Orientation

The intellectual agenda of American political sociology was shaped by
the state-centered debate that emerged in the late 1970s and during the
1980s. Focus on the nature of the modern state became the overriding
emphasis in American political sociology.[23] This focus on state institutions

---

relationships of mutual acquaintance or recognition." See Portes 1998 for an excellent analytical overview of how the concept of social capital has been employed in contrasting ways by its
principal theorists in economics, sociology, and political science.

21. This is particularly the case from the 1970s onward. The student rebellions and
political-left radicalism of the 1960s and 1970s undercut the earlier focus in political sociology
on electoral studies. Growth in a multiplicity of political concerns, such as ethnicities and the
role of ethnic identities in nation building, occurred. In the 1980s and 1990s interest in the
master patterns of change generated renewed focus on nation building as the state became a
central concern (J. C. Jenkins 2000).

22. Voting and electoral behavior formed a central point of departure for academic sociology in the 1950s and 1960s. From the 1970s onward electoral studies became increasingly so-
phisticated methodologically and concentrated in the field of political science (ibid., 11704).

23. Indication of that shift in American political sociology to focus on the modern state
can be found in successive editions of Orum 1989. From the first edition in 1978 to the third

excluded for the most part cultural considerations, or accorded them only a derivative role, and therefore limited interest in the kind of analysis Bourdieu proposed. The debate on state-formation and function pitted neo-Marxist against neo-Weberian perspectives. For the former, culture was considered as an effect of the state and/or economic conditions but not a constituent force in its own right. For the latter, culture played a role only in the analysis of premodern and non-Western states and was limited to formal-legal rationality in the case of modern states. Illustrative of neo-Weberian thinking is Theda Skocpol who in her landmark work *States and Social Revolutions* explicitly rejected cultural analysis by asking researchers to "rise above" the "viewpoints of the participants" (1979, 18).[24] This perspective was further solidified in her influential programmatic introduction, "Bringing the State Back In: Strategies of Analysis in Current Research," to Evans, Rueschemeyer, and Skocpol (1985). Influential in shaping a generation of graduate studies in sociology, this neo-Weberian emphasis on the autonomy of the state from economistic and class-centered approaches relegated culture to a very marginalized position. State-centered and structural Marxist perspectives on politics dominated political sociology until the end of the 1980s (Steinmetz 1999a, ix, 17). For the most part, culture was not taken very seriously as a causal factor or even an object of theoretical reflection, let alone as constitutive of politics and the state. Therefore, there was little interest in Bourdieu's work.

The state-centered analysis did not go without challenge, however. One came from Michel Foucault (1977, 1980b), who argued that the very nature of power needed to be rethought, that power was not centralized in the edifice of state institutions and ideologies but was widely dispersed through capillary networks and disciplinary dispositions. One sees the influence of Foucault on the thinking of the state in the work of Mitchell (1991a, 1991b) and Steinmetz (1993). Another challenge came from globalization and increased acceptance of neoliberal ideology that challenged the autonomy of the nation-state. And yet another challenge came from

---

edition in 1989, Orum notes that "perhaps the major change has to do with the new thinking and research about the modern state" (1989, ix). Prior to 1978 the state was only acknowledged by political sociologists; only in the late seventies and eighties did it become a major object of analysis. His 1989 edition, for example, incorporates many of the new writings on the state, in particular those of Nicos Poulantzas (1973, 1975) and Theda Skocpol (1979, 1981, 1985).

24. One should not underestimate the boundary setting role that Skocpol's work had on political sociology. Writing in 1997 one observer says that "for the past 18 years" Skocpol's work "set the research agenda within sociology" (Berezin 1997, 374).

an emerging "cultural turn" in the social sciences that also contributed to rethinking state-centered analyses of politics (Steinmetz 1999b). Some openness to Bourdieu's analysis of politics began with the "cultural turn" in the social sciences that asserts the constitutive role of culture and occurs more or less simultaneously with the growth of cultural studies.

Bourdieu (1994b, 2004a) did not theorize explicitly the state until later in his work. For example, he did not participate in the lively debates in the seventies over the nature of the state that pitted structuralist Nicos Poulantzas (1973) against instrumentalist Ralph Miliband's (1969) views, or over the degree of state autonomy and contradictions in capitalist economies (Block 1987; Offe 1984; Skocpol 1981). The work of Louis Althusser (1970) and Nicos Poulantzas (1975) contributed significantly to the rise in the 1970s in importance of the subfields of world systems, historical sociology, and Marxist sociology (Orum 1996, 140–41). Bourdieu (1975a) was in fact quite critical of this Althusserian/Poulantzasian emphasis that influenced American political sociology during that period. For Bourdieu, this structuralist Marxism was far too theoretical, devoting little attention to empirical indicators of state structures or practices. Nor did he engage the "state-centered" (Evans, Rueschemeyer, and Skocpol 1985; Nordlinger 1981; Skocpol and Amenta 1986) or "historical institutionalism" (Skocpol and Campbell 1995) approaches that followed. His principal book on the state, *The State Nobility*, originally published in 1989, did not appear in English until seven years later (see Bourdieu 1996d). However, Bourdieu is much closer to the more recent emphasis on social institutions and the history of the modern welfare state that can be found, for example, in the later work of Skocpol (1992; Skocpol and Campbell 1995) and of Charles Tilly (1978) than to the older behavior orientation in political sociology. And Bourdieu has been a sharp critic of rational actor theory (Coleman et al. 1966; Hechter 1987), a rival trend to the new institutionalism.

Elite Studies

Despite ignorance of Bourdieu's work in the United States, portions of it clearly intersect with key currents in American political sociology. Power elite theory and research pioneered in the United States by C. Wright Mills (2000), G. William Domhoff (1983, 1990, 2001) and others clearly overlaps in many ways with power issues researched by Bourdieu. Bourdieu devoted considerable attention to elites and this part of his work overlaps to some extent with the political sociology of elites in the Mills/Domhoff tradition. Yet differences in the nature of the sociology of political power in the two countries helps explain why Bourdieu's work reflects a particular focus that is not found in the United States. Whereas Mills saw American society ruled by powerful business elites, historically WASP capitalists and their dependents, socioeconomic groups from the capitalist class and the military—with this focus being refined and elaborated by Domhoff (1983, 1990) and others—Bourdieu's work focused on state bureaucratic elites more characteristic in France.[25] Still, the overlap in interests has been largely ignored by American elite researchers who have focused primarily on American elites.[26]

Another reason that Bourdieu's studies of elites have not resonated strongly with US students of political elite recruitment and careers stems from differences in the French and American political systems.[27] France developed a strong administrative bureaucracy in which an elite corps of highly trained bureaucrats exercises its authority and power within a centralized state. As in Japan and England, high-level state bureaucrats are recruited directly from elite institutions of higher learning (the Grandes Écoles, particularly the École Normale d'Administration today), pursue their early careers in state administration, and often retire early to positions in big business or run for political office. Bourdieu's *The State Nobility* (1996d) confronted precisely that system. By contrast, high office in the US federal bureaucracy is more permeable through recruitment from the business sector and internal promotion. American researchers have devoted relatively more attention to business and professional elites who are more important to American political life rather than to a fairly autonomous bureaucratic elite as found in France.[28] Both Bourdieu and American researchers working within the tradition of Mills (2000)

25. Domhoff and those working in this power research tradition (e.g., Zeitlin 1974, 1980) have thought it important to demonstrate the active role of the capitalist class in shaping political life in a country where the traditional ideology has long denied the existence of social classes. In France, the existence of social classes is taken for granted.

26. In a private email exchange with one prominent American power structure researcher, mutual disregard of the other's work was personal: since Bourdieu did not cite American research one could not expect Americans to cite his!

27. For exceptions see Swartz 1986 and Useem 1984.

28. However, there has been some comparative elite research with some focus on political elites in particular, such as Carlton 1996; Dogan and Higley 1998; Eldersveld 1989; Inglehart 1997; Putnam 1976.

have examined the circulation between business elites and state elites. In France, the movement is more likely from state to big business than from big business to the public sector as in the United States.

There is, in addition, a key methodological difference separating Bourdieu from many North American sociologists researching the power of elites. In terms of the classic structuralist versus instrumentalist debates over elites and state power, Bourdieu stands closer to the structuralist camp in that he does not focus attention on conscious intervention or organizing. While sharing some affinities with social network analysis, Bourdieu does not limit his investigation to visible contacts or interlocking relations; rather, as will be pointed out in chapter 4, his view of symbolic power and the relational character of power fields stress the invisible effects of domination beyond conscious intervention.

New Directions in American Political Sociology

It is noteworthy, however, that changes in American political sociology over the last several years seem more attentive today to the concerns animating Bourdieu's sociology. American political sociology has experienced a significant shift over the last thirty years from a behavioral orientation to an institutional one (Orum 1996; Robertson 1993). It shifted from behavioral studies of parties, voting, political participation, political attitudes, and so on, toward increased interest in social institutions, particularly the welfare state and social movements. Moreover, studies are increasingly informed by historical perspective. The shift from the view of state institutions as autonomous from social structure to one where the distinction between the political and social is fluid and indeterminate opens an inroad for Bourdieu's thinking. Also the expanded view of power that no longer views it as concentrated in and limited to state institutions may enhance interest in Bourdieu's work.

Social Movement Research

Social movement theorizing and empirical research has been one of the most vigorous and expanding subfields of political sociology since the 1970s. Yet until recently Bourdieu's work is seldom referenced in this exploding literature. In *Sociological Views on Political Participation in the 21st Century* (Dobratz, Buzzell and Waldner 2002), which takes stock of current research of political participation at the beginning of the twenty-first century, Bourdieu is referenced in just one of the ten included papers. And Buechler (2002), who reviews the current theoretical orientations to social movement research, does not reference Bourdieu at all. Crossley (2002), on the other hand, devotes considerable attention to the relevance of Bourdieu for social movement research but Crossley is British and has written elsewhere on Bourdieu (2001). Crossley stresses how Bourdieu can be used to criticize the rational-action perspective in social movement research.

Bourdieu is not known as a social movement sociologist nor has his thinking had significant impact on present-day social movement theorizing and research.[29] Yet his framework is relevant to social movement research. In a case study of the demise of the Workers Alliance of America, a powerful, nationwide movement of the unemployed formed in 1935 and dissolved in 1941, Chad Goldberg (2003) sees in Bourdieu a valuable resource for developing a needed and better synthesis of resource mobilization/political process perspectives with collective identity-oriented analyses of new social movements. Goldberg deftly applies Bourdieu's idea of classification struggles to build a bridge between the two traditions of social movement research, resource mobilization/political process theories and the new social movements' theoretical emphasis on collective identity. Bourdieu's stress on the importance of symbolic power in classification struggles provides an important corrective to each. Goldberg's study illustrates that political mobilization does not presuppose an already established political identity. Nor does political identity require a clear objective base in order to form. Both identity and mobilization can form simultaneously and dialectically out of struggle itself.[30]

Bourdieu argues that collective identities are fundamentally political in that they are constructed identities that involve power relations. This is in part what he means when he stresses that fields are relational. Collective identity in social movements is one area where one might imagine

29. Probably the one Bourdieusien-influenced work that has been most noted by some social movement researchers is Boltanski 1974. When thinking in terms of French social movement research, US researchers are more likely to think of Alain Touraine (1981, 1985) and his collaborators, particularly with regard to the "new" social movements, than Bourdieu.

30. As Neveu (2005, 83–84) points out, Bourdieu's economy of practice can help show how political activism in social movements can be "reasonable" or even "rational" without reducing action to a rigid and oversimplifying cost-benefits calculation. The idea of fields with their *illusio* and actors guided by habitus helps take into account the diversity of social worlds with their own particular sets of goals, rewards, investments, and motivations for engagement that need not stem from conscious calculation of material or symbolic benefits.

scholars drawing some inspiration from Bourdieu. This is illustrated by Irene Bloemraad (2001) in her study of the 1995 Quebec independence movement. Bloemraad draws on Bourdieu's concept of field to argue that collective identity cannot be separated from political mobilization. She sees "parallels" between her concept of "mobilization playing fields" and Bourdieu's concept of field to the extent that field identities are relational and differentiate "them" from "us." In this sense, Bourdieu's longstanding interest in "classification struggles" is directly relevant to social movement mobilization.

Marcos Ancelovici (2010) brings Bourdieu's concept of field to the political opportunity/process framework of social movements as developed by Sidney Tarrow (1996, 1998), Charles Tilly (1978), and Doug McAdam (McAdam 1982; McAdam, Tarrow, and Tilly 2001). Ancelovici redefines the concept of opportunity structures as "field opportunity structures" to permit their application to a far greater range of sites of social mobilization, such as religion, that, while not directly linked to the state or political field, yet are carriers of political consequences. Moreover, Bourdieu's concept of habitus helps us understand why some actors perceive and seize upon certain opportunities whereas other actors do not. There also is overlap between Bourdieu's concept of habitus and Tilly's (2008; Tilly and Tarrow 2007) "repertoire of collective action," notably in the shared criticism of instrumental models of action. While Tilly introduces certain cultural traits with the concept of actor repertoires and proclaims that his "repertoires of contention are ineradicably cultural phenomena" (Tilly 1999, 419), he did not make them the centerpiece of his analysis of social movements, whereas Bourdieu's framework highlights the cultural and symbolic features of group formation and mobilization. (See Emirbayer 2010 for a systematic comparison of the work of Tilly and Bourdieu.) Bourdieu's emphasis on symbolic power and classification struggles also resonates with the "framing" approach to social movements in that both stress the central role of cultural meanings to collective organization (Benford and Snow 2000). Further, Bourdieu's view of capitals overlaps with resource mobilization perspectives that are open to multiple forms of power resources (not just economic) that can animate social movements. However, Bourdieu's emphasis on practical action and the central role played by habitus would not share the resource mobilization assumption that resources are deployed toward well-defined goals. Bourdieu's conflict perspective is more far reaching in that goals themselves are objects of struggle. Social movements can emerge within fields of struggle not only over valued resources but also over how they are to be deployed and for what ends.

Culture and Politics

Bourdieu is receiving greater hearing in the emerging "politics and culture" interdisciplinary site of theory and empirical investigation than in the traditional areas of political analysis, such as states, parties, and voting behavior. Indeed, it is the explosion of interest in culture in American sociology, not the declining fortunes of political sociology, which has made Bourdieu's writings so attractive in the United States.[31] Inclusive of but not reducible to "political culture," this broader arena of inquiry, eclectically informed by theory, history, and anthropology, addresses not only problems of democratization and civil society, but also institutions, such as law, religion, the state, and citizenship, political communication and meaning, and collective action (Berezin 1997). Bourdieu is discussed in Swidler (1986), possibly the most cited work in this broad area, and in Sewell (1992), which has had a major influence on the work with a historical orientation in this area (Berezin 1997, 376). Lamont's (1992; Lamont and Fournier 1992) influential work on boundary making also draws some inspiration from Bourdieu.

Citizenship is another area of recent and growing interest in research that falls within the emerging "politics and culture" research agenda. Brubaker (1992, 35–36), for example, makes a compelling case for understanding the "institution of formal citizenship" as well as the rights and obligations of citizenship since "formalization and codification are themselves social phenomena, with sociologically interesting effects." Though he studies comparatively immigration policy in France and Germany, Brubaker draws from Bourdieu to argue that citizenship is a socially constituted

---

31. By 1995 the Culture Section of the ASA, the fifth-largest section though founded only in 1986, already had 865 members compared to the much older political sociology section of only 549 members (Orum 1996, 147). In *The Handbook of Political Sociology* Hicks, Janoski, and Schwartz (2005) report that the 2003 membership in the ASA Political Sociology section stood at 560, above the 463 average for all sections, but still far below the Culture Section. Orum (1996) observes that by the mid-nineties there is no longer a coherent paradigm in US political sociology. A decade later Hicks, Janoski and Schwartz (2005, 1) note that "the field remains fluid" as the dominance of pluralist, political/economic, and state-centric theories have been sharply challenged by powerful new voices found in Foucault's rethinking power, poststructuralist/culturally oriented theories (they put Bourdieu here), feminism, racialization theory, and rational choice theories creating a number of lively if disparate subfields that broadly reflect political sociological concerns though often without recognition from political sociologists.

boundary-setting device for establishing who is and who is not a member of a polity and that the different ways the French and Germans think about immigration reflects their different political cultures about what constitutes national identity. Citizenship is not a given but a sociologically and historically constituted category (also see Somers 2008).[32] Thus, one can see through Brubaker's widely cited work influence of Bourdieu's thinking on citizenship.

Bourdieu's insights on classification struggles are useful not only for social movement research. Philip Gorski (forthcoming) elaborates this concept for the formation of social groups to help answer the what, when, and why questions relative to nationalism. And in the area of political culture Aronoff (2000, 11642) mentions Bourdieu's concepts of *habitus*, *doxa*, and *cultural capital*, as resources being used by some to shift the focus of political culture analysis to how power is inscribed in "the scripts of everyday life."

Capitals, Fields, and Symbolic Power in Political Analysis

Most promising for political sociology is the application of Bourdieu's concepts of capital, field, and symbolic power. Gil Eyal et al. (Eyal 2000, 2003; Eyal, Szelényi, and Townsley 1997, 1998, 2001) bring Bourdieu's "forms of capital" to bear on their study of the transition from communism to capitalism in Central Europe. Looking at evidence in Hungary, Poland, and the Czech Republic, they show that during the transition period holders of cultural capital used knowledge and symbolic power rather than property to outflank holders of Soviet political capital (i.e., party bureaucrats) and economic capital (i.e., informal entrepreneurs) in the struggle for power. The ascension of cultural capital provided not only knowledge on how to manage the new economic situation but also symbolic power to legitimate the new order. The authors highlight the key dynamic of struggle for control over symbolic meanings in the political power struggles as does Bourdieu in his analysis of the field of power and the state. Bourdieu's concepts help these researchers stress the importance of inter-elite power struggles moving beyond the elites/masses dichotomy in earlier political sociology.

---

32. The social construction of collective identity, including citizenship, can be found in Bourdieu 1990a, 1991d, 1991h.

Eyal (2003, 2005) applies the concept of the political field to analyze political transformation in the post-Communist era in Eastern Europe. He uses Bourdieu's concepts of political field as well as capital to analyze the break-up of the Czechoslovak federation in 1993. Eyal (2005) shows how the 1993 breakup was precipitated not by popular discontent but by political struggle between Czech and Slovak elites. His political field analysis illustrates the idea of the relative autonomy of the political field by its capacity to transpose, invert, and in certain instances subvert the social divisions within the electorate leading to unanticipated outcomes. Stark and Bruszt (1998) also employ the idea of a political field to examine economic transformation and democratization in post-Soviet Eastern Europe.

Though much state-centered political sociology has had a distinctly materialist conceptualization, a growing amount of recent work now devotes more attention to the symbolic dimensions of the state (Adams 1994; Coronil 1997; Corrigan and Sayer 1985; Gorski 2003; Loveman 2005; Steinmetz 1999b) and here Bourdieu's idea of symbolic power has been seminal. As we will see in chapter 6, Bourdieu's view of the state as the central bank of symbolic power and violence suggests that that "top-down" views of the state that focus largely on the means of physical coercion need to be expanded to include a closer examination of the cultural sources of power deeply embedded in civil society. Similar in thrust to Foucault's (1980a, 71–72) view of state power arising from deeply embedded sources of social discipline, Gorski's (2003, 20, 38) emphasis on the Calvinist "disciplinary revolutions" in state formation in early modern Europe, and Mann's (1993, 59) idea of "infrastructural power" as a "two-way street" between civil society and state administrative bodies, Bourdieu's view of the state finds common ground with a growing literature showing more complex patterns of both formation and routine exercise of state power than earlier state-centric accounts suggest. And Loveman's (2005) study of a little-known popular rebellion, the "War of the Wasps," during the nineteenth-century period of Brazilian state formation, shows the crucial role that symbolic power plays in establishing state administrative reach. The nineteenth-century Brazilian state failed to establish civil registration as a legitimate state practice and take its first national census precisely because it failed to accumulate sufficient symbolic power.

Bourdieu's concepts of capital, field, and symbolic power have found significant application in some recent cross-national work. Steinmetz (2007) applies the concept of field to study the colonial states in southwest Africa, Oceania, and Qingdao (Kiaochow in China) under imperial Germany in the late nineteenth and early twentieth centuries. The field concept helps him understand how the colonial states were internally differentiated by struggle among the colonizers over a particular type of symbolic capital, that is, an "ethnographic capital" for the right to impose as the most legitimate characterization of the cultures and subjectivities of the colonized. These field struggles helped the colonial states develop a relative autonomy from the imperial metropole while their intra-elite struggles refracted homologous intra-elite struggles inside the metropolitan German state.

Drawing inspiration from Bourdieu's concept of field and organizational sociology (particularly the new-institutionalism current), Go (2008) proposes the idea of *global fields* to bring a field analytic perspective to international relations. Global fields permits him to compare and contrast two hegemonic empires, that of Great Britain in the nineteenth century and that of the United States in the post–World War II period. Using the global fields analytical framework Go is able to contrast the British strategy he calls "formal imperialism" of direct territorial rule to the "informal imperialism" of the United States through networks and markets. Compared to several competing frameworks, such as realist international relations theory, hegemony/world systems theory, and global cultural structures perspectives, Go shows how a global fields perspective incorporates several of their respective features but goes beyond each to offer a more comprehensive research orientation and a better understanding of how the British and American empires differentiated. His analysis identifies various forms of capital, particularly political capital and symbolic capital, to show the multidimensional character of global fields. Rather than emphasizing either material or coercive factors as realists (Morgenthau 1978) and world systems theorists (Wallerstein 2004) do, or cultural structures as neoinstitutionalists (Meyer 1980, 1999) do, the global fields perspective incorporates both. Thus, even at the core, the dominant states with tremendous economic and military power also struggle for international legitimacy (symbolic capital) and allied support (political capital).

Dezalay and Garth (2002) study how the exports of expertise and ideals from the United States, such as neoliberal economics and international human rights law, were received in four Latin American countries: Argentina, Brazil, Chile, and Mexico. They find that the content of what is exported and how it fares in the receiving counties were profoundly shaped by domestic struggles for power and influence—"palace wars"—in the nations involved. Using Bourdieu's field analytical perspective, these researchers demonstrate that there are national fields of hierarchy and struggle and the export of forms of expertise from one country to another needs to be understood in terms of the structural homologies in the respective national fields of the exporters and importers. National actors pursue international strategies by using different kinds of capital, such as resources, educational degrees, social contacts, legitimacy, and expertise to enhance their state power at home. These international strategies are mediated by field hierarchies and struggles in the respective countries. They reveal imperial processes—the export of neoliberal economics and US conception of the rule of law (an independent judiciary)—mediated by national fields of struggle for state power rather than through direct coercion or imposition of specific programs. These international strategies blur national borders and categories but this does not lead the researchers to discard the state as a key unit of analysis. Indeed, they focus on how the state, itself a field of power struggle, is constructed and redefined through international strategies. Their field perspective on knowledge exports and imports seeks to uncover the micro and macro links neglected by other approaches such as world systems theory.

Despite these new directions in US political sociology and recent examples of Bourdieu inspired research, it remains striking how little of Bourdieu's work is known among American political sociologists and political scientists compared to their colleagues in the sociology of education, culture, social theory, stratification, and in anthropology. A combination of the distinctive interdisciplinary character of Bourdieu's work and American disciplinary boundaries helps explain this lack of familiarity. Though fundamentally concerned with the sociology of power and politics, Bourdieu's work has started only recently to find some hearing among American social scientists sharing similar interests. Recent shifts away from state-centered perspectives toward more culture-oriented views and methods suggest possible openings for Bourdieu's work. These recent shifts in American analysis of politics will likely be enriched by the orientation of Bourdieu's sociology and the American political terrain will offer an interesting test for the applicability of Bourdieu's perspective. His field analytical perspective and his view of politics as struggle for symbolic power promise to inspire new kinds of empirical exploration and theoretical framing. A purpose of this book is to make Bourdieu's political thinking better understood among Anglo-American sociologists and to point to the contributions it can make in political analysis as well as identify some points where elaboration or correction would seem to be appropriate.

CHAPTER TWO

Forms of Power in Bourdieu's Sociology

The analysis of power stands at the core of Pierre Bourdieu's sociology.[1] He proposes a theory of symbolic power, violence, and capital that stresses the active role that symbolic forms play as resources that reflect, constitute, maintain, and change social hierarchies. Bourdieu's perspective challenges the commonly held view that symbolic power is simply "symbolic." His sociology sensitizes us to the more subtle and influential forms of power that operate through the cultural resources and symbolic categories and classifications that connect everyday life to prevailing structures of inequality.

Because of the fragmented reception of Bourdieu's work in the Anglo-American sociological literature (Swartz 2006; Wacquant 1993b), few critics assess the full range of Bourdieu's conceptualization of power.[2] For example, in the revised and expanded edition of his famous work *Power: A Radical View*, Steven Lukes (2005) sees Bourdieu as opening up for investigation important aspects of the "third dimension" of power that Lukes identified in his first edition. The third dimension of power Lukes defines as "the capacity to secure compliance to domination through the shaping of beliefs and desires, by imposing internal constraints under historically changing circumstances" (143–44). It is a systemic power embedded in the

---

1. In a 1972 summary statement of his work and that of his Centre for Eurpean Sociology (*Current Research* 1972), Bourdieu presents his work and that of his colleagues as contributing to a "sociology of power."

2. Loïc Wacquant is one notable exception whose encyclopedic knowledge of Bourdieu stresses the centrality of power in Bourdieu's work. See in particular Wacquant 2004, 2005a, 2005b.

patterns of thought, basic assumptions, linguistic terms and categories, and social relationships that shapes how individuals go about their every-day lives though individuals are rarely aware of its influence. Lukes high-lights Bourdieu's concept of symbolic power and violence as signaling the importance of this third dimension. While certainly a distinctive feature of Bourdieu's thinking on power as domination, there are other aspects that also merit attention, most notably his analysis of valued resources (forms of capital) that are contested in arenas of struggle (fields).

This chapter offers an overview of the key conceptual tools Bourdieu developed in his thinking and research on power. How does Bourdieu con-ceptualize power? What forms of power does he focus on? These are the questions I will address. I begin with how Bourdieu thinks about power in the social order and then describe briefly the forms of power in Bourdieu's sociology and offer a couple of widely voiced criticisms. I situate his think-ing relative to the political sociology tradition and draw out some impli-cations for the analysis of power and politics. This chapter offers only a summary statement; later chapters will probe more in depth the various power dimensions that are simply introduced here.

Bourdieu and the Foundation of Social Order

Bourdieu was a conflict theorist who stressed the conflictual and stratified character of social worlds and who saw them firmly ordered by mecha-nisms and processes of domination and reproduction. His view of order is antifoundational and radically historicist. In terms of classical political theory Bourdieu's view of the roots of political order is clearly closer to David Hume (Bourdieu 1994b, 15; 2000e, 178) and particularly Blaise Pas-cal (1912) than social contract theorists like Thomas Hobbes (1994 [1668]) or John Locke (1980 [1690]) since Bourdieu posits the fundamentally arbi-trary character of any political order.[3] Order is not founded in some innate human reason or naturally endowed right, or in some primitive social con-tract. Though Bourdieu does not systematically engage political theory,

---

3. Recall that Hume, in debunking social contract theory, declares that "almost all the governments which exist at present, or of which there remains any record in story, have been founded originally, either on usurpation or conquest, or both, without any pretence of a fair consent or voluntary subjections of the people." And people "pay obedience more from fear and necessity, than from any idea of allegiance or moral obligation" (1742, II.XII.9, II.XII.22).

which would be contrary to his view of what sociologists should do, one finds nonetheless in *Pascalian Meditations* (Bourdieu 2000e) key elements that show Bourdieu's thinking regarding the basis of social order.[4] Drawing on Pascal, Bourdieu (2000e, 168) says of the origins of law that

> there is nothing other than arbitrariness and usurpation, that it is impossible to found law in reason and right, and that the Constitution—no doubt what most resembles, in the political order, a Cartesian primary foundation—is merely a founding fiction designed to disguise the act of lawless violence which is the basis of the establishment of law.[5]

This historical arbitrariness of law becomes forgotten through custom (by a "genesis amnesia, which arises from exposure to custom") and mythical reasons are invented to become the "founding fiction" of order. Revealing his historicism in extrapolating from Pascal, Bourdieu writes that "the only possible foundation of law is to be sought in history, which, precisely, abolishes any kind of foundation" (94). Every legal order is fundamentally historical. Where Bourdieu disagrees with Pascal is in the implication that the arbitrary foundation of order stems from a kind of Machiavellian "intentional mystification." For Bourdieu, "social order is merely the order of bodies," not the outcome of conscious strategizing.[6]

4. Bourdieu would consider the political theory questions of social order and the foundations of government as scholastic or intellectualist questions that miss a principal insight of his sociology, namely, that order is practically adhered to through the dispositions of habitus and therefore goes for the most part unquestioned (Bourdieu 2000e, 178).

More generally, Bourdieu resists presenting his work as "theoretical" by focusing exclusively on concepts. Most of his theorizing occurs in constructing his empirical objects of sociological research and in response to criticism of his work. Bourdieu 1986 is one notable exception where he explicitly talks "about concepts for their own sake" (255 n. 4).

5. The quote is Bourdieu summarizing Pascal's view as his own. Law as "founding fiction" sounds similar to what Anthony Giddens (1979, 68) characterizes as the "normative irrationalism" of Weber, who along with Nietzsche argued that there are no rational (scientific) grounds for adjudicating conflicting "ultimate value" claims. This leads to the position that Giddens rejects: namely, that "the only recourse open is that of power or might: the strongest are able to make their values count by crushing others." Bourdieu accepts this position in the spirit of historical realism. But Bourdieu also subscribes to the Enlightenment values of rationality that he affirms as universal even if they are historical. This points to a tension in Bourdieu's thinking between historical specificity and normative rationality (see Swartz 1997, 251–53).

6. I agree that Bourdieu points to a key limitation of social contract thinking when he stresses the bodily power foundation of order rather than conscious design. Yet the "order of bodies" seems like a kind of irrational reductionism. Some primitive conscious intention if not design is certainly plausible though unintended consequences can certainly occur. And

But if the foundations of social order are fundamentally arbitrary, lacking any stabilizing universal principles, they are hardly fickle or transitory. If order, right, and law emerge out of violence, they crystallize as custom and are maintained not by conscious design or consent but largely through "learning and acquisition of dispositions." Citing Pascal, Bourdieu argues that "custom makes all authority" and that the social order derives from "the habituation to custom and law that law and custom produce by their very existence and persistence" (2000e, 168). The roots of political order originate in violence but maintain and transmit through bodily dispositions. Rather than in consent or reason Bourdieu thinks of the "primordial political belief"—the *doxa*—of a social order as a "pre-reflexive agreement" rooted in the incorporation of the dominant vision of order in the bodily dispositions of habitus (Bourdieu 1994b, 15).[7] Echoing Pascal, Bourdieu contends that habit not contract is formative of political order.[8] Habit is a powerful driving force in Bourdieu's view of human action and he restitutes to modern sociology the importance of habituated action that was important to the classical thinkers like Durkheim and Weber but evacuated from early twentieth-century sociology through the influence of behaviorism (Camic 1986; Swartz 2002). Political order—indeed social order—is a bodily order, inculcated and incorporated through early socialization. Bourdieu attempts to capture this ordering force through his concept of habitus.

Dimensions of Power in Bourdieu's Analysis

Though Bourdieu sees the objective of sociology as the study of power, he does not offer a typology of the various forms of power as found, for example, in three widely regarded sociological analyses of power: *Power:*

the role of belief, which Bourdieu emphasizes elsewhere, rather than just cynical manipulation also comes into play. The dialectic of mind and body that Bourdieu stresses elsewhere seems lost here.

7. Thus, Bourdieu holds that "the theory of knowledge of the social world is a fundamental dimension of political theory . . . [and that] the most fundamental problems of political philosophy can only be posed and truly resolved by means of a return to the mundane observations of the sociology of learning and upbringing" (2000e, 172,168).

8. Bourdieu writes that "the habituation to custom and law that law and custom produce by their very existence and persistence is largely sufficient, without any deliberate intervention, to impose a recognition of the law based on misrecognition of the arbitrariness which underlies it" (2000e, 168).

A Radical View by Steven Lukes (2005), *The Sources of Social Power*, vols. 1–2, by Michael Mann (1986, 1993), and *Power: Its Forms, Bases, and Uses* by Dennis H. Wrong (1995).[9] Bourdieu is clearly most concerned by power in the form of domination and his sociology focuses on that form of power relationship. As I will note later, Bourdieu does not make a significant distinction between distributive (zero sum) and collective forms of power. He focuses on the distributive. Bourdieu analyzes power in three overlapping but analytically distinct ways: (1) power in valued resources (various types of social, cultural, and economic capital), (2) power in specific spheres (fields) of struggle, and (3) power in legitimation (symbolic power, violence, and capital).[10] I will introduce each briefly here and then analyze them in subsequent chapters.

Power in Valued Resources

In Bourdieu's sociology, power takes the form of valued resources, which he calls *capitals*, that can be created, accumulated, exchanged, and consumed. Bourdieu conceptualizes resources as capital when they function as a "social *power* relation" by becoming objects of struggle (1996d, 264). Capitals are produced through human labor and present themselves in four generic forms: economic (money and property), cultural (information, knowledge, and educational credentials), social (acquaintances and

9. Lukes (2005, 74), for example, sees himself offering a "detailed conceptual map" for thinking about power.

10. Bourdieu's analysis of power is in fact more complex than these three types suggest. Drawing in part from Weber's analysis of modes of domination, Bourdieu also has a historical understanding of increasing differentiation of forms of power with the transition from traditional undifferentiated societies to modern increasingly differentiated societies. (Durkheim's view of the transition from mechanical to organic solidarities is also influential here.) He notes shifts from forms of power rooted in persons, such as clan and village elders, to specialized functions, such as warriors and priests, then to impersonal arenas of competition such as fields; from social systems dominated by single principles and institutions, such a hierocracy, caesaropapism, and the divine right of kings, to modern systems of multiple hierarchies and types of domination; from traditional, relatively homogeneous societies without fields to the development of relative autonomous fields and particularly to the field of power, a sort of meta-field, in modern differentiated societies. To illustrate, Bourdieu (1996d, 386) writes that "no longer incarnated in persons or even in particular institutions, power becomes coextensive with the structure of the field of power, and it is only realized and manifested through an entire set of fields and forms of power united by a genuine organic solidarity, and thus both different and interdependent."

networks), and symbolic (legitimation, authority, prestige) (Bourdieu 1986, 243). His concept of *cultural capital* is most widely known—particularly in the sociology of education and culture—but his work includes a wide array of capitals, such as social capital, economic capital, academic capital, and statist capital.[11] Elaborating upon Max Weber's multidimensional forms of power, Bourdieu's view of capital extends the analysis of power to more subtle expressions beyond that of sheer material advantage and physical coercion. Researchers inspired by Bourdieu's thinking have identified an ever-widening array of types of capital that are unevenly distributed across social groups. Bourdieu's thinking of power resources as forms of capital is developed in chapter 3.

Power in Fields of Struggle

Capitals, as forms of power, exist not in isolation but operate relationally in what Bourdieu calls *fields*. Fields denote arenas of production, circulation, and appropriation of goods, services, knowledge, or status, and the competitive positions held by actors in their struggle to accumulate and monopolize different kinds of capital. Fields are structured spaces that are organized around struggles over specific types and combinations of capital.

Field struggle, for Bourdieu, has two distinct dimensions. On the one hand, struggle occurs over the distribution of capitals within fields. This is struggle to accumulate the more valued forms of capital or to convert one form into another, more valued form. In this sense, capital is a stake in the struggle. On the other hand, struggle also occurs over the very definition of the most legitimate form of capital for a particular field. This is a struggle for symbolic power, a classification struggle, over the right to monopolize the legitimate definition of what is to be the most valued form of capital for a particular field. The cultural field, for example, organizes around the struggle to define and accumulate the most legitimate form of cultural capital, such as scientific or literary capital. There are also specific types of cultural fields with struggle over specific cultural forms such as scientific knowledge. In the field of sociology, individuals struggle over valued resources like research grants, positions in prestigious departments,

---

11. Cultural capital can exist in three different states: embodied, objectified, and institutionalized (Bourdieu 1986, 243–48).

and publication in the flagship journals. They also struggle over theory and methods to define what is the most legitimate approach in sociology.

One particular power arena Bourdieu emphasizes in his sociology of modern societies is the *field of power*. The field of power is that arena of struggle among the different power fields (particularly the economic field and the cultural field) for the right to dominate throughout the social order. It is the arena of struggle among the different forms of power (or capitals) for the power to be recognized as the most legitimate. The concept covers the dominant classes in modern stratified societies. Dominant classes distinguish themselves from other classes by their sheer volume of capital but are also themselves internally differentiated by culturally oriented versus economic forms of capital. Bourdieu (1996d, 266–72) identifies different subfields within the field of power, such as the artistic field, the administrative field, the university field, the political field, and the economic field. Leaders of particular subfields compete to impose their particular type of capital as the most legitimate claim to authority in the social order. For example, artists, writers, and professors compete in the field of power against business leaders to impose their respective capitals (cultural capital versus economic capital) as the most legitimate. The field of power will be examined in chapter 3.

Central to but not synonymous with the field of power is the *state—the bureaucratic field*—which assumes the key role of regulating the struggle within the field of power. It regulates the "rate of exchange" between the various forms of capital. Extending Max Weber's definition of the state as that institution that claims monopoly over the legitimate use of violence Bourdieu stresses the monopolizing role over symbolic as well as physical violence. For Bourdieu the state consists not only of bureaucratic agencies, authorities, ritual, and ceremony but also of official classifications that regulate group relations and are internalized as mental categories through schooling. The state adjudicates the classification struggle among social groups by giving some classifications and categories official legitimation and rejecting others. In this regulatory function, the state institutionalizes its own specific form of capital, *statist capital*, a kind of meta-capital that consecrates and renders official the most legitimate forms of powers.[12] Thus, the state ultimately concentrates the power to designate the most

---

12. Bourdieu writes that this special type of capital, a kind of "meta-capital," emerges with the concentration of other types of capital and "permits the state to exercise a power over the different fields and their particular types of capital, and in particular to the rate of

legitimate forms of capital. I will examine Bourdieu's view of the state in chapter 5.

Power for Bourdieu also appears in a specific form of capital and a specific sphere of activity that are commonly associated with politics: *political capital* in the *political field*. Political capital refers to a subtype of social capital that is the capacity to mobilize social support (Bourdieu and Wacquant 1992, 119). The political field refers to the arena of struggle to capture positions of power using political capital (e.g., parties, occupations, media). It is structured around competition for control of the state apparatus. It roughly corresponds to Max Weber's (1978a) third dimension of stratification, the sphere of politics. The political field will be examined in chapter 3.

Symbolic Power, Violence, and Capital

Bourdieu uses the conceptual language of *symbolic power*, *violence*, and *capital* to talk about a third kind of power, a power that legitimates the stratified social order.[13] This is the most important contribution of Bourdieu to contemporary thinking about power and domination.[14] Bourdieu sees power as a governing dimension of all social life, even where it is not explicitly pursued. He argues that power finds expression in the mundane activities of everyday life. It operates at a tacit, taken-for-granted level in both cognitive and bodily dimensions of human activity. Through the conceptual language of symbolic power, violence, and capital Bourdieu tries to answer the following question: how do stratified social systems

---

exchange between them (and at the same time, the power relations among their holders)" (1993c, 52).

13. These distinctions are my own and are offered here for expository purposes to highlight different aspects of Bourdieu's thinking about symbolic power. Bourdieu himself uses the terminology of symbolic power, violence, and capital with considerable overlap; yet the different aspects I attempt to capture by these analytical distinctions appear in different parts of Bourdieu's work.

14. Wacquant (in Bourdieu and Wacquant 1992, 14–15) affirms that "indeed, the whole of Bourdieu's work may be interpreted as a materialist anthropology of the specific contribution that various forms of symbolic violence make to the reproduction and transformation of structures of domination."

An indicator of the importance of Bourdieu's pioneering work on the idea of symbolic power and violence can be seen in Steven Lukes's (2005, 139) assessment that Bourdieu's conceptualization is useful for helping us better understand the "black box" of power as domination where power is incorporated into the character of individuals.

of hierarchy and domination persist and reproduce intergenerationally without powerful resistance and without the conscious recognition of their members? The answer, he contends, is that the dominated internalize their conditions of domination as normal, inevitable, or natural, and thereby *misrecognize* the true nature of their social inequalities by accepting rather than resisting them.[15]

Symbolic power is not "symbolic" in the popular sense that it is "only symbolic" and therefore less forceful. Bourdieu contends that such thinking rests on the classic idealism/materialism dichotomy and thereby misses what is most notable about the relationship between material and symbolic expressions of power, namely their complex interdependency. Following the thought of Max Weber on the central role legitimation plays in domination, Bourdieu argues that neither brute force nor material possession is sufficient for the effective exercise of power. Power requires justification and belief.[16] Bourdieu elaborates and modifies Weber's concept of legitimation. The language of symbolic power and violence stresses that legitimate understandings of the social world are imposed by dominant groups and deeply internalized by subordinate groups in the form of practical taken-for-granted understandings. *Symbolic power* is the capacity to impose classifications and meanings as legitimate. Symbolic power takes the form of embodied dispositions—what Bourdieu calls the *habitus*—that generate a "practical sense" for organizing perceptions of and actions in the social world. The dispositions of habitus incorporate a sense of place in the stratified social order, an understanding of inclusion and exclusion in the various social hierarchies. Bourdieu puts power at the heart of the functioning and the structure of habitus, since habitus involves an uncon-

15. This is not to suggest that Bourdieu's conceptual framework is rigidly reproductionist in the sense that social structures perpetuate intergenerationally without modification as some critics (e.g., R. Jenkins 1982, 2000) allege. Certainly some of Bourdieu's formulations, particularly in *Reproduction in Education, Society, and Culture* (Bourdieu and Passeron 1977), lend themselves to this kind of easy summary. And as Bourdieu admitted, he was struck by how much continuity there is in the social world in spite of apparent change. Still, Bourdieu devoted considerable attention to the effects of political and economic change on social life, such as in his analyses of colonialism and war in Algeria, the effects of urbanization and the incursion of consumer markets on the traditional French peasantry, massive education expansion on the French university, and the effects of state neoliberal policies on housing, to mention just four cases. Bourdieu's conceptual framework is open to the possibility for social transformation—a topic I take up in chapter 8.

16. Bourdieu posits that "domination, even when based on naked force, that of arms or money, always has a symbolic dimension" (2000e, 172).

scious calculation of what is possible, probable, improbable, or impossible for people in their specific locations in the stratified social order.[17]

Symbolic power creates a form of *violence* that finds expression in everyday classifications, labels, meanings, and categorizations that subtly implement a social as well as symbolic logic of inclusion and exclusion. Symbolic violence also finds expression through body language, comportment, self-presentation, bodily care, and adornment. It has a corporal as well as a cognitive dimension.[18] And *symbolic capital* designates the social authority to impose symbolic meanings and classifications as legitimate that individuals and groups can accumulate through public recognition of their capital holdings and positions occupied in social hierarchies. Symbolic capital is a form of credit and it takes symbolic capital accumulated from previous struggles to exercise symbolic power (Bourdieu 1989d, 23).[19] These distinctions will be further elaborated in chapter 4.

Two key properties of symbolic power are its *naturalization* and its *misrecognition*. Bourdieu's symbolic power does not suggest "consent" but "practical adaptation" to existing hierarchies. The practical adaptation occurs prereflectively as if it were the "thing to do," the "natural" response in existing circumstances. This produces the *doxa* of the social order, the unquestioned acceptance of things as they naturally are. The dominated misperceive the real origins and interests of symbolic power when they adopt the dominant view of the world and of themselves (Bourdieu 2001c, 119). They therefore accept definitions of social reality that do not correspond to their best interests. Those *misrecognized* definitions go unchallenged as appearing natural and justified. Hence, they represent a form of violence. These properties of symbolic power help explain how inegalitarian social systems are able to self-perpetuate without powerful resistance and transformation. Chapter 4 will further explore the processes of naturalization and misrecognition.

---

17. This does not exhaust the dimensions of habitus that Bourdieu calls upon in various places in his work (see Swartz 1997, 95–116, for elaboration). But power is a central feature of this core concept and one that is often insufficiently appreciated by critics of his concept.

18. Symbolic power is "a gentle violence, imperceptible and invisible even to its victims, exerted for the most part through the purely symbolic channels of communication and cognition (more precisely, misrecognition), recognition, or even feeling" (Bourdieu 2001c, 1–2).

19. Wacquant (in Bourdieu and Wacquant 1992, 119) says of symbolic capital that Bourdieu's "whole work may be read as a hunt for its varied forms and effects."

Some Comparisons and Considerations

Bourdieu's interest in power stands within that classical tradition set forth by Max Weber in his analysis of "modes of domination" (see Lagroye 2002, 37). By what forms and through what processes are inequalities accepted by subordinate groups? It is not Weber's classic definition of power, which Bourdieu sees focused too narrowly on an interaction level of analysis and implies intentionality, but Weber's stress on the importance of legitimation in the exercise of power that most influences Bourdieu.[20] Bourdieu's stress on symbolic power, violence, and capital can be broadly seen as an elaboration of Weber's thinking on the role of legitimation in maintaining established power relations. But Bourdieu's analysis of symbolic power also includes a political vision that is more egalitarian and socialist in orientation than that of Weber.

Though similar to the Marxian notions of ideology and the Gramscian variant of hegemony—two forms of cultural power most frequently associated with state-created nationalism—symbolic power and violence stress the practical justification of the established order through taken-for-granted assumptions, classifications, and perceptions rather than specific beliefs, cultural messages, or explicit discourses. Bourdieu's concept of symbolic power and violence points to a layer of pre-existing practical schemes that make ideological and hegemonic messages palatable. The symbolic power of modern educational systems, for example, lies not so much in explicit justification of privilege by dominant groups but in the idea that differential access to the advantages of education is misrecognized as simply express-

---

20. Weber defines power (*Macht*) as "the probability that one actor within a social relationship will be in a position to carry out his own will despite resistance, regardless of the basis on which this probability rests" (Weber 1978a, 53; see also p. 926 for a similar definition: the "chance of a man or a number of men to realize their own will in a social action even against the resistance of others who are participating in the action.") Many sociologists would join Anthony Giddens (1979, 256) and Kate Nash (2000, 1) in observing that Weber's definition of power has been the most influential in sociology. To illustrate, Kimmerling (1996, 154), referencing Dennis Wrong (1995), offers this definition: "Power is the ability of persons or groups to intentionally impose their will and/or interests over others, by controlling different resources including violence." For Bourdieu, this definition captures only a small part of the dynamics of power. Bourdieu focuses more (see, e.g., Bourdieu 1996d) on that "subterranean" realm in civil society that functions for the most part beyond the reach of conscious reflection and instrumental intention as Wrong's definition requires.

ing individual natural abilities and effort rather than reflecting the unequal distribution of inherited cultural capital among social classes. Moreover, in comparison to the Marxian concept of ideology, Bourdieu's language of symbolic power stresses that culture does not simply reflect underlying economic and social relations but is also constitutive of them. Naming and classification, the capacity to use symbolic forms to create associations and divisions, helps bring into existence and give identity to social groups and define their interrelationships. Group making and the central role of symbolic power in that process stand at the heart of Bourdieu's political sociology; symbolic power links politics to the construction of social realities and identities. Culture obtains relative autonomy from the economy.

With the idea of symbolic power, Bourdieu argues that all practices involve power relations. In this respect, he belongs to the current of thought shared by others, like Michel Foucault (1977, 1980b), who stress the central role of power in aspects of social life not usually thought of in power terms—discourse and body language, for example. Both stress how power is embedded in cultural forms. Foucault and Bourdieu share the view that power is implicated in multiple ways, both cognitively and bodily, in the constitution of all areas of social life. Bourdieu's concept of habitus has a corporal dimension that includes the kind of "body politics" that Foucault emphasized. They both focus on what Michael Mann terms "diffuse power" (1986, 8). Yet unlike Foucault, Bourdieu stresses how power becomes embedded in selected kinds of resources that he calls capitals and in particular arenas of human activity that he calls fields. For Foucault, power is diffused throughout the "body politic." For Bourdieu, there are concentrations of power as well, particularly in the field of power and the state as we will see in chapters 3 and 5. Bourdieu's concepts of capitals and fields give him an empirical research orientation that can include but go beyond discourse analysis in the Foucaultian tradition.

Power in the form of symbolic power and violence has not only been Bourdieu's most widely acknowledged contribution to contemporary thinking about power but also the object of sharp criticism. Two frequent criticisms will be mentioned here but developed further in chapters 4 and 5. In modern differentiated societies, Bourdieu stresses that the state, through law, official classifications, and particularly education, institutes fundamental frames of reference, perception, understanding, and memory. It therefore monopolizes the means of symbolic as well as physical violence. But in assigning to the modern state a monopolizing function of symbolic power and violence Bourdieu underestimates the importance of other sources of symbolic power, such as religion, even in modern societies outside of Europe.

Reproduction of social hierarchies likely involves much more than misrecognition. The degree of acceptance and respect for existing hierarchies may be less deeply internalized in numerous instances than the idea of symbolic violence implies. There may be conscious recognition of inequality that leads to tacit forms of contestation or reluctance to resist for fear of reprisal (Scott 1990).

Nonetheless, Bourdieu's perspective challenges the commonly held view that symbolic power is simply "symbolic." Symbolic meanings and classifications are constitutive forces in organizing power relations in stratified social orders. Moreover, the concept of symbolic violence marks a critical break with the view that power has become much more benign and less relevant in societies where the most authoritarian and crudest techniques of coercion have been replaced with persuasion, consent, choice, influence, and negotiation. It reminds us that power remains very much an organizing force in modern societies, though its forms have changed.[21]

Some Implications for Thinking about Power

Though a contested concept (Lukes 2005), power stands at the very heart of political sociology (Kimmerling 1996, 154; Neuman 2005, 11).[22] Since power, particularly in the form of domination, stands at the core of Bourdieu's sociology, it is therefore useful to read Bourdieu as a political sociologist. By making power a central concern in his sociology, Bourdieu joins relatively few other contemporary sociologists, such as Anthony Giddens, Steven Lukes, Michael Mann, Charles Tilly, and Dennis Wrong, who do so.[23] But in contrast to Giddens, Mann, Lukes, and particularly Wrong,

21. One illustration can be found in Bourdieu's (1988b, 194–225) analysis of teacher evaluative remarks on student exams that reach beyond cognitive performance criteria to amount to socially charged slights that stigmatize. Negative epithets, such as "narrow," "mediocre," and "clumsy" as well as negatively slanted complements such as "painstaking," "cautious," and "conscientious" tend to be applied to students from the middle and lower classes.

22. Giddens (1979) argues that all major sociological concepts, not just the concept of power, are fundamentally "contested."

23. Giddens (ibid., 68), for example, sees the orientation of his own work as an important exception in sociology when he writes, "I mean to stress the centrality of the concept of power to social theory." Alexander (2003, 2006), by contrast, does not.

who attempt a classification of all forms of power, Bourdieu does not offer a comprehensive analysis of the concept of power per se. Bourdieu is
fundamentally interested in domination as a type of power for empirical
research. He focused his efforts on empirical research rather than on theoretical classification.

Though Bourdieu's work focuses on power as domination, it would over-
simplify his analysis by making the familiar "power to/power over" distinction and classify him as attending only to the latter.[24] Bourdieu just does
not think in terms of this kind of distinction. He makes no clear distinction
between practices as capacities to empower and those to dominate. Nor
does he distinguish a type of power that is zero sum (distributive) from a
type producing collective benefits.[25] Bourdieu's main concern is not one of
laying out a typology of power. He does not offer a systematic analysis of
all forms of power, or a conceptual map of the various forms of power as
do other scholars like Lukes, Mann, and Wrong. His focus is domination,
indeed, a particular type of domination that he tries conceptually to capture with the language of symbolic power, violence, and capital.

The political sociology tradition has identified four types of power,
though devoting a preponderant of attention to the latter three: (1) physical coercion or the threat of physical force; (2) observable conflict among
competing interests; (3) agenda-setting and nondecisionmaking; and
(4) thought control (Neuman 2005, 12–17). It is the last two forms, particularly control over how we understand the social world, that are the foci of
interest for Bourdieu. It is in what Lukes (2005), in his classic statement
on power, calls the "third dimension" of power that we find Bourdieu's
specific contribution to political sociology.

24. "Power to" is the capacity to create opportunities and advantages that do not necessarily take away from others. "Power over" is the capacity that establishes relations of dependency, often against the best interests of subordinates. Numerous theorists, such as Lukes
(2005), Giddens (1976, 110–11; 1979, 88–93), and particularly Wrong (1995), see analytical
value in the power to/power over distinction. In the 2005 revision of his classic statement
on power, Lukes (2005, 83–84) now acknowledges that the influence of power is not always
negative, zero-sum, or affects the interests of others negatively. Relations of dependency,
implied by domination, need not always mean that power cannot work to the benefit of
subordinates.

25. Parsons (1960) made the distributive/collective distinction in his widely accepted criticism of Weber's discussion of power and domination (Giddens 1979; Mann 1986; Wrong
1995).

Lukes's seminal 1974 statement helped shift attention to the importance of the "third dimension" and in his recent second and elaborated
edition of his 1974 work he sees Bourdieu contributing to a richer understanding of the third dimension of power as domination. Lukes draws on
Bourdieu to help understand how power as domination is internalized as
part of the habitus, particularly Bourdieu's claim that the effectiveness
of power as domination is enhanced by its "naturalization," where what
is arbitrary and unequal appears to actors as natural and objective, and
by the "misrecognition" of its origins and modes of operation. These insights, Lukes believes, offer intriguing avenues for empirical investigation
into how compliance becomes an internalized disposition. Indeed, Lukes
agrees with Bourdieu that the more invisible the third dimension of power
the more effective it is (Lukes 2005, 139–44).

Lukes, however, differs with Bourdieu in weighing the degree to which
symbolic power is effective and causal. Lukes would grant to actors a
greater degree of reflective awareness than Bourdieu does. Power may
not go as undetected as "naturalization" and "misrecognition" suggest,
for actors may hold a high degree of consciousness of oppressive structures and yet consent to comply for some measure of success, happiness,
or security. Moreover, power may elicit more resistance than Bourdieu
seems willing to admit. I concur with Lukes on these critical points and
will return to them in later chapters. Yet, as this overview of Bourdieu's
thinking suggests, Bourdieu's analysis of forms of power goes well beyond
that of Lukes's third dimension to also include power vested in particular
resources (capitals) and as organizing human action in particular arenas
(fields).

In his monumental study of the sources of social power, Michael Mann
(1986, 1–33; 1993, 6–10) identifies four distinct ideal types of power: economic, political, military, and ideological. Bourdieu offers no comparable
typology. He concentrates his attention on what Mann (1986, 8, 22–24)
calls "ideological power," which includes meanings, norms, and aesthetic/
ritual practices and depends more on "*diffused* power techniques," which
are "more spontaneous, unconscious, decentered" than on "definite com-
mands and conscious obedience." Like Bourdieu, Mann rejects materialist
reductionism by stressing that ideology does not merely integrate and reflect existing social arrangements but "it may actually create a society-like
network, a religious or cultural community, out of emergent, interstitial
social needs and relations." However, Bourdieu assigns a greater legitimating force to symbols than does Mann. Bourdieu gives more weight

to the internalized presence of symbolic power (i.e., symbolic violence) than Mann, who focuses more on the *"organizational means"* for achieving social control. For Mann, organization capacity is more important than sheer legitimation in making domination possible. His answer to the key question of why the masses do not revolt is "because they lack collective organization to do otherwise, because they are embedded within collective and distributive power organizations controlled by others." Moreover, he specifies that "one conceptual distinction between power and authority (i.e., power considered legitimate by all affected by it) will not figure much in this book. It is rare to find power that is either largely legitimate or largely illegitimate because its exercise is normally so double-edged" (Mann 1986, 2, 7, 23). Bourdieu, likewise, does not make a significant conceptual distinction between power and authority. He stresses that the exercise of symbolic power requires symbolic capital (authority).

In addition, Mann accepts the distributive/collective power distinction offered by Parsons (1960) and, while acknowledging that the two are dialectically related, Mann emphasizes the importance of collective power relations in creating new capacities, most notably with the emergence of the nation state. This is rather different from Bourdieu's view of domination that stresses the effects of symbolic violence—a distributive power. Bourdieu does not concern himself with collective power as something distinct from distributive power.

Thus, Bourdieu's sociology offers conceptual tools for analyzing three types of power: power vested in particular resources (capitals), power concentrated in specific spheres of struggle over forms of capital (fields of power), and power as practical, taken-for-granted acceptance of existing social hierarchies (symbolic power and violence). Bourdieu's sociology of symbolic power sensitizes us to the more subtle and influential forms of power, which operate through cultural resources and symbolic classifications that interweave everyday life with prevailing institutional arrangements. It calls for looking at expressions of power that radiate through interpersonal relations and presentations of self as well as organizational structures. It suggests an intimate and complex relationship between symbolic and material factors in the operation of power. He also identifies a wide variety of power resources (capitals) beyond sheer economic interests that function as power resources. In so doing, Bourdieu invites sociologists to identify valued resources that may function as forms of power even though they present otherwise. His thinking of power as forms of capital suggests a way for analyzing careers and stances of political leaders in terms of inherited, invested, accumulated, and exchanged varieties of power resources. And his concept of field offers a conceptual language that encourages examination of interrelationships across levels of analysis and analytical units that usually are isolated for specialized focus in empirical research. In the next chapters I will probe these ideas in depth.

CHAPTER THREE

Capitals and Fields of Power

In this chapter I first of all take up Bourdieu's conceptualization of power as forms of capital. Why does he use the economic language of capital to talk about power? Three reasons are offered, and his usage of the term *capital* is compared and contrasted to that found in Marxism, standard neoclassical economics, and human capital theory. His concept of capital is relationally connected to his concept of field. I review the key features involved in field analysis and how Bourdieu thinks about society as an array of fields with specific forms of capital that are objects of struggle. Of central importance to his view of the stratification order and to a political sociology of modern societies is the field of power. I present that concept noting the central role of the state, which I take up in chapter 5. I then turn to Bourdieu's view of political capital in the political field and explore how he uses his concepts of capital and field to analyze the political arena. Finally, I offer some evaluation.

Capitals as Forms of Power

Bourdieu (1986, 243) uses the economic language of capital to talk about many kinds of resources that function as forms of power. Why? Three interrelated reasons can be offered.

First, he uses economic language as a rhetorical device to break with common assumptions about the disinterested character of certain social universes and their characteristics. It is a tool for breaking with received wisdom that many practices appear devoid of interests, such as cultural practices that emphasize individual creativity, giftedness, or political practices stressing individual charisma. The Nobel Prize laureate, the best-selling literary figure, and the MacArthur fellow are heirs and accumulators of various forms of capital. So are most political leaders. Such public figures are usually thought of in terms of their individual capacities but Bourdieu stresses they are also carriers of unexamined social hierarchies—in many cases forms of inherited and accumulated cultural capital. The economic language of capital permits Bourdieu to point up the interested character (power dimension) of these leaders and their social worlds.

Second, the use of economic language is motivated by Bourdieu's desire to develop a theory of practices. The terminology of capital is part of his general science of the economy of practices that views all practices organized around cost-benefit calculations (usually more tacit than conscious) involving the investment, accumulation, expenditure, exchange, and consumption of a great variety of valued resources. Here he breaks with standard economic assumptions that tend to reduce everything to material and monetary interests. Conscious calculation of material rewards is only a small part of a general economy of practices whose calculation is tacit and social rather than explicit and strictly individual, where individuals pursue symbolic as well as material and monetary rewards, and where profits and costs are real but seldom easily quantifiable or reducible to monetary measures. It is a theory of action that is dispositional rather than oriented by rational choice or conformity to social rules or norms; it is fundamentally social in that individual conduct interweaves through social relations. It is a view of action that stresses how individual choices are for the most part tacit calculations based on past experience and accumulated resources as well as opportunities and constraints in structured environments.

Finally, Bourdieu's reach for economic terminology is not just a conceptual or theoretical strategy but also grows out of empirical research in which he is looking for conceptual language to describe certain empirical patterns. One sees this already in his early Algerian work when he participates in critical dialogue and collaboration with French economists charged to gather and evaluate data on the Algerian population during the French Algerian war (Lebaron 2004). There, he combines ethnographic and statistical observations of work, employment, and time structures to identify dispositions toward markets that confound standard neoclassical microeconomic models. Later, his notion of culture as a form of capital grew out of his empirical research showing educational achievement to be more strongly related to cultural background of the family (notably parental education) than to income in France. Employing the term *cultural capital* was for Bourdieu a way of highlighting this finding—novel for the sixties—as well as serving as a tool for breaking with the popular view of educational success as stemming from "natural aptitudes" rather than intergeneration transmission of cultural advantages in families (Bourdieu 1986, 243). I want to elaborate briefly on these interrelated points.

Bourdieu uses economic terminology in a rather different way than is found in standard economic theory. Bourdieu uses the term *economy* in a broader sense—what he calls a "generalized" sense—than the usual and more narrow sense associated with monetary and material goods.[1] He distinguishes between a restricted and generalized economy of practices. He sees this opposition as the "historical invention of capitalism," which categorically divides the universe of human exchanges into those that are economic and therefore materially self-interested and those that are non-economic and therefore disinterested. He contends that "by reducing the universe of exchanges to mercantile exchange, which is objectively and subjectively oriented toward the maximization of profit, i.e., (economically) *self-interested*, it has implicitly defined the other forms of exchange as noneconomic, and therefore *disinterested*" (Bourdieu 1986, 242). This other arena of apparently disinterested practices, such as art, literature, education, and religion, in fact harbors underlying power relations that need legitimation. By developing his general science of the economy of practices Bourdieu examines the complex relationship between the restricted order of economic exchange focused on material and monetary capital and this broader generalized economy that is ostensibly disinterested. He charges that classical economic theory—Keynesian, Marxism, and human capital theory—all employ restricted notions of interest. They all assume a version of economic man who follows self-interested maximization of material and monetary interests. Bourdieu proposes transcending this restricted view of the economy by offering his generalized economy of practices where all practices have an economic logic, though it is a social logic rather than a logic that stems from just individual choice and where interests are multiple and cultural as well as material and monetary.

Thus, his general science of the economy of practices would expand the ideas of interest and capital beyond the usual material and monetary ones. The language of capital permits him to study how different kinds of valued

---

1. Lebaron (2004, 94) observes that Bourdieu gives these economic terms "non-monetary and nonquantitative meaning."

resources can be created, accumulated, exchanged, saved, consumed, and lost. This type of economic calculation is just one of the broader array of economy of practices that involve symbolic, cultural, social considerations as well as monetary and material. Bourdieu (1986, 243, 255 n. 243) speaks of four generic types of capital: economic (money and property), cultural (information, knowledge, and educational credentials), social (acquaintances and networks), and symbolic (legitimation and prestige).[2] His idea of cultural capital is most widely known (see Lareau and Weininger 2004; Swartz 2005) but his work includes a broad array of capitals, such as social capital, economic capital, academic capital, political capital, and statist capital, which are unevenly distributed across social groups.

For the sociology of politics Bourdieu's general science of the economy of practices will be important in several ways. His use of economic language to talk about power will not lead to a political sociology oriented by rational actor or public choice theory. Indeed, he is quite critical of that view of action. His framework points toward social rationalities of politics rather than preferences of individual choice. His framework will also suggest there is a complex interplay between political and ostensibly nonpolitical forms of power, notably through what Bourdieu calls social capital and symbolic capital. This will open up investigation into what Lukes (2005) calls the "third dimension" of power. And, as we will see later in the chapter, actors can invest in, accumulate, and profit from (or lose) political capital, and, under certain conditions, exchange it with other kinds of capital. Wealthy business leaders in the United States transform some of their economic capital into political capital by campaigning for political office. Celebrities with considerable symbolic capital try to transform that into political capital by running for office in the European Parliament (Kauppi 2004). Thus, an important implication for political sociology would be analyzing political careers in terms of inheritance and strategies of accumulation and conversion of various kinds of capital.

2. His 1983 paper "The Forms of Capital" (Bourdieu 1986) is devoted to explaining his conceptualization of capital. Capital, he says, can "present itself in three fundamental guises as economic capital, cultural capital, and social capital" (243). Symbolic capital is only defined in a note but not discussed. Likewise, *An Invitation to Reflexive Sociology* (Bourdieu and Wacquant 1992, 119) presents capital as taking on "*three fundamental species* (each with its own subtypes, namely, economic capital, cultural capital, and social capital." Symbolic capital designates the effects of legitimation for one of the other capitals. I will discuss in chapter 4 the particular properties of symbolic capital that set it apart from the three other generic types.

Bourdieu transforms the meaning of the economic language of capital from that found in Marxism and in neoclassical economics and its human capital variant.[3] While capital functions to enhance economic value, that capacity is not an intrinsic feature of some object or type of private property used to produce something else. Nor does it reside in the intention of actors to employ some resource for future gain by investing rather than consuming it. Rather, Bourdieu thinks of capital as a "social relation of power" that has a differentiating and stratifying effect between individuals and groups. An object becomes a capital when it establishes a social relation of power that differentiates the holder from the nonholder, when it establishes some degree of social closure—a relation of inclusion and exclusion. Thus, Bourdieu's usage of the term *capital* has some affinity with usage in Marxism but is not fundamentally a Marxist concept.

Bourdieu's use of the term *capital* is social and relational, two features found in Marxism, although Bourdieu rejects the economic reductionism found in Marx's thinking. Bourdieu distances himself from Marxism by extending the idea of capital to a great variety of forms of power, whether material, cultural, social, or symbolic. Individuals and groups draw upon a variety of cultural, social, and symbolic resources, not just material, in order to maintain and enhance their positions in the social order. He thus offers a broader conceptualization of capital as a social relation than does traditional Marxism.

This critical conceptual elaboration relative to Marxism needs to be understood in historical context. When Bourdieu went to Algeria in the late 1950s and began his ethnological research and subsequent writing, structuralist Marxism represented a key intellectual pole in France. Economic anthropology of Marxist orientation was of keen interest and posed a central question: how might one apply the conceptual categories of historical materialism to traditional, undifferentiated, noncapitalist societies where markets were embedded in thick social relations?[4] To what extent could economic categories, such as money, capital, exploitation, surplus value, be applied to societies that ostensibly did not differentiate a market or economic sphere from kinship and mythology? Bourdieu's early work enters in that intellectual debate.

3. See Lebaron 2004 for valuable background on Bourdieu's early critical dialogue with French economists. Also see Bourdieu 1974; 1984a; 1996d, 275–76; 1999b; 2000e.

4. See the work of Maurice Goldelier (1972), Claude Meillassoux (1964, 1974), Pierre-Philippe Rey (1971), and Emmanuel Terray (1969).

Bourdieu clearly marks his distance from orthodox Marxism when he employs the term *capital* in his analysis of the Berber. In undifferentiated traditional societies, such as the Berber peasant communities he studied in Algeria, the family patrimony depends not only on its land, animals, and instruments of production but also on kinship relations and networks of alliances that represent "a heritage of commitments and debts of honour, a capital of rights and duties built up in the course of successive generations and providing an additional source of strength which can be called upon when extraordinary situations break in upon the daily routine" (Bourdieu 1977a, 178). In modern differentiated societies, access to sources of income in the labor market depends upon cultural capital in the form of educational credentials and social capital in the form of networks. These forms of power, and their unequal distribution among individuals and groups, explain for Bourdieu why random and perfect competition models are inadequate for understanding social life (Bourdieu 1986, 241). They also illustrate for Bourdieu why a Marxist focus on economic capital, and that of economic theory more generally, is based on a restricted concept of power.

As I point out in *Culture and Power* (Swartz 1997, 74–75), Bourdieu's concept of capital approaches that of Marx when he writes that "capital is accumulated labor," or that "the universal equivalent, the measure of all equivalences" among various types of capital "is nothing other than labor-time (in the widest sense)" (1986, 241, 253).[5] Indeed, Bourdieu's concept of capital appears rooted in a kind of labor theory of value. Yet Bourdieu (245) indicates that scarcity as well as labor is also a factor in determining value and his concept does not include the theory of surplus value. Moreover, his concept, unlike that of Marx, does not distinguish capitalist from noncapitalist forms of labor.[6]

Thus, a key contribution of Bourdieu's generalized conception of the economy of practices beyond Marxism and neoclassical economic theory is to see a much broader range of types of labor (social, cultural, religious, familial, political, to name but a few) that constitute power resources and that under certain conditions and at certain rates can be converted one into another. Indeed, a central focus of Bourdieu's sociology is how and under what conditions individuals and groups employ strategies of capi-

---

5. That would include "labor-time accumulated in the form of capital and the labor-time needed to transform it from one type into another" (Bourdieu 1986, 253).

6. Calhoun (1993, 67–69) makes a similar observation.

tal accumulation, investment, and exchange of various kinds of capital in order to maintain or enhance their positions in the social world. And it represents a foundation for how he thinks about politics.

This suggests some affinity to human capital theory where skills and abilities secured through education and training are considered tools for increasing productivity (Schultz 1961, 1963). Bourdieu's view of power as forms of capital intersects with Gary Becker's (1964, 1976) human capital theory in that both Becker and Bourdieu extend the concept of capital beyond the usual material and monetary terms. Bourdieu in fact casts Becker's human capital within a broader generalized economy of practices. While Becker recognizes, particularly in his later work, cultural and status as well as material and monetary interests, for Bourdieu Becker doesn't extend this idea far enough. There can be social and symbolic profits as well as monetary costs and profits. Profits from education, for example, can be measured not just in income but in tastes, verbal style, manners, and so on (Bourdieu 1986, 243–44, 255). Bourdieu's concept includes but does not reduce to quantifiable measures. Moreover, Bourdieu's concept of cultural capital does not reduce to knowledge and skills directly related to productivity but represents a capacity to make individuals more effective actors within a particular social milieu. Thus, proper types of schooling, reading certain books, acquiring stylized manners, speaking in a certain way, can all function as cultural capital to enhance valued participation in selected social settings. Thus, Bourdieu's concept of cultural capital is broader than human capital, which represents just one type of the former.

Both Bourdieu and Becker present human action in cost-benefit terms, although Bourdieu stresses that his view does not share the anthropological assumptions of a rational actor perspective. Bourdieu's view of practices does not reduce to a utilitarian conception of a form of human capital whereby individuals consciously calculate to maximize the value of a given resource in the market. While Bourdieu uses the economic language suggesting to some critics, such as Alain Caillé (1981, 1992), a utilitarian orientation, his thinking is much closer to the social and anti-utilitarian orientation of Emile Durkheim than the thinking of Jeremy Bentham.[7] These differences, Bourdieu stresses, lead him to distinguish his approach from Becker's economic approach by concluding that they share only "a

---

7. I do agree with Caillé that there is a dimension of utilitarian thinking in Bourdieu, namely that conduct always appears to be oriented toward accruing power and wealth. But it is more of a stratifying orientation rather than one of growing individual and collective good.

number of words" (Bourdieu and Wacquant 1992, 118). Thus, Bourdieu's political sociology does not reduce to an economic sociology. It points to a view that roots politics in a social conflict and stratification perspective—one in which individuals and groups struggle to maintain and enhance their positions in various fields. And Bourdieu stresses the symbolic dimension of practices that escapes most economic sociology. This will become even more apparent when I consider in the next chapter his thinking on symbolic power.

Relations among Types of Capitals

How does Bourdieu think about the relationship between the various forms of capital? He sees the objective of sociology as to examine the multiple forms of power and their complex interrelations. He proposes a general science of the various forms of power as capital and the laws of their interconvertibility. Capitals are interrelated; they need to be conceptualized relationally rather than as separate entities. Bourdieu is a relational thinker like Marx who observes that "capital is not a thing, but a social relation between persons which is mediated through things" (1977, 932). One form of capital obtains significance in relation or opposition to another. The most prominent example in Bourdieu's writings is the cultural capital/economic capital relationship. Economic interest stands against cultural disinterest as one defines the other in a dialectical relationship. Just as Marx saw the working class and the capitalist class as relationally connected historically and conceptually, so also Bourdieu sees cultural capital and economic capital as dialectically interrelated.

In *The Logic of Practice* (1990c, 122, 300), Bourdieu remarks that capital is a kind of "energy of social physics" that can exist in a variety of forms and under certain conditions and exchange rates can interconvert from one into another. This image of capital suggests a conceptualization of power that is multiple and one where no particular form is given theoretical priority over the other. Indeed he offers a quote from Bertrand Russell (1938, 9–10) to suggest that power is analogous to energy in that it occurs in many forms and no one form is more fundamental than the others or can be treated independently of the others.[8] The passage by Rus-

---

8. Bourdieu (1990c, 122) does not push the analogy to social physics very far since he acknowledges that "social science is not a social physics." As I discuss in the next chapter, symbolic power, through the misrecognition of various forms of capital as something ostensi-

sell, where he draws the analogy of power in the social world to energy in physics, is instructive since it offers insight into how Bourdieu himself approaches the analysis of power. Russell writes that

> the fundamental concept in social science is Power, in the same sense in which Energy is the fundamental concept in physics. Like energy, power has many forms, such as wealth, armaments, civil authority, influence on opinion. No one of these can be regarded as subordinate to any other, and there is no one form from which the others are derivative. The attempt to treat one form of power, say wealth, in isolation, can only be partially successful, just as the study of one form of energy will be defective at certain points, unless other forms are taken into account. Wealth may result from military power or from influence over opinion, just as either of these may result from wealth. . . . To revert to the analogy of physics: power, like energy, must be regarded as continually passing from any one of its forms into any other, and it should be the business of social science to seek the laws of such transformations.

In Bourdieu's language sociology should study the various forms of capital (forms of power) and the laws of their accumulation and exchange as humans struggle to maintain and enhance their positions in the social order. The objective of social science is to study the laws of conversion of the different forms of power. Indeed, one of key emphases of Bourdieu's work as political sociology is the study of the multiple forms of power and their interconvertibility.

Capitals are relational and zero sum. As noted in chapter 2, Bourdieu is not concerned with the collective or shared benefits of power, only their private appropriation and zero-sum relations—one capital gains in strength in opposition to another. He casts his thinking about power within the framework of a general science of the economy of practices. Referencing Russell again, Bourdieu writes:

> In accordance with a principle which is the equivalent of the principle of the conservation of energy, profits in one area are necessarily paid for by costs in another (so that a concept like wastage has no meaning in a general science of the economy of practices). The universal equivalent, the measure of all equivalences, is nothing other than labor-time (in the widest sense); and the conservation of social energy through all its conversions is verified if, in each case, one

---

bly other than power, decisively shapes human practices. Perceptions matter in understanding human action.

takes into account both the labor-time accumulated in the form of capital and the labor-time need to transform it from one type into another. (1986, 253)

The emphasis here is not on how some action could create more social energy for everyone but on the economy of practices where every act is a cost, its benefits appropriated privately, and where actors strategize to convert one form of capital into another in order to maintain and enhance their positions in the social order. Bourdieu's capital is a distributive power. It operates in a zero-sum system.

Capitals and Fields

Bourdieu argues that for resources to become forms of capital in modern stratified societies, they must become instruments and objects of struggle in structured arenas, or social spaces that Bourdieu calls fields.[9] Resources turn into capital when they come to function as a "social relation of power" by becoming objects of struggle as valued resources. Capital as a "social relation of power" is constituted in and by a field where it is one of the stakes and instruments of struggle (Bourdieu 1989b, 375). He considers that "a capital does not exist and function except in relation to a field" (Bourdieu and Wacquant 1992, 101).[10]

In discussing cultural capital Bourdieu remarks that "it should not be forgotten that it [cultural capital] exists as symbolically and materially active, effective capital only insofar as it is appropriated by agents and implemented and invested as a weapon and a stake in the struggles which go on in the fields of cultural production (the artistic field, the scientific field,

9. Bourdieu used the language of capital in his analysis of traditional Berber societies before he developed his concept of field. This linkage between capital and field reflects Bourdieu's conceptual development and his shift in focus from what he called traditional, undifferentiated societies to modern differentiated societies. Yet, Bourdieu never stopped reasoning in terms of his early fieldwork experiences in Algeria as his later essay on gender relations attests (Bourdieu 2001c).

10. He specifies that "this is so because, at bottom, the value of a species of capital (e.g., knowledge of Greek or of integral calculus) hinges on the existence of a game, of a field in which this competency can be employed: a species of capital is what is efficacious in a given field, both as a weapon and as a stake of struggle, that which allows its possessors to wield a power, an influence, and thus to exist, in the field under consideration, instead of being considered a negligible quantity" (Bourdieu and Wacquant 1992, 98).

etc.) and, beyond them, in the field of the social classes" (1986, 247). There are as many fields as there are types of capitals, and though one type of capital tends to identify the character of a particular field, fields can be and often are arenas of conflict involving several different capitals. Bourdieu thinks of fields as places of exchange—markets—where different capitals exchange one for the other but also where actors struggle to valorize one form of capital over all others.

Political practices, as all practices, occur in such structured arenas of conflict called *fields*. Elsewhere I (Swartz 1997, 117–36) present the key properties that fields develop as they grow in autonomy so will only summarize them here.[11] Bourdieu defines a field as

> network, or configuration, of objective relations between positions. These positions are objectively defined, in their existence and in the determinations they impose upon their occupants, agents or institutions, by their present and potential situation (*situs*) in the structure of the distribution of species of power (or capital) whose possession commands access to the specific profits that are at stake in the field, as well as by their objective relation to other positions (domination, subordination, homology, etc.). (Bourdieu and Wacquant 1992, 97)

Fields denote arenas of production, circulation, appropriation and exchange of goods, services, knowledge, or status, and the competitive positions held by actors in their struggle to accumulate, exchange, and monopolize these different kinds of capital. Fields may be thought of as structured spaces that organize around specific types of capital or combinations of capital. There are power arenas as well as power resources in Bourdieu's political sociology.

Bourdieu (1993c, 72) speaks of the "invariant laws" or "universal mechanisms" that are structural properties characteristic of all fields. First, fields are arenas of struggle for control over valued resources, which Bourdieu calls *capitals*. Field struggle centers around particular forms of capital, such as economic, cultural, scientific, or religious. Second, fields are structured spaces of dominant and subordinate positions based on types and amounts of capital. Fields are stratified by the unequal distribution of relevant capitals and field struggle pits those in dominant positions

---

11. Bourdieu outlines field properties in many places, including Bourdieu 1993h, 72–77. See Bourdieu 1993h, 118, and Swartz 1997 on the origins of the concept, and see Bourdieu 1996d, 264–72, and Bourdieu and Wacquant 1992, 18, 76–77, on the field of power.

with more capital against those in subordinate positions with less. Third, fields impose on actors specific forms of struggle. Both dominants and subordinates share a fundamental doxa, or set of rules of the game that specify, often tacitly, the specific forms of struggle that are legitimate. Fourth, fields are structured to a significant extent by their own internal mechanisms of development and thus hold some degree of autonomy from the external environment. Cultural fields, for example, develop their own specific laws of exercise that relate to but do not reduce to economic or political interests. Bourdieu uses the language of "relative autonomy" and "structural and functional homologies" to talk about interfield relations in terms of isomorphic patterns, or similarity of function, but devoid of instrumental design.

Each field is internally differentiated by a "homologous structure" of an economically dominant and culturally dominated pole and a culturally dominant and economically dominated pole (Bourdieu 1989a, 383). Two major competing principles of social hierarchy—what Bourdieu calls a "chiasmatic structure"—shape the struggle for power in modern industrial societies: the distribution of *economic capital* (wealth, income, and property), which Bourdieu calls the "dominant principle of hierarchy," and the distribution of *cultural capital* (knowledge, culture, and educational credentials), which Bourdieu calls the "second principle of hierarchy." Bourdieu's field analytic approach to the study of the social world consists of identifying the various forms that this oppositional structure takes in specific arenas of struggle. The chiasmatic structure of economic capital and cultural capital functions as both the bedrock of Bourdieu's field analysis and his understanding of social stratification and politics.[12] Political action is mediated through structural relations of fields.

"To think in terms of field is to think relationally," says Bourdieu (Bourdieu and Wacquant 1992, 96). The concept of field permits Bourdieu to employ relational thinking, which he contends is fundamental to a scientific perspective on the social world. Relationality for Bourdieu means conceptualizing individuals, groups, or even capitals as interdependent units in broad networks of relations that shape human action beyond individual consciousness or even direct contact. Capital and field mutually

---

12. He in fact sees this chiasmatic structure as a "transhistorical" structure whose existence predates the rise of modern industrial societies. At its most general level, this chiasmatic structure represents the "fundamental opposition of the division of labour of domination" across all societies that occurs "between temporal and spiritual powers" (Wacquant 1993b, 24).

define and specify each other. "When one speaks of specific capital, this means to say that this capital is effective in relation to a particular field, and therefore within the limits of that field, and that it is only convertible into another kind of capital on certain conditions" (Bourdieu 1993h, 73).

Further, Bourdieu thinks of fields as a historical process of constitution. Fields can differ in their degree of institutionalization of these structural features and hence in their degree of autonomy. Thus in the primitive phases when a valued resource is just becoming an object of struggle the actual boundaries of the arena of struggle may well be just emerging. Bourdieu (Bourdieu and Wacquant 1992, 98–99) notes that "in empirical work, it is one and the same thing to determine what the field is, where its limits lie, etc., and to determine what species of capital are active in it, within what limits, and so on. (We see here how the notions of capital and field are tightly interconnected.)" It is not a chicken-and-egg conundrum of which comes first; they take form simultaneously.[13]

Fields are arenas of struggle, not functional units in a larger conceptual system. It is the field, not society, that is Bourdieu's macro unit of analysis. Moreover, the unifying factor of fields is not some functional coherence, whether intentional or not, but the sheer fact of struggle, that actors take up positions relationally, in opposition to others, and it is that system of oppositions that gives unity to a field (Bourdieu 1991f, 19). It is important to stress the dynamics of struggle, which differentiates Bourdieu's concept of field from Althusser's notion of state "apparatus" that was popular in French intellectual circles, particular Marxist ones, when Bourdieu was developing his concept (Bourdieu and Wacquant 1992, 101–4). Field struggle, for Bourdieu, has two distinct dimensions. On the one hand, it is struggle over the distribution of capitals relevant to specific fields. This is struggle to accumulate the more valued forms of capital or to convert one form into another more valued form. In this sense, capital is a stake in the struggle. Thus, "the structure of the field is a state of the power relations among the agents or institutions engaged in the struggle, or, to put it another way, a state of the distribution of the specific capital which has been accumulated in the course of previous struggles and which orients subsequent strategies" (Bourdieu 1993h, 73). On the other hand, the struggle is also over the very definition of the most legitimate form of capital for a particular field. This is a struggle for symbolic power (which I

13. However, conceptually Bourdieu developed his concept of capital earlier than that of field.

examine in chapter 4), a classification struggle, over the right to monopolize the legitimate definition of what is to be the most legitimate form of
capital for a particular field. Field struggle, therefore, involves these two
broad types of power struggle: struggle for valued resources and struggle
over defining just what is a valued resource.

Actors get caught up in the logic of struggle and unwittingly reproduce
the structure of power relations within and across fields. They misrecognize the fundamentally arbitrary character of capitals by viewing them and
the struggle over them as necessary. This is an important theme one finds
in Bourdieu's field analysis because it shows that power goes misrecognized not only because of the action of habitus.[14] It is participation in the
struggle as well that contributes to the misrecognition of the fundamentally arbitrary character of what is nonetheless perceived as important and
legitimate. Actors get caught up in the logic of the fields where they are
participants and come to take for granted field boundaries. This insight
has important political implications for it suggests how political participation can unwittingly help create and solidify bounded political options
rather than create new alternatives.

The conceptual language of capital and field helps Bourdieu avoid holistic views of society and political order, such as capitalist society, industrial, or postindustrial society images project. Bourdieu (Bourdieu and
Wacquant 1992, 101–4) rejects a systems view of society such as one finds
in Parsons and Luhman. He views modern society as a configuration of
fields.[15] Similar to Durkheim's view of the growing division of labor leading
to organic solidarity (that creates the broad transition from mechanical to
organic forms of social solidarity), Bourdieu sees a process of differentiation that leads to the development of distinct spheres (fields) of human
practices. He explicitly draws on Durkheim's thinking as he compares the
traditional, nondifferentiated society of Kabyla with modern differentiated society. Yet, the more proximate source of inspiration for his view of
modern societies as complex arrays of fields is Max Weber's view of the
"orders" in societies.

14. A perceptive critic like Steven Lukes (2005) misses this key point as he seems to think
that power goes misrecognized in Bourdieu's thinking only because of the action of habitus.

15. Bourdieu, like Weber, does not work with a holistic view of society. His point of entry
for social structure is the field. Society is an array of fields in Bourdieu's sociology similar in
respects to Mann's (1986, 1) description where "societies are constituted of multiple overlapping and intersecting sociospatial networks of power."

Particular fields that have drawn Bourdieu's attention are the field of social classes (Bourdieu 1984a), the cultural field, particularly the French literary and artistic field (Bourdieu 1993d, 1996c), the university field or French professorate (Bourdieu 1988b), the field of housing (Bourdieu 2005b), religion (French Catholic bishops), French big business (Bourdieu 1996d, 300–369; Bourdieu and de Saint Martin 1978), and the field of power (Bourdieu 1996d). These are all relatively autonomous arenas with their own particular types and mixes of capital though they vary in their degree of autonomy, overlap with, and impinge on others. Only the idea of the field of power provides some overall frame for thinking about how this diverse array of fields interrelates.

Field of Power

Of all fields, the field of power stands out as a central feature of Bourdieu's thinking about how power is distributed in modern societies. It is consequently of central importance for political sociology. The concept dates from the early 1970s but receives its first theoretical and empirical elaboration in *The State Nobility* (Bourdieu 1996d). The idea of the field of power was elaborated by Bourdieu in his historical study of the origins and development of the artistic field in France and several studies of elite schools, the Catholic Church hierarchy, big business leadership, and high-ranking civil servants.[16] This ensemble of studies depicts a constellation of interlinked relatively autonomous yet overlapping arenas of power within which the holders of respective forms of capital (artistic, academic, economic, and legal) struggle to both accumulate and impose their particular form of capital as the most legitimate one for the entire social order.

In Bourdieu 1996d, 264, we find the field of power defined as "a field of forces structurally determined by the state of relations among various forms of power." To stress the relational character of the field of power Bourdieu specifies that "by field of power I mean the relations of force that obtain between the social positions which guarantee their occupants a quantum of social force, or of capital, such that they are able to enter into the struggles over the monopoly of power" (Bourdieu and Wacquant 1992, 229–30). He adds that

---

16. Bourdieu (1998h, 33) says that he developed the concept to explain ambivalent positions of artists and writers vis-à-vis the popular classes and the upper classes.

it is also, and inseparably, a field of power struggles among the holders of different forms of power, a gaming space in which those agents and institutions possessing enough specific capital (economic or cultural capital in particular) to be able to occupy the dominant positions within their respective fields confront each other using strategies aimed at preserving or transforming these relations of power. The forces that can be enlisted in these struggles, and the orientation given to them, be it conservative or subversive, depend on what might be called the "exchange rate" (or "conversion rate") that obtains among the different forms of capital, in other words, on the very thing that these strategies aim to preserve or transform (principally through the defense or criticism of representations of the different forms of capital and their legitimacy). (Bourdieu 1996d, 264–65)

The field of power is that arena of struggle among the different power fields themselves (particularly the economic and cultural fields) for the right to dominate *throughout the social order*. It is in the field of power where the predominate types of capital in each of the fields of struggle themselves become the instruments of struggle, one against the other, for the right to be the legitimate form of domination for the whole society. In the field of power it is no longer a question of struggling to accumulate a particular form of capital or to try to monopolize the definition of one form (such as cultural capital) but a struggle among the different forms of power for the power to be recognized as the most legitimate. It is the struggle over the standard for exchange among all forms of capital. Bourdieu indicates that

> these different forms of capital are themselves stakes in the struggles whose objective is no longer the accumulation of or even the monopoly on a particular form of capital (or power), economic religious, artistic, etc., as it is in the struggles that play out within each field, but rather the determination of the relative value and magnitude of the different forms of power that can be wielded in the different fields or, if you will, power over the different forms of power or the capital granting power over capital. (1996d, 265)

This struggle, as I will discuss in chapter 5, is largely over the control of the state. Bourdieu attributes to the modern state the power to control the exchange rates of capitals between the various fields. The field of power is a level of struggle for control over that institutional function.

The field of power in modern capitalist societies is internally bifurcated by the poles of economic and cultural capital. Particular fields vary in terms of their respective proximity to the two competing poles. At one end stands the economic field, where economic capital predominates. It represents the "dominant pole" of the field of power. At the opposite end lies the artistic field centered around cultural capital. It occupies the "dominated" position within the field of power. The administrative and university fields occupy intermediary positions, with the administrative being situated closer to the economic and the university closer to the artistic. The juridical field, Bourdieu (1987b, 851) observes, obtains less autonomy than the artistic and scientific fields since it is more closely tied to the political field. This means that art and science are less dependent upon the economy and polity than is law for rewarding careers and developing symbolic systems. The religious field is situated near the artistic field since it too organizes around a struggle for noneconomic legitimation. The journalist field, in contrast, is the most dependent upon the administrative and political circles (Bourdieu 1998e). And the political field lies closer to the economic pole than to the cultural pole but intersects with the legal and administrative fields in modern France.

The chiasmatic structure of economic capital and cultural capital functions, therefore, as both the bedrock of Bourdieu's field analysis and his approach to the topic of social stratification and power structure research in modern societies. It serves to mark homologies across different fields. It is an organizing principle both *between* and *within* fields. Bourdieu specifies that "this structural grasp of the field of power makes it possible to see that each of its constituent subfields is organized according to a structure homologous to its own, with, at one pole, the economically or temporally dominant and culturally dominated positions, and at the other, the culturally dominant and economically dominated positions" (Bourdieu 1996d, 270). It also functions as an organizing principle of the social class structure. And it gives homologous structuring to the political field and to the state. In the political field it forms the basis of the struggle between the expert and his or her cultural capital and the party operative and his social/ organizational capital, between those who bring considerable amounts of cultural capital to public policy formulation and those who draw more from popular support and/or bureaucratic inertia.

The political field, which I discuss later in the chapter, is distinct from the field of power though there is overlap. Likewise, the state is also conceptually distinct from the field of power though it is the central organizing mechanism that adjudicates relations among power fields within the field of power. That the state is a key field, or subfield, in Bourdieu's field of power is, of course, of central concern in contemporary political sociology.

In Bourdieu's thinking the two are not equated, yet the state plays a key role of administering relations among the various power fields as they contend for dominance within the field of power as well as over the entire society. Regulating the rate of exchange among different forms of capital has become the role of the modern state. In doing so the state develops its own particular form of symbolic capital—*statist capital*. (I defer discussion of Bourdieu's concept of the state until chapter 5 after having presented his thinking on symbolic power.)

Bourdieu sees two significant historical changes in the field of power in modern France. First is "the increase in the relative importance of academic titles (whether coupled with property or not) with respect to property titles, even in the economic field." His study of French business leadership (Bourdieu 1996d, 261–369; Bourdieu and de Saint Martin 1978) shows this development as there has been a shift in top firm leadership from heirs to highly credentialed managers. The second change he sees is "among the bearers of cultural capital, the decline of technical titles to the advantage of titles guaranteeing general bureaucratic training." Here Bourdieu observes a relative decline of engineering graduates from École Polytechnique in comparison to graduates in finance and public management from École National d'Administration holding top positions in large French corporations as well as in state agencies. These changes typify what Bourdieu means by "modifications in 'exchange rates' among the different forms of capital [that] affected the functioning of the field of power and the field of establishment schools" (1996d, 272). Cultural capital in the form of prestigious educational credentials has become more important in regulating access to positions of power in modern societies and in defining the nature of those positions. Moreover, there has been a shift in France away from the highly technical forms of cultural capital, such as engineering, toward finance and public administration.

Political Capital

> I earned capital in the campaign, political capital, and now I intend to spend it. — George W. Bush after winning the November 2, 2004, presidential election

Of central concern to political sociology are, of course, the power resources that political actors draw directly upon in their efforts to win in the political arena.[17] A power resource that Bourdieu designates as specifically

17. An earlier, shorter version of this section appears as Swartz 2012.

"political" is political capital. Political capital is a subtype of social capital. It represents the capacity to mobilize support for a candidate, cause, party, and so on, that is, the ability to mobilize collective resources.[18] Bourdieu also describes political capital as a form of symbolic capital, a kind of credit that requires collective trust. Political capital refers to a "particular kind of symbolic capital," a "reputational capital linked to notoriety" that is "linked to the manner of being perceived" (Bourdieu 2000a, 64, 65).[19] (I will present Bourdieu's concept of symbolic capital in the next chapter.) He notes that maintaining and increasing political capital involves much political labor to secure the trust, or credit, and avoiding the discredit of the supporting group (1991h, 192–93). Though political capital is a form of symbolic capital, Bourdieu also considers that it takes on objectified forms when it becomes institutionalized as political parties, patronage jobs, and so on (181, 196–97). Just as cultural capital can take on objectified forms as in books and computers, so political capital can obtain its particular objectified forms. He writes that "the delegation of political capital presupposes the objectification of this kind of capital in permanent institutions, its materialization in political 'machines, ' in jobs and instruments of mobilization, and its continual reproduction by mechanisms and strategies" (196). Heads of political machines, parties, unions, and lobbies are powerbrokers of institutionalized political capital, or as "bankers of men" as Bourdieu (194), citing Gramsci, calls them.

TYPES OF POLITICAL CAPITAL.   Bourdieu identifies two broad types of political capital: personal and delegated. The first is attached to the person. It is a personal type of "'fame' and 'popularity' based on the fact of *being known and recognized* in person" and of having a "good reputation" (Bourdieu 1991h, 194). It, in turn, can take two different forms reflecting two distinct origins. It can take on a professional form of specialized

18. Bourdieu defines social capital as "the sum of the resources, actual or virtual, that accrue to an individual or a group by virtue of possessing a durable network of more or less institutionalized relationships of mutual acquaintance and recognition" (Bourdieu and Wacquant 1992, 119). Bourdieu employs the concept quite differently from Robert Putnam's (2000) popular use in political science of the term *social capital*. Bourdieu's concept stresses the stratifying effects of this power resource rather than the integrative force as Putnam emphasizes.

19. As we will see in chapter 4, Bourdieu (1989d, 23) defines *symbolic capital* as "the social authority to impose symbolic meanings and classifications as legitimate and that individuals and groups can accumulate through public recognition of their capital holdings and positions occupied in social hierarchies. Symbolic capital is a form of credit and it takes symbolic capital accumulated from previous struggles to exercise symbolic power."

knowledge or experience accumulated through public service. Or it can assume a "heroic or prophetic" form that resembles Weber's concept of charisma (184, 194). The latter is more likely to emerge in a "crisis situation" when an individual is able to offer a mobilizing discourse that fills the vacuum left by existing political organizations and institutions.

The second type—delegated political capital—refers to the authority granted by a political organization. The political power comes to the individual by means of organizational delegation. It originates in and is attached to organizational position rather than to the individual person. Bourdieu describes the process by which organizational power is delegated to the individual as following a "very specific logic" of "*investiture*, the veritably magical act of institution by which the party officially *consecrates* the official candidate at an election and which marks the transmission of political capital" (1991h, 195). Investiture is a process by which political capital is partly transformed from the collective body to the individual but remains institutional in its source. Delegated power receives considerable attention in Bourdieu's thinking about power. It is not confined to specifically political organizations but operates as a kind of "functional capital" for performing certain organizationally sanctioned tasks, whether that be the delegated power of the priest of the church, the teacher of the school, the official of a government agency, or the leader of a political party (194–96).

These types of political capital are used to distinguish types of political organization and leadership. Bourdieu (1991h, 282) notes that leadership authority among French Communists during the post–World War II period was more likely to be of the delegated type because of the strong hierarchal nature of the party, whereas French Socialist Party leadership was more of the professional type, drawing its leadership more from broader community and professional sources than from within the party itself.

Increasing institutionalization of political capital in the form of jobs, and the material and symbolic benefits associated with political organizations, leads to a shift in objectives from one of representing the interests and capturing the hearts and minds of the electorate and representing their interests to safeguarding and reproducing the political organization itself. Thus political programs and platforms become downgraded in importance and cynically manipulated for the sake of reproducing those organizational interests. With increased institutionalization, the political battle over ideas takes second place—which Bourdieu laments—to the struggle for access to and control over jobs controlled by the political organization (Bourdieu 1991h, 197).

Siding with Weber against orthodox Marxism, Bourdieu does not reduce politics to underlying economic class interests. Political capital is under certain conditions a relatively independent power source from economic interests. However, it is correlated with the amount of leisure time and cultural capital, and the former in particular is related to economic well-being (Bourdieu 1991h, 172). So the autonomy is relative.

HISTORY AND USAGE OF THE CONCEPT OF POLITICAL CAPITAL.   Compared to the other types of capital, particularly cultural capital and symbolic capital, the terminology of political capital appears relatively late in Bourdieu's work. Beyond the 1981 paper "Political Representation" (Bourdieu 1991h) it is noteworthy that "political capital" is not mentioned in his 1983 paper "The Forms of Capital" (Bourdieu 1986), which is devoted to explaining his conceptualization of capital.[20] Political capital does not appear in this paper, although allusion to "political action" does (255). It is also noteworthy that *An Invitation to Reflexive Sociology* (Bourdieu and Wacquant 1992) carries no separate index entry for "political capital" whereas there are separate entries for cultural capital, economic capital, social capital, juridical capital, scientific capital, and of course symbolic capital. Political capital is mentioned in this text only in passing and as a subtype of social capital. "For example," Bourdieu says that

> to account for the shape of social space in old social democratic nations such as Sweden or in Soviet-type societies, one must take into consideration this peculiar form of social capital constituted by political capital which has the capacity to yield considerable profits and privileges, in a manner similar to economic capital in other social fields, by operating a "patrimonialization" of collective resources (through unions and the Labor party in the one case, the Communist party in the other). (119)

The term *political capital* also appears in a footnote to signal the concentration of a power resource that makes it possible for political parties such as the French Communist Party to function like a veritable "apparatus" (the term made famous by Louis Althusser), which Bourdieu sharply criticized and seldom used as he preferred the idea of a "political field" to highlight the dynamics of struggle that pervade even highly centralized

20. The 1981 paper "Political Representation" (Bourdieu 1991h) and Bourdieu 1991a are two key statements from the early 1980s showing Bourdieu's interest in the symbolic aspects of politics.

totalitarian regimes (Bourdieu and Wacquant 1992, 103 n. 155). His early use of the term *political capital* seems related to his critical analysis of the concentration of political power in parties and the correlated disenfranchisement of citizens or party members who lack sufficient cultural capital to challenge party leadership. This describes, he suggested, the organizational reality of the French Communist Party and the formerly Eastern Bloc political establishments.[21] This is not to say that Bourdieu had not developed the ideas of political capital and political field prior to 1992 but that they were not deemed particularly important for presenting his thinking about sociological analysis or for representing important facets of his sociological research by 1992. These concepts had not yet come to figure prominently in his research program by that time.

The Political Field

Like in the case of other capitals and their fields, a social capital becomes a political capital only in the context of a political field. The political field is that arena of struggle for political power where other forms of capital are transformed into the capital of social support such as votes, public demonstrations, and so on.[22] Bourdieu sees it "both as a field of forces and as a field of struggles aimed at transforming the relation of forces" (1991h, 171). Like Weber's political sphere, the political field is a power field where the explicit objective is to capture power.[23] It is that space of competition between agents (individuals, groups, institutions, associations, professionals, and so on) who participate in varying degrees in the struggle for political power regardless of whether they are associated with explicitly political organizations.

21. In important work on the French Communist Party around this time, Bernard Pudal (1988), drawing inspiration from Bourdieu, employed the concept of political capital.

22. The concept of the political field is elaborated in Bourdieu 2000b, 33–80, 93–97. Beyond a few seminal papers (Bourdieu 1991a, 1991h, 1991i, 2000f) Bourdieu's work has not devoted considerable attention to the internal mechanisms of the political field per se. His emphasis has been more on identifying when and how the political field impinges on fields of cultural production.

23. Recall that Weber (1970 [1915], 1978a) conceptualizes the different spheres, such as the economic, the erotic, the religious, and the political, as following distinct logics that stand in mutual opposition. Weber (1978b, 938) characterizes the political sphere as where "action is oriented toward the acquisition of social power."

The political field is a sphere of activity where the conquest of power itself is the central objective. It is an arena of conflict over the definition and implementation of public policies that are struggled over by political professionals who are increasingly linked to the state. The political field can be described as "a game in which the stakes are the legitimate imposition of the principles of vision and division of the social world." In this respect the political field is similar to cultural fields of struggle over symbolic power. Both involve symbolic struggle to impose legitimate standards. Indeed, Bourdieu draws an analogy in this respect between the religious field and the political field. Both are arenas of struggle over belief in what is the legitimate way to characterize how the social world is organized or should be organized. What is distinctively political in Bourdieu's eyes is that the political field involves struggles not just over ideas but for a particular type of ideas, that is, "'force ideas,' which are ideas capable of bringing about collective mobilization." Politics are about the mobilization of public support for particular views of the social world (Bourdieu 2000a, 60, 63, 67).

The political field has a special relationship to social capital that distinguishes it from other fields. Unlike other fields where there is also struggle over ideas, such as the scientific, literary, or religious fields, political capital in the final analysis needs to appeal beyond its boundaries for mass support (Bourdieu 2000f, 39). Political capital is in fact the capacity to mobilize social capital and needs to reach beyond the boundaries of the political field for broader support.

Though analogous to other fields, the political field is a relatively autonomous arena of struggle with its own specific type of capital that has developed historically. But there is occasional overlap in Bourdieu's conceptual terminology that confuses and reflects usage in different contexts. For example, at one point he specifies that the "political field" refers to specifically political institutions and actors (*champ politique*) *and also* [emphasis added] to the whole field of power relations in politics and society (*champ du pouvoir*)" (1988a, 545). Yet Bourdieu usually thinks that the field of power should not be confused with the political field. Nor is the political field the state, although it is structured to a large extent around competition for control of the state apparatus and can include other social fields controlled to some extent by state regulations. Nor should the political field be assimilated to the political party system. The political field includes political parties but does not reduce to them (Lagroye 2002, 175). And finally, as Lagroye (89) notes, Bourdieu's political field is not to be confused with the general terms of political society or what Jürgen Habermas (1962, 1996) means by "the public sphere."

Two key features of French politics that Bourdieu tries to capture with the concept include the differential political participation, particularly with regard to sex and level of education, and the closed character of the political world. He finds considerable variation by sex and level of education in France. Women are much less likely to participate politically than men, and individuals with more education are more likely to participate politically than those with less schooling. Further, the political world functions as a "microcosm" with its own specific interests distinct from those publics it represents. Indeed, Bourdieu stresses the degree of social closure of the French political field, made worse, he argues, by television and political journalism (Bourdieu 2000f, 24–36). As political capital becomes objectified (institutionalized) into positions within organizations, the field becomes increasingly autonomous from electoral sanction. During times of political stability political actors become increasingly integrated into existing political organizations leaving the electorate as a secondary consideration. (As I will point out later in the chapter, Bourdieu is sharply critical of this process of social closure that he feels threatens the foundations of democratic practice.) In rare periods of crisis or rapid political transformation, excessive integration by established political actors into the institutionalized structures of the field can be risky as the spoils are more likely to fall to those outside challengers with external support in the broader public.

RELATIONAL ORIENTATION.   Like the other master concepts in Bourdieu's conceptual repertoire, the political field is first and foremost a research tool rather than a concept designating a particular part of a social system. It embodies the meta-principle of relationality that calls for looking at political life relationally (Emirbayer 1997). This principle understands political action, stances, and programs in terms of oppositions and affinities between the various participants within the political field. The production of politics, whether taking a political stance, outlining a program, making a campaign speech, or participating in some kind of political demonstration, follows a relational logic in which each act is defined "in and through difference" in terms of the universe of competing positions within the political field. Bourdieu offers a relational understanding of field effects on politics by observing that "the field as a whole is defined as a system of deviations on different levels and nothing, either in the institutions or in the agents, the acts or the discourses they produce, has meaning except relationally, by virtue of the interplay of oppositions and distinctions." And "political parties, like tendencies within these parties, have only a relational existence and it would be futile to try to define what they are and what they profess independently of what their competitors in the same field are and profess" (Bourdieu 1991h, 177, 184–88).

INTERNAL DIFFERENTIATION.   The political field is internally structured and differentiated like all other fields by a bipolar opposition. On the one hand are those who defend the status quo, the incumbents, the conservatives, the orthodox; on the other hand stand the challengers, the progressives, the protagonists of change, the heterodox. This binary differentiating structure cross-cuts not only the political field as a whole but permeates individual units, such as political parties, political action committees, and interest groups, within the field. The field of political positions is structured "around the opposition between two poles" and the "field as a whole is defined as a system of deviations" from those poles (Bourdieu 1991h, 185). Agents within the political field struggle over the unequal distribution of political capital. Agents at the dominant pole, the orthodox, hold the most political capital, and challengers at the heteronomous pole struggle to accumulate more, often by drawing on alternative sources of political capital, or other types of capital that are converted into political capital. The orthodox defend the existing order and the heterodox favor change, transformation, and reform. In France, this polarity defines the political opposition between the "left" and "right."

The oppositional logic between transformation and defense of the status quo is a deep "invariant" that Bourdieu finds not only structuring the political field as a whole but each of the units nested within it.[24] Political stances, ideological positions, party platforms, positions, and posturing need to be understood relationally in terms of these struggles internal to the field itself. Agents take up positions relationally, in opposition to or

---

24. The idea of field invariant resonates with the structuralist logic of binary differentiation in which political content is shaped by opposition and can thus undergo interesting reversals or be transposed in different historical circumstances. Thus, Bourdieu (1991h, 185) observes that the "cult of nature" embraced by the conservative and nationalist right against science, progress, and rationalism in both France and Germany between the world wars finds resonance with the more recent ecological movement on the political left.

alliance with (Bourdieu stresses opposition over alliance) other players within the field.

The tendency toward greater autonomy of the political field is counterbalanced, however, by the need to attract outside support. The political field tendency toward greater autonomy and distinctions follows the relational and oppositional logic producing more and more distinctions and group subdivisions into smaller and smaller groups within the field itself. Yet, this differentiating and sectarian tendency is counterbalanced by the need of political groups to mobilize outside support. Bourdieu observes that "the tendency toward fission is limited by the fact that the power of a discourse depends less on its intrinsic properties than on the mobilizing power it exercises" (1991h, 188). Internal sectarianism and division ultimately can succeed only if they are able to garner significant outside support in the electorate. The drive for greater internal distinction is checked by the need for external mobilization and support. However, as I will point out, this counterbalancing need to mobilize outside support is only partially effective. Bourdieu stresses how the French political field has become increasingly closed to large numbers of potential participants. The dynamics of internal referencing and distinction tend to trump the need to be responsive to external demand.

RELATIVE AUTONOMY OF THE POLITICAL FIELD. Thus, Bourdieu approaches the political field as a field of symbolic domination and situates it within the larger context of the field of power. But he stresses, like in the case of other fields, the relative autonomy of the political field. Professionalization and bureaucratization of political life contribute to a growing autonomy of the political field from class, economic, and other outside interests. Professionals pursue their own interests. Those professional interests only need to be able to mobilize sufficient popular support to be successful. He thus defends the idea of the relative autonomy of the political field and argues one cannot reduce political history "to a sort of epiphenomenal manifestation of economic and social forces of which political actors would be, so to speak, the puppets." Such a view misses "the specifically symbolic effectiveness of representation, and of the mobilizing belief that it elicits by virtue of objectification." It also means missing "the proper political power of government . . . via its control over the instruments of the administration of things and persons." On the other hand, Bourdieu also concludes that the political field autonomy poses a threat to genuine democratic life—a consideration we take up shortly (Bourdieu 1991h, 182–83).

THE POLITICAL DOXA. Like other fields, the political field develops its own doxa, or political culture, a "specific competence," which is learned through experience of how to behave politically. To be a serious contender in the political field requires a shared belief, regardless of political affiliation, that politics are important, that it takes experience to be a successful political leader, and that political leadership should be reserved for those with the requisite experience. This political doxa is shared by all political professionals who otherwise compete for political capital (Bourdieu 2000a, 56, 58).

Bourdieu stresses how the political doxa acts as a closure mechanism that erects a barrier to effective political expression for all but the well initiated (2000, 60). While acquired through professional experience, he observes, political culture in France is increasingly dominated by individuals with formal training in a few elite higher education institutions, such as the Paris Institut de Science Politique and the École Nationale d'Administration (58–59). French political leadership has progressively passed from the hands of political activists to political professionals. Bourdieu is highly critical of the contemporary French political field, arguing that it has largely become an enclosed, self-contained universe with less and less contact and understanding of everyday problems faced by French citizens. He sees French political leaders, technocrats, journalists, and intellectuals, all in their particular ways, caught within this closed world and unable to be genuine representatives of the larger public.[25]

One of the effects of a political field is that it delimits the range of possible political ideas and programs, effectively imposing a form of political censorship, from which ordinary citizens as consumers are obliged to choose. The field imposes a "problematic" that defines "what is politically sayable or unsayable, thinkable or unthinkable" (Bourdieu 1991h, 172).

POLITICAL FIELD AUTONOMY: IMPLICATIONS. A key implication of the relative autonomy of the political field is that political professionals (e.g., party leaders, pollsters, political commentators) do and say things not in direct reference to voters but in reference to other political professionals holding different positions in the field (Bourdieu 2000a, 57). Their behavior reflects more directly "the structure of the political field" than

25. As I note in chapter 7 on Bourdieu's own political engagements, one act of protest by Bourdieu against the closure of the French political field was his public support for the right of the French comedian Coluche to become a candidate in the 1981 presidential elections against the established left incumbent Mitterrand.

the interests of their constituencies. Bourdieu writes that "it is the structure of the political field, in other words the objective relationship to the occupants of the other positions, and the relationship to the competing stances that they offer, which, as much as the direct relationship to their mandators, determines the stances they take, i.e., the supply of political products" (1985b, 738). In other words, there is an internal dynamic of self-referencing among political professionals that shapes decisively the array of political options available to the public. Much behavior of political professionals, according to Bourdieu's field perspective, entails more posturing to differentiate positions or enhance their scope of representation than responding to the direct interests of their constituencies. What often passes as "purely personal" battles in fact draw on opposing positions and strategies within the field itself (Fritsch 2000, 23). Growing political field autonomy poses a real challenge to the ideals of democratic process and representation.

Bourdieu (1991h, 180–83) describes "the double game" when professionals in the political field pursue dual interests, the interests of those they represent and their own interests within the field. Political field analysis reveals that political professionals pursue their own specific interests of field position, which do not necessarily reflect the interests of their constituencies (Bourdieu 2000a, 58). There must be, of course, some degree of overlap between the political leadership interests and constituency interests for leadership to maintain a minimum of legitimacy. Unlike the scientific field, which is largely peer-oriented, the political field needs to cultivate broad-based social support.[26] In democratic societies the voting public must be taken into account even if it is the object of considerable manipulation by political elites. Bourdieu acknowledges this, but his analysis emphasizes that increasing institutionalization of political capital and growing autonomy of the political field shift the focus to internal field interests away from the broader interests of public representation. Most important among those interests are the "reproduction of the political apparatus" and maintaining one's position within it. Here he draws an analogy with the Roman Catholic Church. The strength of political institutions, just like that of the Church, lies in their capacity to control positions (66–67). Much political behavior is motivated by the desire to reproduce the political institution by maintaining positions for its members. Thus

26. Bourdieu (1996a) says that the social basis for the political field lies outside since in the final analysis political success is based on the capacity to mobilize broader social support.

the idea of field autonomy and its focus on particular interests present a formidable challenge to the ideals of democratic representations.[27]

The idea that political positions are likely to reflect the immediate professional interests of field position more than broader class or cultural affiliations provides a useful meso-level analysis that improves upon one-sided micro or macro-perspectives. It improves upon the traditional class reductionism of Marxism and the various forms of cultural determinism, such as a functionalist adaptation to societal norms or to the interests of rationally calculating actors. Yet the problems of reductionism and determinism do not go away but re-emerge in a kind of field reductionism and determinism. Bourdieu's politics tend to reduce to field positions.[28] He contends, for example, that

> it is the structure of the political field which, being subjectively inseparable from the direct—and always declared—relation to those who are represented, determines the stances taken, through the intermediary of the constraints and interests associated with a given position in this field. (1991h, 184)

However, Bourdieu also stresses that field positions need not be static. Individuals and groups try to create new ones or modify existing ones; this is the strategy of distinction by challengers and newcomers to the field. Moreover, stances are always mediated by habitus.[29] Where political

27. Bourdieu's view of political leadership as pursuing its own institutional interests resonates with the neo-Marxist view (Block 1977) of the role of state managers with a relatively autonomous state and with democratic elite pluralism (Bachrach 1966; Dahl 1967; Dye and Zeigler 1978). Bourdieu, however, sees the French state as a good deal more unified than pluralists suggest and more culturally determined than Marxists would allow.

28. This field reductionist tendency finds some empirical support in Bourdieu (1988b, xvii–xviii) where he finds that political stances among the Parisian professorate during the May 1968 student revolt originate from their academic field positions rather than from broader class and political influences. Yet his analysis of the literary field seems to guard against this kind of field position reductionism. In this work he says that political stances are mediated more by strategies than by positions alone, that the field of political stances can take on a degree of autonomy of its own since it is generated by strategies of differentiation in a field where to exist means to differ (Bourdieu 1984b, 7; 1991f, 19). Thus, the relationship of strategies to field positions can vary from one field to another and the emphasis Bourdieu himself gives varies by empirical object and the viewpoint Bourdieu is arguing against.

29. Bourdieu writes that "the space of positions finds expression through the dispositions of habitus whereby agents apprehend the space of positions and their position within that space and the perceptions of other agents also engaged in that space" (2001d, 118).

entities become highly bureaucratized, stances by actors tend to reflect fairly directly their positionality. But in less-established political arenas where the dynamic of differential posturing and relational differentiation is accentuated such as, for example, where the media field and political field intersect in opposing dynamics, the space for innovation seems larger. The political field perspective needs to specify the structural conditions (state of historical development) where these kinds of variations are taken into account. It also needs to examine the *social processes* through which political alliance might be formed or broken. Bourdieu's field analysis of politics needs a social movement component that would examine the actual processes of political action and mobilization.

Outside challenges can be brought into the political field by heterodox carriers with new forms of capital but Bourdieu has little to say about how politics might originate beyond fields even though he roots power and politics in social identity itself. The political field perspective stresses a "production of politics" orientation that leaves little space for political initiative to occur outside of the world of elites.

Like the scientific field, the political field is also guided to some extent by the principle of disinterest and universalism that would put the interests of the broader public above those of individual career and organizational clout. Evidence of this is "political scandal," which occurs precisely because individuals are found to be in violation of or transgress the collective interests in favor of personal self-interest (Bourdieu 2000e, 124–25). Yet, unlike in science, the explicit objective of the political field is to win in the power game, to be able to impose one's ideas and programs rather than those of others, and to mobilize sufficient social support even though this goal is usually couched in language claiming the general interest or public good.

While the political field is a force field, like the field of religion it is also an arena of struggle over belief. What distinguishes the political field from other fields (religious, scientific, cultural) is that force relations, the efforts to dominate, are more explicit, more "objectified" in Bourdieu's language (Lagroye 2002, 203). Though both involve struggle over belief, the political field differs from the religious field in its belief in reform, in making society and the political life better, of changing and reforming political life. The political order is seen as "perfectible" (207, 213).

The concept of "force ideas" to distinguish the political from the religious, cultural, or intellectual is not fully satisfying, however. Religious ideas could also be thought of as mobilizing forces; otherwise they secure no following. This would seem to apply particularly to religious evangelization and mission. This points to ambiguity in defining what exactly is in the political field and what is not.[30] Bourdieu acknowledges this ambiguity but contends that the problem lies not in his conceptualization but in political reality itself. There is ambiguity precisely because the boundaries of what is political and what is not are themselves objects of struggle (Bourdieu 2000a, 74). Bourdieu has a point here, for the act of politicizing an issue points up precisely a struggle over field boundaries—a good theoretical point but methodologically difficult to operationalize. Still, the struggle for power in the political field is a good deal more explicit than in the religious, scientific, or other cultural arenas, where the power dimension is more euphemized under the guise of the pursuit of truth, whether scientific or religious. Much more explicitly than elsewhere, actors in the political field struggle for the legitimate manipulation of a comprehensive view of the social world (e.g., Kauppi 2003). Next to journalists and scientists, politicians perform the function of making visible their perceptions, their visions of the divisions of the social world, and they work to transform them into categories applicable for all (Fritsch 2000, 21).

Some Evaluation

Using Bourdieu's concept of political capital can be a useful tool for shifting attention away from the charismatic political figure—the politician as media celebrity—that centers attention on individual characteristics rather than on all the work of social capital accumulation (sociability as investment) needed to be a player in the political arena. Bourdieu's concept of political capital as a form of social capital calls attention to how much political leadership devotes to sociability, solicitation, favors, negotiation, compromise, and garnering support (Bourdieu 1986, 250). Public policy formulation often appears quite secondary, more the preoccupation of think-tanks and academics than political actors themselves, despite rhetoric to the contrary.

One important implication of Bourdieu's field analysis of politics is that he sees the marketplace of political ideas and options, except in periods of crisis, as increasingly limited. Ordinary citizens, the consumers, can

---

30. Fritsch (2000, 29) echoes the criticism that it is difficult to establish the boundaries in Bourdieu's framework between what is political and what is not.

choose from only the few political alternatives (products) offered by the professionalized political field. The current French political field functions like an oligarchy where the supply of political ideals, programs, strategies, analyses, and so on, is determined largely by interelite competition among relatively few specialists and their organizational supports whereas "ordinary citizens . . . are reduced to the status of 'consumers'" and have little say over the array of political choices offered them. This leads Bourdieu to conclude that "the market of politics is doubtless one of the least free markets that exist" (1991h, 171–73). Indeed, "the production of politically effective and legitimate forms of perception and expression is the monopoly of professionals." The constricted choice particularly limits the dominated classes who because of their lack of cultural capital are largely dependent on their political party.

Yet, Bourdieu's field perspective on politics differs significantly from a market perspective. While Bourdieu (1993b, 164) admits that "politics can be described by analogy with the phenomenon of the market," he stresses that that the supply/demand relationship is not direct but mediated by the relatively autonomous structure and history of the field in which politics is produced and consumed. He argues that supply of political options does not develop in direct response to popular demand "but to the constraints peculiar to a political space that has a history of its own" (165). By this he means that the supply of political views is shaped by the positions of the producers of political views in the field of political cultural production less by conscious reference to competitors than by virtue of the competitive positions occupied. Demand likewise is determined by competitive position within the class structure. In both cases one needs to understand the relatively autonomous history of each field. Bourdieu's field analysis of politics entails a broader, more complex analysis than a simple supply/demand equation.

Capitals and fields represent key conceptual tools in Bourdieu's thinking about politics. In the next chapter we turn to one particular type of capital, symbolic capital, which Bourdieu conceptualizes in his argument that power arrangements need legitimation that for the most part operates beyond conscious awareness.

CHAPTER FOUR

For a Sociology of Symbolic Power

The most successful ideological effects are the ones that have no need of words, but only of laissez-faire and complicitous silence.—Bourdieu 1990c, 133

In this chapter I take up Bourdieu's third type of power, symbolic power. This is perhaps the most important form of power in Bourdieu's sociology. Indeed, his sociology can be read as a search for forms of symbolic power (Bourdieu and Wacquant 1992, 14–15). The idea of symbolic power extends his analysis of power beyond specific types of resources (capitals) that are contested in particular substantive arenas of conflict (fields) to a dimension of most all of social life. Symbolic power operates at a different level of analysis than the other types of capital. It is a "diffused form" (Mann 1986, 7–10) of power that legitimates other capitals though it can assume objectified forms. The chapter presents Bourdieu's thinking on symbolic power as a form of domination that elaborates and modifies Weber's emphasis on legitimation. Bourdieu's conceptual language of symbolic power, symbolic violence, and symbolic capital are distinguished, explored, and evaluated. Of particular importance is his analysis of processes of group leadership representation, delegation, and consequent power dispossession of the represented. The chapter concludes with some evaluation.

Domination Requires Legitimation

Bourdieu works in the conflict tradition of sociology (Collins 1994). He offers a stratified view of the social world where individuals, groups, and institutions form inegalitarian structures of hierarchy and domination. Dynamics of competition and conflict pervade those structures. The central underlying preoccupation of his work is how these stratified social systems of hierarchy and domination persist and reproduce intergenerationally without powerful resistance and without the conscious recognition of their members. The exercise and reproduction of class-based power and privilege are core substantive and unifying concerns in Bourdieu's work. How does this work? Bourdieu develops his concepts of symbolic power, violence, and capital in response.

A significant part of Bourdieu's answer to this question lies in his elaboration and modification of Max Weber's emphasis on legitimation. Recall that Weber (1978b, 215) identifies three distinct ideal types of authority to justify domination: rational, traditional, and charismatic. Bourdieu's concept of symbolic power and violence draws significantly from Weber's notion of charisma though it does not fit neatly into just one of Weber's three categories. It is a type of authority that deflects attention away from underlying power resources. It also has the taken-for-granted property of legitimation by recourse to tradition.

For Bourdieu, legitimation rests on common, everyday assumptions— cultural schema—that individuals and groups make about the nature of the social order. Citing David Hume, Bourdieu (1994b, 15) contends that the "fundamental question of all political philosophy" is "the problem of legitimacy."[1] There is, in Bourdieu's (1991b, 127) words, a "doxa" of deeply held, shared representations that express a "kind of original adherence to the established order."[2] Bourdieu writes: "We know that the social order owes some measure of its permanence to the fact that it imposes schemes of classification which, being adjusted to objective classifications, produce a form of recognition of this order, the kind implied by the mis-

---

1. See Bourdieu 2000e, 178, where he references Hume (1994 [1758]), who asserts that it is "opinion" that helps understand this paradoxical phenomena.

2. For Bourdieu, the *doxa*, the Greek term for common belief or popular opinion, is the *Lebenswelt* identified in the phenomenological tradition. It is the taken-for-granted everyday life realities that form the primary experience of the social world. Indeed, Bourdieu (2001c, 1) says that "the whole logic of my research" has been on what he calls the "*paradox of doxa*," namely, "that the established order, with its relations of domination, its rights and prerogatives, privileges and injustices, ultimately perpetuates itself so easily, apart from a few historical accidents, and that the most intolerable conditions of existence can so often be perceived as acceptable and even natural."

recognition of the arbitrariness of its foundations" (127). Bourdieu views legitimation as a kind of practical recognition of existing social hierarchies, but one, as we will see, that misrecognizes their fundamentally arbitrary character.

Like Weber, Bourdieu stresses that domination requires legitimation even when it involves brute force or money.[3] Neither brute force nor material possession is seldom sufficient for the effective exercise of power. "Domination, even when based on naked force, that of arms or money, always has a symbolic dimension" (Bourdieu 2000e, 172).[4] The idea of "naked power" seldom appears in Bourdieu's work; the emperor never goes without clothes as if raw physical constraint or violence might find expression without symbolic trappings. Sheer physical force "can continue to produce an effect once it has ceased to be applied only inasmuch as it always tends to exert an additional, symbolic, effect" (Bourdieu and Passeron 1977, 10). Contrasting symbolic power to "raw force" (*force nue*) Bourdieu (1996d, 383) writes that "in contrast to raw power, which acts according to mechanical efficiency, all genuine power acts as symbolic power, the basis of which is, paradoxically, *denial*."[5] This is not to suggest that Bourdieu believes that physical constraint is seldom used in modern societies. But he does think there has been a shift in ordering mechanisms of social control toward cultural institutions, like schools, that specialize more in internalizing in individuals mechanisms of self-control. This leads Bourdieu to focus on the cultural or symbolic dimension of power. Indeed,

3. Weber (1978b, 213) writes that "*purely* material interests and calculations of advantages as the basis of solidarity between the chief and his administrative staff result, in this as in other connections, in a relatively unstable situation. Normally other elements, affectual and ideal, supplement such interests. . . . But custom, personal advantage, purely affectual or ideal motives of solidarity, do not form a sufficiently reliable basis for a given domination. In addition there is normally a further element, the belief in *legitimacy*. Experience shows that in no instance does domination voluntarily limit itself to the appeal to material or affectual or ideal motives as a basis for its continuance. In addition every such system attempts to establish and to cultivate the belief in its legitimacy." Bourdieu makes a similar argument.

4. Bourdieu writes that "force cannot assert itself as such, as brute violence, an arbitrariness that is what it is, without justification; and it is a fact of experience that it can only perpetuate itself under the colours of legitimacy, and that domination succeeds in imposing itself durably only in so far as it manages to secure recognition, with is nothing other than misrecognition of the arbitrariness of its principle" (2000e, 104).

5. Bourdieu evokes the Freudian term *Verneinung* to signal his intended meaning of "denial."

we may say that it is this dimension of power that is the overriding objective of Bourdieu's sociology. "To be able to discover it in places where it is least visible, where it is most completely misrecognized" (Bourdieu 1991g, 163) has been the central mission of his sociology, a mission that is political as well as analytical.

The Concepts of Symbolic Power, Violence, and Capital

Synthesis of Three Traditions

Bourdieu sees his conceptualization of symbolic power informed by three different theoretical traditions that point to three distinct functions performed by culture. Indeed, he (1999b, 336) sees his work as a synthesis of these three traditions:

- the constructionist tradition that sees symbols as instruments for constructing meanings of the world—a cognitive function
- the structuralist or hermeneutic tradition that sees symbols as instruments of communication—a communication function
- the power tradition that sees symbols as instruments for legitimating force relations—a domination function

Bourdieu (1991g) stresses that these interconnected functions of culture—cognition, communication, and domination—are present in most all cultural expressions. Bourdieu considers it rare that symbolic expressions reduce to just one of these three functions. Rather, they usually contain a complex mixture of all three. Here we see Bourdieu linking a power dimension to structuralist and constructionist perspectives.

His emphasis on the domination function reflects his criticism of the professional ideology of cultural producers who stress the intrinsic value of their work rather than the power dimension. Bourdieu emphasizes the intimate interconnections between the three functions—cognition, communication, and domination—in contrast to other scholars, such as Jeffrey Alexander (1995, 2003), who try to distinguish and isolate specific cultural forms uncontaminated by power and domination. Bourdieu's thinking marks a progress over the self-serving ideology of intellectuals who would divorce culture from power.

Symbolic Power, Violence, and Capital: Conceptual Distinctions and Interrelations

Bourdieu uses the conceptual language of symbolic power, violence, and capital to stress the legitimation of the power function of culture.[6] At times he distinguishes these terms but often uses symbolic power, violence, and capital with considerable overlap since the three dimensions interconnect. Still one can detect different emphases in different parts of his work and for expository purposes I will make the following analytical distinctions: symbolic power, symbolic violence, and symbolic capital. I first offer brief definitions of these terms and then examine each in more detail.

Symbolic power entails the capacity to impose symbolic meanings and forms as legitimate. It is a capacity to shape perceptions of social reality by imposing cognitive categories through which we understand the social world. It is the capacity to conserve or transform social reality by shaping its representations through inculcating classifications, schema of perceptions that hide or reveal the fundamentally arbitrary character of authority relations of the social order. Symbolic power is an imposed power—a cultural expression of domination. It also is a constitutive power, formative of social group identities and intergroup relations. Further, it is a contested power, being both the object and instrument of social struggle among social groups. And in modern societies symbolic power tends to be monopolized by state institutions.

Symbolic power is an internalized or incorporated power, one that resides in both cognitive schemes and bodily expression. It orients individual and collective dispositions that generate practices. As internalized dispositions, it undergoes a process of *naturalization*. It is experienced as a taken-for-granted, natural, inevitable state of affairs, especially on the part of the dominated. The language of symbolic violence is intended to capture this effect of symbolic power. Symbolic violence is misrecognized obedience in that symbolic power is accepted as legitimate rather than as an arbitrary imposition. Bourdieu offers the following definition: Symbolic violence is "a gentle violence, imperceptible and invisible even to its victims, exerted for the most part through the purely symbolic channels of communication

---

6. Key references for discussion of the concept of symbolic power include the following: Bourdieu 1972a, 227–43; 1977a, 171–83; 1989d; 1990c, 112–21; 1991e, 383–85; 1991g, 163–70; 1996d, 383–85; 2000e, 168–82, 240–45; 2001c.

and cognition (more precisely, misrecognition), recognition, or even feeling" (2001c, 1–2).

The exercise of symbolic power requires, however, recognized authority and this dimension is captured by the concept of *symbolic capital*. Symbolic capital refers to the "esteem, recognition, belief, credit, confidence of others" (Bourdieu 2000e, 166) and represents the accumulated authority to be able to exercise symbolic power. It is a form of credit—a publically recognized authority attached to persons and positions—from which symbolic power can be exercised. And symbolic capital designates the social authority that individuals and groups can accumulate through public recognition of their capital holdings and positions occupied in social hierarchies.

Symbolic capital refers to that aspect of symbolic power (form of authority) that can be accumulated and exchanged with other forms of capital. Symbolic violence refers to the internalized effects of symbolic power that distort identity by encouraging the dominated to accept the conditions of their domination as legitimate. The capacity to impose symbolic meanings (symbolic power), the authority to do so (symbolic capital), and the distorting effects upon individual autonomy and interests (symbolic violence) are different but intimately connected aspects in Bourdieu's thinking about the symbolic realm. At times he stresses the imposition capacity of values, norms, beliefs, and so on, by dominant groups and institutions. This emphasis is found, for example, in his writings on the French education system (see, for example, Bourdieu and Passeron 1990). The *cultural arbitrary* is an imposed set of values, beliefs, cultural ideals propagated by the educational system. It is also found in his writings on the state where he stresses that the role of the state is to monopolize symbolic violence. At other times, and receiving the greater emphasis, is symbolic violence, namely, the internalization of dominant views. This is found in his work on the Algerian peasants and particularly in his later formulations in *Pascalian Meditations* (Bourdieu 2000e) and *Masculine Domination* (Bourdieu 2001c).[7] Here the emphasis is on the *effects* of symbolic power, namely,

7. See Mauger 2006 for evidence of these two emphases in Bourdieu's work. Mauger in fact suggests there is a shift in Bourdieu's conceptualization of symbolic violence from one closer to a Marxian view of ideology as an explicit mechanism to impose dominant ideology to a more Durkheimian notion of incorporation that stresses the corporal forms. Certainly Bourdieu's later formulations stress the bodily as well as cognitive expressions of symbolic power that brings him closer to the thinking of Foucault on this point (2000e, 2001c). Despite

how the arbitrary character of power relations goes misrecognized. Yet in other analyses he stresses the accumulation of symbolic authority as a form of credit, symbolic capital, that permits the exercise of symbolic power. But these different emphases are employed by Bourdieu as correctives to opposing views he is combating and as called forth by the empirical objects he is investigating. He in fact views both—capacity for imposition and internalized effects—as fundamental dimensions of symbolic power and violence. Symbolic power and symbolic violence are both an imposed power whose imposition is effective only because of the internalized dispositions of individuals that accept the imposition as a taken-for-granted reality. And the capacity to impose symbolic meanings requires some degree of recognized authority, symbolic capital.

Symbolic Power—Key Features

Symbolic power is a constitutive power and an imposed power. It is also contested but when naturalized and misrecognized it functions as a form of violence (symbolic violence). And it tends to be monopolized by the state in modern societies—a feature I discuss in chapter 5. I now want to examine more in depth each of these key features.

Symbolic power is first of all an expression of domination; it is an imposed power by dominant groups and institutions, notably the state in modern societies. It is usually available only to dominant groups, though Bourdieu does acknowledge that dominated groups, such as sociologists, can in certain situations exercise symbolic power.[8] As indicated in chapter 2, it is fundamentally arbitrary since it resides in force relations rather than standing on some universal principle. His analysis of French schooling (Bourdieu and Passeron 1977) in particular stresses this key feature where he argues that the ostensibly universal standards of educational ideals, values, and practices are in fact arbitrary: they reflect the cultural preferences of dominant groups and the mode of imposition (pedagogy) in French

the variation in emphasis, the effects of symbolic power remain the same: a distortion of one's capacities and best interests.

8. As I will discuss in chapter 6, Bourdieu saw his sociology as a tool of struggle against symbolic violence. Yet he (2008e, 91) also acknowledged that this kind of critical sociology can be thought of as an alternative type of symbolic power, one that contests by debunking the hidden forces of power relations. Bourdieu's socioanalysis brings forth recognition over misrecognition, clairvoyance over mystery.

schools that facilitates the transmission of cultural ideals only to those heirs of cultural capital.

Symbolic power is also formative of collective identities.[9] Symbolic power is a power of naming and classification that group and differentiate social realities. It is a constitutive force in the social world. It is "the performative power of designation, of nomination, [that] brings into existence in an instituted, constituted form . . . a collective of multiple persons . . . [who hitherto had been] . . . a purely additive series of merely juxtaposed individuals" (Bourdieu 1990b, 138). Language is of course central to the exercise of symbolic power. Its "performative" quality points to Bourdieu's critical dialogue with Austin's (1962) view of the performative qualities of speech.[10] There can be performative discourse. Symbolic power is expressed through language but Bourdieu refuses to accord it an intrinsic property of language like he criticizes interpreters of Austin for doing. Bourdieu (1991e, 107–16) stresses two features that distinguish his view of performative discourse from that of Austin:

1. There must be shared, collective meanings for the work of language to be meaningful.
2. The speaker needs some kind of authority to be recognized by the collectivity.

The performative effect depends also on the dispositions of habitus. Both the shared meaning and the authority of the speaker (his or her symbolic capital) need to be recognized by the dispositions of the habitus.[11]

Symbolic power is a "world-making" power in the sense that Nelson Goodman (1978) gives the term (Bourdieu 1989d, 22). Symbolic power finds expression in "social classifications" that "organize the perception of the social world and, in certain conditions, can really organize the world itself" (Bourdieu 1990b, 137). It is a social classification power, or more

9. Wacquant (2004, 6) identifies this as the "second major mode of Bourdieu's political sociology." It is a power of "authoritative nomination and the symbolic fabrication of collectives."

10. By a performative utterance, or what he later calls a "speech-act" Austin identifies statements that do not just describe or state but actually do something, such as "I take this man as my lawfully wedded husband" in the marriage ceremony.

11. Law, for example, is "the form par excellence of the symbolic power of naming and classifying that creates the things named, and particularly groups; it confers upon the realities emerging out of its operations of classification all the permanence, that of things, that a historical institution is capable of granting to historical institutions" (Bourdieu 1987b, 233–34).

precisely a capacity of producing social classifications among groups and rendering them legitimate.

Symbolic power is therefore a stratifying power at the collective level. It is a social reproductive power since "symbolic power relations tend to reproduce and to reinforce the power relations which constitute the structure of the social space." It is a power of domination. Symbolic power is a political power in its capacity to impose as legitimate symbolic divisions that represent social divisions. Indeed, "the power of making visible and explicit social divisions that are implicit, is the political power *par excellence*: it is the power to make groups, to manipulate the objective structure of society" (Bourdieu 1990b, 135, 138).

While symbolic power is an imposed power it does not occur unilaterally but through a context of struggle over the perceptions of the social world. It is also a contested power. It is a tool of struggle among social groups. Bourdieu (1990b, 134) writes that "the categories of perception, the systems of classification, that is, essentially, the words, the names which construct social reality as much as they express it, are the crucial stakes of political struggle, which is a struggle to impose the legitimate principle of vision and division—is, that is, a struggle for the legitimate exercise of the theory effect." He (134) specifies that "symbolic struggles over the perception of the social world may take two different forms."

> On the objective level, one may take action in the form of acts of representation, individual or collective, meant to show up and to show off certain realities: I am thinking for example of demonstrations whose objective is to demonstrate a group, its number, its strength, its cohesion, and to make it exist visibly; and on the individual level, of all the strategies of self-presentation, so well analyzed by Goffman, designed to manipulate one's self-image and especially—something omitted by Goffman—the image of one's position in the social space. On the subjective level, one may act by trying to change the categories of perception and evaluation of the social world, the cognitive and evaluative structures.
>
> On the collective and more properly political level, they include all the strategies which aim at imposing a new construction of social reality by rejecting the old political lexicon, or else aim at maintaining the orthodox view by keeping those words, which are often euphemisms . . . designed to describe the social world.

One form, at what he calls the objective level, includes individual or collective acts of representation designed "to show up and to show off certain realities," to gain visibility or to demonstrate the existence, size, strength of a certain social reality. On could think of political demonstrations, for example. The other form of struggle, at the subjective level, consists of attempting to "change the categories of perception and evaluation." Individuals and groups attempt to manipulate symbols, change the meanings of words, invent new expressions to advance their interests or to shape social realities according to their interests. Here too he (Bourdieu 1990b, 135) distinguishes the "individual struggles of daily life and the collective, organized struggles of political life." From his research on Kabylia he offers an example of how individuals "manipulate genealogy" to enhance their identity much the same way that the classic texts in sociology are used to enhance reputation and visibility in the profession. He acknowledges that collective struggles are usually the ones recognized as political but he does not want to divorce the individual from the collective and therefore connects the political domain to everyday life activities of individuals.[12] Indeed, Bourdieu identifies those "subterranean struggles" as key to political struggles (1996d, 388). He calls these "subjective" struggles (1990b, 134). He stresses the political import to be found in the ethnography of everyday life. Indeed, this is an orienting contribution of Bourdieu's work to the study of politics.

A key implication of Bourdieu's concept of symbolic power is that politics are rooted in group formation and identity. For Bourdieu, the "new" identity politics is not new but goes to the heart of what sociology is about. Nor should it be a separate subfield of theory and research in sociology. Identity politics is new only in the sense that mainstream political sociology lost track of the constitutive force of culture burying it in materialist and structuralist assumptions. For Bourdieu, naming and classification, the use of symbolic forms to create associations and divisions, operates as a constitutive force, not alone, but as a key feature of human sociability that helps bring into existence by giving identity to social groups and defining their interrelationships. This is the cultural bedrock of political life.

Thus, symbolic struggles occur to either maintain and reinforce public perceptions of existing social realities—that is to reproduce them—or to transform those perceptions and in doing so create conditions for social change. As we will see later in the chapter, the struggle for symbolic power

12. He wants to connect the individual and collective levels without collapsing one into the other, which would yield a kind of "everything is political" view.

is a central concern in the political field. The next chapter will examine Bourdieu's argument that symbolic power is monopolized by the state in modern societies.

Symbolic Power as Violence—Key Features

The operation of symbolic power is not an instrumental power whereby dominant social agents intentionally try to impose some propaganda. That can and does happen, but that is not the type Bourdieu has in mind when he employs the conceptual language of symbolic violence. It takes the form of a more subtle, discrete operation whereby power arrangements come to appear as natural and self-evident.[13] Bourdieu writes that "symbolic violence is the gentle, disguised form which violence takes when overt violence is impossible" (1990c, 133). Bourdieu uses the language of *naturalization* to characterize the process of symbolic violence. It "naturalizes" or "universalizes" what in fact is historical and contingent or, in Bourdieu's language, "arbitrary." How does this occur?

Symbolic power is formative of the dispositions of the habitus.[14] Bourdieu argues that structures of power are deeply internalized by individuals from early childhood on and orient all subsequent individual conduct. His concept of habitus calls attention to this phenomenon at the individual level. Symbolic power shapes the habitus and therefore takes the form of embodied dispositions that generate a "practical sense" for organizing perceptions of and actions in the social world. As an expression of habitus, the effects of symbolic power are unconscious and resistant to conscious articulation and critical reflection. They therefore find expression through practices—a practical logic—rather than in sets of explicit beliefs or values. Hence, symbolic violence is incorporated as practical classifications.[15]

13. Bourdieu writes: "The legitimization of the social world is not the product, as certain people believe, of a deliberately biased action of propaganda or symbolic imposition; it results from the fact that agents apply to the objective structures of the social world structures of perception and appreciation that have emerged from these objective structures and tend therefore to see the world as self-evident" (1990b, 135).

14. Much of this section on symbolic power and habitus comes from Swartz 1997, 106–7.

15. Bourdieu (2001c, 37) writes: "The effect of symbolic domination (whether ethnic, gender, cultural or linguistic, etc.) is exerted not in the pure logic of knowing consciousnesses but through the schemes of perception, appreciation and action that are constitutive of habitus."

> Habitus emerges through primary socialization from a practical evaluation of
> the likelihood of the success of a given action in a given situation [which] brings
> into play a whole body of wisdom, saying, commonplaces, ethical precepts
> ("that's not for the likes of us"). (Bourdieu 1977a, 77)

The dispositions of habitus predispose actors to select forms of conduct
that are most likely to succeed in light of their resources and past experience. Habitus orients action according to anticipated consequences. The
dispositions of habitus incorporate a sense of place in the social order, an
understanding of inclusion and exclusion in the various social hierarchies.
Bourdieu emphasizes the stratifying dimension of early socialization:
habitus conveys a sense of place and out-of-place that an individual can
occupy in a stratified social world. Bourdieu writes that

> objective limits become a sense of limits, a practical anticipation of objective
> limits acquired by experience of objective limits, a "sense of one's place" which
> leads one to exclude oneself from the goods, persons, place and so forth from
> which one is excluded. (1984a, 471)

This social, differentiating dimension of habitus can be seen

> in the form of dispositions which are so many marks of *social position* and hence
> of the social distance between objective positions . . . and correlatively, so many
> reminders of this distance and of the conduct required in order to "keep one's
> distance" or to manipulate it strategically, whether symbolically or actually, to
> reduce it (easier for the dominant than for the dominated), increase it, or sim-
> ply maintain it (by not "letting oneself go," not "becoming familiar," in short,
> "standing on one's dignity," or on the other hand, refusing to "take liberties"
> and "put oneself forward," in short "knowing one's place" and staying there).
> (Bourdieu 1977a, 82)

Thus, Bourdieu puts power at the heart of the functioning and the structure of habitus (one of his master concepts), since habitus involves an
unconscious calculation of what is possible, impossible, and probable for
people in their specific locations in the stratified social order. People self-
select into or away from opportunities because of the cultural assumptions
they have internalized regarding the likelihood of successes for people
of their station. As Bourdieu notes, "The relation to what is possible is
a relation to power." The habitus therefore "adjusts itself to a probable

future which it anticipates and helps to bring about because it reads it directly in the present of the presumed world." It thus offers "a realistic relation to what is possible, founded on and therefore limited by power." In Bourdieu's thinking, stratification and politics intersect, separated only by the arbitrary disciplinary boundaries developed in the academy. One can therefore speak of a political habitus (Bourdieu 1990c, 4, 64, 65).

As I will note later, Bourdieu connects this stratifying power of habitus directly to differential forms of political participation. Whether or not individuals, when surveyed or interviewed, have a political opinion is related to the dispositions of their habitus as well as to their cultural capital. Individuals with more education are more likely to respond to political opinion questions on surveys—indeed to have political opinions—than are individuals with less education (Bourdieu 1984a, 397–465).[16] Political sociology and stratification are intimately connected in Bourdieu's thinking and research.

Symbolic violence finds expression above all through language. Language use almost always involves much more than simple communication.

> Quite apart from the literary (and especially poetic) uses of language, it is rare in everyday life for language to function as a pure instrument of communication. The pursuit of maximum informative efficiency is only exceptionally the exclusive goal of linguistic production and the distinctly instrumental use of language which it implies generally clashes with the often unconscious pursuit of symbolic profit. (Bourdieu 1991e, 66–67)

Indeed

> the relations of communication par excellence—linguistic exchanges—are also relations of symbolic power in which the power relations between speakers or their respective groups are actualized. (Bourdieu 1991e, 37)

But symbolic violence also finds expression in bodily gestures, both individual and collective. Religious and secular rituals mark social boundaries as well. And the organization of physical space can convey symbolic significance since

16. The work of Daniel Gaxie (1978, 1990) in France has stressed how political opinion is highly correlated with cultural capital.

space is one of the sites where power is asserted and exercised, and, no doubt in
its subtlest form, as symbolic violence that goes unperceived as violence. Archi-
tectural spaces address mute injunctions directly to the body and, just as surely
as court etiquette, obtain from it the reverence and respect born of distance,
or better yet, from being far away, at a respective distance. (Bourdieu et al.
1999, 126)

This conceptual move by Bourdieu to extend the expressions and effects of power across numerous dimensions of social life stands in sharp
contrast to those wanting to cordon off power as a distinct and less edi-
fying realm of social life. Power and culture do not stand in opposition
in Bourdieu's work, as for example Alexander (1995, 2003) attempts to
do, but as inseparably interconnected. Alexander would sanitize certain
cultural forms from the contaminating influence of power through the
distinction he makes between his cultural sociology and the sociology of
culture. For Bourdieu, such a position amounts to an uncritical embrace of
the professional ideology of academics who see themselves standing above
the contaminating influence of power and politics.

Symbolic power becomes a form of violence that shapes our everyday
classifications. Bourdieu argues that even the cognitive way we understand
the world is informed by power relations. The categories we construct, the
terminology we employ, the logical connections we make, the oppositions
we draw are all operations of power, capacities shaped by habitus. How we
conceptualize the social world is fundamentally political. Cognitive structures are political structures. Bourdieu (1997b, 206) sees himself elaborating the fundamental insight of Durkheim's argument about the connection
between logical conformity and moral conformity. For Bourdieu (2000e,
172) the "the theory of knowledge of the social world is a fundamental
dimension of political theory." This is another implication of his stress on
symbolic power

The violent effects of symbolic power appear in bodily dispositions.
Symbolic violence is corporal as well as cognitive and finds expression in
all forms of body language. It is a "form of power that is exerted on bodies directly and as if by magic, without any physical constraint; but this
magic works only on the basis of the dispositions deposited, like springs,
at the deepest level of the body" (Bourdieu 2001c, 38). We find Bourdieu
stressing this characteristic in his earliest work on the Berber. Bourdieu
observed among the Kabyle that "bodily hexis is political mythology realized, *em-bodied*, turned into a disposition." Regarding gender distinc-

tions, "the opposition between male and female is realized in posture, in the gestures and movements of the body" (Bourdieu 1990c, 69–70). This is a society where the social division of labor and the sexual division of labor are tightly linked and where there is no relatively autonomous domain designated as political. The body embodies "politics."[17] Here the formation of habitus through socialization "instills a sense of the equivalences between physical space and social space . . . and thereby roots the most fundamental structures of the group in the primary experiences of the body." The body, therefore, is the carrier of "a political mythology" in this type of society where the "opposition between masculinity and femininity . . . constitutes the fundamental principle of division of the social and the symbolic world" (71, 78).[18]

Submission to the social order obtains through "respect for form and forms of respect." Even rules of etiquette and politeness governing everyday behavior are invested with power relations. "'Stand up straight' or 'don't hold your knife in your left hand,'" though seemingly insignificant, in fact conveys "a whole cosmology, an ethic, a metaphysic, a political philosophy." Indeed, "the concessions of *politeness* always contain *political* concessions" (Bourdieu 1977a, 94, 95). At the heart of habitus are politics in the sense that our internalized dispositions express fundamental power relations that establish our position in the social world.

The embodiment of politics applies to the modern differentiated societies as well. Where there are relatively autonomous domains of specialized practices the dispositions of habitus stem from and adjust to the structures of various fields. The bodily differentiated patterns may be more varied, complex, and contested in modern than in traditional societies but nonetheless are there. The male/female opposition expressed in the body is to be found "in every society dominated by male values—and European societies, which assign me to politics, history or art, and women to the hearth, the novel and psychology" (Bourdieu 1990c, 77). And

in a society divided into classes, all the products of a given agent, by an essential overdetermination, speak inseparably and simultaneously of his/her class—or,

17. "Power relations" might be the better term in this society that does not recognize politics as some relatively autonomous realm from the rest of social life.

18. "The body language of sexual domination and submission had provided the fundamental principles of both the body language and the verbal language of social domination and submission" (Bourdieu 1990c, 72).

more precisely, his/her position and rising or falling trajectory within the social structure—and of his/her body—or, more precisely, of all the properties, always socially qualified, of which he/she is the bearer: sexual ones, of course, but also physical properties that are praised, like strength or beauty, or stigmatized. (Bourdieu 1990c, 79)

Gender relations embody a "prime example" of symbolic violence, what he calls "masculine domination" (Bourdieu 2001c, 1).[19] In the documentary *Sociology Is a Martial Art* (Carles 2001) Bourdieu offers the example of a woman in a short skirt who, after dropping something, has to enact a carefully controlled posture in bending down to pick up the object and this is carried out without conscious reflection, showing a distinctly feminine way of picking up the object. That, in Bourdieu's view, embodies power relations of male domination.[20]

Symbolic violence is rooted in "the dispositions that the work of inculcation and embodiment has deposited in those who are thereby primed for it." Symbolic violence comes about from "the immense preliminary labour that is needed to bring about a durable transformation of bodies and to produce the permanent dispositions that it triggers and awakens." It requires work of individuals, groups, and especially institutions, such as the state and the education system, which Bourdieu stresses most. It requires *symbolic labor*. Bourdieu stresses that "structures of domination . . . are *the product of an incessant (and therefore historical) labour of reproduction*, which singular agents . . . and institutions—families, the church, the educational system, the state—contribute" (Bourdieu 2001c, 34, 38).

Symbolic violence does not operate out of conscious intention; it is not an instrumental power. Bourdieu's symbolic violence does not suggest "consent" to existing hierarchies but "practical adaptation" to differences in rank.[21] In pointing to gender domination as a key expression of symbolic violence, Bourdieu writes that "symbolic violence accomplishes itself through an act of cognition and misrecognition that lies beyond—or

19. However, in Bourdieu 2000e, 83, he says that rational communication is the "form par excellence" of symbolic violence!

20. See Bourdieu 2001c for suggestive extensions of the gendered body in modern differentiated societies.

21. If by "consent" one means some form of conscious agreement. The "practical adaptation" occurs prereflectively as if it were the "thing to do" or the "natural" response in existing circumstances.

beneath—the controls of consciousness and will" (Bourdieu and Wacquant 1992, 171–72). Indeed, symbolic violence thrives on its invisibility to
participants—the less visible, the most efficacious it is.

The transforming action of symbolic violence on the habitus "is all the
more powerful because it is for the most part exerted invisibly and in-
sidiously through insensible familiarization with a symbolically structured
physical world and early, prolonged experience of interactions informed
by the structures of domination." One can see evidence of this in "relations of kinship and all relations build on that model, in which these durable inclinations of the socialized body are expressed and experienced in
the logic of feeling (filial love, fraternal love, etc.) or duty, which are often
merged in the experience of respect and devotion and may live on long
after the disappearance of their social conditions of production." This process is aided by the bodily incorporation making the dispositions of habitus less visible. The operations and effects of domination occur through
symbolic violence "because the effect and conditions of its efficacy are
durably and deeply embedded in the body in the form of dispositions"
(Bourdieu 2001c, 38, 39).

Another closely related feature of symbolic power is that actors "misrecognize" its true nature. The process of naturalization of inequalities
creates their misrecognition. We have seen that Bourdieu considers the
foundations of any social order as ultimately arbitrary because they are
based on force relations among individuals and groups rather than on universal principles of justice. Actors misrecognize that arbitrary character,
hence, Bourdieu's language of symbolic violence. A property of symbolic
violence is that it abstracts from consideration the context of power relations in which practices occur. Particular practices are separated and
isolated from their context. In education, for example, the pedagogical
relationship between teachers and learners is construed in terms of
communication and efficacy. Lost from view are the social and cultural
inequalities and differential power relationship that are also present. Consider that "if one reduces the relation of pedagogical communication to a
pure and simple relation of communication, one is unable to understand
the social conditions of its specifically symbolic and specifically pedagogic
efficacy which lie precisely in concealment of the fact that it is not a simple
relation of communication" (Bourdieu and Passeron 1977, 7, 23).

Misrecognition occurs for *both* dominant and dominated parties. Symbolic power "is that invisible power which can be exercised only with the
complicity of those who do not want to know that they are subject to it

or even that they themselves exercise it" (Bourdieu 1991g, 164). But it is more insidious for the dominated because as a misrecognized power symbolic violence leads the dominated to participate in their own domination. Dominant and dominated parties do not share equally the doxa, which is that "primordial political belief" that connects people to the established order. The doxa is in fact an "orthodoxy, a right, correct, dominant vision which has more often than not been imposed through struggles against competing visions." The "doxa is a particular point of view, the point of view of the dominant, when it presents and imposes itself as a universal point of view" (Bourdieu 1994b, 15).

A central emphasis of Bourdieu's concept of symbolic violence is the idea that the dominated tend to adopt the dominant view of themselves (Bourdieu 2001c, 119). "To put it as tersely and simply as possible, [it] is the *violence which is exercised upon a social agent with his or her complicity*" (Bourdieu and Wacquant 1992, 167). The dominated participate in their own domination when they

> apply categories constructed from the point of view of the dominant to the relations of domination, thus making them appear as natural. This can lead to a kind of systematic self-depreciation, even self-denigration, visible in particular . . . in the representation that Kabyle women have of their genitals as something deficient, ugly, even repulsive (or, in modern societies, in the vision that many women have of their bodies as not conforming to the aesthetic canon imposed by fashion), and, more generally, in their adherence to a demeaning image of women. (Bourdieu 2001c, 139)

Illustrations that come to mind include Du Bois's (1989 [1903]) portrayal of black self-identity through the eyes of whites and Fanon's (1967) analysis of how through the legacy of colonialism and racial domination the black Caribbean thinks of himself/herself in terms of the standard of the white French. One also thinks of *The Hidden Injuries of Class* (Sennett and Cobb 1972), which documents how blue-collar men in Boston view their failures as a result of their own inadequacies. A more recent and graphic illustration of symbolic violence is offered by Simon Charlesworth, who quotes a working-class man in the English Midlands expressing his sense of inferiority in encountering a middle-class woman:

> I went in to the social [Social Security Office] the other day . . . there were chairs and a space next to this stuck-up cow, you know, slim, attractive, middle class,

and I didn't want to sit with her, you feel you shouldn't . . . I became all conscious, of my weight, I felt overweight, I start sweating, I start bungling, shuf-
fling, I just thought "no, I'm not going to sit there, I don't want to put her out," I
don't want to feel that she's put out, you don't want to bother them . . . they look
at you like you're invading their area . . . you know, straight away . . . you feel "I
shouldn't be there" . . . it makes you not want to go out. What it is, it's a form of
violence. (Quoted in Wilkinson and Pickett 2009, 165–66)

Bourdieu's symbolic violence shares with Weber's view of domination
a voluntary element.[22] In some ways Bourdieu's concept of symbolic violence comes closer to Weber's definition of "discipline" as "the likelihood,
on the basis of an ingrained attitude, that a command will find prompt,
automatic, and blind obedience among a specific group of people" (Kalberg 2005, 179).[23] What differs is that Bourdieu does not limit consideration to a "command" view of power at the interactional level. Moreover,
Bourdieu stresses the social reproduction consequences of this important
dimension of power relations. Bourdieu also stresses the consequences for
personal and collective identity. Unlike Weber's notion of "legitimation,"
Bourdieu's language of symbolic "violence" suggests something stronger
than justification of domination. It is more insidious than the idea of false
or wrong beliefs. It suggests a bending under the weight of domination,
a distortion, a deformation, an assault against the personhood of the individual and authentic identity of the group. Bourdieu goes so far to call
symbolic violence a kind of "possession" because the "miracle of symbolic efficacy" occurs because "possessed individuals" are "predisposed
by prior experience" to "perform the institution's every wish because they
are the institution made man (or woman), and who, whether dominated or
dominant, can submit to it or fully exercise its necessity only because they
have incorporated it, they are of one body with it, they give body to it"
(1996d, 3). This means that domination is deeply rooted in dispositions as
well as in objective structures. By incorporating dispositionally dominate

22. Weber emphasized obedience in his definition of domination (*Herrschaft*). Domination is "the likelihood that a demarcated command will find obedience among a specific circle
of persons" (Kalberg 2005, 179).

23. Weber (in Kalberg 2005, 179) specifies that the "ingrained attitude" suggests that "an
uncritical and unresisting *mass* obedience occurs." Bourdieu uses the language of "natural,"
or "taken-for-granted" to describe a process that occurs "practically" or prereflexively.

views and practices, the dominated unwittingly help sustain those very structures that oppress them.[24]

However, if "the dominated always contribute to their own domination, it is at once necessary to recall that the dispositions that incline them toward this complicity are themselves the effect, embodied, of domination" (1996d, 4). We are not to "blame the victim" (Ryan 1971) but rather recognize that while domination is dispositional it is internalized from objective structures that must be changed. "Symbolic power functions to reproduce the stratified social order. When symbolic power is acknowledged in accordance with the categories of perception that it imposes, the symbolic power relations tend to reproduce and to reinforce the power relations which constitute the structure of the social space" (Bourdieu 1990b, 135). Here Bourdieu stresses that "symbolic struggles, both the individual struggles of daily life and the collective, organized struggle of political life, have a specific logic." It is one of reproducing and reinforcing power relations, not simply reflecting them nor the result of conscious imposition or manipulation.

Bourdieu's understanding of symbolic power and violence overlaps with the processes of boundary work and framing (Gieryn 1983; Kahneman 2000; Kahneman and Tversky 1973; Lakoff 2002; Lakoff and Johnson 2003; Lamont and Molnar 2002). It defines and legitimates social categories in people's minds that orient or permit patterns of inclusion and exclusion in social interactions. The effects of symbolic power on dominated groups limit their capacities to seek alternatives or develop other capacities for self-expression and fulfillment. When symbolic power becomes symbolic violence, the dominated fail to recognize social boundaries as arbitrary and therefore capable of being altered to some extent.

THE SIGNIFICANCE OF "VIOLENCE."   By symbolic "violence" Bourdieu calls attention to the key feature of symbolic power and that is the "violence which is exercised upon a social agent with his or her complicity" (Bourdieu and Wacquant 1992, 167, 168). Dominated individuals and groups participate in their own domination helping to perpetuate it, not out of choice or from external constraint but from the "fit" between the expectations of their habitus and the external structures they encounter. Bourdieu will occasionally refer to symbolic violence as a "soft" form of

---

24. Emirbayer and Johnson (2008, 46–47), for example, present symbolic violence as one of the effects of the operation of habitus whereby actors unwittingly enact their own domination as they conserve and perpetuate the interests of formal organizations.

violence but in doing so he does not intend to suggest that it is somehow not really violence or that it is secondary to physical violence, or especially that it is a form of domination that is purely symbolic and therefore less real than physical forms of control.[25] But rather than intending to make philosophical claims on the relative significance of physical and symbolic violence, in Bourdieu's hands the term is foremost a tool for breaking with received wisdom.

In theorizing about pedagogical action, Bourdieu identifies the concept of "symbolic violence" as a tool to "break with all spontaneous representations and spontaneist conceptions of pedagogical action." By this he wants to call attention to the fundamentally arbitrariness of all pedagogical content and forms of transmission. He says that the theory of symbolic violence is part of a more general theory of violence and legitimate violence that identifies the "interchangeability of the different forms of social violence" (Bourdieu and Passeron 1977, xi–xii). They are interchangeable since they are all rooted in a fundamentally arbitrary characteristic of human existence, namely, that relations of hierarchy and inequality are essentially power relations in that they lack objective foundation in some universal principle of justice. The foundations of social order for Bourdieu, as noted in chapter 2, are fundamentally arbitrary. The language of symbolic violence conveys that view. In later work, when he theorizes the state (as we will see in the next chapter), Bourdieu presents his conceptualization as an extension of Weber's view of the state as that instance that monopolizes the means of physical violence to include the means of symbolic violence as well, notably provided by the educational system. But it can take the form of race, ethnicity, religion, gender, sexual orientation, any cultural standard or set of collective representations that set forth evaluative standards by which to measure identity and position.[26]

In summary, symbolic power is the capacity to impose recognition whereas recognition itself refers to symbolic violence. Symbolic power

25. See Terray (1996, 12–16) for an enumeration of key characteristics of Bourdieu's concept, which overlaps with our analysis above. Terray interprets Bourdieu to say that there is no fundamental difference between physical and symbolic violence since both are rooted in the final analysis in arbitrary power relations that are historical and without an ultimate basis for justification by some universal principles. I, however, would not equate the two in terms of significance for human existence—at least in the extreme form of physical violence leading to death. Rather than making "violence" a catch-all category, Bourdieu's conceptual language is more usefully employed when it delineates particular types or dimensions of domination.

26. He (Bourdieu 2001c, 2) notes here that skin color is "the symbolically most powerful" expression of what he has in mind.

becomes rooted in the dispositions of habitus that orient action. Those dispositions are acquired through socialization that internalize the inequalities of social position and hence capacities from birth on. As deeply seeded dispositions, they stand beyond conscious reflection. They are both cognitive and corporal, finding expression in both symbolic classifications and body comportment that tend to reproduce the internalized patterns. As a consequence these inequalities are misrecognized as natural and inevitable and the social effect is to reinforce and reproduce social hierarchies. Hence symbolic power performs symbolic violence by disposing individuals and groups to accept without contest inegalitarian arrangements. Symbolic power is a pillar of political order.

SYMBOLIC VIOLENCE: PRACTICAL JUSTIFICATION VERSUS IDEOLOGY AND HEGEMONY.   Symbolic violence is similar to the notions of ideology and hegemony, two forms of cultural power most frequently associated with state-created nationalism. The concepts of ideology of Marx and Engels and symbolic violence of Bourdieu both attempt to address the same problem: how to explain why the dominated and exploited internalize their conditions of domination and exploitation as normal or natural rather than resist them. Bourdieu sees his concept of symbolic violence as calling attention to the "effects of legitimation" that the notion of ideology, as sets of beliefs, justifications, and so on, does not fully capture. Bourdieu (1990c, 133) is trying to get at the "practical justification of the established order" rather than an explicit discourse justifying it. Whereas the concept of ideology often suggests the use of specific symbols, the imposition of particular cultural messages, and the inculcation of specific beliefs, such as in the case of state-created nationalism, Bourdieu's concept of symbolic violence points to a layer of pre-existing practical schemes that make such ideological messages palatable.[27] Thus symbolic power and violence facilitate the capacity of states to exercise ideological power but they are not exactly the same thing, as Loveman (2005, 1656) correctly points out.[28]

Symbolic violence suggests a realm of taken-for-granted assumptions that function as a foundation on which more explicit ideological symbols, messages, and formulations make sense. Ideology needs to become em-

27. See Bourdieu 2000e, 168, where he argues that symbolic force acts on the body but not in mechanical ways, but works only if it intersects with dispositions that it "triggers" as sort of springs.

28. My analysis here of the relationship of symbolic power and violence to state ideology follows that of Loveman 2005.

bedded in the dispositions for the imposition of ideas to make sense. The ideas need to exist in an implicit state in order for them to gain recognition. In the case of his analysis of the educational system providing the dominate class with a justification of its domination, it is not so much that a meritocratic ideology is used to justify that domination, but that differential access to educational qualifications is understood in terms of "natural" abilities or gifts, and that the relationship between qualifications obtained and inherited cultural capital is masked and thereby misrecognized. Bourdieu writes that "the most successful ideological effects are the ones that have no need of words, but only of laissez-faire and complicitous silence" (1990c, 133).

Bourdieu's concept of symbolic violence places him within the line of key European thinkers—Lukacs, Gramsci, Mannheim, and the Frankfurt School—to refine Marx's notion of ideology (Neuman 2005, 300–302). Though one does not find Bourdieu drawing in particular from any one of these thinkers, his concept seems to overlap most with Gramsci's notion of hegemony in that symbolic violence is formative of common sense that guides actions.[29] Bourdieu's thinking about symbolic violence follows in the emphasis stressed by Louis Althusser and Michel Foucault who see ideology as more concealed and pervasive than many of the earlier thinkers imagined (certainly Marx and Engels). It is "doxic acceptance of the world, due to the immediate agreement of objective structures and cognitive structures." It is simply rooted in "the *order of things*"—to use Foucault's expression (Bourdieu and Wacquant 1992, 168).

Symbolic Capital: Key Features

Bourdieu speaks of *symbolic capital* to call attention to the social effects of legitimate authority. Symbolic capital refers to socially recognized and approved authority. To exercise symbolic power—that is, the capacity to impose meanings as legitimate—requires some social capital. Bourdieu treats symbolic power as a capacity to impose meanings or representations

---

29. Wacquant distinguishes Bourdieu's thinking about symbolic power and violence from Gramsci's theory of hegemony by stressing the tacit, taken-for-granted character of symbolic violence: "Legitimation of the social order is not . . . the product of a deliberate and purposive action of propaganda or symbolic imposition; it results, rather, from the fact that agents apply to the objective structures of the social world structures of perception and appreciation which are issued out of these very structures and which tend to picture the world as evident" (Bourdieu and Wacquant 1992, 168).

of social reality as legitimate from some authority that forms the basis for that capacity for imposition. He calls that authority *symbolic capital*. The capacity to carry out symbolic action, Bourdieu stresses, stems not from the technical features of symbols or language or from their intrinsic performative capacity, as Austin (1962) emphasized, but from the social authority they are able to evoke.

In parts of his work, Bourdieu conceptually distinguishes symbolic capital from symbolic power while noting their interrelationship: symbolic power as a capacity to impose legitimate means from the authority basis that permits that capacity. They are not one and the same. He suggests that the exercise of symbolic power requires the possession of symbolic capital, a socially recognized authority as a kind of credit and authority to act.

> As any form of performative discourse, symbolic power has to be based on the possession of symbolic capital. The power to impose upon other minds a vision, old or new, of social divisions depends on the social authority acquired in previous struggles. Symbolic capital is a credit: it is the power granted to those who have obtained sufficient recognition to be in a position to impose recognition. (Bourdieu 1989d, 23)

He uses the language of symbolic capital to conceptualize recognized authority, which can be accumulated over time.

Bourdieu speaks of symbolic capital to identify a power property obtained when other capitals take on legitimate recognition. He specifies that symbolic capital is "a form which is assumed by different kinds of capital when they are perceived and recognized as legitimate." "Symbolic capital," he declares, "is nothing more than economic capital or cultural capital which is acknowledged and recognized" (1990b, 128, 135). He extends this logic to all types of capital. Symbolic capital operates effectively because it is perceived as legitimate claims on the services, deference, and respect of others and at the same time disguises underlying interests. It develops out of symbolic practices that deflect attention from the interested character of practices and thereby contribute to their enactment as disinterested pursuits. Activities and resources gain in symbolic power, or legitimacy, to the extent that they become separated from underlying material interests and hence go misrecognized as representing disinterested forms of activities and resources. Individuals and groups who are able to benefit from the transformation of self-interest into disinterest obtain symbolic capital. Symbolic capital is "denied capital"; it disguises the underlying "interested" relations to which it is related giving them legitimation. Symbolic capital is a form of power that is not perceived as power but as legitimate demands for recognition, deference, obedience, or the services of others (Bourdieu 1990b, 118).[30]

Symbolic capital is a reformulation of Weber's idea of charismatic authority that legitimates power relations by accentuating selected personal qualities of elites as supposedly superior and natural. Whereas Weber tended to associate charismatic authority with precapitalist societies, Bourdieu finds it in the form of the ideology of the gifted individual even in modern societies where the rationalized, bureaucratic type of authority predominates. Bourdieu does not think of the concept as an ideal type or restrict it to leadership, as does Weber, but extends the idea as a dimension of all legitimation. For Bourdieu (1980b, 243), charisma is "a dimension of all power" rather than just "a particular form of power." Commenting on Weber, Bourdieu specifies that

> symbolic capital would be no more than another way of referring to what Max Weber called charisma, if Weber, who understood perhaps better than anyone that the sociology of religion is part of the sociology of power, had not been trapped in the logic of realist typologies. This leads him to see charisma as a particular form of power rather than as a dimension of all power, that is, another name for legitimacy, a product of recognition, misrecognition, the belief "by virtue of which, persons exercising authority are endowed with prestige." (1990c, 141)

For Bourdieu, symbolic capital points to a type of legitimation where the vested interests of some authority are misperceived as being disinterested.

Symbolic capital is a kind of power resource in the form of authority that persons carry and can accumulate but often is associated with the authority of positions. While it stems from positions or broader power relations it becomes transferred to and transformed into personal characteristics. An expression of "symbolic power," symbolic capital obtains the capacity to reorient by dissimulating positional properties into personal properties (Bourdieu 1987a, 191). He evokes the case of the pedagogical relationship where the authority of the institution and the cultural arbitrary are masked by the personal authority of the teacher (Bourdieu and

---

30. See Bourdieu 1972a, 227–43; 1990b, 112–21; 1991e, 163–70, for key formulations of this concept.

Passeron 1970, 83). The authority of the teacher comes from the educational institution though it appears to come from his or her personal qualities. System properties are usurped by the individual; individual charisma really owes more to the advantages of position than the intrinsic worth of the individual.

Thus it is wrong to equate Bourdieu's symbolic capital with Weber's legitimation. Bourdieu elaborates and modifies Weber's concept. What distinguishes Bourdieu from Weber is that symbolic capital is not just a matter of belief in the legitimacy or rightness of some authority but *also the misrecognition* that this authority goes against one's best interests. As Loveman (2005) correctly perceives, it is misrecognition that distinguishes this type of power from Weber's concept. It refers to a type of legitimation, one in which one's interests are not best served by the belief in existing power arrangements, and this belief masks those power relations. Bourdieu stresses the idea that his concept of symbolic capital stems from the idea of the misrecognition of resources as capital. Writing of cultural capital that is "predisposed to function as symbolic capital," which means "to be unrecognized as capital and recognized as legitimate competence, as authority exerting an effect of (mis)recognition," Bourdieu notes examples where this readily occurs, "in the matrimonial market and in all the markets in which economic capital is not fully recognized, whether in matters of culture, with the great art collections or great cultural foundations, or in social welfare, with the economy of generosity and the gift" (1986, 245). Misrecognition occurs practically when

> a capital (or power) becomes symbolic capital, that is, capital endowed with a specifically symbolic efficacy, only when it is *misrecognized* in its arbitrary truth as capital and *recognized* as legitimate, on the other hand, that this act of (false) knowledge and recognition is an act of *practical* knowledge which in no way implies that the object known and recognized be posited as object. (Bourdieu 1990b, 112)

Misrecognition is associated with practical, taken-for-granted knowledge that is "inscribed . . . in the immediate relationship between a habitus and a situation" (112). He sees a paradigmatic expression of this when a practical affinity between habitus and situation occurs to produce

> the silence of shyness, abstention or resignation, by which the dominated manifest practically, without even considering the possibility of doing otherwise,

their practical acceptance (in the mode of *illusio*) of the possibilities and the impossibilities inscribed in the field. (Think for instance of the expression "This is not for us" by which the most deprived exclude themselves from possibilities from which they would be excluded anyway.) (112)

In places Bourdieu associates the accumulation of social capital with the logic of social distinction.

Symbolic capital "another name for distinction" is nothing other than capital, of whatever kind, when it is perceived by an agent endowed with categories of perception arising from the incorporation of the structure of its distribution, i.e. when it is known and recognized as self-evident. (Bourdieu 1991e, 238)

And for Bourdieu the logic of social distinction is fundamentally interconnected to the logic of symbolic distinction since

the logic of the symbolic is fundamentally diacritical, distinction is the specific form of profit that symbolic capital procures. Lifestyle, as the exemplary manifestation of symbolic capital, exists only by and for the gaze of the other and as diacritical deviation from the modal, ordinary, common, banal, "average" style, a deviation that can be unwitting or obtained by a "stylization of life." (Bourdieu 1999b, 337)

Bourdieu's concept of symbolic capital closely connects with identity itself, which Bourdieu sees as fundamentally social. Without symbolic capital, there is no identity since identity must emerge from insignificance and this can come only through successful elicitation of recognition from others. Identity comes out of the symbolic struggle for recognition: "it is competition for a power that can only be won from others competing for the same power, a power over others that derives its existence from others, from their perception and appreciation" (Bourdieu 2000e, 241).

It is a power of recognition obtained from others. It is a "power over" others in that it demands their recognition. In an absolute sense, any kind of identity implies some degree of symbolic capital, whether positive or negative, because it requires some kind of social recognition by others. Everyone has some symbolic capital but its social distribution is very unequal. High expressions of this power can be seen in the bureaucratic expression of the "legal act" and in the "prophetic pronouncement" by a charismatic leader. Low expressions take the form of "negative symbolic capital"

corresponding to stigmatized status (Bourdieu 2000e, 241, 242). Referring
to the difficulties faced by foreign-born, notably North African adolescents
in schools and the labor market in contemporary France, Bourdieu evokes
stigmatizing markers of "body hexis . . . proper name, accent, and . . . place
of residence" that function as a *negative symbolic capital*" (Bourdieu
et al. 1999, 185): "The stigmatized pariah who, like the Jew in Kafka's
time, or, now, the black in the ghetto or the Arab or Turk in the working-
class suburbs of European cities, bears the curse of negative symbolic capital" (Bourdieu 2000e, 241). Here Bourdieu's "negative symbolic capital"
overlaps with Goffman's (1986) classic analysis of stigma.

Symbolic Power in the Political Field

We have seen that symbolic power is a constitutive power, formative of
collective identities and realities, the very basis of political life. The performative force of symbolic power is also a stratifying power, one that
generates divisions and classifications. It is a contested power as well, a
tool of struggle among social groups and their representatives either to
enhance their social visibility or to change the perception and evaluation of themselves or others. Nowhere do we see these processes at work
more clearly than in the political field. The power of politicians is largely
symbolic because they are dependent on the credit (trust) extended to
them from those whom they represent. Politicians must constantly engage
in symbolic labor by trying to nourish and sustain their symbolic capital
(credit or trust). And they are particularly susceptible to suspicion and
scandal, anything that can threaten the value of their credit, the bond of
belief and trust between them and those they represent. Indeed, the political field is quintessentially a field of symbolic struggle where symbolic
capital is a foremost concern.

In order to succeed, players in the political field need to develop a practical sense or "feel for the game" that is a political habitus, of specific skills,
competences, sensitivities that are attuned to the particular conditions of
the field. Their behavior becomes shaped by the logic of the field itself, of
political professionals competing one against the other for the power to
impose as the most legitimate their views of the social world. Thus, their
political stances, speeches, and behavior become relational in that they
make sense in terms of the competitive context. This incessant and intense
work to define distinct positions often borders on highly refined and eso-
teric distinctions that leave the lay public indifferent or hostile—not be-

cause citizens do not understand the words but because the hair-splitting distinctions are largely irrelevant to those who are not directly engaged in distinguishing their positions within the field. In this way the field assumes relative autonomy from the larger public and has the effect of imposing boundaries to lay participation.

Leadership Delegation and Lay Dispossession

An important theme in Bourdieu's work going back at least to material published in the seventies in *Actes* and that would find its way into *Distinction* (Bourdieu 1984a) is his concern that French politics in the Fifth Republic was increasingly becoming closed to effective mass representation in spite of the growth and vigor of French political parties, including those of the oppositional left. Political leadership was becoming more and more an elite affair. But rather than focus his attention just on the social origins of French political elites, Bourdieu directed his attention early on to more fundamental sociological processes of delegation in group formation and representation.[31]

One of Bourdieu's principal concerns in analyzing the French political field is the political effects of the *professionalization* and *specialization* of division of labor of symbolic production in modern political life. One effect he stresses concerns the dynamics and consequences of delegated political authority.[32] He examines the mechanism of political delegation by which individual representation and group identity come to be expressed through spokespersons. He explores the complex and circular relationship between the group that selects and creates its spokesperson and the spokesperson who in turn creates the group.

He sees in the delegation of authority a kind of generic antimony between the individual and the group. On the one hand, individuals cannot

31. In the *State Nobility*, Bourdieu (1996d) does in fact research this traditional political sociology topic of access to administrative elite positions in the state. An early and sympathetic critic of Bourdieu's work who captures in just a few pages the essential ingredients of Bourdieu's analysis of the structuring dynamics and growing closure of the political field is John Thompson (1984, 25–31).

32. Delegation is a fundamental concern of Bourdieu's field analysis of politics. Those attentive to the political sociology in Bourdieu's writings, such as Braud (2002), Thompson (1991), and Wacquant (2004, 6), have pointed up the emphasis that Bourdieu gives to the character and effects of delegation in political representation. Bourdieu was not the first to call attention to this dynamic of collective representation but he gave it special emphasis and stressed the political effects of the process. One finds it particularly in Bourdieu 1991a.

exist politically without being part of a group. Delegation is an act of group creation; it is an "act of magic" that enables a collection of individuals to form a corporate body that transcends in significance and purpose individuals (individuals in "serial existence" to use a Sartrean term). On the other hand, by becoming part of a group, individuals "dispossess themselves in favour of a spokesperson" (Bourdieu 1991a, 204, 205, 208). Bourdieu speaks of this process of delegation in the language of "bad faith," "usurpatory ventriloquism," and "usurpation."[33] He analyzes the situation of the delegate as one of a "sort of structural bad faith" in which the delegate conflates personal interests with those of the group, where both individual and group interests coincide. The individual delegate perceives his or her actions solely in terms of group interests and thereby fails to recognize his/her own individual interests at work as well.[34] Individuals become imprisoned by a kind of "political fetishism" when delegates come to think of themselves as the source of their own power and appeal as delegates. Not bad intentions but formative group processes drive delegation and consequent dispossession (205, 209).[35]

Bourdieu (1991a, 205–6) speaks of two mechanisms of delegation leading to dispossession in political organizations. First, the political group sets up its organizational headquarters with both the material and symbolic features of office, positions, bureaucratic organization, logo, and so on—an institutional network of positions. The second act of delegation occurs

33. While Bourdieu appears to see dispossession in virtually all forms of delegation in nonpolitical as well as political groups, he (Bourdieu 1991h, 171, 172) would not assign to the process of dispossession the status of a "natural" and inevitable process much as Michels (1962) described his iron law of oligarchy. Rather Bourdieu would focus on the historically specific social and economic conditions creating the division of labor between those who are politically active and those who are not. Still, he does little to specify conditions that would attenuate the dangers he associates with leadership delegation.

34. The idea of dispossession also reflects the influence of Bourdieu's reading of Weber's discussion of the priesthood/laity conflict where the professional clergy monopolizes salvation goods from the hands of the laity.

35. Bourdieu (1991a, 214) rejects the "cynical view of the delegate as a conscious and organized usurper" as "a very naive view, for all its apparent lucidity." Cynical manipulation of delegated power does of course occur, but Bourdieu stresses that the delegation process is generally perceived as a legitimate process and the "legitimate imposture succeeds only because the usurper is not a cynical calculator who consciously deceives the people, but someone who in all good faith *takes himself to be* something that he is not." My own view is that there is indeed a good deal of cynical strategizing among contemporary political powerbrokers in diverse pluralistic societies though good-faith perceptions are indeed cultivated and believed.

when this organization "mandates" individuals to speak on its behalf. In this second act, what Bourdieu calls the "mystery of the ministry," a process of symbolization occurs by which the individual delegate comes to act as "a substitute for the group which gives him a mandate." The delegate becomes the voice of the group, indeed the group itself; the representative comes to conflate his or her own organizational, career, and personal interests with those of the group. When the person, charm, charisma of the political leader deflects attention away from the real social base, when political capital becomes associated with the person or office concealing its real power base, a veritable "political idolatry" occurs. Dazzled by the enigmatic properties of political person/office, the rank and file become dispossessed of their own political voice.

The effects of delegation are "dispossession" where subordinate groups give up their political voice to delegated representatives who usurp that delegated power in pursuit of their own individual and organizational interests. This process of delegation also becomes a "source of political alienation." Through delegate representation individuals lose their own voices for political action. Dispossession is enhanced by professionalization and bureaucratization. The "specific logic of *delegation*" is one which "tends to dispossess, in favour of professional officials" (Bourdieu 1993b, 166). Dispossession is more severe for those in the dominated classes without much cultural capital. Lacking cultural capital, individuals are more constrained to rely on delegates for their political voice (Bourdieu 1991a, 206). Bourdieu clearly has in mind the French Communist Party and its affiliated labor unions in his analysis of political dispossession through delegation (1991a).[36] Individuals without alternative sources of symbolic identity—the French working class—are more dependent upon their political party than are those with cultural capital. This enhances centralized party power but at the price of individual freedom and local control.

Thus, the delegation of political authority for Bourdieu (1991a, 205) is an important form of political alienation. Ironically, like Michels (1962) in the "iron law of oligarchy," Bourdieu too finds political alienation precisely in those political organizations whose political ideology seems most committed to combating it. In his words, "the concentration of political capital is at its greatest . . . in parties whose aim is to struggle against the

---

36. Those who are most dependent upon their organizations and lacking any alternative source of identity are the "oblats" in the church and the communist party (Bourdieu 2000a, 65–66). These are the more likely victims of symbolic violence.

concentration of economic capital" (1991h, 174); that is, parties on the political left.

The mechanisms of delegation and dispossession are similar in both religious and political spheres. Moreover, they are similar in different kinds of political regimes. Bourdieu notes, for example, that the processes of dispossession through delegation were the same in the centralized party of the former Soviet Union as in democratic parties in Western Europe (2000d, 100–101). Moreover, the same can be found in the church. Leadership in both attempt to monopolize legitimate political discourse and action. What differentiates the case of the former Soviet Union from the Western democracies is the confluence of science and political representation where under the guise of "scientific socialism" and "democratic centralization" symbolic power was effectively monopolized by the state, whereas the greater separation of political and cultural powers in the democracies have not permitted that degree of absolutism.

Bourdieu's analysis of delegation has important implications for political sociology, particularly for the analysis of social movements and governance perspectives in political analysis (Bang 2003). It suggests that social movements and governance perspectives need to be attentive to the potentially stratifying effects of culture in the newly emerging patterns of political arrangements. A shift from administrative centralism of the traditional Western European welfare state need not necessarily signal a radical step toward more democratic life. Traditional welfare-state roles may be displaced by new cultural elites who become significant players in the more decentralized and diversified realm of political life.[37] Yet, the broad masses of people may not find new voice or increased representation—a point not sufficiently appreciated in much governance thinking. And while social movements are likely to include broader representation—at least initially—than state agencies and political parties, they too can quickly become instruments of issue specialization and elite entrenchment.

The concerns Bourdieu points up about the process of delegation and consequent dispossession for political representation overlap some with

---

37. In France, professional politicians since World War II have been increasingly recruited from just a couple of elite schools, such as the Paris Institut d'Etudes Politiques and the École Nationale d'Administration, leaving little room for amateur political activists or citizen legislators (Bourdieu 1996d). However, the more recent advent of the European Parliament opened up somewhat the political space for nontraditional participants, notably women and TV and sports celebrities (Kauppi 1996, 1999, 2000).

the view of democratic elitism made famous by the social-economic theorist Joseph Schumpeter (1975) and embraced by many political scientists and political sociologists (Dahl 1971; Kornhauser 1959; Lipset 1959). This view holds that the emergence of elites in large-scale organizations is inevitable and when in a context of multiple, competing elites this is far better than governance by a single, unified elite, which will become inflexible and nonresponsive, or by the unruly masses who lack the competence to consider the needs of the entire society. Bourdieu, however, does not embrace democratic elitism theory. Bourdieu describes the process of delegation as highly probable—though not inevitable—but is a strong advocate for genuine democratic representation rather than a system governed by elites no matter how multiple. Delegation and consequent dispossession of political capital are to be combated rather than accepted and welcomed for the sake of system efficiency or functionality.

Some Evaluation of Bourdieu's Symbolic Power, Violence, and Capital

Symbolic Capital as Metacapital

Symbolic capital does not have the same analytical status as the other kinds of capital Bourdieu talks about, such as economic capital and cultural capital. Symbolic capital is not a separate form of capital that applies to a distinct class of objects like social capital applies to social acquaintances and their social networks, or economic capital applies to property and income, or cultural capital applies to cultural objects. No one field is organized around symbolic capital like there is for economic capital and cultural capital. Rather symbolic capital functions as a kind of metacapital that parallels other sources of social power and emerges when they become "misrecognized" as power forms, that is, when they become taken for granted and no longer need justification. Symbolic capital does not have its own field; it becomes a dimension of other capitals. As Bourdieu elaborates,

> symbolic capital (male honour in Mediterranean societies, the honourability of the notable or the Chinese mandarin, the prestige of the celebrated writer, etc.) is not a particular kind of capital but what every kind of capital becomes when it is misrecognized as capital, that is, as force, a power of capacity for (actual or potential) exploitation, and therefore recognized as legitimate.

And he continues:

> more precisely, capital exists and acts as symbolic capital (securing profits—as
> observed, for example in the maxim "honesty is the best policy") in its rela-
> tionship with a habitus predisposed to perceive it as a sign, and as a sign of
> importance, that is, to know and recognize it on the basis of cognitive structures
> able and inclined to grant it recognition because they are attuned to what it is.
> (2000e, 242)

There are, however, two important qualifications that Bourdieu makes
to the idea that symbolic capital functions as a metacapital without its specific field. First, as we will see in the next chapter, symbolic capital becomes
concentrated in the state. In describing the formation of the modern state
Bourdieu (1994b, 11) writes that "there is a shift from a diffuse symbolic
capital, resting solely on collective recognition, to an *objectified symbolic
capital*, codified, delegated and guaranteed by the state, in a word *bureaucratized*." Symbolic capital in its objectified form becomes rather different
from the form that simply legitimates other types of capital. Second, this
is particularly the case in the field of law where symbolic capital takes on
an "objectified and codified form" that Bourdieu calls *juridical capital*.
As this concentration of symbolic capital "follows its *own logic*," here too
the authority dimension of other capitals metamorphosed into a distinct
type of capital with its own field. Thus, usage of the term modifies its analytical significance in different applications, suggesting that the versatility
of the terminology of capital glosses certain important distinctions while
also capturing key features of the dynamics of power, such as their interchangeability under certain conditions.

   This points to a conceptual difficulty in Bourdieu's language of capital,
one that he acknowledges when he writes that

> every kind of capital (economic, cultural, social) tends (to different degrees)
> to function as symbolic capital (so that it might be better to speak, in rigorous
> terms, of the *symbolic effects of capital*) when it obtains an explicit or practical
> recognition, that of a habitus structured according to the very structures of the
> space in which it has been engendered. (2000e, 242)

Here he acknowledges the problematic conceptual overlay where the idea
he is after is a social recognition of some power resources that are perceived as legitimate and as something whose worth does not reduce to

power. A change in conceptual language might better grasp those effects of power.

Consider the relations between economic capital and symbolic capital. The concepts of symbolic power, violence, and capital play an important role in Bourdieu's thinking for both assigning some priority to economic capital and yet avoiding the charge of economic reductionism (Bourdieu 1991g). We have seen that in spite of Bourdieu's emphasis on the multi-dimensionality of power in the forms of many kinds of capital, not all are equal in his assessment of how modern societies operate. He argues that economic capital is the root of all forms of capital although they are not reducible to it. Some goods and services can be obtained directly and immediately through economic capital. But other goods and services are accessible only through social capital or cultural capital. In other words,

> the different types of capital can be derived from *economic capital*, but only at the cost of a more or less great effort of transformation. . . . So it has to be posited simultaneously that economic capital is at the root of all the other types of capital and that these transformed, disguised forms of economic capital, never entirely reducible to that definition, produce their most specific effects only to the extent that they conceal (not least from their possessors) the fact that economic capital is at their root, in other words—but only in the last analysis—at the root of the effects. (Bourdieu 1986, 252)

The effects of symbolic power through misrecognition play a key role in hiding the economic basis of other forms of capital. However, the degree to which underlying economic interest is present or at work varies considerably by situation and by other types of capital at stake as Bourdieu seems to suggest. In very autonomous cultural universes, such as poetry and mathematics, economic interest would seem to play a less significant role than in the political field. Clearly the interplay between politics and funding is different than between science and funding.

While Bourdieu says that other capitals (economic, social, and cultural) can also function as symbolic capital, he notes that cultural capital is more likely to obtain symbolic capital value ("is predisposed to function as symbolic capital") than economic capital "because the social conditions of its transmission and acquisition are more disguised than those of economic capital" (1986, 245). That the term *capital* also applies to the symbolic or legitimation effects of other kinds of capitals points up limitations in this kind of conceptual strategy. The effects that one can accumulate are more closely tied to cultural and social resources than economic, a point that Bourdieu himself acknowledges. Symbolic capital is relatively more important to the field of cultural production than it is to the field of economic production. Legitimation is more important to the functioning of cultural and social resources than to economic, as Bourdieu points out. Yet the conceptual language of capital tends to put all on the same plane whereas the relationship is more complex suggesting differences in types rather than just forms.

And political capital as a form of symbolic capital is precarious indeed. It is the "supremely *free-flowing* capital" that "can be conserved only at the cost of unceasing work which is necessary both to accumulate credit and to avoid discredit." Since "the politician derives his political power from the trust that a group places in him," he (or she)

> like the man of honour, is especially vulnerable to suspicious, malicious misrepresentations and scandal, in short, to everything that threatens belief and trust, by bringing to light the hidden and secret acts and remarks of the present or the past which can undermine present acts and remarks and discredit their author. (Bourdieu 1991h, 192–93)

This helps explain the highly euphemized character of political discourse of the politician. Because of "the extreme vulnerability of political capital," the "accomplished politician . . . can be measured in particular by the high degree of euphemization of his discourse" (1991h).

The idea that political capital is a form of symbolic capital and therefore is particularly vulnerable to the changing winds of reputation, rumor, and so on, points to Bourdieu's efforts to identify specific characteristics of forms of political power. The capacity to mobilize support for one's cause, to represent a collective body, to cultivate public recognition, point to power resources that do not reduce to economic interests. But this insightful effort to offer a more refined analysis of forms of power also points up the difficulty of his conceptual language. As I noted earlier, any form of capital, including economic capital, can become symbolic capital. Symbolic capital is a form of other capitals. It designates a power effect when other capitals take on recognized authority. But might they not be differences in *types* rather than forms, as the conceptual language implies? Bourdieu acknowledges a particular relationship between political capital and symbolic capital that one does not find in the case of economic capital or even in the institutionalized forms of cultural capital. This shows Bourdieu's efforts to identify the more subtle expressions of power. But while the language of symbolic power as capital points up certain characteristics that suggest an analogy to economic capital, it also becomes an awkward conceptual tool when trying to distinguish other features. The term *capital* suggests more similarity and interchangeability than there in fact is.[38]

Historical Shift toward Symbolic Forms of Domination

The idea of power expressed through symbolic violence reflects Bourdieu's belief that there has been a historical shift toward symbolic forms of domination in modern differentiated societies. Bourdieu is not alone in making this observation. One finds classic formulations of that claim in Elias (1978) and Foucault (1972). This does not mean that traditional societies were without symbolic violence. Indeed, Bourdieu first uses the idea in his analysis of Berber society. Yet the term plays a critical role for Bourdieu in his conceptual strategy for analyzing modern societies.

One needs to understand this claim in light of Bourdieu's view of the general transition in modes of domination found in traditional, undifferentiated societies where domination passed largely through personal relations to modern, differentiated societies where symbolic as well as material resources become more objectified as "social facts" of power that connect power to positions and titles.[39] Thus, it seems important to note that in spite of this transition to more symbolic violence, Bourdieu sees symbolic capital and power expressed in traditional societies as well. The transition is one of increasing objectification and differentiation of power resources.

38. Indeed Braud (2002, 369) points to the limits of assimilating the dynamics of politics to those suggested by the idea of a market. Political capital is really not analogous to economic capital because the resources used by political leaders are only partially material but depend more on the positive representations of their identity, which in turn are based on shared beliefs. Notoriety and popularity are as important in politics as money is in economic activity, a point that Bourdieu stresses in the 1981 paper "Political Representation" (1991h). Therefore Braud considers it a metaphor rather than a scholarly concept.

39. Bourdieu (1990c, 133) links "modes of domination" to the degree of objectification that material and symbolic resources take on. So symbolic capital and power in undifferentiated societies, where power resources have not objectified into concrete forms with some degree of autonomy from the persons holding them, are embedded in personal relations. But in the differentiated societies where forms of capital emerge with relative autonomy from other forms, power, including symbolic power, becomes attached to positions rather than persons and the kinds of qualifications required to occupy particular positions.

While Bourdieu affirms the shift toward "softer" symbolic forms of violence in the Western tradition, he also strongly affirms the need to transcend the material/idealism dualism. Bourdieu sees his work as transcending the traditional opposition between the material and symbolic dimensions of power. His materialist economy of symbolic goods represents his attempt to find a conceptual language that will transcend this traditional antinomy. Hence his concept of symbolic power links the material and the symbolic in a relational way: as power resources each requires the other.[40]

Is there a contradiction or tension here in Bourdieu's thinking? Clearly Bourdieu—by his own affirmation—is on the materialist side of the traditional debate over the relative importance of material/physical and symbolic power resources, but he wishes to transcend that traditional opposition by rejecting both crude materialist and idealist versions of it.[41] He characterizes as a "radical misinterpretation" of his concept of symbolic violence the criticism that it minimizes the important role of physical violence—a criticism that I make in this book. He contends that this is in fact based on a commonsense reading of the term *symbolic* and a "crude" materialistic view of the realist/symbolic opposition (Bourdieu 2001c, 34).[42] He charges that such criticism reflects a reductive and impoverished view of the importance of the symbolic realm for ordering social life. He defends his emphasis on the symbolic, and the numerous formulations that stress that form of control, as a necessary corrective to the crude materialism he was reacting against.

Nonetheless, it is significant that Bourdieu has focused on education institutions rather than prisons, such as Foucault or on the military. France remains a highly militarized country and the United States stands out for its degree of incarceration and militarization. Given the strong claims Bourdieu makes for the role of education in modern stratified societies, this different focus from Foucault could not simply flow from an intellectual division of labor. When he writes that "the symbolic efficacy of the

---

40. See Terray (1996), whose reading of Bourdieu stresses how symbolic and material violence are but flip sides of the same coin—fundamentally violence.

41. He affirms offering a genuinely materialist view of the social world but one that is not crudely reductionist in that material interests could not function without symbolic support, just as the page 113 quotation beginning "the different types" suggests.

42. His 1977 paper "On Symbolic Power" (Bourdieu 1991g) makes it clear that his "materialist theory of the economy of symbolic goods" is constructed against "crude materialism."

prevailing mode of domination tends to increase, and physical coercion and repression tend to give way to the milder dissimulated constraints of symbolic violence, with the police and the prison system, privileged by adolescent denunciation and its extensions in scholarly discourse, becoming much less important in the maintenance of the social order than the school and authorities of cultural production" the United States stands in sharp contrast (1996d, 386–87).[43] Here he seems to downplay the persistent forms of physical violence and constraints found at least in American society. Clearly inspired by Bourdieu's thinking, Wacquant's (2009b) work on prisons offers a compelling view that connects symbolic violence and physical incarceration in a way that shows their intimate connection.

Still a tension becomes apparent if one considers the importance Bourdieu assigns to the socialization of habitus in the formation of orderly conduct.[44] If order were as widely internalized as the emphasis on habitus implies and as naturalized as symbolic violence would have, then one would expect a smaller prison population even for differentiated societies—even a highly differentiated order. There is at least an empirical discrepancy between the magnitude of some key indicators of symbolic capital and those of physical coercion and perhaps a conceptual difficulty as well. In the United States, at the very citadel of capitalist development where education, advertising, and the mass media give perhaps the greatest opportunity for symbolic power to find expression, the prison appears

43. Bourdieu (2000e, 96) suggests here that the properties of symbolic violence can be illustrated by a well-trained and appropriately responsive civilian police force that makes one forget that it is ultimately a force that has been converted into legitimate violence, and because it is thus misrecognized as such, it converts legitimate violence into symbolic violence. There are many countries today or regional/local situations where police forces lack that taken-for-granted respect.

44. Bourdieu, and Wacquant after him, have talked about the "differentiated" habitus to try to take into account differentiating conditions of socialization that set up conflicting dispositions in individuals. That shows their willingness to be attentive to variation in empirical conditions. In discussing the contradictions of inheritance experienced by the son relative to the father who occupies a dominated position, Bourdieu (in Bourdieu et al. 1999, 511) describes a "habitus divided against itself, in constant negotiation with itself and with its ambivalence, and therefore doomed to a kind of duplication, to a double perception of self, to successive allegiances and multiple identities." Yet the idea of the differentiated habitus stands in tension with the unifying and homogenizing thrust of habitus as a "structuring structure" that helps create homologies across different fields and that is so emphasized in Bourdieu's earlier work. Not a fractured but a unitary force of habitus across different fields characterizes the emphasis of most of his work.

to be assuming a growing power function (Wacquant 2009a; Western 2006). Physical as well as symbolic violence increasingly haunts significant segments of the American population.

Symbolic Power Internalized: How Does It Actually Work?

Bourdieu's dispositional view of practices holds that these are prediscursive patterns of "power exerted on bodies" with the "inscription of social structure into bodies." He challenges social scientific researchers to identify ways in which these linkages are made. Numerous studies employing various methodologies have suggested ways in which social positions appear to find expression in bodily form. See, for example, the very insightful work on boxing by one of Bourdieu's students, Loïc Wacquant (2003), or the classic ethnographic observations of Goffman (1959). The "political body" carried and projected as "studied observance" (a variation on Goffman's notion of "studied nonobservance") by professional politicians is ripe for ethnographic study. Nonetheless, as Lukes (2005, 142–43) notes, Bourdieu raises the very interesting and complex topic of the interplay among the social, the symbolic, and the physical, and the interpenetration of the social, the biological, and the cognitive of which we still know very little. Moreover, as Lukes queries, we often do not know when these prediscursive dispositions set limits to discursive learning or are themselves set into place by discursive input from religion, the mass media, and so on. The impact of decades of feminism, for example, may well have brought about significant changes in the ways some women today express their bodily identity.

Bourdieu stresses that symbolic power goes misrecognized because it becomes naturalized by taking on a natural, given, taken-for-granted appearance. Symbolic violence is symbolic power misrecognized. Yet he also acknowledges that symbolic power is a contested one; it finds expression in the context of struggle over the right to name and classify for legitimate authority. These can be doxic struggles over fundamental assumptions and categories that characterize a particular field. There is a tension, therefore, between these two aspects of symbolic power since conflict and struggle would seem to disrupt the taken-for-granted or naturalizing qualities of symbolic power. Might there not be more room for conscious awareness of power constraints than Bourdieu's concept of symbolic violence would suggest? Overt political conflict can challenge fundamental assumptions of participants, leading to more conscious reflection on, invention of, and strategizing around expressions of symbolic power.

Dominant expressions of symbolic power may not always be as fully internalized as Bourdieu's language of symbolic violence suggests. While dominated individuals and groups may outwardly adapt to prevailing social perceptions, they can work inwardly to undermine the dominant conceptual and social order in small and sometimes large ways. Moreover, at times dominated individuals and groups can work actively to resist and subvert the imposed social definitions (Scott 1985, 1990). Bourdieu does think of the class struggle as a classification struggle where the framing terms and social boundaries are contested. But the overwhelming emphasis in his work is the subtle but gripping ways that symbolic violence operates through our everyday understandings of the social world. Too little attention is given by Bourdieu to those inward and outward forms of resistance that shape the social order in small and large ways. This is a promising avenue of investigation for political sociology and one that would contribute to a fruitful, critical elaboration of Bourdieu's work.

Power to–Power over Distinction

Bourdieu's concept of symbolic power seems clearly to be a kind of "power over" that points to the capacity to impose a social vision of the world as the most legitimate one. Though domination is the focus of his concern, his thinking draws as well on the more generic capacity of "power to" act. The generative dispositions of habitus suggest the capacity to act, or power as capability. His analysis of symbolic struggle at the "subjective" level whereby individuals and groups can "act by trying to change the categories of perception and evaluation of the social world, the cognitive and evaluative structures" (1990b, 134) opens up creative potential for new forms of power to accomplish certain things. Symbolic power is also a constitutive power.

The "power to/power over" analytical distinction is undercut by Bourdieu's conflictual view of the social world in which struggles for distinction are a fundamental dimension of social life. To garner recognition from others implies the capacity to exercise some influence on the attention of others. The "power to" implies in Bourdieu's view of the social world "power over" since we are all involved in the struggle for identity that involves efforts to garner the attention of others. Cultural power institutionalized, as in educational credentials, imposes that recognition

(Bourdieu 1986, 248). Moreover, his dispositional view of action holds that the habitus, which embodies power as a capacity to act, connects to stratified social structures.

Nonetheless, Bourdieu's focus on domination leaves unattended those forms of power that generate resources and effects that are influential and enhance the capabilities of a collectivity rather than being just zero-sum. Bourdieu does not make the distributive/collective power distinction that Parsons (1960, 199–225) did in his widely accepted criticism of Weber's discussion of power and domination (Mann 1986, 6–7; Wrong 1995, 237–47). Further, Bourdieu does not consider cases of "power over" relations that may be beneficial to subordinates. The power of the sports trainer over his or her trainee—a relation that Bourdieu sees as an appealing analogy for learning the craft of sociology—can be a power over that produces positive benefits for the subordinate. These are distinctions worth making, yet need not detract from Bourdieu's singular focus on power as a capacity to dominate, including its more subtle iterations.

False Consciousness and Misrecognition

Typical of the "power over" perspective, symbolic power and violence suggest a form of "false consciousness." Bourdieu distances himself from the language of false consciousness discredited by the history of its usages by Marxist parties and regimes. But his alternative language of "recognition-misrecognition" retains the fundamental idea that actors often fail to see their best interests and therefore are unable to act on them. While the shift in terminology and critical posture toward the perverse usages of the idea by Marxist leadership organizations is helpful, it nonetheless leaves open the troublesome issue of who is able to determine the best interests of groups. Bourdieu avoids some of the traditional baggage that comes with this issue by stressing how interests are multiple, including cultural and symbolic as well as social and economic, and they are fundamentally contested, as field analysis is able to show. But the external standpoint found in the traditional Marxist view is there and potentially problematic. Analytically, in our view it is quite justified: often an external standpoint is needed to determine the overriding, vested, or best interests of insiders (inside actors) caught up in the internal practices of their particular social worlds. Indeed, as Bourdieu suggests with the idea of an epistemological break, the social scientific perspective is by definition to some extent that of the outsider. Politically, however, the external posture stands in tension with democratic participation. It can embody a form of elitism if grounded on the assumption that insiders, because of misrecognition, are incapable of perceiving their own best interests. Reflexivity is needed to guard against the analytical and political from becoming uncritically conflated.

While Bourdieu merges the analytical and political in ways that may be troublesome, given Bourdieu's critical posture and reflexive orientation I find little in his work that would effectively legitimate some vanguard leadership. Indeed, as I document in chapter 7, Bourdieu's own anti-institutional political practice on the "left that is Left" should assuage that concern. More problematic in my view would be whether Bourdieu's critical voice could ever become an effective mobilizing tool in struggle for greater equality. The shift from debunking to mobilizing would seem to call for leadership delegation and representation that Bourdieu finds so problematic.

How Deep Does It Go?

The concept of symbolic violence is designed as a critical break with the view that power has become much more benign or less relevant in societies where the most authoritarian and crudest techniques of coercion have been replaced with persuasion, consent, choice, negotiation, and influence. Bourdieu's concept reminds us that power remains very much an organizing force in modern societies though its forms have changed. Power has not disappeared from modern social relations but simply taken on nonauthoritarian, more egalitarian, therapeutic, personal forms. Even in societies where fields of cultural production, circulation, and consumption have emerged relatively autonomous from direct economic and political influence, power remains an organizing dynamic. Indeed, for Bourdieu power relations, through more comprehensive and intensive forms of socialization, have become more insidious and effective. Perhaps they also have become more contested. If so, have they become more objects of critical reflexivity than Bourdieu thinks since a state of contest would likely heighten awareness of the arbitrary character of positions of authority, of their bounded nature rather than universalizing spread?

Bourdieu's view of symbolic domination (and violence) offers one compelling answer to the question why the dominated in modern democratic societies do not resist more their conditions of domination. It is an answer that falls within the range of what Lukes calls the "third dimension" of power. Yet, it is but one from the checklist of seven possible answers to the question Charles Tilly (1991, 594) provided some time ago. They include some degree of clairvoyance of the arbitrary character of subordination, some calculation of the costs of rebellion, and some capacity to extract some benefits from the condition of subordination. Bourdieu's analysis stresses the misrecognition of the arbitrary conditions contributing to subordination. But the reasons need not always be mutually exclusive and may well exist in complex combinations, as Tilly suggests, whether it is James C. Scott's (1990) proverbial Ethiopian wise peasant who "bows deeply and silently farts . . . when the great lord passes" or Adam Przeworski's (1985) subordinated worker who nonetheless extracts some material rewards.

CHAPTER FIVE

Bourdieu's Analysis of the State

Having introduced the master concepts in Bourdieu's political sociology, particularly his analysis of the political field, the field of power, and his concept of symbolic power, I turn in this chapter to his analysis of the state, that is, the institutions of central government. Previous chapters have shown the central role Bourdieu assigns to symbolic power, violence, and capital. With these ideas he develops a powerful argument for how capitals are legitimated in fields of struggle. Capitals become legitimate, he argues, when they are naturalized and misrecognized as something other than power sources, when their arbitrary character is perceived in legitimate terms, that is, as forms of disinterested objects and pursuits. The conceptual language of symbolic power and violence permits Bourdieu to examine the dynamics of power at micro as well as macro levels and across a broad array of fields. In modern differentiated societies, however, symbolic power tends to be centered in one key institution, the state. This chapter examines Bourdieu's analysis of the modern state.

The chapter begins by noting that Bourdieu theorized the state relatively late in his career. It identifies the key influence of Max Weber and Norbert Elias on Bourdieu's thinking and notes the point where Bourdieu believes he moves beyond Weber and Elias. The chapter also identifies how Bourdieu's thinking regarding the state is an extension of his broader sociology of culture, particularly his conceptualization of symbolic power, of class struggles as classification struggles, and his field analysis. It examines how Bourdieu thinks of the origins of the modern state, its leadership and ideology, and situates his view of the state relative to his concept of the field of power and the political field. The chapter highlights Bourdieu's emphasis on the classificatory power of the state and notes his criticism of unitary, state-centric views of political life. His alternative language of bureaucratic field challenges realist conceptions of the state as a clearly bounded, self-evident institution. Yet, the strength of Bourdieu's emphasis on the symbolic dimension of state power also points to its limitation. The chapter concludes with some evaluation of Bourdieu's thinking about the state, including comparisons to other leading theoretical perspectives on the state.

Later Conceptual Concern

While many political sociologists during the seventies and eighties put the state-society relationship at the center of their analysis of power, Bourdieu did not—at least not explicitly.[1] With the notable exception of his sharp condemnation of French colonial state power in Algeria, Bourdieu offered an explicit analysis of the state relatively late in his career. Indeed, he seldom used the term "state" in his early writings; it is only in the 1980s that he began to theorize explicitly and critically the concept of the state (Bourdieu 2012, 595–98).[2] He did not participate in the major paradig-

1. He devoted little attention to government organizations, administrative agencies, political parties, elected representative bodies, and so on (Swartz 2006). However, on the broader topic of the state, his early focus on French schooling certainly concerns the state-society relationship because of the centralized place of public, state-administered education in France. I discuss in chapter 7 how his early work in Algeria documented the destructive effects of French colonial state power. Indeed, he rooted the ultimate source of violence of the French Algerian war in the colonial system itself.

2. One of the first expressions of Bourdieu's thinking on the state as a field of struggle can be found in Bourdieu 1980b, 7, where he briefly asserts that even under absolutism, the monarch, who holds the reins of power (*L'Etat c'est moi*), engages in ongoing struggle to maintain and balance the divisions and tensions within his court. In Bourdieu 1988b, 42, and 1990b, 136–37, he articulates his view that the state monopolizes legitimate symbolic violence. Yet in his 1987 paper "The Force of Law" (Bourdieu 1987b) he discusses the properties of the juridical field without connecting them explicitly to the state as a bureaucratic field—terminology he uses only later. In an interview reflecting on the 1989 publication of *The State Nobility*—his first book on the state—Bourdieu remarks that "I had been aware for quite some time that I would eventually have to confront the problem of the state" (Wacquant 1993b, 40). The most comprehensive guide to Bourdieu's thinking on the state can be found in his 1990–91 Collège de France lectures published in *Sur L'État* (Bourdieu 2012). That book appeared just after this manuscript was submitted to the publisher for copy editing and I was therefore unable to incorporate all of the relevant material from those lectures into this book. But *Symbolic Power, Politics, and Intellectuals* does take into account most all of Bourdieu's published statements regarding the state that are referenced in these lectures. Other key references on the state include Bourdieu 1990b, 1994b, 1999a, 2004a, 2005c; Bourdieu and Wacquant 1992, 111–14.

matic shift starting in the seventies among many political sociologists that would place the historical origins and administrative reach of state power at the center of their analyses (Block 1977; Carnoy 1984; Evans, Rueschemeyer, and Skocpol 1985; Skocpol 1979; Therborn 1978; Tilly 1975). This is striking since Bourdieu developed his sociology of culture and power in France during the sixties when the theoretical influences of Louis Althusser (1971) and Nicos Poulantzas (1973) were strong and focused on the state.[3] The work of Althusser and Poulantzas contributed significantly to the rise in importance in the 1970s of the subfields of world systems, historical sociology, and Marxist sociology (Orum 1996, 140–41). Bourdieu was in fact quite critical of this Althusserian/Poulantzas emphasis that influenced American and British political sociology during that period.[4] Indeed, he (1990b, 3–55) reports making a conscious choice to focus on the sociology of culture, an area of investigation he considered neglected at the time, rather than on the more popular and widespread topics of class stratification and theories of the state motivated by the dominant force of Marxism in France during the sixties and seventies.[5] Nonetheless, the state is ever-present in Bourdieu's thinking even if in his early work it is not explicitly theorized with the kind of emphasis one finds in state-centered work in political sociology.

There are educational, intellectual, and early career reasons why Bourdieu did not focus on the state as a privileged topic for his early sociological investigations. His educational training had been in the elite academic culture of École Normale Supérieure (ENS) where he studied philosophy and not political science or political sociology in one of the political science institutes, such as the famed Paris Instituts d'études politiques. He developed a particular interest in phenomenology, not political theory. At the time there was no comparable national competitive exam in

3. Following Althusser's (1971) lead, Poulantzas (1973) proposed a structuralist theory of the state by arguing that market competition fragments the capitalist class, which requires the state to operate as a relatively autonomous institution that gives overall direction and unity to capitalists while restraining the power of organized labor.

4. Bourdieu (Bourdieu and Wacquant 1992, 111) would sidestep the debate over the relative autonomy of the state as being too scholastic since such discussion assumed a unitary view of the state that he rejected and in his view failed to encourage empirical research.

5. Bourdieu is much closer to the institutional approach of Michael Mann (1986, 1993), the organizational network perspective of Laumann and Knoke (Bourdieu and Wacquant 1992, 113; Laumann and Knoke 1987; Bourdieu 2012, 178), and particularly to the recent "cultural turn" from state-centric and class-based models of politics toward an emphasis on cultural politics (Nash 2000; Steinmetz 1999a).

political sociology or political science such as the *agrégation* in philosophy for teaching positions in French lycées. And following the practice of many ENS graduates, Bourdieu passed the rigorous *agrégation* exam and began his first teaching position in philosophy in a lycée.

Bourdieu's first fieldwork occurred in Algeria during the horrible French colonial war in which he documented and condemned the destructive effects of colonial state power on a traditional society. But that early military and political experience did not lead him to formalize a theory of the state or participate in the debates over the state that animated considerable sociological attention during the sixties and seventies. Other early empirical objects drew his attention: the traditional Berber peasant communities without a centralized state, the effects of urban migration on traditional French peasant marriage patterns, social class patterns in photography and museum attendance, and student social and cultural inequities in educational expansion. His early concern for a sociology of power, in fact, examines expressions of power beyond the explicitly political and state arenas. An early summary of his research until 1972 (Current Research 1972) shows a clear interdisciplinary thrust across the sociology of education, culture, power, and economics but no focus on political organizations per se. His early research on the ruling class focuses on cultural elites, not state administrators or political leadership. Indeed, his concept of symbolic power did not require immediate focus on the state. The concept, as noted in chapter 4, did not originate in state-centered theory. Further, he in fact develops the concept of fields and the field of power against a unitary concept of the state. His concept of power as a form of capital that becomes both the means for and object of struggle in fields leads him to investigate forms of power spread across the field of power in complex relations within and between fields. Indeed this capital/field orientation suggests that power is not concentrated in the state per se but in the field of power and the broad array of relatively autonomous fields, such as science, literature, and the universities.[6]

There is therefore a certain affinity in the direction of Bourdieu's work on power and that of Foucault. Though the study of power is central to their respective intellectual projects, neither Bourdieu nor Foucault made the state the focus of analysis, particularly in their early work. Indeed, Foucault (1991, 103) contends that too much attention has been focused on this abstract, unitary object, the state. Bourdieu stresses that power is

6. The idea that the primary locus of power is the field of power and not the state per se can be found in Bourdieu 1996d, 386, 388.

not concentrated in the state per se but in the field of power. Bourdieu (1996d, 386) writes that

> no longer incarnated in persons or even in particular institutions, power be-comes coextensive with the structure of the field of power, and it is only realized and manifested through an entire set of fields and forms of power united by a genuine organic solidarity, and thus both different and interdependent.

He goes on to say that

> power is primarily wielded invisibly and anonymously, through 'mechanisms' such as those that achieve the reproduction of economic and cultural capital, in other words, through the apparently anarchical, yet structured, actions and reactions of networks of agents and institutions that are both in competition and complementary, and involved in increasingly long and complex circuits of legitimating exchanges.

Bourdieu thus describes the distribution of power as forms of capital dis-tributed over a set of field arrangements and in an increasingly diversified field of power. He in fact sees educational institutions playing a key role in the distribution of power in modern societies.

Thus both Bourdieu and Foucault develop a conceptualization of power that extends well beyond the confines of the state. Both are critically react-ing against the Marxist preoccupation with state power. Yet, unlike Fou-cault, Bourdieu, particularly in his later writings, considers the state as a particular concentration of power worthy of critical analytical attention.[7]

Some of Bourdieu's apparent late concern with the state is, however, due to North American perceptions shaped by academic disciplinary special-ization and boundaries. In addition to documenting the effects of French colonial violence in Algeria, Bourdieu devoted attention to forms of state power in his early work on education, although national tradition and disci-plinary boundaries in North America have obscured that dimension of his work. North American sociology tends to view the sociology of education and political sociology as distinct subfields with their own distinct courses, curriculum, professional literature, and section within the American So-ciological Association. While some sociology of education concerns public

---

7. Foucault (1980a, 166–93) eventually admitted that the state required special attention and he continued to use the term *state* in his writings on governmentality (Foucault 1991). But he never saw in the state the concentration of powers that Bourdieu did.

policy issues, the profession has tended to demarcate the political dimension off from other topics of concern. Since an early conduit of Bourdieu's work in North American sociology was through the sociology of education, his concepts of cultural capital and habitus were made the key conceptual tools of interest for they directly spoke to the social stratification concerns of North American education researchers. Their political import often became secondary considerations. Yet, with a strong tradition of centralized public education at all levels in France, analysis of education for French sociologists, and particularly for Bourdieu, was in fact analysis of an important state institution.[8] It is clear that Bourdieu's landmark work *Reproduction in Education, Society and Culture* (Bourdieu and Passeron 1977) does not divorce the sociology of education from an analysis of state power.[9] His later book, *The State Nobility* (1996d), which is largely devoted to the state and the recruitment of state elites, opens with an analysis of academic classifications. Bourdieu clearly saw his analysis in *The State Nobility* of the elite secondary school track as an analysis of the French state and its reproduction. So Bourdieu's ostensible neglect of state power in fact lies in part in North American perceptions shaped by a strong federalist national tradition that does not focus on a strong centralized state and by strict disciplinary boundaries and academic traditions that separate knowledge units into distinct subunits.[10] Still, compared to the work of many of his contemporary political sociologists at the time, Bourdieu's early work did not lift out the state per se for theorization or empirical investigation.

The State as Monopoly over Symbolic Power and Violence

Bourdieu conceptualizes the modern state as an elaboration of Weber's classic and widely used institutional definition of the state as holding the monopoly of physical violence over a specific territory. Weber writes that "a compulsory political organization with continuous operations . . . will be called a 'state' insofar as its administrative staff successfully upholds the claim to the *monopoly* of the *legitimate* use of physical force in the enforcement of its order" (1978b, 54).

---

8. One might recall that education was one of Althusser's (1971) key state apparati.

9. Still, the focus of that work is really a sociology of the pedagogical relationship rather than a reflection on the state per se.

10. Indeed my own early presentation of Bourdieu to North American sociology of education reflects that professional disciplinary orientation (Swartz 1977).

Bourdieu sees Norbert Elias (Elias 1978; 1982, 104–16, 149–61, 201–25) as elaborating from Weber to stress the monopolizing power of the state over the means of coercion and taxation to eliminate competition in a given territory. While both Weber and Elias include the "legitimate" means of violence in their definitions, Bourdieu argues that neither probes sufficiently all the consequences of legitimation that Bourdieu tries to capture with his concept of symbolic violence (Bourdieu 2012, 204). Bourdieu (1994b, 3) defines the state as that institution that "successfully claims the monopoly of the legitimate use of physical *and symbolic violence* over a definite territory and over the totality of the corresponding population" (emphasis added).[11] This definition points to Bourdieu's understanding of power, one clearly influenced by Weber and Elias in that power must be *legitimated* in order to be exercised in any enduring and effective way.

Bourdieu's analysis of the state, therefore, focuses on the symbolic dimension of the state, but he understands that in terms of positions, interests, beliefs, and strategies of agents in fields. He draws on his field analytical perspective, which stems in part from his reading of Weber's sociology of religion (Bourdieu 1987c, 1991c), to develop his concept of the religious field and his field analytical framework more generally.[12] This field perspective is extended to his understanding of the state. The state is

> an ensemble of administrative or bureaucratic fields (they often take the empirical form of commissions, bureaus and boards) within which agents and categories of agents, governmental and nongovernmental, struggle over this peculiar form of authority consisting of the power to *rule* via legislation, regulations, administrative measures (subsidies, authorizations, restrictions, etc.), in short, everything that we normally put under the rubric of state policy as a particular sphere of practices. (Bourdieu and Wacquant 1992, 111)

11. This definition of the state as the "holder of the monopoly of legitimate symbolic violence" is found several places in his work (Bourdieu 1989d, 22). For example, in Bourdieu and Wacquant 1992, he defines the state as "the ensemble of fields that are the site of struggles in which what is at stake is—to build on Max Weber's famed formulation—the *monopoly of legitimate symbolic violence*, i.e., the power to constitute and to impose as *universal* and *universally applicable* within a given 'nation,' that is, within the boundaries of a given territory, a common set of coercive norms" (112).

A similar 1984 formulation can be found in *Homo Academicus* (1988b).

12. Indeed, as Calhoun (1993, 85) rightly notes, it is Bourdieu's approach to religion, inspired in part by Weber's sociology of religion, that anticipates how Bourdieu will later develop his approach to the state.

In other words, the state is a "set of partially overlapping bureaucratic fields" (Bourdieu and Wacquant 1992, 113) that constitute an instituted arena of struggle over the functions of social regulation in a society. Thus, the conceptual language of bureaucratic field permits Bourdieu to break with unitary views of the state and technocratic images of official classifications and regulations. It breaks with a hyperrational view of state action suggesting consensual direction rather than conflicting interests. Political struggle stands at the very center of state power for Bourdieu.

The state is also a field of ideological production. Bourdieu speaks of the "effect of the universality" as the "symbolic dimension of the effect of the state" and presents this in terms of the interests and strategies of civil servants producing a "performative discourse" that both legitimates and constitutes the state as the guardian of the public interests and therefore wielder of considerable symbolic power in the struggle to dominate the social order (Bourdieu 1994b, 16). Thus, appeals to civic mindedness, public order, and the public good are seen as flowing from the interests and strategies of agents of the state as they struggle to enhance the administrative reach of their government agencies. This illustrates Bourdieu's way of thinking about ideology by focusing on the producers of ideology and their field positions and interests. And their most immediate ideological interests do not trace back to location in the social relations of production (as theorized in Marxism) but to location in the social relations of symbolic production (Bourdieu 1994b). Hence, the state becomes a field of ideological production and develops relative autonomy from both civil society and the economy and the actions of state actors need to be understood primarily in terms of their positions and capital holdings and strategies within the array of bureaucratic fields Bourdieu considers as the state. This view of the state sets Bourdieu apart from both Marxists who view the state as the executive committee of the bourgeoisie and from pluralists who view government officials as neutral referees called upon to adjudicate conflicting private interests for the sake of the larger good.

Origins of the State and State Nobility

Statist and Other Forms of Capital

One finds the first sustained effort by Bourdieu (2012) to theorize explicitly the state in his January 1990–December 1991 Collège de France lectures. In those lectures he reviews a considerable body of theoretical writings and historical investigations relative to modern state formation. The lectures address numerous issues relative to conceptualizing modern state origins and power. He devotes particular attention to the models of Max Weber (1978b), Norbert Elias (1982), Charles Tilly (1992), and Philip Corrigan and Derek Sayer (1985) as he formulates his own model. In a 1993 paper, "Rethinking the State: Genesis and Structure of the Bureaucratic Field" (Bourdieu 1994b, 4), which grows out of those lectures, he proposes a "model of the emergence of the state." He sees the modern state emerging from the

> culmination of a process of concentration of different species of capital: capital of physical force or instruments of coercion (army, police), economic capital, cultural capital or (better) informational capital, and symbolic capital. It is this concentration as such which constitutes the state as the holder of a sort of meta-capital granting power over other species of capital and over their holders.

In describing the logic of modern state development, Bourdieu sees progressive concentrations of physical capital (physical coercion), economic capital, informational (or cultural) capital, and symbolic capital. From these concentrations emerges *statist capital*, a special type of capital, a kind of metacapital, that "enables the state to exercise power over the different fields and over the different particular species of capital, and especially over the rates of conversion between them (and thereby over the relations of force between their respective holders)" (Bourdieu 1994b, 4). Statist capital represents an emergent metacapital, a regulatory power over the field of power and the broader society. It is state authority.

Thus he follows Weber's and Elias's lead in conceptualizing the modern state as fundamentally concerned with monopolizing the means of violence over a particular territory and corresponding population. But he extends the monopolizing function to the means of symbolic violence, an emphasis Bourdieu sees as distinct from that of Weber and Elias. Mobilization of forces of order (warriors, army, police) requires justification, building solidarity, and obtaining social recognition, which in Bourdieu's view validates his emphasis on the importance of legitimation.

The state emerges as there develops a specialized corps (e.g., police, army) of agents who wield violence. The concentration of physical capital in the hands of a few is paralleled by the concentration of economic capital through taxation. Bourdieu (1998i) sees these processes as occurring simultaneously or "dialectically" rather than sequentially. They are "interdependent." He stresses how the processes of unification of a territory and people through a concentration of the means of violence and through a national economic market are paralleled by a concentration of "symbolic capital." The processes of assembling police, military, and economic resources become operative only as they obtain social recognition and hence legitimacy. He stresses that even the concentration of armed forces and economic resources necessary to maintain the emerging state does not occur without a parallel concentration of symbolic capital. Taxation, for example, which must develop in order to pay for armed forces, raises the issue of legitimation. Indeed, the thrust of Bourdieu's argument suggests that in order for the state to monopolize physical violence it must have already captured considerable symbolic capital, that is, considerable legitimacy in order to do that (1994b, 4–8).

Bourdieu (1994b, 5; 2012, 203–16) indicates agreement with Weber, Elias, and Tilly on the coercive and economic foundations of modern European state formation. Tilly, perhaps the most important contributor to the literature on state-formation in recent decades, in particular, stresses the dialect relation between war and taxation in early state development. Bourdieu acknowledges this contribution, particularly Tilly's examination of cases beyond France and England (Bourdieu builds his model after just the French and English cases), but argues that all three miss the important development of statist capital and the process of monopolization of that symbolic power by the state nobility. Indeed, Bourdieu (1998i, 22) considers symbolic capital to be "the most important" in the process of concentration of powers in early state formation.

In a secondary analysis of several key works on the early European dynasties Bourdieu (2004a) constructs a "model" of the process of historical transition from the early dynastic regimes to the modern bureaucratic state. The rise of the state is assimilated to the rise of a bureaucratic field. This transition consists of an extension of the patrimonial mode of management and reproduction characteristic of the dynastic form (Bourdieu 2004a, 34–40). Bourdieu stresses the linkages between the traditional monarchy and the emerging modern bureaucratic field rather than a sharp break with the past. The concerns and problems of dynastic control give rise to and extend into modern bureaucratic leadership and organization.[13]

---

13. Bourdieu describes as the "fundamental law of this *initial division of labor of domination*" that he sees operating in the transition from dynasties to modern bureaucracies as "between the heirs, dynastic rivals endowed with reproductive capacity but reduced to politi-

The modern bureaucratic state emerges initially from the ambiguities of governance within the dynasty and the successive attempts to deal with those ambiguities through law (Bourdieu 2004a, 34–48). The emergence and consolidation of power by legal authorities are key to this process. Jurists play a leading role in this process (Bourdieu 1994b; 2004a, 43–48).[14] Ideas such as sovereignty and kingship eventually come to be understood as something above and beyond the person of the king. The problems of hereditary succession, palace wars, and so on, lead to the development of forms of authority independent of kinship and the royal household. This is the beginning of the "impersonal" character of bureaucracy.

Bourdieu describes this process of "progressive dissociation" of dynastic authority and bureaucratic authority that occurs as a differentiation process through the increasing creation of new links of delegation of authority and responsibility (2004a, 48–51). Here he elaborates directly from Elias. As this occurs the locus of power shifts from the person to that of the field. This lengthening of the chain of authorities and responsibilities creates a "veritable *public order*." Each chain becomes a center of relatively autonomous power, or a new power field. There is a shift from power vested in persons to power vested in positions and fields. The state then becomes that metafield that attempts to regulate all the other emergent fields.[15]

Origins of the State Nobility and Ideology of Public Service

A state nobility emerges with the development of the modern state (Bourdieu 1996d, 379). The rise of the state is connected to the ascent of a corps of civil servants. Bourdieu argues that it is impossible to distinguish the emergence of bureaucratic positions from those who preside over them. He connects the development of the modern state with the simultaneous

---

cal impotence, and the oblates, politically powerful but deprived of reproductive capacity" (2004a, 23).

14. Out of this historical emergence of competing and differentiating forms of power (capitals) opens up a space in which "clerks" and jurists attached to the dynastic state create a social space for themselves through their writings. They help create the distinct features of the modern bureaucratic state, which is that "set of impersonal public institutions officially devoted to serving the citizenry and laying claim to authoritative nomination and classification" (Bourdieu 1994b).

15. Wacquant (Bourdieu and Wacquant 1992, 111) refers to Bourdieu's conception of the state as "a sort of meta-field."

rise of a corps of bureaucrats. The ascent of the state nobility is also linked to the emergence of public educational institutions and particularly to the development of an elite track within French public education leading to top positions within the state. Bourdieu thus sees the origins of the modern state rooted in a gradual shift in type of mode of succession, from one founded on hereditary and bloodline to one founded on individual merit (education). The transition from the dynasty to the modern state is also a change from a family to the education mode of reproduction (Bourdieu 1997a, 61, 67).

Bourdieu also emphasizes the ideological dimension of the rise of the modern state. The ascent of the modern state nobility is described in terms of the transformation of the culture of the old aristocracy of "service to the king" to the new ideology of "public service" (1996d, 379). With the state nobility appears a disinterested ideology toward universal ends. The state nobility is a new form of nobility with a new form of ideology ("sociodocy," to use Weber's term) to justify its privileged existence, that of public service. Thus, Bourdieu describes the cultural and social production of modern French administrative elites, the modern French technocracy, with the historical analogy in mind of the production of the aristocracy under the Old Regime. The technocratic elite (members of the *grands corps* emanating from École Polytechnique and especially École Nationale d'Administration are the highest expressions) are the contemporary structural and functional equivalents of the old aristocratic nobility.

Bourdieu's cultural emphasis in understanding the origins of the modern state is part of more recent attention being given to the cultural dimensions of modern state formation (Adams 1994; Coronil 1997; Corrigan and Sayer 1985; Gorski 2003; Loveman 2005; Steinmetz 1999b; Torpey 2000). This cultural explanation of the origins of the modern state contrasts with earlier accounts that stressed the materialist and bellicist accounts summarized by Tilly's (1975, 42; 1992) early and widely affirmed assertion: "War made the state, and the state made war."[16] For Bourdieu, however, the modern state, even in its formative stages, needed to secure considerable symbolic power and capital in order to legitimate its use of physical force.

16. In later work Tilly broadens his view of state-linked social processes to include "repertoires of contention [that] are ineradicably cultural phenomena . . . [and that] provide splendid illustrations of culture's general place in state-connected political processes," bringing him closer to Bourdieu (Tilly 1999).

Bourdieu's understanding of the rise of the modern state also reflects the European experience where state development is tied to a professionalized civil service trained by elite educational institutions. Indeed he formulates his model of modern state formation specifically from the French and English cases (Bourdieu 2012, 216, 588). It does not generalize completely to other experiences of state formation where leadership is not nearly as homogeneous as for example in the United States.

Field of Power and the State

Bourdieu's conception of the state is linked to his concept of the field of power, which represents the upper reaches of the social class structure where individuals and groups bring considerable amounts of various kinds of capital into their struggles for distinction and power. Those struggles are polarized between holders of economic capital and cultural capital. The state, however, is an arena of struggle for statist capital, which is power over other types of capital, including economic capital and cultural capital, over their ratio of exchange and their reproduction (Bourdieu 1994b, 4). The state functions as a kind of metafield, with statist capital representing the capacity to regulate relations among other types of capital.

The field of power and the state appear to overlap conceptually. The state seems to be a particular set of agencies and organizations—an ensemble of bureaucratic fields—within the broader arena of the field of power. On the one hand, Bourdieu says that the development of the state parallels the development of the field of power (they emerge together) as an arena of struggle where holders of different kinds of capital struggle for control over the state, that is, struggle for statist capital (Bourdieu 1994b, 4; Bourdieu and Wacquant 1992, 114). The field of power is "defined as the space of play within which holders of capital (of different species) struggle in particular for power over the state, i.e., over the statist capital granting power over the different species of capital and over their reproduction (particularly through the school system)" (Bourdieu 1994b, 5).[17] The struggle in the field of power is, in fact, struggle for control of the state.[18]

17. See Bourdieu and Wacquant 1992, 114–15, for a similar definition.

18. Bourdieu writes that "a growing number of struggles within the field of power are of this type, notably those aimed at seizing power over the state, that is, over the economic and

On the other hand, Bourdieu sees the state as an arena of struggle for control over the field of power when he writes that "the state as the holder of a sort of meta-capital granting power over other species of capital and over their holders." This is the struggle to gain statist capital for power over other forms of capital and their reproduction (Bourdieu 1994b, 4). It is in the state where the struggle for power is in fact a struggle for control over relations of other fields in the field of power. Thus the state functions to regulate the rate of exchange among the various forms of capital in the field of power.[19] The state as a distinct field generates its own particular sets of interests. Thus, Bourdieu thinks of the state as a kind of metafield, with its own relative autonomy, that mediates the struggle for the dominate principle of legitimation among the various power fields, such as the cultural field, the economic field, and the scientific field.[20]

Bourdieu therefore sees the state "marked by a profound ambiguity." On the one hand, the modern state functions as "a relay . . . of economic and political powers which have little interest in universal interests" represented by the ideology of public service (Bourdieu 2000e, 127). Here one sees the influence of dominant groups, particularly those strong in economic capital, shaping activities of the state. As I will note later, this feature of the state in Bourdieu's thinking overlaps with the power structure school in political sociology. On the other hand, the state functions as a kind of neutral "referee" (Bourdieu 1990b, 137) that enforces the rules of the game in the field of power; that is, it adjudicates power relations between competing groups. Those rules reflect in part the historical struggles leading to the welfare provisions of the state. This orientation of the state is more favorable to the ideals of justice and dominated groups than would be the free reign of economic interests. Later in his career Bourdieu (1998a, 1999a) comes to see this latter function more and more threaten by neoliberalism and he becomes a staunch defender of the welfare state against globalization.[21]

---

political resources that enable the state to wield a power over all games and over the rules that regulate them" (ibid., 99–100).

19. This analysis is echoed in other parts of Bourdieu's work such as in ibid., 114–15.

20. An important implication from the above analysis of the state in terms of capitals and fields is, as Wacquant (2004, 8) points out, that Bourdieu does not see political conflict directly linked to class interests but more differentiated and mediated in that it involves conflicts among elites with different kinds of capitals, and different modes of capital reproduction.

21. Bourdieu writes that the state acts "as a neutral body which, because it conserves, within its very structure, the trace of previous struggles, the gains of which it records and

Political Field, Field of Power, and the State

The political field is that arena of struggle for access to positions within the state. As noted in chapter 4, struggle in the political field is concerned primarily with symbolic power and social capital. The struggle for political capital is for a reputational power resource that mobilizes support among citizens. The political field intersects with the field of power and the state but does not reduce to either. The field of power brings into play struggle over different types of capital as the most legitimate in a society. The concept is broader than the political field since the latter is explicitly concerned with accumulating political capital, which gives access to positions of power with the state. Much political leadership, of course, recruits out of the field of power but in the modern democracies political leadership needs to reach beyond for legitimation in the vote. The struggle for power is more visible in the political field than in the field of power though the latter shapes much of the agenda in the political arena. While Bourdieu describes the political field as an arena of struggle to impose a vision of the world as legitimate, the state is the end result of struggle in the political field for it is the state that represents those ideas, classifications, values that become official—the winners (Bourdieu 2000f, 63–64). While Bourdieu does make an analogy between the religious field and the political field—both are arenas of struggle for the most legitimate vision of the world—the state is the end point of struggle in the political field whereas in the Western democracies competition among religious groups for adherents is not directly concerned with control over the state. This, of course, is not the case in theocratic regimes.

Power of Classifications

Bourdieu stresses that "one of the major powers of the state is to produce and impose (especially through the school system) categories of thought that we spontaneously apply to all things of the social world-including the state itself" (1994b, 1). He emphasizes the impact of state power upon

---

guarantees, is capable of acting as a kind of umpire, no doubt always somewhat biased, but ultimately less unfavourable to the interests of the dominated, and to what can be called justice, than what is exalted, under the false colours of liberty and liberalism, by the advocates of laissez-faire, in other words the brutal and tyrannical exercise of economic force" (2000e, 127).

mentalities. He argues that the state imposes cognitive classifications of the social world that encourage taken-for-granted acceptance of the social order. To the extent there is consensus in modern societies it is largely through "state forms of classification" (13). More than any other modern institution, the state holds the power of nomination.[22] When Bourdieu speaks of the "very mysterious power . . . of nomination" (10–12) he is thinking of the capacity of state officials to exercise power through bestowing honors or titles, such as the titles of nobility in the Old Regime, or through the various categories of official acts, such as education and marriage certificates, in modern societies.[23] The state is the "holder of the monopoly of official naming, correct classification, and the correct order" (Bourdieu 1985c, 734).[24] It is the state that has the power to "impose and inculcate all the fundamental classification principles, according to sex, age, 'competence,' etc." (Bourdieu 1994b, 13).[25] The state, therefore, creates a political doxa, that is, an array of official classifications that become practical, taken-for-granted understandings of the social order, accepted as the natural order of things (60).[26] The state is the "holder of the monopoly of legitimate symbolic violence" (Bourdieu 1985c, 732).

The official discourse imposed by the state performs three interrelated functions:

> Firstly, it performs a diagnostic, that is, an act of cognition which enforces recognition and which, quite often, tends to affirm what a person or a thing is and what

22. Nomination is a key mechanism of social identity formation in Bourdieu's social constructionist perspective. Naming helps bring individuals into group identity and maintaining and enhancing the legitimacy of the group name is vital for its existence.

23. John Torpey's 2000 study of the passport illustrates how modern states develop and exercise symbolic power through classification.

24. Bourdieu (1985c, 732) points to the role of the INSEE (the National Institute of Economic and Statistical Research) in France as exemplar in this activity.

25. He writes, "Through classification systems (especially according to sex and age) inscribed in law, through bureaucratic procedures, educational structures and social rituals (particularly salient in the case of Japan and England), the state molds mental structures and imposes common principles of vision and division, forms of thinking" (Bourdieu 1994b, 7).

26. This sounds somewhat similar to Althusser's (1971) "state apparatus," which Bourdieu rejects as too objectivist. Bourdieu frequently gives more stress to the state as an arena of struggle rather than of coordination or unilateral imposition. (See next section of this chapter.) Yet, in spite of the claim that the state is a human construction, the discussion in Bourdieu 1994b does not emphasize that the state can itself be an arena of struggle (except between fractions in the field of power) or that classification struggles and their transformations can occur in civil society outside of the imposing power of the state.

it is universally, for every possible person, and thus objectively. It is . . . an almost divine discourse, which assigns to everyone an identity. In the second place, the administrative discourse, via directives, orders, prescriptions, etc., says what people have to do, given what they are. Thirdly, it says what people really have done, as in authorized accounts such as police reports. (Bourdieu 1990b, 136)

Official discourse conveys a power of identification, an administrative directive power, and a power of authorization and sanctioning. One can see an illustration of this kind of state power in immigration. Categories such as legals, undocumented, political refugee, illegal, green-card holder, and citizen give certain rights and responsibilities. These rights include access to education, social welfare services, voting, fair treatment in the labor market, and so on. State classifications are crucial in making possible or denying access to material resources. But they also play a key role in self and group identification, since individuals and groups come to define themselves and each other through such official classifications. Immigrants' self-definitions, for example, are decisively shaped by official classifications that become internalized as part of their self-understandings as well as public labels that guide their social interactions with others.

Bourdieu offers, then, the image of the state as a big cognitive machine. It is not manifest in just bureaucracy, visible authority, and ceremony. It is also internalized in fundamental mental categories that shape tacit judgments as well as official classifications. The state exists "internally" as well as externally. State authority is most visible in the obedience it enforces through the judicial system. But Bourdieu stresses that more fundamentally state power resides in symbolic violence for it obtains obedience "for the most part from the docile dispositions that it inculcates through the very order that it establishes" (2000e, 168). The state legitimates the official classification categories of a society[27] and the education system[28]

27. Wacquant (Bourdieu 1996d, xviii) insightfully draws a parallel between Bourdieu's thinking about the state and Durkheim's when he evokes Durkheim's description of the state as a "social brain" that has "the essential function is to think" and that it is a "special organ entrusted with elaborating definite representations valid for the collectivity." The big different between Bourdieu and Durkheim, as Wacquant rightly points out, is that Bourdieu, unlike Durkheim, stresses how those collective representations elaborated by the state are in fact called ideologies. The "scholastic forms of classification" that provide social integration for the nation-state for Durkheim are for Bourdieu class ideologies that serve particular interests even though they are perceived as universally valid.

28. The state exists as state-sanctioned mental categories acquired via schooling. Bourdieu writes that "the State institutes and inculcates common symbolic forms of thought, social

plays a key role in developing and transmitting those cognitive categories that legitimate power. In the last chapter of *The State Nobility* (1996d), education is referenced as the principal instrument of symbolic power of the state. Bourdieu argues that "the educational institution is thus one of the authorities through which the state exercises its monopoly on legitimate symbolic violence." It exercises this symbolic violence in two ways: by "consecrating" individuals with special rights, responsibilities, and recognition and by "condemning" those excluded from the class of academic title holders. French schooling helps make the state a big cognitive machine (377).

Central to Bourdieu's analysis of the French state is his analysis of the elite sectors of French education that prepare state elites. Bourdieu says that "the top academic nobility is a state nobility" legitimated by academic credentials with an ideology of "public service" (1996d, 375). Thus, one can see that Bourdieu's early work on French schooling does not fall simply within the sociology of education; it is also a political sociology of state power. His focus on education—indeed, his principal work on the state, *The State Nobility* (1996d), is in large part an analysis of how the elite tracks of French secondary and higher education feed into the field of power and the state—represents one of his distinctive contributions to contemporary thinking about the modern state. *The State Nobility* documents the formation of a technocratic elite at the helm of state power in France.

This does not mean, however, that state monopoly over symbolic classifications is ever complete. Bourdieu acknowledges that "the holders of bureaucratic authority never establish an absolute monopoly" because "there are always, in any society, conflicts between symbolic powers that aim at imposing the vision of legitimate divisions" (1989d, 22). The state itself is a site for ongoing struggles between groups and bureaucratic agencies, each attempting to impose its understandings of the social world as legitimate. Yet even if the monopolizing work of the state through the educational institution is always contested, the educational credential stands as a reference that must be taken into account even by those who contest it. The fundamental assumptions and cognitive classifications we bring to our understanding of the modern social world are for the most part, Bourdieu argues, imposed by the state, particularly through the educa-

---

frames of perception, understanding or memory, state forms of classification or, more precisely, practical schemes of perception, appreciation and action" (2000e, 175).

tional system. The symbolic power of the state is formidable in Bourdieu's analysis. Our "state of mind" is the "mind of state."[29]

Bourdieu connects the monopolizing symbolic power function of the state to the classification struggles of social classes. He argues that "one of the major stakes in [the class struggle] is the definition of the boundaries between groups" (1987d, 13). Just as there are "individual struggles of daily life" in which actors try to "impose a representation of themselves through strategies of presentations," so also there are "properly political collective struggles."[30] In the collective struggles, the ultimate aim is to obtain a monopoly over legitimate symbolic violence which in modern societies means control of the nomination power of the state. He writes that

> in these struggles whose ultimate aim, in modern societies, is the power to nominate held by the state, i.e., the monopoly over legitimate symbolic violence, agents—who in this case are almost always specialists, such as politicians—struggle to impose representations (e.g., demonstrations) which create the very things represented, which make them exist publicly, officially. Their goal is to turn their own vision of the social world, and the principles of division upon which it is based, into the official vision, into *nomos*, the official principle of vision and division. (1987d, 13)

Despite the social construction emphasis in much of Bourdieu's work—an emphasis suggesting that politics is a struggle over classifications, meanings, and boundaries—one finds a growing emphasis in his later work on the dominating role in politics played by the centralized French state.[31] The state is the ultimate source of symbolic power. It is the

29. I use the expressions "state of mind" and "mind of state" to get at the effects of the monopolizing power of the modern state on mentalities. The expression "mind of state" plays on the French title of "Esprits d'état: Genese et structure du champ bureaucratic" (Bourdieu 1993c), which was translated as "Rethinking the State: Genesis and Structure of the Bureaucratic Field" (1994b). Bourdieu argues in this paper that the challenge to think social scientifically (therefore critically) about the state is to resist allowing state thinking (official classifications) and power to shape unwittingly our sociological analysis. "State of mind" usually suggests something more psychological than the sense of cognitive categories that Bourdieu intended.

30. I discuss Bourdieu's view of political action later.

31. The dominating role of the French state in Bourdieu's analysis of politics undoubtedly reflects the particular type of state formation in France, reflecting a long national tradition of a highly centralized state with its origins extending back to the Old Regime. Yet this emphasis also stands in tension with the social constructionist orientation of his other work that stresses

ultimate referee of all classification struggles. Thus, the state contributes to the unification of a national cultural market (Bourdieu 1994b, 7); it is the basis of a national culture. It is, as Bourdieu puts it, the "central bank of symbolic credit" (1996d, 376) [32]

The omnipresence of official categories and classifications legitimating social divisions poses a fundamental problem for the critical sociologist whose objective is to break with received views of the social world to construct genuine sociological objects of research. How does the sociologist develop a critical distance from this all-pervasive power in order to analyze its foundations? For Bourdieu "thought on the state (*pensée de l'Etat*) is always liable to be a state thought (*pensée d'Etat*)." By this he means that to conceptualize the state runs the risk of uncritically accepting official state categories and thereby miss the most fundamental truth of the state, which is to designate certain conceptual categories as legitimate. A critical sociology must not do as Durkheim did in certain of his texts on the state where one gets the distinct impression that "it is the state which is thinking itself through the state thinker, the civil-servant sociologist (*sociologue-fonctionnaire*)" (Wacquant 1993b, 40).

Bourdieu's answer to this dilemma is first to exercise a "radical doubt" that would "question the very existence of this nominal entity": "*what if the state was nothing but a word, upheld by collective belief*?" (Wacquant 1993b, 40–41). The state is not a unitary thing but a human construction of many different and often divided administrative and legislative bodies. Second, one must question the very basis of the state by doing a social history of state formation. State claims for functional necessity can be relativized by historical perspective. And third, Bourdieu would bring a field analytical perspective to the analysis of state power. Understanding state power as one of conflict and struggle can moderate overrationalized views of the state. Critical posture, historical perspective, and field analysis combine for Bourdieu to obtain critical purchase on the tremendous symbolic power exercised by the state and to make possible a genuine sociology that does not simply reflect the prevailing categories of state power.

---

the micro level of human agency. Bourdieu aims to incorporate and transcend micro and macro levels of analysis in his sociology. Yet, this part of his political sociology is decidedly more macro in orientation.

32. In Bourdieu 1994b, 12, he refers to the state as the "bank of symbolic capital." In Bourdieu 1990b, 137, "the state thus appears as the central bank which guarantees all certificates."

State Division and Unity

Bourdieu's approach to the state may be contrasted to those institutional perspectives that point toward a unitary conception of the state.[33] Bourdieu (1998g) sees the French state divided between its welfare functions (education, social assistance, lower-level courts), which he calls its "left hand," and its financial side of the Ministry of Finance, École Nationale d'Administration graduates, ministerial cabinets, which he calls its "right hand." This division corresponds roughly to underlying differences in cultural and economic capital, the same differentiating structure that polarizes the field of power. The welfare side tends to be based more exclusively on cultural capital, whereas the financial side in modern France includes considerable amounts of both cultural and particularly economic capital. This division also reflects different social class representations. The welfare side recruits largely from the "minor state nobility" whereas the financial side recruits from the "senior state nobility" (1998g, 2).[34]

This internal division within the French state helps explain the rise of the contemporary neoliberal ideology in France, which Bourdieu sees beginning in the 1970s. Free market ideology did not come just from the private sector. His study of French housing markets (2000c) shows that the financial wing of the French state under the leadership of President Giscard D'Estaing and high-ranking French government officials in the finance ministry and housing ministry actively contributed to both thinking and policy following neoliberal lines. More generally, the French state was divided between those ministries and services focused on health, education, and welfare and whose leadership oppose privatization of those

33. In discussing his research on single-family housing and the state, Bourdieu criticizes the image of the state as "a well-defined, clearly bounded and unitary reality which stands in a relation of externality with outside forces that are themselves clearly identified and defined" (Bourdieu and Wacquant 1992, 111). His (Bourdieu 2005c, 112) analysis of housing markets and public policy in France reveals a complex intersection of public and private organizations and agencies that in his view undermines a conception of the state as a unitary institution with a clear private/public division of powers.

34. Bourdieu (2001c, 88) also observes that the "archetypal division between male and female" overlaps the left hand/right hand opposition of the state since men largely populate the financial ministries and agencies concerned with industry and commerce whereas women are "linked to the left hand as its administrators and as the main recipients of its benefits and services."

services, and state officials in the financial ministries who favor market-based public service reform, notably by the withdrawal of state aid from public housing. Thus, a segment of the French state itself promoted the ideas and policies of neoliberalism. The modern French state is divided against itself. But the division is also marked by a relation of domination as the right hand dominates the left hand.

The 1981 electoral victory of François Mitterrand held the promise of the left hand of the state reasserting its authority; indeed, the initial program by the Mitterrand government of expanded welfare benefits and increased regulation and control of the financial and industrial sectors suggested this shift in power to be under way. But this political program barely got off the ground when in response to international economic pressures the Mitterrand government abruptly changed course, giving renewed power to the right hand of the state by curtailing regulation and cutting welfare provisions.[35] Bourdieu was sharply critical of this reversal in policy by the French socialists, as will be pointed out in chapter 7.

Thus Bourdieu breaks with a unitary vision of the state. The state is a differentiated field of struggle situated within the broader field of power that it both attempts to regulate and is itself simultaneously the object of control by agents in the field of power. The state is a contested arena as well as an institution of control in the field of power. Bourdieu sees a fundamental division between the welfare and financial sections. Undergirding that division is the cultural capital/economic capital opposition one finds in the field of power.[36] Thus, while Bourdieu's political sociology of state power is one of domination, he offers a more differentiated view of state power than one where conflicts occurs between dominant and subordinate groups. He stresses the importance of the internal conflict between different categories of dominant groups themselves. And he connects their conflicts to a broader historical transition of changing modes of social re-

35. The landmark election of President Obama in 2008 in the wake of the financial crisis suggests a potentially interesting contrast to the first Mitterrand government using Bourdieu's analyses. Lacking a strong coalition of Socialists, Communists, and a left-oriented labor movement to press for employment, housing, and other welfare concerns, the right hand of the American state was able to assert immediate control to protect the dominant financial interests in spite of the unpopularity of Wall Street.

36. Bourdieu does not consider more extreme cases of internal differentiation beyond this dichotomy. While his view of the state is not unitary, it does not dissolve into a chaotic array of fragmented and competing agencies and factions. Bourdieu's state does not "Balkanize" (Alford and Friedland 1985, 202–22; Evans, Rueschemeyer, and Skocpol 1985).

production: from the traditional hereditary system based on property to the school-mediated one in modern credential society.

Some Evaluation

Symbolic Power: Top Down or Bottom Up

Two radically different portraits of the state reside in uneasy fit in Bourdieu's writings. On the one hand, Bourdieu stresses in parts of his work state power that "imposes and inculcates all the fundamental principles of classification, based on sex, age, 'skill,' etc." (1994b, 13). In "Rethinking the State: Genesis and Structure of the Bureaucratic Field" Bourdieu emphasizes the capacity of the state to impose its classifications (1994b). The state is a major instrument of symbolic power and violence. Here Bourdieu does not stress as much the idea of the state as an arena of struggle as he does in other places such as in "The Left Hand and the Right Hand of the State" (1998g). For example, Bourdieu begins "Rethinking the State" with a warning that it is very difficult to do critical sociological analysis of the state (i.e., construct the state as a sociological object of study) without uncritically accepting categories and definitions of issues imposed by the state (1994b, 1). Bourdieu stresses in this essay the extensive power of the state in shaping our mentalities. He argues that the state imposes cognitive classifications of the social world that encourage taken-for-granted acceptance of the social order. Following a top-down logic, the state creates a political doxa, a practical, taken-for-granted understanding of the social order, accepting it as the natural order of things. It creates symbolic violence. Here the state appears to have considerable agency, but it is a structural agency mediated primarily through educational institutions rather than by elite manipulation. Here the state takes on the character of an actorless presence that is all pervasive—a reach that one finds in Althusser's ideological state apparati, Foucault's episteme, and Gramsci's hegemony.

In other parts of his work, however, the emphasis is different. He qualifies the top-down logic of classification by saying that state monopoly over the legitimate exercise of symbolic power is never complete but always contested. One area where he points to the contested nature of state power is his analysis of the state divided between the social welfare sector and the financial, pro-market sector (Bourdieu 1998g). This image of an arena of struggle where state created classifications are contested suggests potential limits to state imposed symbolic power and violence. However, this possibility does not receive much attention in Bourdieu's work though, as I will point out in chapter 7, his political activism late in his career aimed to do just that, namely, challenge state-sponsored symbolic power and the violence of neoliberalism. Moreover, one does not find in Bourdieu much bottom-up movement showing how classification struggles in local groups or organizations might generate categories that become adopted as state-sponsored categories. His frequent criticism of intellectuals embracing populist ideals suggests that he sees very limited capacity for nonelites to challenge successfully state-imposed categories. Nor does one find much discussion of middle levels of state administration. Middle and lower levels of state officials appear simply to implement the symbolic violence created by state elites. As Mounier (2001, 255–56) perceptively suggests, it is as if Bourdieu accepts without criticism Weber's view of the rational bureaucratic state by limiting his analysis to the normative codes regulating the occupants of middle- and lower-level administrative positions without investigating how that organizational rationality is actually implemented at the lower levels. Bourdieu looks at nominal and symbolic power rather than how power is carried out through the actual behavior of its agents.[37] Such cases and levels of analysis merit exploration.

Excessive Emphasis on Symbolic Violence

Bourdieu's argument that the state also includes an important symbolic dimension whereby fundamental classifications of social life explicitly and tacitly order social life is a useful and fruitful elaboration of Durkheim's view of the state as the "social brain" whose "principal function is to think" and bring about cognitive and moral integration, "a communion of minds and wills" (Durkheim 1992, 51, 69). However, Bourdieu overstates his case in claiming that official categories are effectively internalized and assume a taken-for-granted status. After all, he sees the school system as the principal institutional means for inculcating those cognitive dispositions. Yet judging from the number of school failures and the contested order of public education, particularly in the United States, one wonders if that political socialization is as extensive and enduring as Bourdieu warns. The United States may be exceptional in this respect but the issue invites cross-national comparison. Moreover, the practice of physical incarcera-

---

37. Bourdieu et al. 1999, however, does offer some testimony of the perverse effects of neoliberalism on former middle- and lower-level state officials.

tion that is rapidly growing in the United States and includes a significant proportion of the population, particularly among minorities, suggests the effectiveness of symbolic power to be more limited than Bourdieu thinks, or at least varies considerably by country and segment of the population. Though Bourdieu (1990b, 137) admits that state control over symbolic power is never complete, he devotes little attention to other arenas or sources of symbolic power in modern societies, most notably in organized religion.[38] Yet in numerous countries religion rivals as well as joins forces with state power. As Loveman (2005, 1653) remarks, the fact that Bourdieu still looks to the state as the primary locus of symbolic power and neglects religion suggests that his theorization may reflect a period of secular power of the French republican tradition that does not generalize well to other national contexts.[39] Moreover, contemporary challenges by Islamic minorities suggest that the symbolic reach of the secular French state is not what it once was.

Bourdieu sees his contribution going beyond that of Weber as one of emphasizing how the state tries to monopolize not only the means of physical violence but also the means of symbolic violence (1994b, 5). At times, however, this emphasis takes on its own autonomy so that later in the same article one reads: "In order truly to understand the power of the state in *its full specificity*, i.e., the particular symbolic efficacy it wields . . . [emphasis added]" (12). Here the monopolizing power over symbolic violence becomes the state's most distinctive feature. Bourdieu goes on to say that one must transcend the opposition that views social relations in terms of purely physical force or in terms of pure forms of communication with only semiological significance.[40] Yet, he himself stresses that the most brutally physical power relations are "always simultaneously

38. Bourdieu qualifies the claim for monopolization by noting that "in the struggle for the production and imposition of a legitimate vision of the social world, the holders of bureaucratic authority never obtain an absolute monopoly, even when they add the authority of science, as do state economists, to their bureaucratic authority" (1990b, 137). But he does not explore much that qualification.

39. Indeed, Loveman (2005) shows that the nineteenth-century Brazilian state failed to accumulate symbolic power and establish civil registration and take its first national census in part precisely because it tried to follow the French secular republican model and neglected religion.

40. This corrective to Weber is part of Bourdieu's broader project of transcending all subjective/objective dualisms, in this case the "physicalist vision of the social world that conceives of social relations as relations of physical force" and the "semioloigcal vision" that portrays social relations "as relations of symbolic force" or "relations of meaning or relations of communication" (Bourdieu 1994b, 12).

symbolic relations" and that "acts of submission or obedience are cognitive acts" (12–13). What we do not find him arguing with equal emphasis is the view that in certain situations sheer physical coercion trumps its symbolic justification, or that some symbolic acts are simply that, purely symbolic with no enduring consequences. His stress upon the symbolic character of power relations, while insightful, does not quite transcend the opposition he rejects. One does not find a commensurate exploration of the physical dimension of symbolic communication, particularly where physical coercion is employed. In his effort to "twist the stick in the other direction," to correct for the excessive materialist and objectivist emphasis he finds in the social sciences, Bourdieu stresses the symbolic and thereby falls short of transcending the very dualism that he denounces.

Like Anthony Giddens (1987, 18), Michael Mann points out that most states of the past did not actually "monopolize" the means of physical violence and "even in the modern state the means of physical force have been substantially autonomous from (the rest of) the state" (Mann 1993, 55).[41] So likewise Bourdieu's use of the language of "monopolization" seems excessive for symbolic violence to adequately describe the situation in many countries.[42] Nonetheless, while his emphasis on the capacity of the modern state to monopolize symbolic power and violence is overstated and calls for more comparative testing, Bourdieu's view of the state as a principal source of symbolic power and violence represents a useful corrective to those state-centric views stressing only the physically coercive and materiality of state power. It opens up for fruitful investigation a broader range of the effects of state power in the everyday lives of citizens.

Compared to Other State Theories

In evaluating Bourdieu's thinking about the state it is useful to situate him relative to the leading traditional frameworks in political sociology and theories of the state: class, pluralist, and elitist (Alford and Friedland

---

41. Likewise Tilly's early definition of states as "*coercion* wielding *organizations* that are distinct from households and kinship groups and exercise *clear priority* in some respects over all other organizations within substantial *territories*" (cited in Steinmetz 1999a, 8) does not insist on complete monopoly of coercion.

42. Bourdieu (2001b, 27) acknowledges that in the United States the state does not monopolize the control of the means of physical violence—the right for citizens to bear arms is considered by many a sacred right and the National Rifle Association is an important political lobby—but treats it as very much an exception among the developed countries.

1985). Like many other theorists of the state Bourdieu cannot be easily classified into just one of these three theoretical streams. He in fact draws upon features of each but transcends all three. Compared to Marxist class perspectives (e.g., Jessop 1982; Miliband 1969; Poulantzas 1973, 1975; Zeitlin 1974, 1980), Bourdieu may accept the modern French state as capitalist but he does not dwell on this feature. His state does not reduce to economic structure or to capitalist class interest. He sees his definition of the state as applicable to former East European socialist states—where the bureaucratic field was particularly salient—as well as Western democratic ones. He draws from the class-struggle model to suggest that ideas, agendas, and symbols are contested particularly by competing groups within the field of power. He sees class struggle in politics but his focus is much more on intra-elite struggle than interclass conflict related directly to the ownership and control of the means of material production. He does not emphasize capitalist class control of the state but stresses the cultural and symbolic dimension of state power rather than its function relative to perpetuating capitalist social relations of production.

Relative to pluralism (e.g., Dahl 1961, 1967, 1971), Bourdieu accepts multiple power actors in competition in the field of power. Moreover, the state itself is a "site of struggles" (Bourdieu and Wacquant 1992, 112). But he does not see that struggle, involving multiple segments of the dominant class, creating a shifting array of power relations that eliminates hierarchy and enduring patterns of domination. The current opposition between economic capital and cultural capital is skewed toward the former putting Bourdieu closer to Marxist thinking than a thoroughgoing pluralist polyarchy (Lindblom 1977).[43] Moreover, he rejects the pluralist faith in voting and shared norms as sole protectors of democratic life. The unequal distribution of capitals (cultural as well as social), the pervasive effects of symbolic violence, and the dynamics of delegation and dispossession severely compromise democratic practices. Bourdieu sees greater and more enduring centralization of power than pluralists do putting him closer to the elite perspective.

Though Bourdieu researched state elites (e.g., *The State Nobility*) he did not stress their autonomous powers over society as one finds among

43. Though their thinking on politics in democratic societies has never been compared, Lindblom's argument that choices and competition in the modern democratic polity are limited by the "privileged position of business" finds echo in Bourdieu's claim that economic capital dominates in the field of power.

elite theorists. Like Michael Mann (1993, 44–54), Bourdieu rejects a Millsian-like power structure framework (Mills 2000) that treats societies as integrated wholes and states as cohesive directional units that fulfill key social functions. Thus, Bourdieu does not embrace the power-structure model in which there is a ruling class that shapes national politics. Domhoff (1967, 1978, 1990, 2001), for example, argues that American capitalist class interests articulate through policy planning networks concerned particularly with economic issues. The ruling class via the state is thereby able to give direction to American politics. For Bourdieu, states are divided and intersect and overlap with the field of power where elite factions of the dominate class struggle for power. States lack the cohesion, coherence, and direction suggested in the power-structure framework. Nonetheless, there is overlap in Bourdieu's analysis of the right hand of the French state and Domhoff's power-structure perspective. Yet Bourdieu seems closer to the structuralist and institutionalist model of state-societal relations. Instead of seeing an active ruling class that directly manipulates or controls ideas, ideological assumptions, attitudes, and beliefs, these symbolic meanings are built into the fabric of cultural institutions and prevailing social relationships.

In her path-breaking study *States and Social Revolutions*, Theda Skocpol (1979, 27) defined the state as "a set of administrative, policing, and military organizations headed and more or less well coordinated by an executive authority" and initiated a neo-Weberian state-centric focus that has shaped much political sociological thinking about the state over the last twenty-five years. She depicts states as actors with their power radiating outward from their center to the periphery. The state is an "autonomous structure" with its own "logic and interests." Bourdieu differs from the state-centric school initiated by Skocpol on three key claims. Like Mann's (1993, 44–54) criticism of the state-centric paradigm, Bourdieu rejects monocausal arguments—including that of the state as the key independent variable—and embraces a multidimensional analysis of social power. He sees several forms of power (notably economic capital, cultural capital, and social capital) organizing the entire social space as well as structuring the field of power. In this respect, both Mann and Bourdieu are closer to Weber than to Marx, yet different from Skocpol et al., who find also inspiration in Weber. Whereas Skocpol privileges key cases of social revolution for understanding power and states, Bourdieu concentrates not on the few moments of rupture in established relations but on their conditions for social reproduction. And whereas Skocpol champions the comparative-historical method, Bourdieu calls for field analysis and a social historical method that does not treat entire societies as unitary bodies for comparison.

While her earlier work on revolutions offers the image of states as actors, Skocpol's more recent work with associates (Weir and Skocpol 1985) on welfare policy in the United States stresses the effects of the logic of state institutions, such as federalism and the party patronage system, on all political actors. Bourdieu is relatively closer to this more recent work since he emphasizes the logic of the field rather than the independent action of elites though he stresses more the symbolic dimension and pictures the state as a site of intersecting fields that comes closer to an organizational network view. Bourdieu (Bourdieu and Wacquant 1992, 113; Bourdieu 2012, 178–80), in fact, says that his position is closer to the organizational network perspective of Edwin Laumann and David Knoke (1987). Here the state is conceptualized via network analysis. No sharp distinction is made between the private and the public, between the state and society as in the state-centric model. Nor is there an image of the state as the generator of political action. However, in contrast to a network view of the state, Bourdieu stresses the differentiating logic of fields that situates individual and groups in terms of "competing powers or species of capital" that Bourdieu thinks can be best captured by correspondence analysis (Bourdieu and Wacquant 1992, 114).

Relative to more recent perspectives that initially developed outside of political sociology but show growing influence on how political sociologists think about and explain politics and states—constructionism, rational choice, and new institutionalism (Neuman 2005, 83–120)—Bourdieu is clearly closer to the constructionist and new institutionalist views and sharply critical of rational choice models. His emphasis on culture as integral to politics, on the symbolic dimension of social identities, and on the state as a source of legitimate classifications connects with themes in the constructionist camp. That he connects state formation and exercise to the efforts of particular social groups, such as jurists, who construct their distinct identities and interests, shows his social constructionist orientation. Moreover, he frames this social-cultural-political process as ongoing struggle between groups that create, accumulate, and convert different kinds of power resources to make the state an arena of power conflict rather than a unitary center of decisionmaking.

By contrast, Bourdieu is sharply critical of rational choice theory. His field perspective of the state rejects the notion of a unitary actor capable

of making rational cost-benefit decisions. While there is an underlying rationality to state development, it cannot be assimilated to rational choice
embodying conscious intention.[44]

Some new institutionalists have drawn inspiration from Bourdieu's
concept of field and habitus so he has contributed, if indirectly and unin-
tentionally, to this more recent perspective originating in organizational
sociology. Bourdieu's work resonates in particular with those new institutionalists, following the lead of Paul Dimaggio and Walter Powell (1991,
8), who reject rational-actor models, emphasize cognitive and cultural factors, and elevate institutions (fields) over individuals, groups, or organizations for analysis. Like many new institutionalists, Bourdieu rejects simple
dichotomies between state and society, states and markets, and the symbolic and material aspects of social life. Political action, including that involving the state, grows out of complex intertwining relationships among
states, societies, markets, symbols, and material resources. For example,
his criticism of neoliberalism and the destructive effects of free market
ideology and practices on the social fabric focuses on how the French
state itself incorporated and propagated the market within its own practices. Bourdieu, along with Mann (1986, 26–27), therefore parts company
with Foucault when they hold that state-centric models of political power
are not wrong in seeing political power centralized and territorial. But
state-centric models wrongly limit consideration to that form of power,
relegating all others to secondary status.

Finally, Bourdieu does not include a geopolitical dimension in his conceptualization of the state. On this point Bourdieu has considerable company because much sociological theory tends to ignore the geopolitical
organization connecting states. Yet, as Mann correctly points out, "it is an
essential part of social life and it is not reducible to the 'internal' power
configurations of its component states" (1986, 27).

Clearly Bourdieu's thinking about the state falls within the emerging
culture/state problematic that has grown out of the broader "cultural turn"
in the social sciences (Steinmetz 1999a). Unlike state-centric and mate-
rialist/coercive perspectives on the state, Bourdieu weaves in culture as

44. His criticism of rational choice theory helps explain his sharp attacks against mainstream political science and why that discipline has virtually ignored Bourdieu's thinking
about politics. By the mid-1990s rational/public choice held a dominating position in American political science, illustrated by the fact that nearly 40 percent of the articles in the *American Political Science Review* were cast within that framework (Hedström 1996, 278).

constitutive as well as reflective of state power rather than as a secondary variable or appendage. Yet, his constructionism does not reduce to processes of individual interactions or group identity formation but situates those processes within a structured framework of unequal distributions of capital, hierarchy and domination. His is a *structural constructionist* approach (Ansart 1990; Kauppi 2004, 319).

Bourdieu's thinking on culture/state relations avoids three flaws that Steinmetz (1999a, 12) sees in earlier theorizing of culture/state relations. First, Bourdieu does not treat culture and symbolic power as a kind of "dependent variable" or ideological effect of the state. Symbolic power is a constitutive force in the historical process of growing concentration of various powers within the state. Second, he does not restrict culture to a kind of "political culture" that restricts consideration to values, ideas, forms of expertise, or individual behavior within political institutions. Bourdieu sees culture as constitutive of those institutions themselves. And third, he does not elevate culture to a kind of foundational status that one finds in national character and culturalist sorts of arguments where the state disappears in a diffused cultural analysis. Bourdieu avoids a radical culturalism that would make the state indistinguishable from more general mechanisms of cultural constructivism. For Bourdieu, the modern state does concentrate various forms of power unlike any other institution. Yet this particular institution is also a field of power relations that take on crystallized bureaucratic forms but are formed and transformed by social groups struggling for advantage.

CHAPTER SIX

For an Intellectual Politics of Symbolic Power

B ourdieu offers not only a sociology of politics but also a politics of so-ciology. There is a political project in his sociology that for the most part goes overlooked in its reception in North America. For Bourdieu, doing sociology is doing politics in a different way. Acts of research are political acts. Sociology is not just analysis of power relations but also a form of political engagement; it is to be *scholarship with commitment*. This chapter will examine this normative vision for the political vocation of the sociologist. The following chapter will look at his political engagements.[1]

Bourdieu holds that sociology should be politically relevant but that as a science sociology should not take its marching orders from political causes or bend to political expediency or the whims of relevance. Yet a sci-entific sociology can yield important progressive political consequences. How does Bourdieu conceptualize sociology as science and what political consequences does he draw from that view? What should be the role of the sociologist in the modern world? How do the sociological vocation and the political vocation intersect? How does Bourdieu address the tension between the claim that sociology is to be a science but also one that has political consequences? Would that not make sociology just another form

---

1. In examining Bourdieu's normative vision for the sociological vocation, I draw selec-tively from my earlier treatment of Bourdieu's view of intellectuals and politics (Swartz 1997, chaps. 9–10). There I argued that it is useful to look at Bourdieu's work from the standpoint of a theory of intellectuals. I continue that line of argumentation here by elaborating and modifying certain points to focus on the politically normative role Bourdieu envisages for sociologists.

of symbolic power wedded to some political cause? Bourdieu believes he has an answer to this classic dilemma, an answer that charts a distinctive position relative to other prevailing views and that invites us to rethink this tension, though perhaps not fully resolve it. It comes in three related arguments: the science of sociology is to play a critical debunking role rather than a technocratic or political advocacy role, it must be practiced reflexively, and its institutional integrity must be defended. The first part of this chapter will develop those ideas.

How Bourdieu thinks about the relationship of sociologists and politics contrasts to several other role models that intellectuals can play in the modern world. This chapter also compares briefly Bourdieu's model intellectual with several other prevailing models. In particular, I compare and contrast Bourdieu's thinking with the vision by Michael Burawoy who has relaunched widespread discussion and debate in recent years on public sociology. In chapter 7 I will examine Bourdieu's own political practice as a critical social scientific intellectual and show that there was some change in his own political practices that corresponded to his change in thinking about how to intervene effectively in the public arena in the age of neoliberal domination.

Science: The Great Disenchanter

We have seen in earlier chapters that the analysis of power stands at the core of Bourdieu's work. Bourdieu assigns a central place to symbolic power in maintaining social order. Symbolic violence points to those unacknowledged, practical, taken-for-granted adaptations to existing hierarchies. Yet for Bourdieu it is in the very nature of scientific inquiry to critically challenge taken-for-granted assumptions about the social world.[2]

2. In the spirit of Marx's line from his 1844 letter to Arnold Ruge, Bourdieu embraces the "ruthless criticism of everything existing" (Tucker 1978, 13). Like Marx, Bourdieu calls for a "radical doubt" that questions the fundamental presuppositions of the object of analysis. But going beyond Marx, Bourdieu calls for a reflexive questioning of the fundamental presuppositions held by the social scientist in defining objects for scientific examination.

There is a more personal character—Bourdieu would root it in his habitus—of the contrarian disposition that leads Bourdieu to go against the tide, whether that be prevailing intellectual currents or political movements that take "the form of a politically correct espousal of good causes" (Bourdieu 2004b, 112). Part of this is personal in deeply rooted rebellious dispositions from childhood and early school socialization, as he admits in a posthumous

The logic of science is an ongoing process of critical challenge of existing explanations, both lay and intellectual. By conceptualizing science as a rational process that questions common assumptions and received categories of the social world, Bourdieu attributes to the very logic of scientific discovery a debunking or disenchanting force against the taken-for-granted character of social worlds that "conceal power relations" (Bourdieu 1993h, 12).[3] Science desacralizes the sacred (1975b). This disenchantment of the social order is profoundly political, for it strikes at the very efficacy of relations of domination.

Further, critical social science not only has the capacity to disenchant but also to "provoke" or "makes trouble" (*dérange*) and will frequently evoke hostile reaction from those most accepting of taken-for-granted arrangements. It reveals not only the "hidden" but "sometimes *repressed* realities that provoke resistance. Bourdieu calls his critical sociological analysis "socioanalysis"; akin to psychoanalysis, it probes the social unconscious as psychoanalysis probes the individual unconscious and in doing so provokes reactions of resistance.[4] Sociology cannot count on "business leaders, bishops, or journalists to praise the scientific character of work that unmasks the hidden foundations of their domination, nor on those who profess to produce common sense" to help diffuse its findings (Bourdieu 1993h, 9).

Social science is not simply descriptive; it is not just a constative but also a "performative" knowledge, one that produces what Bourdieu calls

---

biographical note (2008e, 84–110). However, it is not just personal but also institutional, as Bourdieu suggests in his field analysis of several leading critical French thinkers who were his contemporaries, such as Althusser, Barthes, Deleuze, Derrida, and Foucault. They all shared an "anti-institutional disposition" stemming in part from their marginal positions within the French academic establishment in spite of their considerable symbolic and intellectual clout at home and abroad (Bourdieu and Wacquant 1989, 13–14). And it is also intellectual, as Bourdieu (2008e, 384–88) situates this critical attitude within the philosophy of the Enlightenment running from Voltaire to Zola, from Gide to Sartre, Foucault, and Bourdieu himself.

3. Bourdieu does not define what science is so much as describe the intellectual movement that characterizes scientific thought, a logic described by his intellectual mentors, Gaston Bachelard and George Canguilhem, as an ongoing, struggle against prescientific, epistemological obstacles, misleading taken-for-granted views (Swartz 1997, 30–35).

4. Bourdieu (1993j, 23) writes that "sociological discourse arouses resistances that are quite analogous in their logic and their manifestations to those encountered by psychoanalytical discourse." Grenfell (2005) attempts to capture this feature of Bourdieu's sociology with the book title *Pierre Bourdieu: Agent Provocateur.*

"theory effects" on the social order.[5] These are the effects of "imposition of the principles of di-vision which occurs whenever an attempt is made to make something explicit" (Bourdieu 1991b, 132). By bringing to awareness a logically coherent and empirically founded description of some aspect of the social world, which was only implicit or repressed in people's consciousness, science transforms the representation of the world that guides practices and therefore affects practices. He writes: "Even the most strictly constative scientific description is always open to the possibility of functioning in a prescriptive way, capable of contributing to its own verification by exercising a *theory effect* through which it helps to bring about that which it declares" (134).

Even scientific description can function as "prescription" by encouraging practices oriented toward what it describes. He illustrates his point with an example of the debate over how to conceptualize social differentiation, as a stratification structure or as a social class structure. He argues that science cannot offer a straightforward answer to this question without producing theory effects.

> Nothing would be more open to refutation by reality, and therefore less scientific, than an answer to this question which, considering exclusively the practices and dispositions of the agents at the moment in question, failed to take into account the existence or non-existence of agents or organizations capable of working to confirm or invalidate one vision or the other, on the basis of more or less realistic pre-visions or predictions of the objective prospects for one possibility or the other, predictions and prospects that are themselves liable to be affected by scientific knowledge of reality. (1991b, 135)

In a 1970 interview, Bourdieu outlines the kind of political impact he believes science can have (Bourdieu and Hahn 1970). Following the view of the French philosopher of science Gaston Bachelard (1949, 1980, 1984; Tiles 1984) that scientific discovery reveals the "hidden," Bourdieu argues that by unmasking taken-for-granted power relations, "genuine scientific research embodies a threat for the 'social order'" (Bourdieu and Hahn 1970, 15).[6] Because symbolic power by its very nature is hidden from the

---

5. The term *performative* Bourdieu draws from Austin's 1962 work on language to stress the social effects of discourse.

6. Bourdieu (1993h, 10) frequently quotes Bachelard saying "There is no science but of the hidden." He draws on Bachelard to stress the historical, constructionist, and agonistic

everyday understandings of actors and goes misrecognized as natural understandings invested by arbitrary power relations, its exposure strikes at
the very core of its efficacy. Scientific research, therefore, "inevitably exercises a political effect."[7] Since the power relations that sociology reveals
owe part of their strength to the fact that they do not appear to be power
relations, "all sociological discourse has a political effect, even by default"
(19). Thus, "social science necessarily takes sides in political struggles"
and this is usually against the interests of dominant groups (Bourdieu
1975c, 101; Bourdieu and Wacquant 1992, 51).[8] Clearly, Bourdieu invests
in his understanding of scientific inquiry a progressive political project that
he tries to legitimate in the name of scientific authority. Science can become a symbolic capital for political transformation.

There is, therefore, a political dimension to Bourdieu's conception of
science and what sociology should do in the modern world. It is political
in the sense that for Bourdieu a key objective of social scientific research
is to struggle against all forms of domination. Bourdieu thinks of sociology
as a weapon of struggle ("a martial art") for emancipation from symbolic
domination.[9] He thinks of the intellectual vocation as a social scientist in
an activist sense. Acts of research, no matter how seemingly mundane,
are acts of struggle, conquest, and victory over the taken-for-granted assumptions of social life: scientific research is a struggle against all forms
of symbolic domination. By exposing through research the arbitrary and
taken-for-granted mechanisms of social life that maintain power relations,
the social scientist is able to challenge the legitimacy of the status quo. As
existing power relations lose their taken-for-granted character, possibilities for alternative ways of constructing social relations open up. Thus for

---

character of scientific reason. Science is empirical but not positivist. Like Bachelard, Bourdieu
argues that evidence is not simply there waiting to be discovered. Social scientific knowledge
is consciously constructed against taken-for-granted knowledge of the social world (Bourdieu
and Wacquant 1992, 235). For Bourdieu, science progresses from new critical insights into the
taken-for-granted world of power relations rather than by an accumulation of facts.

7. This theme appears throughout Bourdieu's work as he writes some eleven years later
that "science is destined to exert a theory effect" (Bourdieu 1991b, 133).

8. Bourdieu admits that effects of scientific analysis of the social world can reinforce domination when they appear "to confirm or intersect with the dominant discourse"—notably
when they show how the dominated participate in their own domination (Bourdieu 2001c,
113, 114). But he clearly counts on the effects going in the other direction.

9. "A martial art" is how he describes it in the documentary *Sociology Is a Martial Art*
(Carles 2001).

Bourdieu politics and science combine in the very objective of the social scientific vocation. "Acts of research"—to borrow from the title of his journal—are for Bourdieu fundamentally "political acts."[10] Sociological research is another means of doing politics.[11]

This is not to say that Bourdieu believes that one can extract a political program from social scientific work. Science cannot offer direct purchase on which course of action to follow in the political arena. In this respect Bourdieu's view resembles that of Weber in "Science as a Vocation" (1970). But he goes beyond Weber by pointing to the political effects that go beyond personal clarification of ultimate commitments. Weber recognized the disenchanting effects of social science; Bourdieu stresses their political consequences.

The debunking power of science benefits not only the sociologist by permitting him or her to gain some measure of critical distance from the imprisoning grasp of symbolic violence. This view of science also suggests a key role that sociologists can play in modern societies. Sociologists can play a "liberating function" by offering "others the means of liberation"

---

10. Accardo (1983), Grenfell (2005), Lane (2000, 2006), Pels (1995), Robbins (1991), and Wacquant (1992b) are others who have caught this activist sense of Bourdieu's conception of social scientific research. It also appears in the documentary *Sociology Is a Martial Art* (Carles 2001).

11. Bourdieu's view of a political dimension inherent in social scientific practice is not dissimilar from Althusser's (1970) justification for doing theory: doing social science becomes a form of politics just as doing theory becomes a form of political practice. One of Althusser's contributions to French left thinking close to the French Communist Party of the 1950s and 1960s was to legitimate theoretical work beyond the traditional, orthodox, and simplistic materialist reductionism that characterized official party thinking at that time. Althusser's theorizing of the relative autonomy of superstructural instances from the infrastructural base offered in France a break from orthodox reductionism. Althusser's work was important for it helped open up some degree of autonomy for intellectuals within the French Communist Party and made possible a larger number of fellow travelers.

I would not argue, however, that this fundamental orientation by Bourdieu represents a direct lineage from Althusser to Bourdieu. Bourdieu clearly found inspiration from a long tradition of intellectual political activism in France that preceded Althusser. But the idea of this kind of theoretical practice as a form of political practice was in the air during Bourdieu's formative period while a student at the ENS. While a sharp critic of the Althusserians (Bourdieu 1975a), Bourdieu held the view that one of the overlooked contributions of Althusser to the French intellectual milieu at that time was to get *Normaliens* (students at the famous École Normale Supérieure where Bourdieu studied) to read Marx beyond the few official passages sanctioned by the French Communist Party (Bourdieu, interview with author, November 23, 1993).

(Bourdieu 1993h, 44). Indeed, "the sociologist unveils and therefore inter-venes in the force relations between groups and classes and he can even contribute to the modification of those relations" (Bourdieu and Hahn 1970, 20). Identifying "classes on paper" can contribute to the formation of classes in social reality (Bourdieu 1985b, 1991i). That a critical social science can potentially modify relations between social classes amounts to a strong claim for the power of sociological knowledge in modern strati-fied societies and for the vocation of the social scientist as an intellectual. Indeed, a normative vision for the political effects of social scientific re-search characterizes Bourdieu's sociological project. This normative vision calls for protecting the autonomy of the scientific field from the distorting effects of politics while simultaneously orienting one's scientific research so that it will have the maximum effect in the public arena. It also calls for a reflexive practice of sociology, one that does not import the logic of political struggle into the scientific arena yet is able to produce symbolic effects that can shape political life.[12] In Bourdieu's words, the challenge is to "think politics without thinking politically" (1988c, 2).[13] A sociology of intellectuals informs Bourdieu's reflexive practice of the sociological craft and his political activity.

Good Science Produces Good Politics

The theme that doing good social science means doing good politics reso-nates strongly throughout much of Bourdieu's work. This reasoning points to an extraordinary idealism in Bourdieu's thinking about the role of the social scientist in the modern world. That Bourdieu believes that a critical and professional sociology can modify relations among the social classes amounts to a phenomenal claim for the power of sociological knowledge in modern stratified societies. It also points to a remarkable Enlighten-ment faith in the emancipatory effects of science, a view that came to be contested by postmodernism and the radical social constructionist view of science—two intellectual currents that Bourdieu vigorously opposed.

12. See Bourdieu and Wacquant 1992, 247–83, for a fuller discussion.

13. Another expression of this ideal is to be found when Bourdieu points to the same chal-lenge particularly in thinking critically about the state. He writes that "to endeavor to think the state is to take the risk of taking over (or being taken over by) a thought of the state, i.e. of applying to the state categories of thought produced and guaranteed by the state and hence to misrecognize its most profound truth" (1994b, 1).

Though Bourdieu (1975c) offers a critical sociology of the scientific field, he parts company with the "strong programme" by critics of science, such Barnes (1974; Barnes and Bloor 1982), Bloor (1976, 1983), Gilbert and Mulkay (1984), Knorr-Centina (1983), Latour (1987, 1988; Latour and Woolgar 1979), and Woolgar (1988a, 1988b), who Bourdieu (2004b) believes completely relativize scientific knowledge.[14] He eschews radical views (e.g., Feyerabend 1978) that depict science as simply some alternative form of knowledge on par with religion, magic, and so on. These radical cognitive relativists throw out the proverbial baby with the bathwater. While Bourdieu (1975c) locates the practice of science within an intellectual field, with interests, conflicts, and hierarchies analogous to other cultural fields, he nonetheless distinguishes between a "false" or "official" science and a "genuine" science.[15] Though historical in its development, the scientific field nonetheless has developed a kind of symbolic power that distinguishes it from all other cultural fields. It is a social universe where "in order to be 'right' [*avoir raison*], one has to put forward reasons, demonstrations recognized as consistent, and in which the logic of power

14. Bourdieu (2004b) responds to some of his critics of his 1975 paper (1975c), particularly Knorr-Cetina. Though the 1975 paper argues that science is a field of struggle that shares some properties with other autonomous cultural fields, such as literature, he argues that his 1975 argument has frequently been misinterpreted by critics. He argues that his field analytical approach to science, accompanied by his dispositional view of human action as represented in his concept of habitus, guards against two forms of reductionism he finds in the work of his critics, particularly Latour and Knorr-Cetina. First, the scientific field has developed a degree of autonomy and specificity that does not reduce to characteristics of other fields. Struggle within the scientific field is about power but is not the same kind of struggle found in the world of politics. External economic and political influences do indeed influence scientific practices, but they do not reduce science to money and political power. Moreover, the world of science cannot be assimilated to the world of rhetoric or semiology, as Latour suggests, as if it were no more than just another language competing on the same level as others. Second, the struggle for distinction in science that motivates scientific investigation does not reduce to a kind of conscious, rational pursuit of self-interests that are primarily social, as Latour and Knorr-Cetina allege. Here Bourdieu invokes his concept of habitus and accompanying dispositional view of human action to argue that such an interpretation of scientific behavior is precisely the kind of simplistic rationalism that he has long argued against. The scientific field imposes a logic for the search for the best description and verification of the "real" that cannot be found in other cultural fields.

15. In doing a sociology of science, Bourdieu (1975c, 2004b) wants to identify the social conditions in which scientific activity occurs so as to enhance greater objectivity in science, that is, to improve social scientific practices rather than relativizing them and discrediting their legitimacy. He sees the radical program as a pseudo-philosophical, high-handed theoretical dismissal of science as a kind of fiction.

relations and struggles of interests is regulated in such a way that the 'force of the best argument' (as Habermas puts it) has a reasonable chance of winning" (Bourdieu 2004b, 82).[16] In this exceptional social universe

> symbolic power relations take a quite exceptional form such that, for once, there is an *intrinsic force of the true idea*, which can draw strength from the logic of competition; in which the ordinary antinomies between interest and reason, force and truth, etc., tend to be weakened or to disappear. . . . [Scientific] truth presents itself as transcendent with respect to the consciousnesses which apprehend it and accept it as such . . . because it is the product of a collective validation performed in the quite singular conditions of the scientific field, that is to say, in and through the conflictual but regulated cooperation that competition imposes there, and which is capable of enforcing a supersession of antagonistic interests and even the obliteration of all the marks linked to the particular conditions of its emergence. (82, 84)

Though historical in character, "the truth recognized by the scientific field is irreducible to its historical and social conditions of production" (84).

Bourdieu cites three reasons why the scientific field is both "a field like others, but one which obeys a specific logic." First, like other autonomous cultural fields it imposes "closure" where the researcher's audience is her professional peers. "Each researcher tends to have no other audience than the researchers most capable of listening to him but also of criticizing and even refuting and disproving him." Second, unlike other cultural fields the competitive struggle within the scientific field aims to monopolize "the scientifically legitimate representation of the 'real' and that researchers, in their confrontation, tacitly accept the *arbitration of the 'real.'*" And third, and distinctive of the scientific field, is the "immense collective stock of equipment for theoretical construction and empirical verification or falsification which all participants in the competition are required to master" (2004b, 69–71).

In the interview referenced above, Bourdieu admits that even though sociology can weaken power relations by unveiling them, sociology can be

---

16. If this vision for the work of scientific exchange sounds familiar to Habermas's ideal universe of rational communication, Bourdieu (2004b, 82) acknowledges shared agreement on this point. Where Bourdieu differs from Habermas is that Bourdieu stresses the historical emergence of this type of human communication under specific social conditions rather than emphasize transcendental reason as a property of human nature. For Bourdieu, scientific reason is *both* historical and transcendental.

accommodated and recuperated by dominant groups for their own interests (Bourdieu and Hahn 1970, 20). In revealing the hidden mechanisms
of power, science may be of service to dominant groups in that it may lead
to better and alternative modes of manipulation and social control. Those
in dominant positions are better situated to benefit from the existing hi-
erarchical order and thus meet the threat from science of having their
privileged positions exposed. Their advantaged resources also give them
opportunities to find alternative sources of legitimation for their privileged positions. But Bourdieu is banking on the other possibility, namely
that when prevailing power mechanisms are exposed, they will lose their
efficacy to the benefit of those subordinate individuals and groups who
have access to and are able to use this knowledge.[17] For Bourdieu, science
is on the side of subordinate individuals and groups.

Though he is a sociologist, Bourdieu's claim for a potentially emanci-
pator role of critical social science seems to be interdisciplinary. The first
required step is to break with the received views of the social world where
naturalization and misrecognition of symbolic power play out. Bourdieu
privileges social history as a tool for constructing the field of a particular
object of analysis but other methods, such as ethnographic observation,
interviews, experiments, and statistical analysis, can be employed—and
theory, too—regardless of their academic disciplinary moorings. Yet,
despite the interdisciplinary openness and methodological pluralism,
Bourdieu assigns to sociology a privileged position in this political project
of debunking status quo power relations.[18]

Tensions in Bourdieu's Thinking: Debunking or Advocacy

The idea of science as a performative force that debunks taken-for-granted
power relations points up a number of tensions in Bourdieu's thinking
about the relation of science to politics. This line of argument points to

17. This does not mean that for Bourdieu the debunking effects of critical social science
automatically connects to the demands, needs, and mobilizing potential of dominated groups.
Whether and how subordinate groups can gain access to this liberating message of sociology is a key question, however, and points to an important tension in Bourdieu's thinking.
Bourdieu acknowledges this difficulty but offers little insight on how the message of science
can be effectively communicated to those without the requisite cultural capital. I return to this
important issue below.

18. The privileged role of sociology can be vividly seen in his sharp criticism of political
science as a "false science" lacking for the most part the characteristics of a critical social
science.

the central role that Bourdieu assigns to symbolic power and violence (legitimation) and its misrecognition in the maintenance of power relations. It also assigns a key debunking role to science. This role presupposes that science holds considerable authority in order to produce this kind of debunking political effect. This type of scientific authority can come only from increasing the autonomy of the scientific field from outside interests. Indeed, the kinds of political effects he seeks would seem possible only so long as science enjoys a legitimacy superior to politics.[19] However, this points to a complex if not ultimately contradictory position in which Bourdieu finds himself. To achieve the desired political effects, belief in science as a form of disinterested knowledge and inquiry must exist. Yet, the thrust of Bourdieu's (1975c) own work on the scientific field emphasizes the very political character of that social universe. In that work, Bourdieu argues that the scientific field is "a social field like any other, with its distribution of power and its monopolies, its struggles and strategies, interests and profits." Though they "take on specific forms" and thereby do not reduce to sheer politics, even in science "epistemological conflicts are always, inseparably, political conflicts" (19, 21).[20] And though intellectual politics are undoubtedly different than electoral politics, they nonetheless are politics.[21]

19. Bourdieu advances the following proposition to speak of the political effects of increased field autonomy: "The greater the intellectuals' independence from mundane interests because of their specific expertise (e.g., the scientific authority of an Oppenheimer or the intellectual authority of a Sartre), the greater their inclination to *assert* this independence by criticizing the powers that be, the greater the *symbolic effectiveness* of whatever political positions they might take" (1989a, 100).

Thus membership in a relatively autonomous field of cultural production is crucial, for, in Bourdieu's thinking, it seems to generate a propensity to contest the power of holders of economic and political capital and a capacity (symbolic capital) to do so with greater effectiveness.

20. By this Bourdieu does not mean that the practice of science simply reduces to political power. As I note above, he rejects radical deconstructionist and postmodernist claims that science is but another kind of knowledge (extreme relativism) imposed by the strongest (knowledge/power connection). For Bourdieu, the field of science is organized around the particular interest of the search for objective truth even if that search is inseparable from a social and political dimension. Knowledge is inseparably linked to power, but not all types of knowledge are equal in Bourdieu's eyes.

21. By pointing to the "political" character of science I do not mean to suggest that Bourdieu's scientific field reduces to the political field. Although they are both power fields, the political field and scientific field have different interests. In contrast to Habermas, Bourdieu sees scientific practice as itself an interested pursuit, but one that occurs in a regulated social universe that does not appeal for mass support as is the case in the political field. Individual

One finds another tension as Bourdieu recurrently warns social scientists against partisanship in the social struggles they study. Social conflicts are to be objects of study, not occasions for choosing sides. The field analytical perspective focuses on the conflict itself rather than advocating for any particular position. It offers a more comprehensive view than any one of the parochial interests involved. Yet no field analysis is ever complete. Field boundaries themselves can be permeable and their demarcation frequently contested. Indeed, one of the strengths of Bourdieu's political field analysis is to show that the very definition what is labeled "political" as opposed to "bipartisan" is itself a struggle over field boundaries. But in that strength lies a weakness: conflict can be a moving target, making it very difficult for the social scientist to set limits on his or her investigation. Moreover, the viewpoint of the social scientist itself stems from an intellectual field position that limits attainment of a fully objective view—a criticism Bourdieu himself stresses in his call for a sociology of sociology as a necessary tool for assessing the limits of the scientific view.[22]

Nevertheless, Bourdieu believes that science necessarily sides with the interests of subordinate groups since by exposing the mechanisms of power science renders them less effective for dominant groups. Yet, subordinate groups realize with considerable difficulty those benefits from science. Dominated groups often lack the cultural capital needed to grasp the findings of good, critical social scientific work.[23] Moreover, it is not clear

---

interests for distinction and power must be transformed into scientific interest that is realized in a normative universe where peer recognition is given for the most convincing theoretical and empirical demonstration. Nonetheless, the criticism that science is an interested pursuit in disinterest poses a legitimacy problem for science that cultivates the prevailing ideal of objectivity that transcends all parochial interests.

22. Bourdieu offers an occasional passing reference to Leibnitz's image of God—that ultimate viewpoint over all other viewpoints—a viewpoint that identifies the points and their connections in geometric space. This is Bourdieu's ideal of the scientific view but one "which science can only indefinitely approach" (Bourdieu 2004b, 95).

23. Indeed, Bourdieu remarks that critical sociology lacks a ready audience among those who need its liberating message most because they lack the cultural capital necessary to appropriate its message. He writes that "the sociologist's misfortune is that, most of the time, the people who have the technical means of appropriating what he says have no wish to appropriate it, no *interest* in appropriating it, and even have powerful interests in refusing it . . . whereas those who would have an interest in appropriating it do not have the instruments for appropriation (theoretical culture, etc.)." And "scientific truth is very likely to reach those who are least disposed to accept it and very unlikely to reach those who would have most interest in receiving it" (1993j, 23).

that scientists on the whole tend to support political opposition parties as Bourdieu's view hypothesizes. Indeed, there are likely to be important variations among types of scientists (e.g., pure versus applied research, government versus private industry funding) and from one country to another.[24] Furthermore, there is no "organic" connection between critical social scientists and dominated groups, only a "structural homology" by virtue of their respective positions of subordination: scientists subordinated in the field of power and dominated social groups in the social class structure. This poses a real problem for disseminating the debunking message of critical social science to the larger public.

Bourdieu's thinking about this tension between science and politics evolved over time, making it even more problematic. In a key 1990 text

Bourdieu's style of writing and complexity in argumentation make direct access to a lay audience virtually impossible. This is one reason why he adopted in his later years, as I will note in the next chapter, a less scholarly mode of publication and dissemination of his research findings and thinking. However, Bourdieu's work is for the most part not aimed at the rank-and-file masses but at intellectuals and the educated laity, at teachers, union leaders, and political activists who do have sufficient cultural capital to decode the message and can implement political practices consistent with the insights Bourdieu's sociology offers. In a sense Bourdieu's sociology would help facilitate that "process of dissolution going on within the ruling class" that Marx and Engels describe in *The Manifesto* (Tucker 1978, 481). Nonetheless, this points up a tension in Bourdieu's sociology as politics, between a critical discourse that can challenge dominant groups and one that is also inaccessible to the most dominated in society.

24. As evidence of this Bourdieu reports in *Homo Academicus* (1988b, 66) that in general members of the Parisian science faculty at the time of the May 1968 university crisis were more likely to lean to the political left than were faculty in the humanities and medicine, except for a visible left-wing minority.

Bourdieu's claims for a greater critical disposition among natural scientists toward the status quo invite historical and cross-national comparisons. In reviewing several surveys of the American professorate Ladd and Lipset (1976, 72) find that "all the natural sciences . . . are significantly more conservative politically than the social sciences." In the United States strong business/corporate interests influence funding and research in the natural sciences and thereby introduce, in Bourdieu's terminology, more "heteronomy" in the natural scientific field. Yet, among the natural sciences there is important variation; Ladd and Lipset find physics to be more liberal and the more applied sciences such as engineering and chemistry to be more conservative politically. This contrasts with findings that natural scientists in the former Soviet Union were notably more free and universalistic in views than the social scientists who were more committed to sustaining the regime (73).

This also invites cross-national comparisons of political attitudes and practices of scientists. Gross and Fosse (2012) find that American professors in general tend to be more liberal than the general American population and social scientists to be the most liberal of all.

Bourdieu (2000d) reflects on the relationship between sociology and politics from a changing historical perspective. He recalls that sociology, emerging in the nineteenth century, was primarily concerned with social problems and reform. During this early period sociology and socialism were connected in the eyes of many. However, in order for sociology to gain legitimacy as a science, sociology had to develop its own norms of validation and define its own social scientific problems as an autonomous intellectual enterprise rather than simply take up the prevailing social and political agendas of the day. Durkheim's *Rules of Sociological Method* (1966) and Weber's ideal of "ethical neutrality" were important expressions of the development of sociology as an intellectually autonomous discipline worthy of scholarly recognition. However, in order to gain scientific respectability sociologists had to expunge social reform and political dimensions from their work. The development of a professional sociology with scientific status came with a price, that of censoring from consideration politics (Bourdieu 2000d, 104).

Observing that sociology had successfully achieved scientific status and considerable autonomy from outside influence, an autonomy where much sociological work was oriented toward its own professional audience, Bourdieu became concerned during the eighties and nineties that the public arenas where political agendas are set up and maintained no longer receive any significant input from a critical scientific perspective. Moreover, in Bourdieu's (2000d, 104) view, scientific professionalization had the effect of relegating the political function sociology once assumed historically to "the less scrupulous and less competent sociologists or to politicians and journalists." Bourdieu grew increasingly concerned by the growing influence of the mass media and economic forces on intellectual life and the power of neoliberal thinking to dominate political discussion. These constraining forces called for more aggressive resistance. In his view, the urgency of the contemporary situation no longer permitted the strict science/politics separation that had been important for the development of sociology as a legitimate scientific practice. This separation, he concludes, is no longer necessary or tenable. "I believe that nothing can justify that scientistic abdication, that ruins any political conviction, and that the time has come when scholars need to intervene in politics with their competence in order to impose utopias based in truth and rationality" (105). Weber's idea of "ethical neutrality" that Bourdieu says represented a fundamental advance in the professional ideology of sociology to obtain scholarly legitimacy, including Bourdieu's own use of Weber's principle, seems to be no longer acceptable (Bourdieu 2000f, 104).[25] Sociologists must engage more directly the political arena.

Despite this shift in emphasis Bourdieu does not propose a return to the sociology of the nineteenth century where social reform and social science intermingled without clear distinction. He has no interest in resurrecting a scientific socialism or Marxism of yesteryear. The autonomy of science is to be protected from political and economic encroachments. He wants to reaffirm science and rationality but also the political function of intellectuals. He still sees no "antinomy between autonomy and engagement, between separation and collaboration" (2000f, 105). Yet, the tension, if not contradiction, in his thinking does not go away and becomes accentuated by some of his public pronouncements and public interventions, particularly in his later life.[26] His ideal, as we will see in the next section, is of the intellectual who intervenes in politics, like the French literary figure Emile Zola, as someone whose intervention is legitimated by his accomplishments in an autonomous area of expertise, such as art, philosophy, and science. The authentic intellectual derives his intellectual authority entirely from his intellectual work, not from political activities or journalistic or media visibility, and intervenes politically as Zola did with an intellectual competence and authority. Bourdieu cites Noam Chomsky (linguist) and Andrey Sakharov (physicist) as two contemporary illustrative examples.[27]

25. For enhancing sociology as science, Bourdieu affirmed Weber's call for "ethical neutrality" against the moralizing of social philosophy but rejected the idea that "value neutrality" of research techniques were "epistemologically neutral." Indeed, Bourdieu considers that the idea that a social science can be politically and ethically neutral "is a fiction" (Bourdieu and Wacquant 1992, 51). Following Bachelard, he (Bourdieu, Chamboredon, and Passeron 1991, 40–41) called for the exercise of "epistemological vigilance" in all aspects of scientific practice, not to relativize the knowledge claims of science but to make them more robust.

26. Critics such as Mounier (2001) see some of Bourdieu's "political" texts and public engagements late in his career as compromising his scientific legitimacy. Certainly the line between debunking existing power arrangements and advocacy for the cause of certain dominated groups becomes blurred by some of Bourdieu's public engagements in his later years. But the predominant mode of Bourdieu's public engagements remains at the level of speaking to other intellectuals, to the media, to political elites, to the nation, rather than developing "organic" relationships with particular subordinate groups. See Poupeau and Discepolo 2004 and Swartz 2003a for accounts of his public political activities. I examine his public political life in the next chapter.

27. The natural science model of course dominates in the work of Sakharov and Chomsky in ways that it cannot in sociology, as Bourdieu himself admits. Still he holds the view that the specificity of sociology as an intellectual practice is that it embodies key features of rational

It is therefore useful to look more closely at the kind of political vocation he sees for the sociologist as an intellectual.

Intellectual Roles in Politics: Bourdieu's Collective Intellectual

Bourdieu's view of social science and the ensuing political function of sociologists it entails suggest a model for intellectual political activism that can be contrasted with other prevailing views. While Bourdieu defends the autonomy of intellectual and cultural fields, particularly science, he is ultimately interested in the political effects of science rather than just science for science's sake.[28] He therefore rejects the *ivory tower model* of the intellectual role. The sociologist is to engage the public sphere. On the other hand, Bourdieu is sharply critical of the sociologist as *technocratic expert* who sells his or her services to outside groups, such as the state, foundations, political parties, or corporations. To allow external groups to set the research agenda sacrifices intellectual and scientific autonomy.

While Bourdieu rejects the intellectual role of service to established powers, he also rejects intellectual subservience to parties and social movements attempting social transformation. He has been a sharp critic of the Gramscian idea of the *organic intellectual* who connects "organically" to classes and social movements in order to bring about social transformation.[29] Echoing concerns about intellectual autonomy voiced by the

---

exploration and empirical verification associated with natural science. Sociology, he declares, "seems to me to have all the properties that define a science" (1993h, 8).

28. Though as I have suggested, Bourdieu argues that it is only by engaging in science for science's sake that the social scientist can accumulate the symbolic capital necessary to make an impact in the political arena.

29. He charges that many so-called organic intellectuals are in fact pseudo-intellectuals who, being unable to compete successfully in the scientific arena, go find receptive non-intellectual audiences to propagate an anti-intellectual and anti-elitist ideology (2008f, 381). Bourdieu's relationship to Gramsci is complex. In terms of the political sociology of power, Bourdieu can certainly be situated broadly along with Gramsci in stressing what Lukes calls the third dimension where domination is built within cultural categories and institutions (Lukes 2005; Neuman 2005). Yet, Bourdieu claimed only a late acquaintance with the writings of Gramsci and never devoted systematic attention to his work. Bourdieu says that "the most interesting thing about Gramsci, who, in fact, I did only read quite recently, is the way he provides us with the bases for a sociology of the party apparatchik and the Communist leaders of his period—all of which is far from the ideology of the 'organic intellectual' for which he is best known" (1990b, 27–28).

French literary scholar Julian Benda (1927), Bourdieu sees organic intellectuals as surrendering their autonomy to the party. He also fears they
will usurp leadership of dominated social groups and manipulate their
identity and interests.[30]

Preserving more critical attachment than the organic intellectual, the
fellow traveler intellectual is the model made famous by Jean-Paul Sartre,
who for a period of time conceptualized his relationship to the French
Communist Party in these terms. This does not entail membership or a
close working relationship as the organic intellectual formula does but
an independent status that retains some critical distance though in public
solidarity with the party. For Bourdieu, this stance nonetheless sacrifices
too much critical independence and tends to blunt needed criticism of the
party for politically strategic reasons.

But maintaining an autonomous and critical posture does not mean that
the intellectual is without interests and that he or she is able to transcend
all parochial interests as the popular image of Mannheim's *free-floating
intellectuals* suggests.[31] Bourdieu's intellectuals function in fields of spe-

---

Other brief references to Gramsci can be found in "Political Representation" (Bourdieu
1991h) and "Delegation and Political Fetishism" (1991a) and in "The Uses of the 'People'"
(Bourdieu 1990e).

Bourdieu's passing criticism of the organic intellectual role often associates it with the
"professional ideology of cultural producers" wedded to the political apparatus (Bourdieu
2000d, 105). These he contrasts with his ideal of the "authentic intellectual" who is "capable
of being collaborative and still separate." Yet, it should be noted that Bourdieu never really engages seriously Gramsci's thinking about organic intellectuals. The few references in
Bourdieu's work to the term are dismissive and serve as foils to heighten the distinction of
Bourdieu's own model of the intellectual that he builds from his view of Emile Zola and the
Dreyfusards. See, for example, Bourdieu 1996b, 348, where he refers to the organic intellectual as a myth without further explanation. It is juxtaposed to the mandarin.

30. Between the dangers of vanguardism (where, for example, Bourdieu describes the
problems of delegation, discussed in the previous chapter) or subservience to the party line,
Bourdieu sees no possible middle ground. But, as Burawoy insightfully points out, Bourdieu
overstates these critical dangers that Gramsci himself warned against while advocating for the
organic intellectual role (see Burawoy's lectures "Conversations with Pierre Bourdieu," at
the Havens Center, University of Wisconsin–Madison, 2008, and at the University of Witwa-
tersrand, Johannesburg, 2010 available online at http://burawoy.berkeley.edu/Bourdieu.htm
[accessed May 4, 2012]). While appearing to reject the organic role, Bourdieu paradoxically
appears to assume a form of it in his own political activism in his later years. In *The Weight of
the World* (Bourdieu et al. 1999) he does adopt a kind of organic intellectual role by giving the
"voice of science" to experiences of social suffering.

31. Though commonly attributed the image of the free-floating intellectual, Mannheim
(1955, 1956) himself believed that intellectuals are only "relatively" free of their class inter-

cific interests; they pursue their particular interests in the competition to advance their own positions within the scientific field and their interests in the struggle over the definition of what is legitimate science. However, in this struggle to advance the cause of science they also advance universal interests insofar as science debunks power relations and therefore opens up the possibility for thinking beyond existing social arrangements.

Mannheim's view received little attention by Bourdieu.[32] But Sartre's view of the role of a *total intellectual* received much critical comment. Sartre epitomized on the political left (Raymond Aron on the politically center-right in France) the intellectual activist who draws on his notoriety as an intellectual to speak out of conscience on all the issues of the day. Bourdieu was sharply critical because he thought this kind of public intellectual role failed to bring any grounded expertise to the public debate or sufficiently challenge the very terms of the debate.[33]

---

ests—a point he stressed in response to criticism of *Ideology and Utopia* (1955). Mannheim does envisage a kind of self-critical though technocratic vision of the intellectual role that would be sufficiently freed from political commitments and parochial interests in order to grasp a view of the totality and thereby be better able to represent the general interest. Mannheim seems more willing to accept some form of the technocrat role whereas Bourdieu is categorically critical. Even in his own political practice, Bourdieu showed little inclination to be a "service intellectual" to the state—including the French Socialist state from 1981 to 1994. Bourdieu does share with Mannheim, however, the idea that the social scientist can achieve to an appreciable extent an overview of particular social universes. Field analysis is precisely an attempt to grasp a total vision of a particular arena of conflict. However, for Bourdieu the effects of field analysis are limited to demystification of powers relations. Field analysis does not lead to a common interest solution transcending all parochial interests as one might imagine from a Mannheimian perspective.

32. Bourdieu did note in passing that the idea that the individual social scientist armed with the sociology of sociology could completely free himself from all ideological contamination in his research was a "utopian hope" that should be abandoned (Bourdieu, Chamboredon, and Passeron 1991, 74). Bourdieu admonishes the social scientist to struggle against the "illusion of absolute knowledge" where the social scientist becomes in Durkheimian fashion the one "who grasps the whole and is a sort of god compared to the mere mortals who understand nothing" (250). Bourdieu's reflexive practice of sociology focused more on making the field of sociological practice more scientific rather than finding individual escape routes from politics for sociologists. While Bourdieu is critical of positivist objectivity as a form of elitism, his social constructionist perspective does hold to an ideal of objectivity that can be approached though never fully attained through reflexivity.

33. In the United States a version of Sartre's total intellectual can be found in the idea of the "public intellectual" brought into academic discussion by Russell Jacoby (1987) who criticizes contemporary American academics for being excessively preoccupied by professionalization and specialization and thereby largely irrelevant to public debate. Jacoby calls

In contrast to Sartre's generalist view of the intellectual's political vocation, Bourdieu's preferred view comes much closer to Michel Foucault's idea of the *specific intellectual* who intervenes in the public arena only on those issues that his specialized knowledge permits him to speak with authority.[34] It is the authority of specialized knowledge, not individual conscience, which guides where and how the intellectual will enter the public debate.

Like Foucault, Bourdieu thinks the proper role for the intellectual is to attack the foundations of symbolic power, to question the fundamental assumptions made when people think politically. Foucault says that

> the role of an intellectual is not to tell others what they have to do. By what right would he do so? . . . The work of an intellectual is not to shape others' political will: it is, through the analyses that he carried out in his own field, to question over and over again what is postulated as self-evident, to disturb people's mental habits, the way they do and think things. (1997, 131)

In Bourdieu's language the intellectual is to expose the doxa of fields of power, those taken-for-granted assumptions of social life invested with power relations but misrecognized as natural and legitimate types of authority. What is a sociologist as a "specific intellectual" to do? The sociologist is to contribute to public debate in a way that is compatible with the authority of the specific expertise the sociologist can legitimately claim. In Bourdieu's language of capitals, the sociologist must convert the symbolic capital obtained from recognition for his scientific contributions into political capital.

One of the special types of expertise that the sociological perspective can bring to the public arena is the capacity to analyze the conditions making possible political discourse, even in those areas not explicitly viewed as political. Bourdieu's social constructionist perspective on political discourse asks critically what creates the terms of public debate and how it is framed.[35] In other words, the critical intellectual work for the sociologist is

---

for a return to generalist intellectuals in the tradition of C. Wright Mills to intervene on a wide range of public concerns. Bourdieu rejects this model.

34. Bourdieu's appropriation of Foucault's specific intellectual draws on only part of it. Foucault uses the image not just to limit public intervention to a particular field of expertise but also to reject any claims for universality. Bourdieu (1996b), however, retains a vision for the universal, even if it is historically specific and socially constructed.

35. There is overlap here with William Gamson's (2006) work on framing of political discourse and that of George Lakoff (2002).

essentially a symbolic work, one of deconstructing and thereby demystifying the jargon of domination (the doxa) of official political discourse. One early example of this is the 1976 analysis of dominant ideology in France (Bourdieu and Boltanski 1976). In that work Bourdieu (with Luc Boltanski) analyzed the newly emerging technocratic vocabulary among the younger French administrative elite who combined neoliberal ideology with technical know-how in proffering policies that would sacrifice traditional welfare state guarantees for promises of market-oriented flexibility and efficiencies. In later years, this emphasis led Bourdieu to focus more and more of his attention on the role of journalism and the neoliberal assumptions present in much journalistic political debate (Bourdieu 1998e). The model of the scientific intellectual who attends primarily to critical analysis of political discourse would also seem to lead naturally to concern with the media and we see this shift in concern later in his career (Swartz 2003a).[36] In fact, when reflecting on the social movement of the mid-nineties, of which he was one of the leading intellectuals, Bourdieu (2008f, 380–83) rejects any sharp distinction between the roles of the scholar and the political activist. He advocates "scholarship with commitment." He presents the relationship between the researcher and the social movement as one where the researcher helps by providing instruments of analysis (created out of the autonomous logic of the scientific field) to use against the symbolic effects produced by experts working for those multinational organizations promoting globalization. He distinguishes this role of providing critical conceptual tools for demasking symbolic violence from that of ideological control or prophetic pronouncements, which he finds to be key dangers for organic intellectuals.

In an effort to respond to shortcomings of the Foucaultian model, such as the highly individualistic character of intellectual work, and the increasing intellectual specialization and the overwhelming dominance of mass media in public debate, Bourdieu develops the idea of the *collective intellectual*. He proposes a model of collective work by intellectuals on a small number of common objectives. We find an early formulation of the idea

---

36. Earlier critics had often pointed up Bourdieu's neglect of the mass media in central works such as *Distinction*. For example, Garnham (1986), a sympathetic critic, points to the neglect of media in *Distinction*. Bourdieu's focus traditionally was on enhancing and protecting the autonomy of intellectual fields, particularly the scientific field. When the media appear to threaten that autonomy and when the public debate becomes bereft of genuine scientific input, Bourdieu begins devoting more and more attention to the media. See the next chapter where we discuss his book on TV journalism in which he describes the growing threat of the mass media to democratic life.

of the collective intellectual in the late 1980s.[37] The 1992 postscript "For the corporatism of the universal" to *The Rules of Art* (Bourdieu 1996c, 399–448) appears as a kind of manifesto that outlines an activist strategy calling for the collective organization of intellectuals, a call that "takes a normative position based on the conviction that it is possible to use knowledge of the logic of the functioning of the fields of cultural production to draw up a realistic programme for the collective action of intellectuals." It defines an activist role for the scientific intellectual that Bourdieu sees going back to the example set by Emile Zola during the Dreyfus Affair and that Bourdieu would more and more employ for the remainder of his life.[38]

Bourdieu's model for the political vocation of the sociologist is rooted in the intellectual role he sees incarnated by Emile Zola and the Dreyfusards "when they intervened in political life *as intellectuals*, meaning with a specific authority founded on their belonging to the relatively autonomous world of art, science and literature, and on all the values associated with that autonomy—disinterestedness, expertise, etc." (Bourdieu 1996b, 340–41). Bourdieu argues that intellectuals have found themselves conflicted between autonomy and exclusive focus on their cultural work on the one hand, and commitment, political engagement, and relevance on the other hand. It was Zola and the Dreyfusards who brought together the two poles of this opposition into a model that we can use today. This model embraces both autonomy and commitment.[39] Intellectuals need to enter the political arena not as political actors but as intellectuals who engage their specific authority of expertise, rationality, and disinterestedness. In his words:

37. See Bourdieu 1989a and 2008c, 209–17.

38. The Dreyfus Affair was a political scandal that divided France in the 1890s and early 1900s. Captain Alfred Dreyfus was wrongly accused and imprisoned by a military court for alleged espionage. The renowned writer, Emile Zola, and other leading intellectuals published an open letter, *J'accuse* (I accuse), denouncing the cover-up and this led to a new trial and Dreyfus's exoneration. The affair saw the emergence of "intellectuals" and an important historical reference point for writers, artists, and academics who subsequently would rally on grounds of higher moral principles against injustices, such as French military torture in the French-Algerian war (Le Sueur 2005).

39. Bourdieu's understanding of Zola was informed by Bourdieu's (1996c) own study of the rise of the literary field in nineteenth-century France, which became a model for how he thinks of intellectual field autonomy. Bourdieu's work on nineteenth-century French intellectuals was both informed and elaborated by his student Christophe Charle (1987, 1990).

My dream would be to create an *international* of artists and scientists which would become an independent political—and moral—force capable of intervening, with authority and with a competence founded on their autonomy, about problems of general interest (such as nuclear power, education, or the new bio-technologies). They would not rule but, while remaining in their place, they would constitute a very serious control over rulers, especially in those domains where they know a great deal, if only by saying that we do not know enough. (Wacquant 1993b, 38)

Likewise, sociologists need to bring to the public arena their particular expertise on the social world that Bourdieu believes, if done critically, will pose a fundamental challenge to taken-for-granted assumptions and prevailing views on how the world is organized.

Bourdieu's model of a collective intellectual became institutionalized to some extent during his lifetime as a loose array of networks and centers across several organizational settings primarily but not exclusively within the French academic research and cultural world. It included contacts with former students, researchers, publishers, and academic circles.[40] It represented a kind of "anti-political politics" model where Bourdieu as the intellectual did not assume an administrative position within government or function as a kind of "counselor to the prince" or to any political party, but operated as a permanent anti-establishment critic of the establishment, whether it was left or right, against injustice.[41] Indeed, though politically left, Bourdieu proved to be a sharp critic of the French Socialists soon after they came into power in 1980. This model contrasts to the positions by the sociologist Anthony Giddens, who became an advisor to the Tony Blair regime in the United Kingdom, to Václav Havel, who became an elected official in the Czech Republic, and to the sociologist Fernando Cardoso, who became president of Brazil.[42]

40. *Raisons d'Agir* (http://www.homme-moderne.org/raisonsdagir-editions/index.html) is one enduring expression of Bourdieu's collective intellectual vision.

41. The term *anti-political politics* is suggested by Dick Pels (1995), which he borrows from George Konrád (1984). Bourdieu had an acute political sensibility and a penetrating awareness of forms of power. But he was not a political organization person nor did he outline political platforms or propose alternative policies. It is this duality—political sensibility but little organizational engagement—that the "anti-politics politics" expression is intended to convey.

42. See Garcia 2004 for an analysis of how Cardoso followed certain capital accumulation and conversation strategies to interweave a pathway between the intellectual and political field in Brazil under military rule.

Comparison of Bourdieu and Burawoy on Public Sociology

In this section I compare Bourdieu's vision for sociology in the public arena to the efforts by Michael Burawoy to launch a debate over public sociology. Burawoy's considerable efforts have found receptive ears, particularly in American sociology. His advocacy for a public sociology struck a chord within the profession and in fact become a matter of "public" discussion for a time within the profession. His presidential leadership of the American Sociological Association (ASA) and his keynote address "For Public Sociology" at the 2004 ASA meetings clearly marked an event in the life of the professional association.[43] In that address, Burawoy called for sociologists to step out of the ivory tower and to engage various nonacademic publics in support of their causes. He proposed mobilizing the entire discipline for this enterprise. He identified four subtypes of sociology—academic (produced for professional peers to accumulate knowledge), expert (oriented for bureaucratic demand notably by government agencies), public (oriented for nonacademic publics), and critical or reflexive (oriented for self-critical analysis of the methods and programs of the discipline itself)—as distinct but complementary practices that could all be mobilized in service of his overall program for public relevance. Several symposia in professional journals ensued: the *American Sociologist* (Fall/Winter 2005), *Social Problems* (February 2004), *Social Forces* (June 2004), *Critical Sociology* (2005), the *British Journal of Sociology* (June 2005), and *Contemporary Sociology* (November 2008) have carried numerous commentaries on Burawoy's arguments and the theme of public sociology.[44]

Some of Burawoy's views overlap with those of Bourdieu. Burawoy published in Bourdieu's journal, *Actes de la Recherche en Sciences Sociales*, and Burawoy draws inspiration in some of his ideas from Bourdieu, explicitly referencing Bourdieu in his ASA presidential address and more

43. The call for public sociology in the American tradition, however, does not originate with Burawoy. Herbert Gans (2002) made the diffusion of sociological knowledge beyond the academy a key theme in his 1989 ASA president address. And of course it is a central theme, though not the term itself, in C. Wright Mills's *The Sociological Imagination* (1959) and Robert Lynd's *Knowledge for What? The Place of Social Science in American Culture* (1986 [1939]).

44. Numerous additional commentaries appear in Blau and Lyall Smith 2006, Clawson 2007, and Nichols 2007.

extensively in subsequent papers on public sociology.[45] However, Burawoy would not describe himself as a devoted follower of Bourdieu; indeed, he differs with Bourdieu on certain key points. Burawoy draws inspiration from Gramsci and does not share Bourdieu's fundamental misgivings about the organic intellectual role. It seems appropriate, therefore, to compare Bourdieu's vision for a politics of sociology and political vocation of the sociologist to the kind of public sociology advocated by Burawoy and that has received so much recent attention, particularly in the United States.

Burawoy argues that it is important today to develop a public sociology, a type of sociological work that in dialogic exchange with certain publics would help formulate and give voice to their concerns. He defines public sociology as "taking sociology to publics beyond the university, engaging them in dialogue about public issues that have been studied by sociologists. Indeed, it is a triple dialogue—a dialogue among sociologists, between sociologists and publics, and most importantly within publics themselves" (2005c, 4). It is one of four types of sociological practice that he sees emerging historically through four different phases that characterize the relationship between sociology and its publics.[46]

The first phase, prior to World War I, finds early sociology closely connected with social reform movements. Sociology started historically as public sociology. "Social science and social reform were seen as inseparable" (2005c, 1). The second phase, roughly from the 1920s to 1960s, brought the development of professional sociology and policy sociology. Professionalization separated sociology from social reform in an effort to achieve scientific legitimacy and recognition as an autonomous body of knowledge within the academy. Over the same period policy sociology developed, in which government became a key client for sociological expertise. This was the period of development of the welfare state. In the third phase, beginning in the 1960s, there emerged critical sociology that challenged the policy sociology connections to the welfare state, the corporate order, and the ideological basis of structural functionalist theory of professional sociology. Social movements challenged both the universities and wider society contributing to this critique of mainstream sociology. Critical sociology "had antecedents" in the work of Robert Lynd (1986 [1939]) in the 1930s but "it crystallized in C. Wright Mills's *The*

---

45. See n. 30 above for Burawoy's lectures.
46. See Burawoy 2005c, 1–4, for a brief sketch of this argument.

Sociological Imagination (1959).[47] Gouldner (1979) "and others carried the critical mantle forward into the 1960s and 1970s" (Burawoy 2005c, 3). A new wave of social movements emerged, shifting sociology, universities, and, to a lesser extent, society, to the political left. Professional sociology adopted, however, by accommodating the critical perspectives into many subspecialties within the profession.

Sociology is currently entering a fourth phase very much tied to broader developments of globalization, the decline of traditional social movements, cutbacks in public funding, and recourse to market mechanisms and private donations to provide public goods such as health and education (privatization, corporatization, and marketization). There has been a conservative reaction to the sixties and early seventies; social movements of this period have ebbed and the labor movement "forcibly repressed" (Burawoy 2005c, 4). In the developed countries, particularly in the United States and the United Kingdom, public welfare and state regulation have come under sharp attack. Moreover, Burawoy contends that the state has increasingly given up its regulatory function and adopted market ideology in launching an attack on civil society. Burawoy associates the rise of sociology with the rise of civil society. Now sociology must take up defense of civil society that the state has abandoned to the vicissitudes of market deregulation. The contemporary period calls for a new commitment to public sociology as a mechanism for the defense of civil society.

Public sociology in the fourth phase differs from that of the first phase because it can now draw on the wealth of methods, theories, and accumulated experience of professional sociology. This calls for "a renewed dialogue between professional and public sociology" (Burawoy 2005c, 4). Moreover, Burawoy does not present public sociology as simply advocacy knowledge for particular groups. Beyond the defense of particular publics, public sociologists are to become organic intellectuals for the defense of civil society more generally.

From this historical development of sociology, Burawoy sees the emergence of the four distinct types of sociology identified earlier: professional, policy, critical, and public. Burawoy sees the four types as distinct cognitive practices that stand in mutual opposition but also need each other. One does not reduce to the other; each can enrich the other.[48] The four types

47. For Burawoy, "Mills is Bourdieu draped in 1950s American colors."
48. The four types and their interrelationships receive the most systematic attention in Burawoy 2005a.

can be classified according to two key questions: sociology *for what* and *for whom*. In terms of knowledge *for whom*, policy sociology is oriented to external, extra-academic clients, particularly governments, corporations, and foundations that set the agenda of issues to be studied. Professional sociology, by contrast, is internally focused among academic peers on advancing sociology as a science. Critical sociology is also for academic peers but it examines the fundamental value assumptions of professional sociology. Public sociology draws on the wealth of methods, theories, and accumulated experience of professional sociology to help identify and articulate the concerns of external publics. In terms of knowledge *for what*, Burawoy sees commonality between policy and professional sociologies because they represent forms of "instrumental" knowledge to achieve particular ends (client interests and scientific advancement) whereas critical and public sociology demand a "reflexive" sociology that reflects on the purposes to which sociology is to be used. Burawoy takes the normative position that the four are "mutually interdependent and invigorating," yet analytically he sees American sociology as a "field of power" in which "instrumental knowledge dominates reflexive knowledge" (2005c, 7, 14). By contrast, Burawoy advocates for a critical and public sociology in particular.

Burawoy's embrace of the idea of public sociology, a form of public intellectual, draws some inspiration from Bourdieu's thinking, overlaps with some of his concerns, and shares some of his views. Burawoy's sketch of the historical shift from nineteenth-century social reform to professionalization overlays with Bourdieu's analysis of sociology's lost political function that I identified earlier in the chapter. Both want to recapture a political function for sociology though they understand that project in somewhat different terms. However, their respective positions originate out of quite different historical contexts that shape their respective postures. Burawoy speaks in a national context where intellectuals, particularly literary, humanistic, and social scientific (with the exception of some economists), have generally not played a significant part in shaping national political debates. Burawoy's advocacy for public sociology occurs in a national context where sociologists have frequently lamented their lack of voice in public debate.[49] Some long for the return or emergence of a new C. Wright

49. It is worth recalling the climate of the times in which Burawoy's 2004 ASA presidential speech occurred. The ASA had recently passed by a large majority a resolution, though strongly contested by some, condemning the American military intervention in Iraq. Many of

Mills (Jacoby 1987). Burawoy fits within this stream of thinking, though, as we will see, his call for a public sociology is not without some important qualifications. Bourdieu, by contrast, is both heir to and reacts against a long tradition of French intellectuals assuming prominent positions in public life. To be a prominent artist, writer, or teacher, and on the political left (though there were some on the political right as well) meant almost by definition taking on a public role of signing petitions, participating in public demonstrations, writing op-ed pieces, and appearing on TV in recent years. Bourdieu (1963) was frequently critical of French intellectuals for this kind of intellectual/political activism that was based on individual conscience, commitment to a cause, or desire for public notoriety, rather than on scholarly expertise. Indeed, Bourdieu's (1980c, 1993a) criticism of Sartre as a total intellectual and Bourdieu's espousal of a specific and collective intellectual reflect this position.

Further, the very notion of public sociology is rather foreign to most sociologists beyond the US borders, as Burawoy himself acknowledges. Sociology for most outside of North America is by definition public. Only in the United States, where there is an extreme division of intellectual labor and where the positivist tradition has been quite strong, does the call for public sociology as a new kind of practice stand out.

Their differing views on how the sociologist should engage the public area stem in part from their different positions relative to the professional bodies in their respective countries. They reflect different intellectual and professional strategies. Burawoy is writing and mobilizing within the American sociological profession. He is an advocate for the discipline, the professional association as a whole. Indeed he held the presidency of the American Sociological Association in 2004. While Burawoy clearly

the leaders of the discipline, including Burawoy himself, had been activists against the Vietnam War some thirty years earlier and experienced an acute disjuncture between their political and value aspirations for attacking the problems of injustice and the growing political isolation of the discipline. There was a strong sense of growing isolation over the last thirty years from the public arena where investigative journalism, key news editorialists or commentators (both in the print and TV media), and hybrid intellectual output of think-tanks were more successful in shaping the terms of the public debate (Medvetz 2009). Even within the discipline itself the degree of specialization and professionalization and fragmentation into fairly autonomous subfields or specialized knowledge sections made dialogue across the discipline difficult. In this climate Burawoy's call for a public sociology came as a veritable challenge to the discipline and judging by the multitude of reactions to it, many of them quite critical, it struck a timely and sensitive chord within the vocational identity of the profession.

prefers the critical and public sociology types, he stresses how all four are needed and ultimately complementary despite different cognitive orientations. He takes the normative position that there should be "reciprocal interdependence among the four types" (2005a, 15, 17). By contrast, Bourdieu stood for the most part outside of the French professional association. He seldom published in the French professional sociology journals or participated in the life of the professional associations.[50] He created his own institution. He devoted his energies to those activities that bear directly his imprint rather than attempt to animate an entire profession with all its diversity.

Bourdieu did not distinguish the four types of sociologies as Burawoy does.[51] Burawoy's types would be too compartmentalized, too suggestive of essentialist-like features in Bourdieu's thinking. When Bourdieu does analyze sociologically the field of sociology itself he casts it within his field analytical perspective relative to the other disciplines in terms of "academic power" (control over teaching positions and institutional resources) and scholarly prestige (recognition of the discipline and scholarly work). In Bourdieu's (1988b, 77–84) field analysis of the Parisian professorate during the sixties, sociology and the social sciences in general had relatively little academic power and scholarly prestige whereas philosophy and particularly classical literature and ancient history were rich in both. And were he to look at internal differentiation within sociology itself, he would identify those tendencies toward more heteronomy (e.g., external funding) in contrast to those toward disciplinary autonomy (peer review and intellectual agenda setting).[52]

Moreover, one cannot divide Bourdieu's own work up into these different types. Burawoy acknowledges that the work of some sociologists in fact overlaps to varying extent his four distinct types, yet contends that most sociologists tend to concentrate in one or two types. The kind of sociology Bourdieu did would indeed overlap with the critical, professional,

50. Except for a few early papers (Bourdieu 1966, 1971a, 1974; Bourdieu and Bourdieu 1965; Bourdieu and Passeron 1968), Bourdieu did not publish in the mainstream *Revue Française de Sociologie* of French professional sociology.

51. Though Burawoy sees a parallel between his four types of sociological knowledge (professional, policy, public, critical) and Bourdieu's (1996c) four types of art (pure art, bourgeois art, social art, and avant-garde) (personal communication, January 2011).

52. Burawoy uses Bourdieu's language of "field of force" to describe sociology but does not give a systematic field analysis of the discipline, either in his ASA address or in subsequent writings. And Bourdieu himself does not offer a detailed field analysis of French sociology.

and public types that Burawoy delineates. We can see Bourdieu centrally concerned, particularly early in his career, with professional sociology to enhance the scientific status of sociology. Yet, Bourdieu most always designed his work to have a public effect. He oriented his work toward "public" issues, such as decolonization, class inequality, education, and housing (Bourdieu 2008e; Swartz 2003a). Indeed, Bourdieu saw all of sociology to be public sociology and would object to identifying it as just one subfield of specialization within the discipline. He saw himself as forging concepts and developing analyses that political activists could use in particular domains, such as education in particular. However, seldom did Bourdieu work on policy issues. His two reports from the Collège de France to the Socialist government on educational reform are notable exceptions.[53] He spoke as a "critical sociologist" being sharply critical of other sociological approaches and calling for the reflexive practice of all sociology.

While Bourdieu did not identify with the kind of terminology Burawoy employs, Bourdieu would see himself closer to Burawoy's ideal of a public sociologist than that of a public intellectual. Indeed, both see their vision for sociology as distinct from that of the public intellectual.[54] The public sociologist limits his public commentary to areas of established expertise. Bourdieu early on was a sharp critic of sociologists who played public intellectual roles without first firmly establishing their social scientific authority. Bourdieu's public sociologist seems closer to Foucault's specific intellectual, with which Bourdieu was relatively more sympathetic, than it does to Sartre's total intellectual, which Bourdieu sharply criticized.

Burawoy wants critical sociology to be separate from professional sociology, not just a dimension of the other types of sociology; indeed, he argues that "you need someone outside of its practice to develop a critical perspective" (2005b, 425). By "critical" Burawoy means the capacity to do two things: "question the basis of our research programmes" and "interrogates the extra-scientific foundations of science." By contrast, Bourdieu would situate Burawoy's critical sociology at the very core of what good sociology is to be—not simply as a kind of normative corrective internal to the discipline but as a key epistemological characteristic of sociology *as science* and to be directed toward all objects of investigation not just

53. "Propositions pour un enseignement de l'avenir" (1985) and "Principes pour une réflexion sur les contenues d'enseignement" (1989).

54. Burawoy (2005a) references Herbert Gans (2002), who makes a similar public sociologist/public intellectual distinction in an earlier call for more public sociology.

the internal dynamics of the discipline. Burawoy's critical sociology seems to cover some of what Bourdieu means by *reflexivity*, but for Bourdieu reflexivity is a necessary dimension of *all* sociological practice; it is not to be reserved for some specialized subfield of sociology.

Both Bourdieu and Burawoy see the rise and increasing dominance of neoliberal thinking as a threat to be combated, a threat against sociology, and more important as generating more inequality in modern societies. Bourdieu is sharply critical of its increasing prominence in public discourse in the media, in political leadership, as well as among a growing number of academics. And he sees sociology well equipped to carry out this critique.

But they differ in thinking about state, market, and civil society relationships. Burawoy sees these as quite separate spheres with sociology identified with civil society, which was to be protected with the help of public sociology against intrusions by the state and markets. Burawoy sees sociology as rooted in and defending the interests of civil society against the state and the market (2005a, 24). Bourdieu, by contrast, does not see the fundamental state/civil society dichotomy that Burawoy does. Bourdieu sees the need to protect the welfare state as a way to preserve civil society. Bourdieu sees defense of the welfare sector of the state as key for preserving the social benefits obtained in previous struggles against capitalism. Burawoy seems to focus exclusively on defending civil society. Bourdieu (1984a) stresses the socially stratified character of civil society so much that it is difficult to imagine him embracing civil society as a whole to be defended by sociology.

Again national context is important in understanding their differing views. The fight against neoliberalism in Europe meant opposing American state and corporate dominance and in France this meant using the French state to defend national interests. Writing from the country exercising world dominance in military, political, and economic power, Burawoy is less likely to see the state as a protector of civil society.

Burawoy charges public sociology with the vital task of defending civil society as a whole against the state as well as the market since the state has increasingly become an "agent and partner" in market expansion it no longer checks. Conceptually Burawoy treats the three as separate entities but increasingly in the modern period the state and market are encroaching on civil society and threatening its very existence. Burawoy writes that "the state, either directly or indirectly through the market, takes the offensive against labor and social rights won in previous periods, establishing a very different terrain for sociology that can no longer collaborate with the state for a policy sociology. Instead sociology must directly defend civil society, against the twin forces of state and market" (2005d, 157). Bourdieu shares with Burawoy his critical analysis that the state has increasingly embraced market ideology. Bourdieu (Bourdieu and Boltanski 1976) was in fact an early critic of the increasing adoption by French state elites of free-market ideology. However, Bourdieu does not divide up the social order into three distinct entities and does not pit civil society and sociology against the state as an undifferentiated unit. As noted in chapter 5, Bourdieu (1998g; 2008e, 245–52; Bourdieu et al. 1999) offers a differentiated analysis of the French state,[55] one divided into the "left hand" that supports social welfare programs and the "right hand" that embraces free trade ideology. Thus while Burawoy categorizes the state as a separate sphere that today has embraced neoliberalism in opposition to civil society, Bourdieu's analysis of the state would support what he calls the left hand of the state as respective and supportive of civil society.

Both share a vision for the reflexive practice of sociology, not as some subspecialty of theory but as a necessary dimension for the practice of all good sociology. However, there are differences. Reflexivity for Burawoy means the critical evaluation of "ends," particularly the value presuppositions underlying policy and public sociology. Moreover, Burawoy doesn't confine reflexivity capabilities to just sociologists. "A dialogue about ends" can be carried out with various publics as well (2005a, 11).

Bourdieu goes beyond exposing value presuppositions to stress how sociological analysis is shaped by the cognitive orientation that reflects the social conditions of the researcher. Bourdieu is centrally concerned with controlling the distorting effects of the position of the sociologist as outsider on analyzing the social world of the insider. The "scholastic view" formalizes and thereby distorts the informal logic of practice. Moreover, he stresses the need to break with insider views of their social worlds rather than, as Burawoy emphasizes, implement a kind of dialogue with insiders as a necessary process for being able to grasp what is sociologically relevant about their social worlds. Burawoy's reflexivity includes a dialogic dimension with external publics that one does not find in Bourdieu, with

---

55. In discussing his research on single-family housing and the state, Bourdieu criticizes the image of the state as "a well-defined, clearly bounded and unitary reality which stands in a relation of externality with outside forces that are themselves clearly identified and defined" (Bourdieu and Wacquant 1992, 111).

the exception of the interview work in *The Weight of the World* where Bourdieu gives voice to and probes how individuals experience social exclusion and isolation. In Burawoy's thinking Bourdieu's sociology is very much a traditional public sociology, whereas Burawoy would stress the organic public intellectual mode. Bourdieu's public sociologist is to be a "catalyst of public debate and discussion" (Burawoy 2005c, 5) rather than one who "is intimately and directly connected to publics" and gives voice to their local concerns. This difference in the leadership role of the public sociologist becomes more apparent in their respective views on how sociology can promote social change.

Bourdieu's own efforts as a public sociologist to promote progressive change stand in sharp contrast to aspects of his theory of symbolic power and violence. He saw his sociology as an effort to denaturalize and render less deterministic the social world, which he tried to communicate to people. But given the powerful force of habitus to operate beyond the reaches of conscious decisionmaking, it is not clear how the debunking force of sociology could be effective against the unconscious force of habitus and the dynamics of misrecognition it reinforced. Indeed, Burawoy (2005c) charges that Bourdieu fails to theorize the conditions of his own practice as a public sociologist.[56]

56. Burawoy's criticism here of Bourdieu is similar to the familiar criticism that Marx could not explain himself, or that he undertheorized the claim in *The Manifesto* that a portion of intellectuals would shift allegiance to the working class in times of crisis. Bourdieu acknowledges that it is very difficult to break out of the grips of symbolic power and violence. He (1994b) notes, for example, in his analysis of the state that it is very difficult to break with state-imposed schemes of classification. Yet Bourdieu identifies one source of change as emerging when disjuncture occurs between habitus and field. This clearly happens in Bourdieu's own case as a cultural and social outsider in origins in the world of a privileged Parisian intellectual elite. And he suggests a similar understanding of the anti-institutional dispositions in the work of Foucault and Derrida. So Bourdieu's own self-image as well as his conceptual framework is not devoid of some understanding of the origins of critical intellectuals like Bourdieu himself, as Burawoy charges. However, in Bourdieu's case the conditions of disjuncture between habitus and field could have produced an "oblat" who would uncritically embrace the institution that recruited and consecrated him as frequently happened in the case of the village priest. But Bourdieu himself "bit the hand that fed him." He did not become a cheerleader for the educational institution that offered him upward social mobility; he in fact became one of its ardent critics. As noted earlier, Bourdieu (2008e, 84–110) also suggests that some of his oppositional dispositions stem from the particularities of early family and school socialization in a period of rapid decline of the traditional French peasantry.

As I note earlier in the chapter, Bourdieu's thinking regarding how the sociologist should carry out his political vocation appears to have changed in the later years. Bourdieu came to adopt a more overtly advocacy posture in many of his public engagements. To use Burawoy's terminology, the intimate linkage between professional sociology as a science and public sociology shifted toward more emphasis on public sociology in Bourdieu's later career.

A point of divergence between Bourdieu and Burawoy concerns the role sociologists as public intellectuals can play in fostering social change. Burawoy sees a distinct difference in their views and I think he is right in identifying that difference. Here is how Burawoy (2005b) sets up his criticism of Bourdieu.

Bourdieu's sociology of science begins with a rupture with common-sense understandings. While agents are not dumb—they follow a logic of practice—they misrecognize its true nature, namely, that it is vested with unequal power relations that establish arbitrary hierarchies between individuals and groups. Only science can reveal the conditions of misrecognition. There is no significant provision in Bourdieu's thinking for recognition of the conditions of misrecognition outside of the insights of science.[57] How common sense embodies patterns of domination becomes accessible to lay people only through the insight offered by science. This allocates to the social scientist a formidable role in creating the cultural conditions for social transformation. This line of reasoning also implies that one must therefore defend the autonomy of science at all costs because by defending the corporate interests of science one also defends the universal interest of humanity by providing a means for freeing people from the clutches of misrecognition. As Burawoy critically observes, this is "quite a leap from science to the public defense of humanity" (2005b, 429).[58]

57. Bourdieu does stress that disjuncture between the expectations of habitus and the actual opportunities of field gives cause for critical reflection and protest. But it is not clear how such a disjuncture giving rise to frustrated expectations relates to the critical inquiry of science. Can individuals and groups come to a critical assessment of their own taken-for-granted acceptance of their conditions of domination without the benefit of social scientific insight? Bourdieu downplays that possibility in his sharp criticisms of popular culture theorizing by intellectuals.

58. The theme that doing good social science means doing good politics resonates strongly throughout much of Bourdieu's work. He embraces the idea that defending the interests of science amounts to defending the universal interests of humanity. Burawoy, like Gouldner, is more skeptical and suggests that Bourdieu's vision for an extraordinary role for his "collective

By contrast, Burawoy draws inspiration from Gramsci to say that "in the final analysis . . . truth can only be elaborated in dialogue with agents themselves who are endowed with 'good sense' within their common sense . . . [and that] social change comes from intellectuals working in close connection with agents, elaborating local imaginations of what could be, and struggle for their realization" (2005b, 430). He acknowledges the kinds of criticisms voiced by Bourdieu, as noted earlier in the chapter, of organic intellectuals sacrificing their intellectual autonomy for popular opinion (populism) or setting themselves up as a kind of leadership vanguard. But one cannot conclude, therefore, that all agents' understandings of the social world are so distorted and unreliable by misrecognition that they should be summarily discarded.[59] Nor can one conclude that the sources of change therefore reside solely in the hands of enlightened social scientists, as Bourdieu's argument implies. It is not clear that Bourdieu would want to make such a claim for it suggests a kind of intellectual elitism that Bourdieu himself denounced in this criticism of sociologists playing the charismatic role of a social prophet. Yet the logic of his argument and his embrace of sociology as scientific knowledge point in this direction. Might not situations of crisis or radical transformation generate among insiders critical reflections that could possibly inform and be informed by the critical insights brought from the outside world of social science? Certainly, this is the "dialogical" model put forth by Burawoy. One finds a few such moments in some of Bourdieu's own work, such as *The Weight of the World* (Bourdieu et al. 1999), but their acknowledgment is not given the force of partners in social transformation that Burawoy seeks. Indeed Bourdieu's technique of "participant objectification" resembles a Socratic

intellectual" in social transformation looks like what constitutes in Gouldner's (1979) terms a "flawed universal class." (Bourdieu was quite critical of Gouldner's new class theorizing [Swartz 1998].) Perhaps, as Burawoy (2005b) suggests, Bourdieu's view here misrecognizes "its own particularism as universalism."

59. Affirming Durkheim's well-known skepticism of the scientific validity of actors' common-sense perceptions, Bourdieu rejects the "illusion of immediate knowledge" by arguing that "social agents do not have innate wisdom." "Common sense . . . has to be mistrusted" (Bourdieu, Chamboredon, and Passeron 1991, 250). Yet Bourdieu also rejects the opposite extreme, the "scientistic illusion, the illusion of absolute knowledge" that he also finds in Durkheim. For Bourdieu, doing a sociology of sociology as an "integral part of sociology, is indispensable for calling into question both the illusion of absolute knowledge which is inherent in the scientist's position, and the particular form that this illusion takes depending on the position that the scientist occupies in the space of scientific production." Still, Bourdieu gives little reflexive agency to ordinary actors in their everyday worlds.

dialogue where the social scientist and the interviewee are not on equal footing. From the superior position of science, the sociologist does not so much "give voice" to the individual experiences of social exclusion as give the "voice of science" that probes and constitutes into rational discourse the social class and status factors shaping those experiences.

Thus, Bourdieu offers not only a sociology of politics but, more important, a politics of sociology. Embedded in his view of sociology as science is a vision for attacking the foundations of power relations, namely, their taken-for-granted acceptance. His concepts of symbolic power, violence, and capital are tools for understanding the powerful force of legitimation of power relations. This conception of the sociological vocation intersects with a political vocation that Bourdieu believes the sociologist should embrace. I have pointed out how Bourdieu's vision for the public sociologist compares and contrasts with several other views on the role of intellectuals in politics, particularly the recent project by Michael Burawoy for a public sociology. The next chapter examines how Bourdieu implemented his vision in various public interventions during his career.

CHAPTER SEVEN

Critical Sociologist and Public Intellectual

On December 12, 1995, Pierre Bourdieu took up a megaphone and addressed striking railroad employees at the Lyon train station rally, culminating in the largest street demonstrations in Paris since May 1968.[1] He proclaimed solidarity of French intellectuals with the striking workers. This intervention was the first of a series of highly visible public positions Bourdieu would take against neoliberalism and in support of the welfare state that would make him a key figure in the antiglobalization movement in the 1990s. By the mid-1990s, and until his death in 2002, the French sociologist had become the leading public intellectual in Europe.

Bourdieu (along with Jean-Claude Passeron) had achieved some fame already in the mid-sixties with the publication of *The Inheritors: French Students and Their Relation to Culture* followed by *Reproduction in Education, Society, and Culture* in 1970 (see Bourdieu and Passeron 1977, 1979). Yet these widely influential works did not lead Bourdieu to assume an active public intellectual role typical of so many French intellectuals. He rarely signed petitions, editorialized in newspapers, or participated in public demonstrations. In fact, his later years of public political activism seem to contrast with the earlier years of following a professional career as a social scientific researcher. Indeed Bourdieu's relative silence during the May 1968 student uprising was conspicuous for virtually all other leading French sociologists at the time took public positions regarding the

---

1. Earlier and shorter versions of this chapter appeared in Swartz 2003a, 791–823; 2004, 393–411; 2010. Key sources for discussion in this chapter of Bourdieu's political activism are Bourdieu 2008e; Poupeau and Discepolo 2005.

student movement.[2] But in the 1990s Bourdieu clearly became a kind of public intellectual that he had not been before. A change occurred in both form and frequency of his political activism; he increasingly undertook a series of highly visible political engagements, whereas he previously had been quite critical of these forms of political activism by French intellectuals, notably of the "total intellectual" figure represented by Jean-Paul Sartre.[3] Bourdieu had stressed the need to develop sociology as a scientific discipline and was highly critical of those sociologists he thought were too oriented toward the mass media.[4] So what changed? How did Bourdieu become the leading European public intellectual by the time of his death in 2002?

I consider in this chapter the process by which Bourdieu became a public intellectual by focusing on both the intellectual field conditions and his sociological work that permitted this development. This analysis is informed by Bourdieu's field analytical perspective. I argue that changes in Bourdieu's position within the French intellectual field and changes within the intellectual field itself relative to other fields set the stage for Bourdieu's strategic choices in political involvement. Bourdieu's experience of those changes led him to shift emphasis in the way he understood the relationship between sociology and politics and the kind of role he could play in the public arena. The chapter offers, therefore, a cultural/

2. Bourdieu and several colleagues at the Center for European Sociology did draft a May 1968 statement criticizing the social selectivity of the university system and calling for democratic measures to address directly that issue. (See Bourdieu 2008a, 41–45). But he did not participate in the May '68 demonstrations as did Michel Foucault (see Eribon 1991 on Foucault's participation). He did not publish analyses of the May 1968 events in the immediate aftermath as did Raymond Aron (1968), Raymond Boudon (1969, 1970), Michel Crozier (1969), and Alain Touraine (1968), nor did he editorialize in the French press on the significance of the events as many French intellectuals did. His assessments would come later in Bourdieu 1988b and Bourdieu, Boltanski, and Maldidier 1971, but only as elements of analyses focused on the French university teaching profession. In that work he argues that the political positions taken by faculty during the May '68 events reflected their field interests within the academic world.

3. A key difference between the political activism of Bourdieu and that of Sartre is that Bourdieu entered the political arena with an intellectual practice directly related to the public issues he addressed whereas Sartre as philosopher and literary figure did not. For example, Bourdieu's defense of the welfare state against privatization stemmed in part from what he learned while researching for *The Weight of the World* (Bourdieu et al. 1999) the negative social and economic effects on those most directly affected by downsizing the welfare safety net. See Bourdieu 2005b; Bourdieu et al. 1999.

4. See Bourdieu 1963. On developing sociology as a scientific discipline see Bourdieu, Chamboredon, and Passeron 1991.

political field explanation rather than a personal/psychological one, an explanation where personal intellectual strategy is framed and modified in changing institutional settings. The chapter does not offer an exhaustive account of Bourdieu's political engagements but presents a selection of his works and public involvements that exemplify the modes of political involvement he undertook during his career as a sociologist.[5]

Science and Politics

Sociology as Scientific Craft

Before 1990 Bourdieu rarely made public political declarations in the tradition of Parisian intellectuals.[6] His efforts during his early years focused on developing a critical social scientific research orientation as distinct from both the academic sociology taught in the universities and the media-oriented pop sociology that flourished in French intellectual circles. French sociology during the 1950s and 1960s was a dominated discipline.[7] There existed few programs in sociology and little specialized training. It was either taught as strictly academic theory akin to social philosophy or practiced as applied empirical research with little connection to theory.

In this early period Bourdieu believed it necessary to distinguish between internal intellectual field struggles and external political struggles and focused his efforts largely on the internal struggles to build up the scientific status of sociology in France.[8] Enhancing intellectual autonomy from outside forces would be an enduring theme throughout his career and much of his later political activism was rooted in this basic concern. He wanted to transform sociology into a rigorous research enterprise

5. See Bourdieu 2008e for a more detailed account of Bourdieu's political interventions.

6. To be sure, Bourdieu had on a few occasions made highly visible political statements. He had joined Michel Foucault in protesting the Russian clamp down on Solidarity in Poland in 1981. He had supported the French comedian Coluche's right to enter the 1981 electoral race against the Socialist François Mitterrand for the presidency. On a couple of occasions during the 1984–90 period he played the role of expert by preparing reports on educational reform for the French Socialist leadership in government. But in comparison to the public political activism of Michel Foucault, and particularly Jean-Paul Sartre, and the customary appearance on French television of many other leading French intellectuals, Bourdieu was strikingly absent from the front stage of the Parisian French intellectual politics prior to the 1990s.

7. See Swartz 1997, 21, for more on French sociology during the period.

8. A point also made by Pinto 1998.

that would be critical though not prophetic, theoretical though empirically researchable, and scientific though not positivist.[9] Thus he devoted his energies to creating a research center (the Centre for the Sociology of Education and Culture, which in part grew out of Raymond Aron's Center for European Sociology), to founding and directing a sociological journal (*Actes de la Recherche en Sciences Sociales*), and to forming an international network of researchers who would institutionalize and legitimize his vision for sociological inquiry.

In his work Bourdieu argues that there should be a clear separation between sociology as a science and politics as distinct arenas of struggle. The first task of sociological analysis is to break with received views of the social world, including political views, and to develop its own scientific analysis of the social world.[10] If sociology is to become a legitimate science, then it must develop an autonomous set of intellectual practices distinct from external constraints. The sociologist is not to take marching orders from political parties or interest groups. Sociologists are not philosophers or moralists who offer prophetic insights on all the important issues of the day as Sartre frequently did. Sociology is a scientific craft that constructs a distinct type of knowledge. Sociology must establish its own intellectual agenda. It must accumulate symbolic capital as science.

Politics Nevertheless

Yet even Bourdieu's earliest work has a political dimension.[11] While drawing a sharp distinction between politics and the scientific work of soci-

9. Bourdieu and colleagues (Bourdieu, Chamboredon, and Passeron 1991) outlined an ambitious program for setting sociology on firm epistemological grounds and for developing an approach to the study of the social world that seemed no less ambitious than that of Emile Durkheim (1966) in the early twentieth century. The parallel to Durkheim has been drawn by several observers, such as Michel Offerlé (1999) and Loïc J. D. Wacquant (1992a).

10. Bourdieu embraced a critical epistemology rather than positivist objectivity in his thinking about the relationship between science and values. One central theme in his early methodological writings (Bourdieu, Chamboredon, and Passeron 1991) is epistemological, not political. Sociology needs to be set on firm epistemological grounds as a science. But, as Wacquant (1992a, 50) points out, for Bourdieu "even epistemology is fundamentally political." Bourdieu writes: "The theory of knowledge is a dimension of political theory because the specifically symbolic power to impose the principles of construction of reality in particular social reality is a major dimension of political power" (1977a, 165). In other words, the cognitive is political.

11. This is a view shared by many who have examined the ensemble of Bourdieu's writings and political activities. See, for example, Calhoun 2005a; Fritsch 2000; Grenfell 2005;

ology, Bourdieu insists on the political relevance of sociology. Bourdieu is sharply critical of the "ethical neutrality" often attributed to Weber (1970), which he dismisses as "a mere non-aggression pact with the established order" (Bourdieu and Passeron 1977, 218). He reasons as follows. Sociology is to be the study of power. Since effective exercise of power requires legitimation, the practice of sociological research has the effect of unmasking and debunking hidden, taken-for-granted power relations shaping social life. By demasking taken-for-granted power relations, "genuine scientific research embodies a threat for the social order" (Bourdieu and Hahn 1970, 15; see also Swartz 1997, 249–55). Scientific research exposes the hidden interests of the established powers.[12] Once power relations are exposed, new possibilities for individual and collective arrangements become possible.

This view of science suggests a key role sociologists can play in modern societies: "The sociologist unveils and therefore intervenes in the force relations between groups and classes and he can even contribute to the modification of those relations" (Bourdieu and Hahn 1970, 20).[13] That a critical social science can potentially modify relations between social classes amounts to a strong claim for the power of sociological knowledge in modern stratified societies and for the vocation of the social scientist as intellectual. Indeed, a normative vision for the political effects of social scientific research characterizes Bourdieu's sociological project.[14] And a

---

Lane 2000; Mauger 1995, 579–80; Pinto 1998; Wacquant 1992a, 47–59. This is also the view of Franck Poupeau (personal communication, Paris June 6, 2002), one of the editors of the most complete set of Bourdieu's political writings (Bourdieu 2008e).

12. In a particularly pointed formulation of this idea of the political effects of science Bourdieu and Passeron (1977, 218) write: "If there is no science but of the hidden, then the science of society is, per se, critical, without the scientist who chooses science ever having to choose to make a critique: the hidden is, in this case, a secret, and a well-kept one, even when no one is commissioned to keep it, because it contributes to the reproduction of a 'social order' based on concealment of the most efficacious mechanisms of its reproduction and thereby serves the interests of those who have a vested interest in the conservation of that order."

13. I discussed in the last chapter how Bourdieu thinks that the sociologist, armed with the tools of critical science, can and should have a responsibility for playing a key role in modern political life. Also see Swartz 1997, 247–69.

14. His vision calls for protecting the autonomy of the scientific field from the distorting effects of politics while orienting one's scientific research to have maximum effect in the public arena. It calls for a reflexive practice of sociology, one that does not import the logic of political struggle into the scientific arena yet is able to produce symbolic effects that can shape political life. See Bourdieu and Wacquant 1992; Swartz 1997.

sociology of intellectuals informs Bourdieu's reflexive practice of the sociological craft.

Algeria: A Decisive Experience

For Bourdieu, choice of research topics is guided by moral and political considerations: inequality, suffering, and domination.[15] At times the sheer force of circumstances also shapes one's intellectual enterprise. This is certainly the case of Algeria for Bourdieu. Bourdieu's early Algerian research embodies themes, concerns, and conceptual issues that animate his later work as several critics have noted (Calhoun 2005a; Goodman and Silverstein 2009; Lane 2000; Loyal 2009; Robbins 1991; Wacquant 2002; Yacine 2008a).[16] It was in Algeria where he shifted from being a philosopher, for which he was trained at the École Normale Supérieure, to a social scientific researcher.[17] While he never abandons some of the themes and topics that animated his young philosophical mind and training—indeed he (1990b, 3–33) says of sociology some years later that for him it was in fact "fieldwork in philosophy"—his intellectual activities shift to social scientific investigation. Algeria was also influential in shaping his thinking about relations between sociology and politics and the role of the social scientist in public life. It sets a pattern that characterizes much of his career: political engagement but in a scholarly way.

Algeria achieved its political independence from France in 1962 after eight years of horrific struggle that Le Sueur (2005, 1) describes as "one of the bloodiest wars of independence of the twentieth century." The war mounted "unprecedented violence—torture, terrorism, and military actions" and penetrated all of French and Algerian political, cultural, so-

15. In this respect he follows Max Weber (1970) who argued that choice of research topic is informed by ethical and political considerations (see Bourdieu, Chamboredon, and Passeron 1991, 149). Bourdieu stresses, however, that choice of research object is shaped not only by value and political commitments of the individual researcher. Intellectual fields also class certain objects as legitimate for intellectual attention but depreciate the value of others. One objective of Bourdieu's critical sociology is to challenge established intellectual hierarchies by bringing into consideration the less prestigious but sociologically significant objects of research (Bourdieu 1975b).

16. See Goodman and Silverstein 2009 for an illuminating collection of papers on the intersections of theory, method, politics, and habitus in Bourdieu's Algerian experience and research. In French, see Yacine 2008b.

17. Indeed, Bourdieu (2008g, 58–59) notes that "my Algerian experience is no doubt the pivotal moment" contributing to "the transformation of my vision of the world that accompanied my transition from philosophy to sociology."

cial, and intellectual life.[18] By the war's end, Algeria had achieved political independence but its infrastructure was in complete ruins, over 400,000 were dead, six prime ministers had resigned, France's Fourth Republic had collapsed, and De Gaulle's Fifth Republic was struggling for stability (including several assassination attempts that he narrowly escaped). The war polarized French political and intellectual life and continues to reverberate even today.[19]

It was in this war-torn environment that Bourdieu began his social scientific career and his thinking about political engagement as a social scientist. At age twenty-five, after teaching philosophy one year in a lycée, Bourdieu was called into military service in 1955. Refusing to enter the Reserve Officers College, the route taken by many of his highly educated peers, he was nonetheless assigned to a relatively comfortable position with the Army Psychological Services in Versailles. His outspoken opposition to French colonialism earned him reassignment to Algeria as punishment. Following a brief ground assignment with an aviation unit in the Chelif Valley, he was reassigned an office job in Algiers with the information and documentation services of the colonial administration that had the most complete library in Algeria (Yacine 2003, 337). There he gained access to numerous historical, ethnological, and administrative reports on Algeria and met a number of French and Algerian teachers, researchers, and students. Upon completion of military service, he secured a teaching assistant position in philosophy and sociology at the University of Algiers (1958–61) and from there was able to begin fieldwork that included ethnographic observations, interviews, photos, and two large-scale studies on the transformation of Algerian social structure under colonialism and the war. The fieldwork and surveys document traditional village life among the Kabylia (a northern mountainous region east of Algiers) peasants and more significantly its disruption by the forced migration into the urban areas of much of the population by colonialism, the war, and the French army resettlement policy.[20] His opposition to the war, his association with certain

18. It is important to note that officially—and in the minds of many French and some Algerians as well—Algeria was considered an extension of the French territory, not a colony, and more than a million French citizens lived there at the time of the war.

19. Le Sueur (2005, 286–322) documents how the legacy of that violent chapter in recent French history, particularly the debate over torture by the French military, continues into the twenty-first century.

20. This research resulted in two coauthored books, *Travail et travailleurs en Algérie* (Bourdieu et al. 1963) and *Le déracinement* (Bourdieu and Sayad 1964), and numerous articles. It also forms the basis for three subsequent and widely acknowledged books: *Esquisse*

Algerian intellectuals, and his fieldwork in certain militarily contested areas drew the attention of certain military and civilian authorities. Blacklisted (put on the "red list" of those susceptible to arrest by the French military) he returned France in the fall of 1959 with the help of Raymond Aron, who helped him secure university teaching assistant positions in Paris and Lille.[21]

Even prior to his military service, as well as during it, Bourdieu opposed French colonialism and favored Algerian independence. The extremities of the colonial war and military service forced on Bourdieu a choice: how could a young French intellectual having just completed military service in Algeria respond? Some years later he remarked that "I couldn't be content with just reading books and visiting libraries in a historical situation in which every moment, every political statement, every discussion, every petition, the whole reality was at stake, it was absolutely necessary to be at the heart of events and form one's own opinion, however dangerous it might have been—and dangerous it was" (Honneth, Kocyba, and Schwibs 1986, 39).

Bourdieu (2008e, 18) would respond by becoming a social scientist.[22] He would carry out social scientific research to inform the public of the local realities—an option that he would later contrast sharply to those who responded as public intellectuals by signing public petitions, editorializing against the war, and participating in public demonstrations with Sartre

---

d'une théorie de la pratique (Bourdieu 1972a), its revised and updated translation, *Outline of a Theory of Practice* (Bourdieu 1977a), and *The Logic of Practice* (Bourdieu 1990c), which is a revision and elaboration of *Outline*. Published posthumously is a remarkable set of photographs taken during his 1957–60 Algerian period. They did not appear publically at that time but surely helped frame Bourdieu's sociological eye for the transitions and dislocations experienced by many Algerians during that period of tremendous upheaval. Several give vivid depictions of "dissonant realities" that Bourdieu tried to capture photographically, such as the veiled woman riding a scooter and the visible discomfort of a peasant selling some goods in a city (Schultheis and Frisinghelli 2012, 7–33). As would characterize much of his later work, Bourdieu combined the visual with the textual and statistical in revealing the hidden forces of power.

21. Bourdieu reported in 1994 to Le Sueur (2005, 368) that he needed to go into hiding several times and eventually had to leave Algeria for his own safety, which he also reported to me (interview, Paris, November 1993). See Bourdieu 2008g, 37–58, where Bourdieu recounts a few incidents that his opposition to the war incurred during his military service.

22. Bourdieu's entry into social science was practical and self-taught rather than through formal instruction. This contributed to his interdisciplinary focus, drawing from economics, sociology, ethnology, and anthropology.

being the most prominent example.[23] Reflecting back on that tumultuous period, Bourdieu reports:

> I came to Algeria when I was in the army. After two arduous years during which there was no possibility of doing research I could do some work again. I began to write a book [*The Algerians* (1962a)] with the intention of high-lighting the plight of the Algerian people and, also, that of the French settlers whose situation was no less dramatic, whatever else had to be said about their racism, etc. I was appalled by the gap between the views of French intellectuals about this war and how it should be brought to an end, and my own experiences; the army, the embittered "pieds noir," as well as the military coups, insurrections by the colonizers, the inevitable recourse to de Gaulle, etc. I did of course agree with the actions of some intellectuals—I am thinking here of Sartre, Jeanson, Vidal-Naquet—against torture and for peace, and I tried to contribute in my own way. I was however concerned about the associated utopianism since in my view it was not at all helpful, even for an independent Algeria, to feed a mythical conception of Algerian society. Here again I found myself between camps as far as intellectual life was concerned. (Honneth, Kocyba and Schwibs 1986, 38)

He would use social science to address burning issues surrounding the French-Algerian war.

Doing fieldwork, ethnographic observations, and administering surveys Bourdieu was able to develop an empirically informed social scientific account of both traditional village life among the Kabylia peasants and its disruption and destruction by the colonial system and war. His two earliest "political" texts, "Révolution dans la révolution" (Bourdieu 1961) and "Les sous-prolétaires algériens" (Bourdieu 1962b), spoke directly to the colonial situation and French military involvement in Algeria as he documented the destructive effects of colonialism and the struggle for independence. They were published in two of the most influential public intellectual journals in France at that time: *Esprit* and *Les Temps Modernes*, both carrying articles opposing the war. But these political texts were based on a significant amount of field and survey research. What does his fieldwork during his Algerian period show? I do not attempt an exhaustive presentation of Bourdieu's Algerian work but limit

---

23. The Manifesto of the 121 (September 6, 1960) was the most famous public petition by 121 French intellectuals denouncing torture by the French military and supporting the right to conscience objection to military service. Sartre and De Beauvoir signed.

consideration to just a few important themes that illustrate his emerging political sociological orientation.[24]

A first objective was to give testimony to the plight of those suffering most from the colonial regime and the war. Reflecting back on his Algerian research forty years later Bourdieu says that it was motivated not simply by political but also "civic" reasons (Bourdieu 2008e, 21).[25] His 1958 book, *The Algerians* (1962a), was a politically pedagogic text, which he wrote in order "to tell the French, and especially people on the left, what was really going on in a country of which they often knew next to nothing" (Bourdieu 2008g, 39–40).[26] It was work that combined specifically intellectual concerns with public issues. In the background one can see some of his Algerian research reflecting the political sociology theme of transition from traditional to modern societies. It is informed by classical conceptual traditions that attempt to interpret that transition in terms of the Durkheimian distinction between mechanical and organic solidarity and the Weberian debate with Marxism over the relative significance of culture and economic factors in historical change. What seems key and relevant for political sociology is that his discussion of contact between civilizations, cultural assimilation, and integration is situated within the context of a colonial system based upon economic superiority, cultural imperialism, and brute force. He documented how traditional peasant life was rapidly undergoing transformation by the imposed market economy, contact with Western culture, and particularly by the war itself. There were also the disorienting effects of the French military's forced resettlement policy of uprooting peasant villages and herding villagers into camps organized under French military surveillance and control.[27] Peasants also

24. See Calhoun 2006, Goodman and Silverstein 2009, Lane 2000, and Yacine 2008b for a more complete assessment of Bourdieu's time in Algeria. Go (2011) makes a compelling argument that in his Algerian work Bourdieu articulates a "*theory* of colonialism" that offers for the time original "insights into racial domination and colonial cultures."

25. But as Bourdieu (2000e, 186) would later stress, a civic mission of informing is nonetheless a strategy in the symbolic struggle for how best to understand the social world and therefore an expression of symbolic power. It is political.

26. In a 1994 interview Lévi-Strauss expressed a similar view: too many French intellectuals entered the debates over the French-Algerian war without any informed knowledge of local social and cultural conditions in Algeria (Le Sueur 2005, 366–67).

27. Bourdieu documents the social and cultural effects of this French military pacification program but his work did not enter into the public debate over these camps. Michel Rocard (the same age as Bourdieu) was at the time a senior public official and published a report in April 1959 revealing to the French public the reality of the resettlement camps, where among

flocked to impoverished conditions in the old quarters and new shanty-towns in the coastal cities in search of employment (though there was in fact very little) and to escape the conflict in the countryside. This created a tremendous internal migration; Bourdieu estimated in 1958 that since 1954 one in three Algerians no longer occupied their home residence.

Bourdieu documented the disorientation, fatalism, and despair that resulted from this massive population displacement. The colonial system and the war uprooted large portions of the Algerian population from their traditional social and cultural moorings, turned them into objects of contempt, and devastated their prospects for the future. French colonial practices treated the Algerians as either without a distinctive cultural base or one that that was negatively charged and needed to be changed; either Algeria lacked a culture or it was hopelessly backward. The image and identity of the Algerian was filtered through that system of domination. It had the effect of creating fatalistic attitudes toward events and developments over which the people had little control. But it also elicited resistance. While Bourdieu did not engage much in recent debates over identity politics, he was clearly attentive to the importance of individual and collective identity in political life and that is quite visible in some of his early fieldwork observations in Algeria. Writing before the contemporary debates surrounding "identity politics" began, Bourdieu observes already in 1958 how in the face of French colonialism and military occupation recourse by many Algerians to "traditional traditionalism" (Bourdieu 1962a, 155) functioned as expressions of resistance to the externally imposed values and rules of conduct imposed by colonialism. Emblematic of this resistance was the use of the veil. Bourdieu notes that

> the veil has the role of a symbol that expresses both an alliance and an exclusion; it is primarily a defense of the inner self and a protection against any intrusion from without. But in addition to this, by the wearing of the veil, the Algerian woman is also creating a situation of non-reciprocity; like a cheating gambler, she can see without being observed; and it is through her that the whole of this dominated society is symbolically refusing to establish any reciprocal relations, is looking on without letting itself be observed. The veil

---

other things children were dying of malnutrition (Yacine 2003, 344). Rocard almost lost his job as a result but he continued as a key leader in Socialist politics and eventually became a prime minister under Mitterrand and won Bourdieu's respect for some of his policies, particularly his positive response to the movement for independence in New Caledonia.

is the most obvious symbol of this closing in upon oneself, and the Europeans have always obscurely felt it to be such. In this way it becomes evident why all attempts at assimilation have taken the discarding of the veil to be their primary objective. (158)

His insight anticipates some of the issues debated today in France about the veil.

In "The Revolution within the Evolution" (1962a, 145–92) Bourdieu argues that the conflict was not a civil war or a war between France and Algeria but a tragedy stemming from the colonial system itself; it was an expression of revolt against the tremendous inequalities and loss of identity generated by this structure of domination. Bourdieu placed blame for disruption and violence directly on the colonial system. In doing so Bourdieu challenged the prevailing French ethnology of the time that simply accepted the colonial arrangements.[28] Bourdieu was one of the few French ethnologists at that time to expose through social scientific analysis the effects of the violence created by the colonial system and the war on everyday life.[29]

But the aim of his research was not only to address great intellectual issues or to inform French and Algerian leadership of the suffering of Algerian peasants. Bourdieu also engaged in his research key issues animating the intellectual left debate in France over the war. Vidal-Naquet (1986) identifies among French intellectuals and antiwar activists three ideal types of opposition to the French-Algerian war: Dreyfusards, Bolsheviks, and Third Worldists.[30] The Dreyfusards, inspired by the historical struggle of Emile Zola and other leading intellectuals in defense of Captain Dreyfus, wrongly accused of treason in the late nineteenth century, saw the colonial war—particularly the torture and massacres carried out by French forces—as violating fundamental national values of equality and liberty of the French Republic. They were initially mobilized by the French military torture of two French civilians, Henri Alleg and Maurice

28. He opposed Jacques Soustelle, then governor-general of Algeria and an anthropologist, who promoted the official idea of "integration" rather than independence.

29. George Balandier (1970, 1985) was another of the early French sociologist/anthropologists who broke with established French ethnology by condemning French colonialism in Sub-Saharan Africa.

30. Vidal-Naquet presents these as ideal types emphasizing important variations within each camp and that numerous individuals crossed the boundaries.

Audin. The Bolshevik current brought a Marxist class analysis to the conflict and viewed the war as an expression of international revolution that drew inspiration from the Russian October revolution. They tended to support the FLN (Front National de Libération) and included the Francis Jeanson network that clandestinely channeled financial, material, and personnel support for the FLN. The Third World current emphasized Algerian nationalism and saw the war as a national struggle for liberation, emphasizing the specific conditions of Algeria as a third world country. Many Third Worldists drew more inspiration from Maoism than the October Revolution. They tended to accept uncritically Algerian nationalism as a unifying and driving force for independence. Here is where Vidal-Naquet situates Jean-Paul Sartre and Frantz Fanon.

Because of the imposed upheaval on traditional society, Bourdieu sees the potential for revolutionary change in Algeria, but his fieldwork also identifies a number of social and cultural conditions that do not fit with a Marxist class analysis, nor does he celebrate violent struggle centered on nationalism. The Marxist analysis of Algeria, whether inspired by idealized images of the Russian or Chinese revolutions, might animate left political debate in Paris, but fundamentally misunderstood the social and cultural conditions in Algeria. Bourdieu does not see the struggle in strictly class terms; indeed, the colonial system he describes as a kind of caste system that sharply segregated along racial lines Algerians from French whites. Indeed, it was a racialized system of violence. Moreover, he sees the national struggle limited by deeply seeded cultural and fractured identities, the continuing importance of Islam, and a disenfranchised subproletariat whose material conditions and corresponding vacillating consciousness between resignation and revolt compromised its potential to confront realistically the challenges of founding a genuinely new social order. The Algerian subproletarian, an uprooted peasantry, did not constitute a revolutionary force as theorized by Fanon and the FLN.[31] Bourdieu saw Fanon's celebration of violent Third World nationalist struggle as a dangerous utopian vision that masked the underlying legacies of cultural traditionalism, albeit diverse, and the profound disorienting and uprooting experience of the war itself. Bourdieu had researched Algerian peasant attitudes toward time and found that they were simply not the incipient revolutionaries that many—particularly those influenced by Maoism—in the anticolonial

31. At the time the writings of Fanon (1965, 1967), particularly *The Wretched of the Earth* (2004), were widely discussed and followed by many.

struggle assumed or theorized them to be (Bourdieu 2008e, 22–23). Again combining theoretical and political aims, he viewed his research as

> trying to find out something that had not previously been clarified in the theo-retical tradition: what, ultimately, distinguishes the proletariat from the sub-proletariat? I have tried to show that this difference resides on the level of the economic conditions of the possibility of modes of action based on rational anticipation, with revolutionary expectations being one of its dimensions; this view was arrived at through the analysis of the economic and social conditions underlying the emergence of economic-calculative orientations in relation to actual economic activities, as well as fertility, etc. (Honneth, Kocyba and Schwibs 1986, 39–40)[32]

The sociology of knowledge question concerned under what conditions does a rational, calculating attitude toward the future occur?

But the political implications were obvious: the Algerian uprooted peasantry and urban disenfranchised masses were not revolutionary in the sense they could be assimilated into the Marxist view of the revolutionary potential of the industrial working class or of a revolutionary peasantry popular in Maoist thinking. Nor did they fit into a kind of black national-ism that Fanon idealized. For Bourdieu this Marxist analysis did not apply to Algeria, and French intellectuals like Sartre were responding in opposi-tion to the French Algeria war more through the lens of Marxism and a utopian vision of life after the revolution than by an informed social and cultural understanding of the consciousness and practices of uprooted and disenfranchised Algerian masses.

The Algerian experience created important methodological implica-tions as well for Bourdieu's subsequent work and for political sociology. Doing fieldwork in a war-torn situation instilled in Bourdieu a keen at-tentiveness to the complex relationship between the observer and the ob-served, the interviewer and the interviewee, and heightened therefore the need for a reflexive practice of social science that became a trademark of his sociology. As he (2008g, 50) put it,

---

32. His theoretical interests reflected his earlier interest as an École Normale Supérieure student in Husserl's phenomenological reflection on time and his reading in Max Weber's *Protestant Ethic and the Spirit of Capitalism* on changing attitudes toward time and work that accompanied capitalist development.

to conduct sociological fieldwork in a situation of war compels one to reflect on everything, to monitor everything, and in particular all that is taken for granted in the ordinary relation between the observer and the informant, the interviewers and the interviewed: the identity of the interviewers, even the composition of the interviewing unit—one or two persons, and, if two, a man and a woman, an Algerian man and a Frenchwoman, etc.

It is therefore understandable that this critical vigilance would later find professional opinion polling and its use in social scientific inquiry so problematic. If knowledge reflects the conditions of its creation, observation, and formalization, the critical implications for opinion polls and formal surveys of political opinion are obvious: opinion polls reflect constructed knowledge by elites rather than genuine views of the public. Bourdieu would later on offer some research showing public opinion to be correlated with the unequal distribution of cultural capital, social classes, and gender roles (Bourdieu 1984a, 397–465).

Doing social scientific study during the colonial war in Algeria disabused Bourdieu of the idea of positivist notions of neutrality (Bourdieu 2008b, 5). Social science could not be freed of all ethical and political content in a colonial situation. From this "shock of Algeria" Bourdieu would extend this thinking to other objects of empirical inquiry. However, Bourdieu does not give up on science because of value commitments or because of his acute awareness of the gap between the social scientific observer and the person observed. Rather than moralizing on the limits of social investigation as science, he calls for a critical reflexivity to enhance the science of critical observation. Rather than giving up on social science because it cannot escape the effects of power, Bourdieu proposes to make power itself the object of social scientific investigation.

Despite Bourdieu's considerable social scientific efforts, his work had no visible impact on French policy. Nor was Bourdieu a public figure in the mobilized political opposition to the war. He did not sign petitions, participate in public demonstrations, or editorialize in the newspapers and his classic works *Outline of a Theory of Practice* and *The Logic of Practice* that develop his theory of practice draw on the traditional social structures and culture of Kabyle society largely independent of French colonialism.[33]

33. This opens his Algeria work to the charge that he neglects an adequate analysis of colonialism but Go (2011), who offers a more informed evaluation of this early work, discounts this criticism.

Reflecting back on his 1958 book he concluded that it "made no impact at all . . . ; it was the poor attempt of an outsider" (Honneth, Kocyba, and Schwibs 1986, 39). Still, the Algerian experience proved decisive for him. He would return to his Algerian research again and again such as he does in *Masculine Domination* (2001c). He would support the work of his colleague Abdelmalek Sayad (2004) and other Algerian social scientists like Tassadit Yacine (1993). He would in 1985 support Mouloud Mammeri in founding the Berber Studies journal, *Awal*, at the Centre for the Study of Amazigh Culture (CERAM) in Paris. He would organize support for Algerian intellectuals persecuted by the subsequent authoritarian regime in Algeria. And his own subsequent work and political involvements would reflect themes, dispositions, and strategies forged in his early experience in that country.

The Class Politics of French Education

In spite of the political tumult of the French-Algeria war and the ensuing fall of the Fourth Republic, the French economy entered a period of rapid modernization and growth following the humiliating defeat and occupation in World War II. Under the guidance of centralized state planning the economic boom brought promises of a more equal and inclusive society. Educational expansion was one key public policy instrument implemented during that period.

Bourdieu (and Passeron) was one of the first sociologists to take a critical look at the popular post–World War II public policies of expanding educational opportunity in order to reduce social inequality. In spite of the popular view of education as an instrument of opportunity and mobility for the naturally talented, Bourdieu's sociology of education documented the persistent class inequalities in French educational achievement and he laid much of the blame on traditional pedagogical practices that reproduced cultural inequalities rather than reducing them. Traditional pedagogical practices, Bourdieu argued, actually contribute to the maintenance of an inegalitarian social system by allowing inherited cultural differences to shape academic achievement and occupational attainment. One of Bourdieu's first works on French education, *The Inheritors* (Bourdieu and Passeron 1979), documents the striking overrepresentation of middle- and upper-class students in French universities despite years of education expansion. Numerous subsequent analyses and publications furthered that critical assessment of French education and helped animate broad debate

among social researchers, state planners, teachers, and the broader educated public over education policy and inequality. While Bourdieu's sociology of education did not foster significant public policy reform by state
administrators and political leaders, it did sensitize particularly educators and education researchers to the unfulfilled promises of the postwar
education expansion. Indeed, it provoked sharp debate as *Reproduction*
was widely criticized for being too fatalistic about the social-class consequences of expanded educational opportunity. But many educators and
researchers accepted the criticism as an accurate account of what needed
to be changed. His data and arguments debunked the cherished belief in
the "liberating" effects of educational opportunity.[34] Here, as in Algeria,
Bourdieu spoke to a critical public issue through his sociological research
not through public petition or demonstration. But one work, *The Inheritors*, did have an unexpected effect on the public—the May 1968 student
revolt.

May 1968 ushered in a series of student protests and a general strike that
brought France to a standstill and eventually obliged President Charles
de Gaulle to dissolve the National Assembly and call for new parliamen-
tary elections. Bourdieu himself remained very ambivalent about the student movement whereas many other French intellectuals, such as Michel
Foucault and Alain Touraine, actively embraced it. While Bourdieu was
sharply critical of the conditions in which students and professors worked,
he rejected the strong utopian elements of the student movement and remained skeptical of any real significance it might have for effective and
lasting political change. Nevertheless, his book *The Inheritors* (Bourdieu
and Passeron 1979) contributed to the growing critical consciousness of
class inequalities in French higher education and contributed to the May
1968 student movement.[35] That work documents a striking statistical relationship between social origins and school success and shows that those

34. It is important to recall the symbolic importance of the role of secular public education
in France at the time when Bourdieu and Passeron offered their criticism. The secular and
tuition-free public education system (from primary to university and graduate and professional schools) was a crowning achievement of the Third Republic in its conflict with the
Church, the monarchy, and conservatism. In the eyes of many French, the school was a symbol
of egalitarianism against elitism, of democracy against the monarchy, and of liberty against
the control of the Church and the dominant classes. Bourdieu and Passeron attacked these
fundamental assumptions through critically argued empirical assessment of actual behavior.

35. *The Inheritors* contributed to French student-leader political awareness of social and
cultural inequities within the French university system (Lindenberg 1975, 13). Raymond Aron

students endowed with cultural capital from their family background are most favored by the school system. Moreover, a meritocratic ideology whereby the school ostensibly rewards students on the basis of their natural talents and efforts masks the process by which social privilege is reinforced by the transmission of cultural capital and thereby legitimates the inegalitarian social order. *Reproduction* (Bourdieu and Passeron 1977) continues and expands empirically and theoretically this unmasking work by informing a generation of labor leaders and activists as well as students, teachers, and sociologists of the subtle inequalities in education. That work argues that May '68 had little effect on the authoritarian structure of pedagogical relations in the French university. *Reproduction* provoked considerable debate both within the scholarly community and beyond.

Numerous articles and two key books, *Homo Academicus* (Bourdieu 1988b) and *The State Nobility* (Bourdieu 1996d) on French education would follow. *The State Nobility* in particular would document the increasing social elitism of French higher education and the recruitment of its high-ranking civil servants and corporate leaders. That work is significant in showing Bourdieu's understanding of the French state and political field and I return to it later in the chapter.

Opinion Polling: Undemocratic Action

Early work on the social and cultural origins of public opinion emphasizes a sharp division between political professionals and lay persons over who actually produces political opinion (Bourdieu 1971b, 1972b). This work inaugurates a political sociology theme that will be developed later: the social closure of French political life to only those with the requisite cultural capital and social competence to participate.[36]

In a 1971 paper, "Public Opinion Does Not Exist," Bourdieu (1993g) formulates key themes that would characterize both his critical analysis of established political processes and institutions in the modern liberal democracies and a course of action for the critical intellectual.[37] They also show the kinds of public intellectual posture he will adopt.[38] He

---

would later characterize *The Inheritors* as one of the catalysts of the May student movement (Poupeau and Discepolo 2005, 68).

36. See Bourdieu 1977b; 1984a, 397–465.

37. The paper was reprinted in *Les Temps Modernes* 318 (1973): 1292–1309.

38. These arguments are echoed and elaborated in Bourdieu 2000b, which was delivered in November 1973 before the French Association of Political Science, in "Questions de poli-

challenges three fundamental assumptions of opinion polling; namely, that everyone can and does have an opinion, that all opinions are equal, and that there is a prior consensus on the issues worthy of being discussed. Examining nonresponse rates Bourdieu finds that responses depend on political competence (knowledge of political issues) and socially recognized authority (the status right to hold a political opinion), which vary by social class, education, and gender.[39] Not all opinions are equal since opinion is constructed, not simply elicited, and opinion makers are better situated than ordinary citizens to shape what is considered to be worthy of being opined. The aggregation of all opinions into an average distorts that reality. Moreover, pollster questions do not simply gather or elicit opinion; they create it by imposing questions that are deemed worthy of being asked. Questions are imposed by polling agencies. They do not measure what respondents spontaneously consider to be important to their lives. Furthermore, polling agencies are too subordinated to political interests. They poll what is of interest to the political career preoccupations of professional politicians. Therefore, public opinion polls in fact measure an "*artifact* of public opinion," not the real thing (1993g, 157). "In real situations, opinions are forces and relations between opinions are power relations between groups" whereas what currently passes as public opinion "is a pure and simple *artifact* whose function is to disguise the fact that the state of opinion at a given time is a system of forces, tensions, and that nothing more inadequately expresses the state of opinion than a percentage" (155).

These criticisms lead Bourdieu to conclude that opinion polling is seldom an objective instrument measuring political knowledge. It is not simply a technical instrument for encouraging and measuring democratic expression. Rather, it is a form of political action designed to shape public debate along the interests of the political class and to devalue other

---

tique" (Bourdieu 1977b), and in the "Culture and Politics" chapter in *Distinction* (Bourdieu 1984a).

39. Bourdieu writes that "the propensity and ability to raise interests and experiences to the order of political discourse, to seek coherence in opinions and to integrate one's whole set of attitudes around explicit political principles, in fact depends very closely on educational capital and, secondarily, on overall capital composition, increasing with the relative weight of cultural capital as against economic capital" (1984a, 417–18).

He identifies three different modes of producing explicitly political discourse: the first mode would originate from the "class ethos" that would generate responses from the practical, everyday considerations of social existence; the second mode would reflect a political "slant" from a systematic and explicitly held political view; and the third mode would be the party line provided by a political organization.

possible forms of democratic action such as demonstrations, strikes, and sit-ins, those most frequently employed by social movements that challenge the monopolizing control of established political leadership. Polls are in fact used by political and administrative elites to justify their claims to authority. Opinion polling Bourdieu views as a political weapon against the demobilized masses. Opinion polling, like voting, contributes to the political dispossession of the mass of citizens. This criticism anticipates the growing gap that Bourdieu increasingly criticizes between the class of political professionals and citizens who become dispossessed of their authentic mode of political expression and therefore depoliticized. He would later see his work in *The Weight of the World* (Bourdieu et al. 1999) as a more genuine expression of the experience of social suffering and isolation than what French pollsters were picking up. Through probing interview questions ("participant objectification") Bourdieu and colleagues worked to get interviewees to come to terms with their experiences of social exclusion.

This critical political sociology of the dominant ideology through opinion polling occurred in the 1970s when the modernization of French capitalism was in full swing. Numerous "administrative researchers" and "scientific researchers," operating from within scholarly institutions, were in fact responding to state demands for aid in that overarching political project. Bourdieu sees them as an expression of heteronomy within and threat to the autonomy of the scientific field. At stake for Bourdieu is the autonomy of sociology as an academic discipline that should develop its own research questions at a critical distance from immediate and direct political and social demand. Bourdieu contends that public-opinion polling is too subordinated to political and administrative demands and dominated by an applied orientation represented in the 1970s by Jean Stoetzel, a social psychologist, who imported into France survey research techniques from the United States.[40]

Bourdieu's defense of the autonomy of sociology as science and the social scientist as a critical intellectual finds expression in his sharp criticism of those he dubs the "doxosophists," those political journalists, media intellectuals, pollsters, and political commentators who intervene in public debate not as scholarly experts but as "semi-scholars" with general ideas and borrowings from social science to achieve media-oriented symbolic capital rather than to meet the challenges of scientific peer review

40. Jean Stoetzel (1919–87) was the founder not only of the *Revue française de sociologie* (the main journal of the French professional sociological association) but also of the French Institute of Public Opinion (IFOP), a leading polling firm in France.

(Bourdieu 1972b; 2008c, 216).[41] They manufacture, manage, and propagate ideology serving dominant group interests by giving to political and state administrative powers a legitimating authority over the terms of public debate and public opinion. The challenge of critical social science is to mark its distance from pseudo-scholarly justifications of the social order such as opinion polling.

In a 1973 paper, "Forms d'action politique et mode d'existence des groups," delivered to the French Political Science Association, Bourdieu (2000b, 81–88) draws on Durkheim's familiar individualism/corporatism opposition to identify two general forms of political action: a statistical aggregation of atomized individual choices versus a collective interactional model in which opinions are produced out of collective interaction and delegated representation so that individual and collective interests are forged and represented.[42] While not subscribing to Durkheim's corporatism, Bourdieu argues that Durkheim raises the key political philosophy question: what is or should be political action? And for Bourdieu, liberal political theory does not provide a satisfactory answer. He writes that

> liberal philosophy identifies political action with solitary, even silent and secret, action, whose paradigm is voting, the "purchase" of a party offering in the secrecy of the voting booth. In doing so, it reduces the group to the series, the mobilized opinion of an organized or interdependent collectivity to the statistical aggregation of individually expressed opinions. One thinks of the utopia of Milton Friedman [for whom] political action finds itself reduced to a form of economic action. The logic of the market, or of voting, which is to say the aggregation of individual strategies, imposes itself whenever groups are reduced to the state of aggregates—or, if you prefer, whenever they are demobilized." (Bourdieu 2000b, 83; my translation)

Genuine politics begins for Bourdieu with group mobilization in which interests are collectively formulated into discourse and given representation by delegated leadership.

41. Paraphrasing Plato, Bourdieu describes them as those who "appear to be scientists or are scientists of appearances" (Bourdieu 2008c, 216). Likened to the Trojan horse, they introduce heteronomy into the field of cultural production and represent "the worst threat to the autonomy of cultural production." They introduce media visibility and public notoriety into the cultural arena without sufficient regard for peer review. Bernard-Henri Lévy epitomizes in Bourdieu's view this kind of heteronomy in the field of cultural production.

42. The text Bourdieu cites is Durkheim's discussion of democracy in Durkheim 1958, 105–6.

This early 1973 statement outlining the two forms of political action and Bourdieu's clear preference for the collective mode signals that Bourdieu's preferred line of political activism will not follow an electoral strategy but more that of social movements. Consistent with this view he spent little time studying elections and political parties. His focus would be more on those fundamental social conditions that he found to be blocked or under-represented by the normal political channels in France but would pro-vide on key occasions resources for significant social movements. Though Bourdieu is not known as a social movement theorist his criticism of estab-lished processes of political representation through the vote and opinion polls and his public intellectual activism of his later years show him to be much more oriented toward social movements than usually thought.

Defending the Autonomy of the Intellectual Field

Bourdieu's Change in Intellectual Field Position

During the 1960s and 1970s Bourdieu's position within the French intel-lectual field changed little by little. He accumulated intellectual prestige from his extensive critical social scientific investigations and publications, not university teaching or administration. He invested entirely in scholarly and intellectual capital that crossed traditional disciplinary boundaries yet remained oriented primarily for peers. He did virtually no applied work for industry or government.[43] These efforts were institutionally successful. He developed his center, introduced his journal, and expanded consider-ably his edited series with Éditions de Minuit. He helped increase the scientific legitimacy of sociology and his own central position in French social science. His efforts were aided by the rising fortunes of the social sciences in France during the sixties and seventies with the considerable expansion in funding and recruitment of researchers, teachers, and stu-dents in the social sciences.[44]

43. One exception is the research on photography reported in Bourdieu et al. 1965 that received financial support from Kodak-Pathé. However, the book is thoroughly sociological without the kinds of market indicators that would interest a private firm.

44. This was the golden age of post–World War II French sociology. The social sciences captured much of the attraction that had previously been accorded to philosophy and the humanities.

In 1981 he was elected to the chair of sociology at the intellectually prestigious Collège de France.[45] The Collège provided him additional institutional resources and considerable symbolic capital. Access to the Collège was made possible by his tremendous publication output, such as *Distinction* (Bourdieu 1984a), *Outline of a Theory of Practice* (Bourdieu 1977a), and *The Logic of Practice* (Bourdieu 1990c), considered classics in twentieth-century sociology.[46] Entry into the Collège represented an important step in securing the scientific legitimation of his work. The Collège secured for him a prestigious institutional position from which he also could speak beyond the community of intellectual peers. It facilitated his capacity to play the leading public intellectual role that he would come to play in the nineties. His central position in the French scientific community was further solidified in 1993 with the Centre national de la recherche scientifique (CNRS) Gold Medal award by which the French scientific community gave recognition to sociology as a science and to Bourdieu as its most recognized spokesperson.[47]

Intellectual Field Changes

Bourdieu's accumulated symbolic capital within an enlarged social scientific field accompanied a broader mutation in the French intellectual field. Sartre had made intellectual political activism a virtual rite of necessity for French left intellectuals after World War II. The humanist and literary culture that provided the basis for Sartre's notoriety came under attack from the rising social sciences and particularly the success of structuralism. Increased intellectual specialization and the displacement of the humanities by the social sciences, particularly by structuralism, in relative importance in French education undercut the traditional cultural base for Sartre's

45. The Collège stands at the summit of the research sector of French intellectual life. Bourdieu was elected to the Chair of Sociology, a position held earlier by Marcel Mauss and Raymond Aron.

46. An International Sociological Association 1997 survey placed *Distinction* (1984a) as the sixth most important social scientific work of the twentieth century. *The Logic of Practice* (1990c) was ranked fortieth and *Reproduction* forty-eighth. The only other French works to make it into the top fifty were Emile Durkheim's *The Elementary Forms of Religious Life* (thirteenth), *The Division of Labor in Society* (thirty-fourth), and *The Rules of Sociological Method* (thirty-fifth), and Michel Foucault's *Discipline and Punish: The Birth of the Prison* (sixteenth). http://www.ISA-sociology.org/books/ (accessed August 17, 2009).

47. Lévi-Strauss is the only other social scientist having received this coveted award.

style of the public intellectual in France. Following Sartre, Foucault had been able to build from that declining traditional base but only by following a "specific intellectual" model of limited, specialized involvements in selected public issues, such as prison reform, rather than imitating the "total intellectual" model of speaking on all the issues of the day as idealized by Sartre. But with Foucault's death in 1984 that tradition of a public intellectual in France was called into question. Who would replace him? Was the French tradition of the leading intellectual, epitomized by Zola, Sartre, and Foucault, finished?[48] Some asked if Bourdieu might be next in line but the answer would not come immediately but would await further intellectual field and political developments (Ross 1987).

The French intellectual field changed in other ways, leading Bourdieu to devote more attention to struggles external to the research community. Expanding cultural markets also contributed to weakening the institutional base of the critical intellectual tradition. Careers in the media, management, and advertising became more attractive to highly educated French men and women than secondary school and university teaching. Moreover, the expansion of student enrollments without commensurate expansion of facilities and support services plus extensive politicization of the university milieu after May 1968 led many to see the universities as undesirable places for careers.

This growth in possibilities for cultural consumption and production beyond the walls of the university changed the structure of power and control of cultural life in France. Prior to the 1960s the university professor could enter public debate under controlled conditions where he or she could exercise some control over the mode of transmission and reception of his views. The rapid expansion and diversification of cultural markets changed that. Symbolized by the events of May 1968, the traditional monopolizing power for the academic intellectual was lost.[49] French cultural and political life became more mass media–oriented: the number of potential competitors in the public arena increased considerably, television played a greater role, and journalists increasingly shaped the form and content of intellectual debate in France. Numerous highly educated French men and women broke down the traditional boundaries between the university, government administration, and private and

48. This was the view, for example, of Raymond Boudon (personal communication, Paris, 1988).

49. This point is suggested by Mounier (2001, 217–18).

public enterprise by taking on multiple roles of teacher, consultant, and journalist.[50] Growing numbers of academics oriented their writing toward high-visibility media outlets. In Bourdieu's view, intellectual work became increasingly corrupted by being oriented toward the media rather than scholarly peer review.[51] Whereas the traditional critical intellectual was rooted in the elite academic culture of École Normale Supérieure, the new participants in public debate were increasingly graduates of École Nationale d'Administration and Institut des Sciences Politiques (Paris) who shared cultural orientations more favorable to markets and rational management.[52] Also emerged several policy oriented think-tanks, such as the Foundation Saint-Simon, which cultivated close contact among corporate executives, senior government officials, journalists, and policy consultants.[53] This new type of cultural orientation came to overshadow the critical discourse of the political left intellectual and the institutional order that had fostered it. For Bourdieu, this institutional shift facilitated the rise in neoliberal thinking in the french media and political field that he so sharply criticized in his later years.

The role of the mass media, particularly television, became vastly more important in French political life through the eighties and nineties. Bourdieu saw increasing interrelations between politics and the media, between the journalistic field and the political field. His research colleague Patrick Champagne (1979) documented that increasingly tight nexus leading Champagne to refer to the "journalistic-political field." Champagne's

50. See Boltanski 1973.

51. It became more acceptable to a growing number of French academics (particularly those teaching within the political studies institutes) to write for and appear in the mass media. Attitudes had changed considerably from when Raymond Aron's appointment at the Sorbonne in 1955 had caused concern among some French scholars precisely because Aron wrote for the leading center-right newspaper, *Le Figaro*.

52. See "Le pouvoir n'est plus rue-d'Ulm mais à l'ENA" where Bourdieu (1989c) indicates that underlying the monopolizing power of corporate and administrative elites is a shift in power from the École Normale Supérieure (formative site of traditional intellectuals, such as Sartre, Foucault, and Bourdieu himself) toward the École Nationale d'Administration (formative site of senior public and private managers in France today).

53. The Fondation Saint-Simon was created in 1982 at the initiative of François Furet, Pierre Rosanvallon, Emmanuel Le Roy Ladurie, Simon and Pierre Nora, Alain Minc, and Roger Fauroux. The objective was to build bridges between the academic world and that of big business and top-level state administrators. Participants generally favored relying more heavily on market mechanisms than state regulations to distribute valued resources. See Halimi 1995, Laurent 1998 for critical descriptions.

work shows that this media/political arena became increasingly insulated from external influences and conflicts as it grew more and more homogeneous sociologically and unified ideologically. By a kind of "circular logic," politicians and journalists fed off of each other: both reacted to public issues they themselves had constructed, often through opinion polling. Bourdieu himself analyzed this evolution in some of his work, as have others, such as Régis Debray, whose denunciation of the media orientation of many French intellectuals follows in many respects Bourdieu's views.[54] In this newly developing intellectual market the implicit critical dimension of the scholarly social scientific text became eclipsed by other contenders more able to attract attention in the new mass-media arena of public debate.

Disillusionment with the Political Left in Power during the 1980s and 1990s

Changes in his institutional position and the broader social/political context only partially explain Bourdieu's rapid ascendency to the public intellectual position that seemed to many to be in line with that previously held by Sartre and Foucault. Personal experience, reflection, and choice in both research and in relationship to the François Mitterrand presidency shaped a change in view and strategy of relations between sociology and politics, a change in the form of strategic action Bourdieu believed a critical sociologist should take.

Bourdieu had always been on the political left and hence in the political opposition during the center-right governments of the Fifth Republic up until the election of François Mitterrand in 1981. The arrival of the socialist-communist coalition to power in 1981 opened up the possibility of a more effective rapport of communication between left intellectuals and the new left government; it created the possibility of implementing Bourdieu's ideal of more rational and scientific based public policy less governed by parochial economic and political interests. During the Mitterrand years Bourdieu did contribute two different reports on education. In 1985 he published the Collège de France report "Propositions pour un enseignment de l'avenir" (Propositions for an Education of the Future) in response to the request by Mitterrand that the Collège reflect on the

54. See Bourdieu 1985a, 1998e; Debray 1981.

fundamental principles of education.[55] With François Gros, he presided
over a commission set up by the Socialist minister of education, Lionel
Jospin, on the contents of education and published its report "Principles
pour une reflexion sur les contenues d'enseignement" (Principles for a
Reflection on the Contents of Instruction) in 1989.[56] Thus, on a few occasions during the 1980s Bourdieu functioned as an expert advising political
authority under a socialist government. But one could hardly characterize
him as assuming a major advisory role to the left government. Bourdieu
himself was far too critical of power and too fearful of falling into an intellectual servitude role to political leadership to join in any official way the
Mitterrand government.[57] Indeed, he proved to be a sharp critic of the
various left governments formed under Mitterrand and later in "cohabita-
tion" with the center-right leadership of Jacques Chirac as prime minister
under the Mitterrand presidency. He became disillusioned with the left
government, coming to the conclusion that it was no better able than the
right to hear the voice of reason and science. The political class of the left
socialist government was as socially and ideologically closed as was that of
the previous center-right regimes.[58] His disillusionment with the French

55. Bourdieu later sharply criticized the way this report was used by Mitterrand largely
to legitimate his presidential campaign in 1988 while failing to adopt any substantial reforms
proposed by the report. The report received considerable attention both in France and abroad
but brought no policy reform by the Socialist government. However, the report was acknowledged and approved by the CFDT (the socialist-oriented trade union in France) and supported by the SGEN (a teachers' union).

56. Bourdieu accepted work with the commission despite his frustration with the first
report because of his respect for the socialist prime minister Michel Rocard (personal communication, Franck Poupeau, Paris, June 6, 2002). This report proposed greater interdisciplinary
collaboration and improved pedagogy to reach a wider spectrum of students but the Socialist
government failed to implement its recommendations.

57. In this respect, he was quite different from Britain's leading sociologist, Anthony Giddens, who accepted a formal role in Tony Blair's labor government in the United Kingdom.

58. His reluctance to break totally with the regime before the early 1990s can be seen in
the famous statement, "La virtue civile," which he wrote in September 1988 in *Le monde* in
which he came to the support of Prime Minister Michel Rocard (1988–91) for the way Rocard
handled the movement for independence in New Caledonia. The statement, however, also
reflects a growing concern of his relationship to the Mitterrand presidency, a concern that asks
what are the necessary conditions—and how can they be created—for the voice of science
and rationality to be heard by political leaders. This theme shows both his growing skepticism and lingering hope for the French left at the end of the 1980s and very early 1990s to do
something different from the previous center-right regimes.

Socialists helped prepare him for the public intellectual role he would play in the 1990s.

A Shift in View and Strategy

Personal experience of having researched the social effects of neoliberal economic policies in France and growing disillusionment with the left government under Mitterrand led Bourdieu to modify his view of the political effects of critical social scientific research. The ideal that a sociology of power would unmask and debunk power relations and lead to their transformation came to appear overly optimistic. This ideal had guided the work on the French elite system of the *grandes écoles* culminating in the 1989 publication of *The State Nobility*. That research exposed as never before the power relations buttressing the elite system of the grandes écoles. The book received considerable media attention but no significant response from French Socialist political leadership. No significant reform of the grandes écoles was undertaken in response to their increasingly class-based character, in recruitment, curriculum, and pedagogy that Bourdieu critically documented. Something more needed to be done.[59] While Bourdieu never backed away from the debunking ideal of critical social science as an act of resistance, he began to seek out more direct forms of political intervention and work increasingly toward developing collective expressions of intellectual criticism of existing power arrangements.

Indicative of Bourdieu's changing consciousness regarding the political vocation of the sociologist is his observation that the professionalization of sociology as science resulted in the loss of the classical political function emphasized by the early social theorists. Bourdieu writes in 1993 that

> in fact, one can say, to simplify a little, that the social sciences paid dearly to gain recognition as science (which remains contested). By a self censure that constitutes a veritable self-mutilation, sociologists—beginning with me, who frequently denounced the temptation of social prophesying and philosophizing—refused all opportunity to propose "ideal and global" representations

59. I recall a conversation with Bourdieu in Paris on November 23, 1993, when in response to my query about the reception of *The State Nobility* he shrugged and pointed out that while nothing significant had happened in France, by contrast, the book was receiving considerable attention in Germany!

of the social world, as if such would signal a lack of sufficient embrace of scientific morality and thereby discredit the author. (Bourdieu 2000f, 104; my translation)

Here Bourdieu speaks of that loss in terms of a regrettable sacrifice both personally and professionally. By the early 1990s, he no longer accepts this "scientistic abdication, which ruins political conviction," and argues that "the time has come when scholars are needed to intervene in politics, with all their competence, to impose utopias based in truth and rationality" (104–5, my translation).

While critical of the "total intellectual" role played by Sartre, Bourdieu nonetheless valued the critical intellectual tradition dating back to Emile Zola.[60] Part of his willingness to assume this kind of public intellectual role was in response to the apparent decline of the critical intellectual tradition in France.[61] The image of the leading public intellectual in France thrived during the Cold War period. Situated on the political left, most French intellectuals carved out a distinct identity as critics of colonialism and capitalist imperialism. Algeria and Vietnam were rallying issues for the left. But with the fall of the Berlin Wall in 1989 marking the end of the Cold War, a growing number of French intellectuals began to argue that the time for the role of the "critical intellectual" was over and that it was time to defend and manage better markets and democracy. A growing number of intellectuals began cultivating more cooperative relationships with political and economic leadership and the mass media in the roles of advisor, expert, political analyst, and TV commentator.

This shift in orientation was made easier by the loss of political legitimacy of the left parties. The attack against welfare state provision by Margaret Thatcher in England and Ronald Reagan in the United States spread to Western Europe. To Bourdieu's considerable disgust even the French Socialists began to advocate market-oriented reforms that would reduce the size and responsibilities of the welfare state. In 1983 the Mitterrand government made an about-face in French political economic

60. See Charle 1990 for a history of that intellectual tradition.

61. Mauger (2004, 385) observes that with the decline of Marxism as an intellectual force in France, the kind of critical sociology that Bourdieu offered came to fill a position in opposition to rising popularity of the French "new philosophers" and neoliberal thought. There was a growing demand for his critical sociology that might have in the earlier period been satisfied by Marxism.

policy by shifting abruptly away from the traditional *dirigest* tradition of economic policy characteristic of the Fifth Republic. It began dismantling with considerable rapidity some of the centralized administrative power of the French state. The 1982 nationalizations by the newly elected socialist-communist government gave way to the 1983 policy of privatization. Even firms remaining under government control were held to standards of profitable performance. Significant private sector policy initiatives increased. Restructuring of French industry created massive layoffs that were to be absorbed largely through early retirements with benefits. Socialist Party leadership during the Mitterrand presidency had adopted a number of macro-economic policies of accommodation to international financial markets. Scandals, failed initiatives, and economic crisis plagued various governments under the Mitterrand presidency. Socialists therefore became less able to rally support around their traditional role of ideological resistance toward capitalist trends. This kind of economic realism Bourdieu would sharply contest as spineless abdication to the forces of globalization.

Bourdieu devoted more and more time and attention in later years to giving organizational expression to protecting the autonomy of the intellectual field from outside economic, political, and religious forces. This concern became more important in his later years because he believed that autonomy to be increasingly threatened by a new and growing media-oriented intelligentsia. Unlike in the early years, when Bourdieu was willing to distinguish between internal intellectual field and external political struggles and focus on the former, his concern and activities in his later years suggests he no longer believed this to be possible. While he always distinguished between internal and external struggles Bourdieu's analysis of the changing relationship of the intellectual field to outside political and economic constraints led him to conclude that an intellectual/political strategy focused entirely on internal issues was no longer viable. The distinction between internal and external struggles became less convincing.[62] The autonomy of intellectual life was more and more threatened by the mass media and more diverse cultural markets. Bourdieu came to the conclusion that to defend the former he must challenge directly the latter. Thus, despite a change in type and frequency of public activism, there was continuity in the kind of concern expressed. The same concern

---

62. Pinto (1998, 182–83) makes a similar point.

for intellectual autonomy remained but it was as if his intellectual concern now had to be fought out in the larger public arena, not just within peer networks.

As a consequence we observe a shift in intellectual strategy, particularly in his publications appearing in the early 1990s. He started publishing small paperbacks that were accessible to a broader audience in terms of price and writing style and that were collections of interviews, short speeches, and essays devoted largely to criticism of neoliberal globalization.[63] This strategy brought a wide readership beyond the university as well as within but also provoked a sharp debate in the French media.[64]

He also lent his support to several high-profile forms of protest against established powers. He supported, for example, the French peasant protest movement against neoliberalism, attending the trail of the leader José Bové. Believing that the arena of public discourse had become narrowly framed by the logic of neoclassical economic assumptions, Bourdieu tried to find ways to break through that iron cage of ideological determinism. He also looked to the work of artists, such as Karl Kraus and Hans Haacke, as privileged sources of creative intervention to expose the enclosed world of political leadership and discourse.[65]

One can also observe the shift in strategy as he devoted more and more energy to developing the idea of and organizational means for a "collective intellectual." The idea was not entirely new; one can find expressions of it in the late 1980s and early 1990s.[66] The 1992 postscript "For the corporatism of the universal" to *The Rules of Art* (1996c) appears as a kind of manifesto that outlines an activist strategy that he would more and more employ throughout the 1990s. It defines an activist role for the "scientific intellectual" that calls for the collective organization of intellectuals, a call that "takes a normative position based on the conviction that it is possible to use knowledge of the logic of the functioning of the fields of cultural production to draw up a realistic program for the collective action of intellectuals" (Bourdieu 1996b, 339). Here the work of social science

63. See Bourdieu 1998a, 2001a.

64. See Champagne 2004 for an account of relations between Bourdieu and journalists, which is discussed later in this chapter.

65. See Bourdieu and Haacke 1994. I am indebted to Gérard Mauger (personal communication, Paris, November 26, 2002) for bringing to my attention how much Bourdieu looked to the artistic world as a way of breaking through the taken-for-granted assumptions of power relations.

66. See Bourdieu 1989a, 1992, 1993e, 2008e.

is presented in strikingly instrumentalist terms as a tool for the political efficacy of intellectuals.

Bourdieu tried to implement this "realpolitik" of the collective intellectual in several practical ways. He created in 1989 his own European review of books, *Liber*, in an effort to develop a European intellectual tradition modeled on the Encyclopedists of the Enlightenment. With the fall of the Berlin Wall and the European Union under construction Bourdieu saw reason for defending intellectual autonomy at the international as well as national level. *Liber* was to disseminate to a large readership a broad range of literary, artistic, and scientific avant-garde works not readily available because of language barriers, slowness of translations, and national traditions.[67] In one issue, for example, Jürgen Habermas (1992) is interviewed about the negative effects of German reunification after the fall of the Berlin Wall.

In the early 1990s he devoted attention to an "International of Intellectuals" and joined in Strasbourg in November 1993 with other intellectuals, such as Jacques Derrida, Toni Morrison, Susan Sontag, and Salman Rushdie, in the creation of an International Parliament of Writers. This initiative was to establish a "critical counter-power" by organizing "a concrete solidarity with threatened writers" in certain countries as well as reflect "on new forms of engagement" for defending intellectuals.[68] Salman Rushdie was elected president of the new group in February 1994. In efforts to protect intellectual autonomy the group created a number of safe havens across many countries for intellectuals threatened with persecution and organized press conferences about Rwanda, Algeria, Sarajevo, asylum rights, and so on (Bourdieu 1993f). The strategy of organizing international conferences of intellectuals became a favorite one of Bourdieu and he participated in several until just before his death.

In 1992 he issued a call, "Appel à la communauté des universitaires et des chercheurs" (Appeal to the Community of University Faculty and Researchers), to the university and research communities for renewed at-

67. *Libre* 1 (October 1989): 2, reprinted in Bourdieu 2008e, 205. *Liber* appeared first as a supplement to four major European newspapers (*Frankfurter Allgemeine Zeitung*, *L'Indice*, *Le Monde*, *El País*) but then, because of financial constraints and disagreement with *Le Monde* over editorial control, became a supplement to *Actes de la Recherche en Sciences Sociales* in 1991 and continued until 1999.

68. It was announced in *Libération*, November 3, 1994, and was reprinted in Bourdieu 2008e, 289–92.

tention to the problems of French higher education. This led to the creation of the Association de réflexion sur les enseignments supérieurs et la recherche (ARESER) (Association for Reflection on Higher Education and Research), which published in 1997 *Quelques diagnostics et remèdes urgents pour une université en péril* (Paris: Liber-Raisons d'Agir). The group aimed to provide key information to help arrest loss of control over teaching and research to state administrators. In conjunction with this group Bourdieu published in the 1990s several opinion pieces in the national press showing his ongoing concern for educational reform (see, e.g., Bourdieu et al. 1997; Bourdieu, Baudelot, and Lévy 1994).[69]

He created in June 1993 the Comité international de soutien aux intellectuels algériens (CISIA) (International Support Committee for Algerian Intellectuals) to offer support to Algerian scholars, journalists, teachers, and writers threatened by attack and assassination in the civil war in that country. The committee sought to aid in finding suitable exile for threatened intellectuals and to disseminate information on the violence threatening intellectuals. Bourdieu editorialized in the French press rooting the origins of the civil war in Algeria in the legacy of French colonialism and calling for the need to establish basic cultural and political liberties. He also criticized the French government for restricting immigration from its former colony (Bourdieu and Derrida 1994, 1995; Bourdieu and Leca 1995).

The Struggle against Neoliberalism

Though traditionally critical of centralized and bureaucratized state power, Bourdieu came to view the new era of globalization and fiscal constraints on state spending as even more threatening to the well-being of communities. This represented a remarkable shift in views attested to by many. But it was not just that Bourdieu stepped in to fill a gap in French intellectual space left by the death of Foucault in 1984. The issue of globalization had become a major issue in France of the 1990s. No other single issue had so galvanized France since May 1968. By the early 1990s the French became obsessed with globalization. There were prominent factory closings. Bookstores were filled with book titles on the subject. TV programs and news regularly featured the issue. José Bové and the direct

69. Under the leadership of Christophe Charle ARESER continued periodic publications through 2008.

political action of the peasant movement and protests received high media visibility. Bourdieu attended Bové's trial in July 2000 and offered his support. Globalization became in France not just a matter of intellectual debate but the source of considerable social agitation. Thus, Bourdieu did not just fill a gap in the intellectual arena in the 1990s following the death of Foucault. He entered the arena on a hotly debated issue. Globalization became a unifying national issue, making it easier for intellectuals to find an issue on which they could expect to be heard. Without a unifying national issue like globalization Bourdieu's political engagements in his later years might well have been quite different.

Another contributing factor to the rise of Bourdieu as a leading public intellectual was the conjuncture that occurred between the burning public issues that emerged during the 1990s and Bourdieu's own research. Bourdieu's attack on neoliberalism took the form of polemical essays and public declarations. It was also based on sociological research. And this distinguishes his public intellectual activism from that of other French intellectuals, such as Henri-Bernard Lévy, who oriented their essayist rather than scholarly style of work toward media visibility. In sharp contrast, Bourdieu drew on his authority as a social scientist and generally intervened in only those public issues that he had researched.

His support for the social movement strikes in 1995, and the issues they represented, was anticipated already in his 1993 publication of *The Weight of the World*. This massive work of almost a thousand pages documented through interviews and portraits the social suffering of a diverse array of lower-middle- and lower-class individuals and their families. The book documented the social suffering of those left unprotected by the vicissitudes of markets and by explicit public policy by state planners who had become practitioners of neoliberal ideology. *The Weight of the World* documents extensive testimony of the social effects of reduced welfare state protection. The book quickly became a key reference for social movement activists challenging those policies and achieved enormous public success. It challenged directly the closure of the French political elite, out of touch with the realities of social disenfranchisement created by their policies. It amounted to a stinging indictment of Socialist government policies focused on "fiscal responsibility" rather than fortifying traditional state welfare and safety net functions that corresponded to long-standing demands of the left parties.

The experience of researching social suffering and exclusion for *The Weight of the World* sharpened Bourdieu's awareness of the disenfranchised and marginalized individuals and groups who experienced directly the dislocation, precariousness, and constraints imposed by reduced state social services. This research experience gave him a new appreciation of their plight and motivated him to give voice to these social groups he found without effective representation in the national debate over economic and political policies. The tremendous success of the book, both in terms of sales (it sold over 100,000 copies) and public debate and media attention it provoked, brought to Bourdieu a new level of public visibility as a public intellectual. Theater groups staged performances based on the book's interviews and ethnographic exploration of social suffering. This success opened for Bourdieu the possibility of a new and effective political role based on his scientific authority. It suggested the possibility of new more direct forms of political engagement that had not been previously possible and he seized that opportunity.[70]

The 1995 Strikes and Beyond

The massive 1995 political mobilization in France in response to erosion of public policies upholding traditional welfare state functions is important for understanding the visibility that Bourdieu achieved in his later years as a public intellectual. He was mobilized by a social movement that made it possible for him to intervene politically with considerable symbolic capital in ways not possible in earlier years.[71] But as we have seen, the public political activism of his later years was but a change in form of political intervention.

Late 1995 was a period of intense labor agitation in France. A broad range of labor unrest, particularly in the public sector, and demonstrations in the universities generated the most significant political crisis in France since May 1968.[72] The strikes were precipitated by the Juppé plan, which

70. Indeed, at this time he saw his increased public interventions as a way of helping to get across the message of the work, that is, to increase awareness of the conditions of suffering in France and to call to account the Mitterrand presidency and French Socialists under whose watch these conditions had increased (interview, Paris, November 23, 1993).

71. It is ironic that Bourdieu, whose sociological investigations had not focused on social movements, as for example had his rival Alain Touraine, became in his later years politically catalyzed by a social movement just as it was also enhanced by Bourdieu's presence.

72. The social movement of December 1995 had its origins in three different crises: beginning in November, student protest in the universities, a strike by railway employees against government plans to institute cutbacks in retirement benefits, and protests against Prime

attempted a reform of the social security system and a modification of the retirement benefits for employees of the Parisian transportation system (RATP) and railroad employees (SNCF). Salaries of public service employees had already been frozen and other measures limited or decreased the traditional benefits granted to public service employees. Massive railway employee strikes broke out and spread throughout the public sector, bringing France to a standstill. The political crisis gave new life to the more radical political and labor union elements that rapidly gathered new support. Bourdieu supported the strikes.

Earlier in November of that year, a public petition with a list of signatures of prominent French intellectuals around the review *Esprit* and the Fondation Saint-Simon—including sociologist Alain Touraine—came out in support of the leadership of the Confédération Fédérale des Travailleurs (CFDT) that supported the Juppé plan.[73] Bourdieu was furious that his long-standing antagonist *Esprit* had come out against the strikes. He mobilized and published a second list of signatures in early December supporting the strikes.[74] These events marked the start of a series of highly

---

Minister Juppé's plan to reform social security by reducing public expenditure in this area (Duval et al. 1998, 12–14).

73. *Esprit* is a monthly journal that assembles a network of progressive thinkers of humanist and Christian left perspectives interested in the intersection of culture and political issues with a general liberal reform perspective. It was founded in 1932 by Emmanuel Mounier, a well-known advocate of personalism. Though Bourdieu published one of his overtly political papers in the journal, *Esprit* became sharply critical of Bourdieu and the kind of social science he represented. It published sharp criticism of *Reproduction* and *Distinction*. For Bourdieu, *Esprit* was a center of dialogue and exchange of dominant ideas but insufficiently critical of them. An analysis in *Actes de la Recherche en Sciences Sociales* (Bourdieu and Boltanski 1976) of dominant ideology gave *Esprit* a central role in circulating dominant ideology ideas. Bourdieu was further left politically and more critical of existing institutions than *Esprit* contributors. Bourdieu's sharp criticism of the established left made him an attractive voice for many radical left groups, much to the consternation of the *Esprit* group.

74. See Duval et al. 1998 for an insightful if controversial sociological analysis of the two lists. These researchers and colleagues of Bourdieu find that the pro-strike list includes relatively more university professors, researchers, women, and intellectuals from the provinces, whereas the reform list includes relatively more senior civil servants and managers and liberal professions. Moreover the analysis shows significant secondary oppositions within each of the two camps. For example, within the pro-strike list (p. 93) one finds those who owe their presence more to political activism, often with a radical left party or labor groups, in opposition to those who come with scientific prestige. These patterns resemble those found by Bourdieu (1988b) in his field analysis of the French professorate. Politically, the lists generally divide on the traditional opposition between the radical left and the reformist left in French politics,

visible, media-catching public appearances by Bourdieu that continued in a variety of forms until his death in January 2002. To many observers in the French media this period marked the beginning of a very "political" Bourdieu.[75]

At the December 12, 1995, rally at the Lyon train station in Paris, Bourdieu delivered his famous "Against the Destruction of Civilization" speech, in which he spoke not to the particular grievances of the strikers but argued that they represented something more fundamental: defense of a type of social security that had been protected, albeit imperfectly, by the traditional welfare state (Bourdieu 1998b, 30–33). Bourdieu would reiterate this theme across a wide range of public protests and social unrest over the next seven years. He became a strong public advocate for the protection of pensions, job security, open access to higher education, and other provisions of the welfare state that were achievements of social struggles earlier in the twentieth century. He argued against social security budget cuts and scaling back welfare provision in the name of free markets and international competition. He began to sign public petitions, participate in demonstrations, editorialize in newspapers, grant more interviews, appear on television, and work overtly with political protest groups.[76] He became

---

with Bourdieu siding with the former. But the general finding that the scholarly and scientific communities were clearly more present in the pro-strike list provoked sharp critical reaction from voices on the other side arguing that Bourdieusians were using science for political sectarian purposes. That scientists tended to disproportionally appear on the pro-strike list is consistent with Bourdieu's view of science as a critical debunking force of existing power relations. This view of the scientific profession invites further comparative research.

75. One can find this and other popular criticisms of Bourdieu's political activities in the late nineties in the *Magazine Littéraire* (October 1998). There emerged in the French press a debate over the "two Bourdieus," the earlier social scientist with considerable scientific stature and the later "political" Bourdieu who compromised his scientific legitimacy by public interventions late in his career. The charge was in fact political, reflecting differences in views on whether and to what extent market mechanisms should replace tradition state services in allocating certain state services and whether changing economic conditions warranted significant downsizing of the public sector. The argument of this book has hopefully demonstrated that Bourdieu was "political" from the very outset of his social scientific career beginning in Algeria and that in his view economic questions were ultimately political considerations. See Boschetti 2005, Bourdieu 2008e, and Mauger 2004 for convincing testimony refuting the "two Bourdieus" thesis.

76. This is not to suggest that Bourdieu became in his later years a "mediacrate" shuttling from one public appearance to another in the manner of some French intellectuals—though some critics would accuse him of that. His own view was that he in fact interviewed relatively little and then quite selectively turning down invitations daily (interview, Paris, November 23,

the primary public intellectual of major scientific status at the head of the antiglobalization movement that emerged in France and other Western European countries in the 1990s.

In 1995 he organized Raisons d'Agir, a group of progressive social scientists who publish critiques of neoliberal public policies as a way of counteracting those conservative think-tanks, such as the Fondation Saint-Simon, that celebrate market mechanisms.[77] In the same year he launched a publishing venture that eventually assumes the same name. This enterprise attempts to regain control over the conditions of intellectual production from growing commercial interests in the French publishing world and is designed to bring sociological analyses of contemporary civic issues to a broader public. The first publication in 1996 was his own controversial best-seller *On Television* (Bourdieu 1998e).[78] A broad and sharply critical debate broke out in the French press over Bourdieu's criticism in this book on TV journalism. In the April 8, 1998, issue of *Le Monde* he published his famous "Pour une gauche de gauche" (For a left that is Left) in which he criticizes "la troika neo-liberal Blair-Jospin-Schroder" and the socialist government under Lionel Jospin for betraying the ideals of the left.[79]

In January 1998 Bourdieu publically supported the movement of unemployed whose forms of direct action captured considerable media attention. When supporters of the movement occupied the École Normale Supérieure, Bourdieu's alma mater, he met with protesters and delivered

---

1999). This was echoed later by Franck Poupeau (personal communication, Franck Poupeau, Paris, June 6, 2002), who interviewed Bourdieu extensively while preparing edited collection of Bourdieu's "political" texts (Bourdieu 2008e).

77. The Raisons d'Agir association is the most successful, continuing expression of Bourdieu's vision for the "collective intellectual." Dedicated to the goal of bringing social scientific research into the public arena for advancing the cause of the political left, affiliated members have published numerous books and reports and been moderately successful in entering public debates in France. In 2003 the association launched a new journal, *Savoir/Agir*, which at the time of this writing was in its seventh edition. See the Raisons d'Agir website for both a history and a current agenda of political actions since Bourdieu's death: http://www.raisonsdagir.org (accessed April 3, 2009).

78. A second publication by Serge Halimi (1997) also became a best seller, reaching over 100,000 copies within two months.

79. The article was cosigned with Christophe Charle, Frédéric Lebaron, Gérard Mauger, and Bernard Lacroix and was elaborated within the framework of the Raisons d'Agir group. The op-ed piece elicited considerable debate in the French press and an avalanche of written correspondence.

a public defense of those who he considered to be dispossessed and excluded politically and economically by the process of political closure that he had been criticizing for years (Bourdieu 1998f).

In 1999 Bourdieu gave his open support to the Action Critique Médias (ACRIMED), an association devoted to defending France Culture (the French equivalent of PBS), against state efforts to make the cultural programming of this public station more commercially profitable. Bourdieu strongly opposed such state leadership efforts to impose market thinking and evaluation criteria that could only enhance the power of dominant groups (Bourdieu 2002a).

By the late nineties, particularly beginning in 1998, Bourdieu himself came under sharp attack in the French media for his highly visible political stances opposing government policies. Indeed the subsequent debate sometimes reduced to whether one was for or against Bourdieu! One can find in the popular press numerous personal attacks as well as highly polemical denunciations of both his sociological research and political activism.[80]

In 2000 Bourdieu published *The Social Structures of the Economy* (2005b)—earlier portions of this book had already appeared in *Actes de la Recherche en Sciences Sociales*—in which he deconstructs neoliberal economic discourse by showing that the housing market for individual dwellings was in fact shaped by public policies. The book analyzes various parts of a large-scale study conducted in the early 1990s of France's single-family housing market, offering a polemical attack against neoclassical economics by arguing that economic phenomena are always embedded in broad social and political phenomena. The individual decision to purchase a dwelling is not simply individual but brings into play a range of social and political conditions—including public policy—that make it possible or impossible. Thus housing provision is not simply a product of invisible market forces as technocratic and neoliberal discourse would have it, but results from political decisionmaking and political interests

---

80. One finds sharp attacks in publications such as *Esprit, Marianne, L'Evenement du jeudi,* the *Magazine Littéraire,* and *Le Nouvel Observateur.* Several critics appeared in the September 18, 1998, issue of *Le Monde.* The polemical character of the criticism is reflected in titles, such as "The Devil and Bourdieu" and "Does the Left Need Bourdieu"; perhaps the most virulent, *Deconstructing Pierre Bourdieu: Against Sociological Terrorism from the Left,* came from a disaffected follower, Jeannine Verdès-Leroux (2001), who accused Bourdieu of intellectual terrorism against all who would oppose him.

that Bourdieu wished to highlight. Against the determinism of market necessity, Bourdieu attempted to create a broader debate on the idea that
markets are socially constructed and, albeit constraining, are always open
to some political alternative.[81] This research made it possible for him to
intervene politically as an expert having researched the social effects of
neoliberal policy in France.

Bourdieu's Criticism of Media Journalism

The forgoing discussion helps explain Bourdieu's attack on media journalism that generated much of the criticism of his political activism in the late
1990s. His sharply focused criticism in his little "red book," *On Television*
(1998e), of neoliberal bias in media journalism was a major publishing
coup and provoked sharp debate over the role of the mass media in France.
The book is based on two courses filmed at the Collège de France and
an article, "L'emprise du journalism" (The Stranglehold of Journalism),
that had appeared in *Actes de la Recherche en Sciences Sociales* (Bourdieu
1994a). It sold over 140,000 copies and was for several months at the top
of the best seller list in France. The book placed Bourdieu at the center of
a national debate over the role of the mass media in France, particularly
television journalism. Sharply critical of the celebrity-making machine of
the media, the book had the paradoxical effect of making Bourdieu himself all the more a celebrity.

Bourdieu was not against journalism per se even though some of his
sharpest criticism suggested as much. Indeed, he attributed to journalism the important function of keeping the claims and actions of political leadership under public scrutiny and thereby holding political leaders
accountable for their actions or inactions.[82] Rather, it was his defense of
the autonomy of the intellectual field and criticism of the closure of pub-

81. There is a certain irony here in contrasting Bourdieu's political aims with some criticism traditionally leveled against Bourdieu's sociological theory of action. Many critics (Alexander 1995; R. Jenkins 1982, 2000) have charged his sociology with being too deterministic.
His sociology of reproduction seems to offer only limited chances for change. Yet Bourdieu's
attacks against neoliberalism seemed both to call attention to the determining forces of globalization and to raise the hope of choosing some alternative course of action rather than their
sublime acceptance.

82. However, he did not favor tabloid scandalism as a sort of check on the excesses of
politician power.

lic discourse that motivated his attack. He believed that the intellectual field was rapidly being undermined by the invasion of a media-oriented intelligentsia where intellectual prestige was determined more and more by media visibility than by traditional peer group review in professional publications. At the same time the terms of public discourse were becoming narrowly framed by neoliberal economic terminology and assumptions. While a long-time critic of media-oriented intellectuals whom he dismissed as superficial, without enduring intellectual qualities, and who contributed to a kind of "cultural fast food" consumption, Bourdieu became increasingly convinced that the marketing orientation of cultural and political life had so advanced that it had become virtually impossible for alternative viewpoints to gain a fair public hearing. He viewed the arena of public debate as increasingly monopolized by technocrats and journalists, pushing out artists, writers, and scientists. The voices of grassroots activists, immigrants, the unemployed, and labor activists were too easily dismissed as "irrational" and "unrealistic" in the climate of globalization and austerity that were justified in the neoliberal language of financial necessities. Measures of "flexibility" and "fiscal responsibility" were presented as the rational and necessary steps to take, when in fact they were but a euphemized way of justifying unemployment, reduced retirement, and medical benefits, and so on. He denounced as the "neoliberal scourge" the euphemized language of financial rigor and efficiency as harboring the market interests of dominant groups. And the voices of those most directly affected by those policies were seldom listened to and generally dismissed as representing vested corporatist, sectorial interests, and unfair advantages, rather than as genuine needs of the common good. Against this Bourdieu proclaimed an emphatic "no" and much of his political activism in his later years can be seen as a series of protests against the rigid neoliberal framing of public discourse.[83]

83. In a November 23, 1993, interview, when *The Weight of the World* was receiving widespread attention, Bourdieu stressed to me how important it was for critical intellectuals to become effective in using the media rather than have journalists impose their own journalistic categories.

Clearly his attitude and strategy had changed from what they were prior to his entry into the Collège de France in 1981. In the same interview he admitted that he was then intervening publically as much as possible so that *The Weight of the World* might have the largest political impact possible. In his view it was important to heighten awareness of the experiences of social exclusion and to call to accountability the French Socialists for losing touch with the conditions of sufferance in France under the Mitterrand presidency.

Bourdieu came to believe in the urgency of assuming an active public role as a critical intellectual and social scientist to speak forcefully against the neoliberal discourse that increasingly exercised a powerful censoring effect on public debate. He found himself increasingly in the paradoxical position of assuming a high-profile public intellectual role for which he himself had expressed strong reservations. Indeed, as one scene in the Pierre Carles documentary on Bourdieu, *Sociology Is a Martial Art*, suggests, some of the celebrity visibility seemed to be more of an embarrassment than a relished experience for Bourdieu. More important, he believed that his more direct political involvements did not compromise his rigorous and objective practice of sociology as science. In his words, the challenge was to "think politics without thinking politically" (Bourdieu 1988c). Yet, the tension between science and politics that he hoped to sidestep in his vision of "science with commitment" did not go away as his critics would point out. His early emphasis on building up sociology as a legitimate science and accumulating symbolic capital as a very successful social scientist stood in contrast to the more publically visible engagements as he himself admitted. There had been a change in form and strategy in response to changing circumstances.

It is difficult to offer a precise measure of the impact Bourdieu had as a public intellectual during the 1995 crisis and subsequently. In the short term, some indicators suggest that the impact was substantial. Clearly, Bourdieu's name, signature, and perceived support were used by activists during the 1995 strikes and, subsequently, by social movement activists. Bourdieu brought considerable symbolic capital to the social movement.[84] He brought to the movement the prestige of the Collège de France, of his scientific reputation, of his moral force from having previously spoken to the issue of social exclusion and suffering in *The Weight of the World*, and of the relative rarity of his name appearing on public petitions.[85] For a short time Bourdieu and the social movement represented a formidable force, providing some check to further erosion of welfare safety net functions by the French state. But his efforts appear to have been more "acts of resistance" than successful long-term reorientations of public policies

---

84. Duval et al. 1998, 60–61.

85. A petition would be sometimes referred to simply as the "Bourdieu list." As Michel Offerlé (1999) notes, there was considerable anecdotal evidence of activists using the "support of Bourdieu" to rally support in meetings.

in France.[86] The shift to increasing reliance on market mechanisms for the delivery of public goods and services in France continues to this day, though perhaps at a different rate and in a different way than had Bourdieu and the social movement of the 1990s never existed.

It is striking that Bourdieu, who was frequently criticized for being a deterministic reproduction thinker, saw in neoliberal globalization a powerful threat to traditional welfare arrangements but not one whose success was a foregone conclusion. Consistent with his constructionist view of agency and collective identity, even those seemingly powerful economic forces grew out of collective struggles where actors had some choice in the matter. Bourdieu's own political activism in his later years demonstrated that fundamental faith that the reproduction of forces of domination could be strategically resisted in certain times and places.

Whether Bourdieu's efforts, and those of the social movement he helped lead, end up being only a blip on the ascending curve toward increasing market determination of the distribution of public goods and services or a more significant alternation in that pattern remains to be seen. The current fascination with markets and the taken-for-granted view of their determining constraints seems hardly to have run their course.[87] If several years hence the 1995 social movement appears to have been nothing more than a short-lived political event, then there would be no harsher critic than Bourdieu himself who, reflecting on the significance of May 1968, credited that crisis with having little effect on the most fundamental structures of domination in modern France.[88]

Far from sheer personal ambition to become another Sartre or Foucault, Bourdieu's rise to the role of leading French and European public intellectual grew out of a conjuncture of institutional influences and changes that set the stage for personal choices. Bourdieu's movement to a leading position in the changing French intellectual field, his research and

86. Poupeau and Discepolo note that the initiative of the General Assembly of the Social Movement "had no further sequel after 1996" (Bourdieu 2008e, 272).

87. In the summer of 2003 large street demonstrations again responded to a new initiative by the Chirac center-right government to implement similar kinds of welfare state reforms as were proposed in 1995.

88. In a brief reflection published in May 1983 in *Lire*, Bourdieu (2008e, 40) assesses the significance of May 1968 as entirely of the "symbolic order" with "almost nothing" changed in the political field. However, as already noted, Bourdieu and Passeron's critical analysis of the French university culture and social selectivity contributed to student awareness and mobilization in May 1968.

publications, the growing influence of the mass media in French political and cultural life, the failures of the French Socialists in power, a cultural legacy of leading critical intellectuals in France, a unifying national issue of globalization, and the political conjuncture in 1995 all intersected in ways that opened a path for Bourdieu to choose new and more frequent forms of political action. His responses to that combination of factors at different moments reveal both a striking continuity in desire to preserve the autonomy of intellectual life and a change in view and strategy on how best to do that.

Contrary to the widespread media view that Bourdieu had suddenly become "political" during his later years in the antiglobalization movement, Bourdieu expressed ongoing interest in politics throughout his career. Indeed, although in only one did he come to play a leading public intellectual role, Bourdieu confronted at least three burning national crises in his lifetime: the Algerian war of the late 1950s, the university crisis of May 1968, and the crisis of the welfare state in the 1990s. He offered a political response to all three but the forms of those responses differed. He responded as a social scientist through his research and writing identifying key political issues that shaped each of those crises. But only in the welfare state crisis did he also come to play a public intellectual role. His move to a preeminent position in the French intellectual field and his accumulation of considerable symbolic capital made it possible for him to lead a social movement in a way that he could not have done during the Algerian War or May '68. Nevertheless, at different times, with different resources, and from different locations within the French intellectual field Bourdieu addressed in different ways national political issues throughout his career. He offered a political sociology that was simultaneously a politics of sociology.

CHAPTER EIGHT

For Democratic Politics

I have argued in the earlier chapters that Bourdieu's sociology should be read as both a sociology of politics and a politics of sociology. Though he is not known for his political sociology, Bourdieu's analysis of power in the form of domination stands at the heart of his sociology. He offers conceptual tools for analyzing three types of power: power vested in particular resources (capitals), power concentrated in specific spheres of struggle over forms of capital (fields), and power as practical, taken-for-granted acceptance of existing social hierarchies (symbolic power, violence, and capital). Bourdieu's sociology of symbolic power sensitizes us to the more subtle and influential forms of power that operate through cultural resources and symbolic classifications that interweave everyday life with prevailing institutional arrangements. His concepts of symbolic power, violence, and capital, together with his concept of habitus, stress the active role that symbolic forms play in both constituting and maintaining social hierarchies. They call for looking at expressions of power that radiate through interpersonal relations and presentations of self as well as in organizational structures. They also point to an intimate and complex relationship between symbolic and material factors in the operation of power.

Bourdieu's perspective challenges the commonly held view that symbolic power is simply "symbolic." He identifies a wide variety of resources (capitals) beyond sheer economic interests that function as power resources. In so doing, he invites political sociologists to consider all valued resources, including cultural and social as well as material and coercive, that may function as forms of power even though they present otherwise. Individuals and groups struggle over the very definition and distribution of these capitals in distinct power arenas Bourdieu calls fields. He sees concentrations of various forms of capital in particular areas of struggle, such as the field of power, the political field, and the state. His concept of field offers a conceptual language that encourages examination of inter-relationships across levels of analysis and analytical units that usually are fragmented for specialized focus in empirical research.

Key in Bourdieu's sociology is how power resources (capitals) and the field struggles over them become legitimated (misrecognized) as something other than power relations. The struggle for symbolic power in the political field for gaining access to state power is particularly salient. In addition, he examines critically how leadership representation and delegated authority dispossess individuals of their effective voice in political life. His analysis of the state as an ensemble of bureaucratic fields in which actors struggle for regulatory power (statist capital) and attempt to monopolize legitimate classifications in society holds potential for more refined analyses than offered in state-centric views that stress only material and coercive powers. Finally, Bourdieu offers not only a sociology of politics but also a politics of sociology. Sociology as science can challenge a key foundation of power relations—their legitimation—and thereby open up the possibility for social transformation. One finds in his work a vision for what he thinks the practice of social science can do for democratic life and a critical role he assigns to social scientists as public intellectuals.

The implications for the analysis of politics are numerous and I have identified several studies in earlier chapters that offer compelling applications of Bourdieu's work. Recall just a few. Public opinion (Champagne 1979, 1990) is socially and culturally constructed and political participation (Gaxie 1978) depends far more on cultural competence than commonly believed. For analysis of social movements Goldberg (2003) offers a promising framework for how Bourdieu's ideas of symbolic power and his emphasis on classification struggles can bridge two traditions of social movement research, resource mobilization/political process theories and new social movements with their emphasis on collective identity. Indeed, Bourdieu-inspired work can be found in the analysis of social movements (Bloemraad 2001; Crossley 2002; Goldberg 2003; Ancelovici 2010), the analysis of social and citizenship boundaries (Brubaker 1992; Lamont and Fournier 1992), the analysis of nationalism (Gorski forthcoming), and the analysis of political culture (Aronoff 2000). Benson and Neveu (Benson 1999; Benson and Neveu 2005) draw on the concept of field and symbolic capital to suggest an innovative way of looking at the mass media. Calhoun (2005c) uses the idea of field in his analysis of political radicalism. Eyal (2003, 2005) applies the concept of the political field to analyze political transformation in the postcommunist era in Eastern Europe. Stark and Bruszt (1998) use the idea of a political field to examine economic change and democratization in post-Soviet Eastern Europe. Loveman (2005) points to the central role of symbolic power in the formation and operation of the modern state. Steinmetz (2007) considers the colonial state as a field in his analysis of German colonialism. Drawing inspiration from Bourdieu's concept of field, Julian Go (2008) proposes the idea of "global fields" to bring a field analytic perspective to international relations. Kauppi (2004) employs the concepts of political capital and political field to study European integration. And Wacquant (2005c) indicates ways in which Bourdieu's thinking and research can invigorate the practice of democratic politics. These are but a few examples of a growing and diverse body of political analyses that draw inspiration from Bourdieu's sociology.

Beyond providing tools for political analysis, I have argued that Bourdieu's sociology also provides ways for enhancing progressive politics. What possibilities does Bourdieu see in his critical sociology for enhancing action toward greater democratic participation? This concluding chapter explores and evaluates those normative considerations.

Thinking about Change

Some critics (e.g. Alexander 1995; R. Jenkins 1982, 2000) charge that Bourdieu lacks a theory of change, including political change. They contend that his sociological framework limits consideration to the analysis of how social orders reproduce themselves intergenerationally. The topic of social change in Bourdieu's work has evoked considerable criticism. I address that issue in *Culture and Power* (Swartz 1997, 211–17) and will not review here that whole debate. Clearly, significant pieces of Bourdieu's empirical investigations concern the effects of change: the French Algerian war, the French peasantry confronting urbanization and rising consumer markets, rapid and massive educational expansion, and the shift toward neoliberal policies. And it is obvious that Bourdieu does not conclude that the old world simply reproduces itself across all these vastly different cases! He sees important continuities but also change. It is worth highlighting, however, a few key points that shape how Bourdieu thinks about political action and change.

Bourdieu clearly stresses in his analytical framework the reproduction of social order. But this is an emphasis, not one that excludes the possibility for resistance and change. While he does not elaborate an explicit theory of change, his conceptual framework leaves open the possibility for transformation. Take, for example, his idea of the doxa of established fields. The concept certainly stresses the idea of an underlying, deeply shared, if unconsciously so, understanding of the social world that contributes to its reproduction. Indeed, as he admits, "the whole logic of my research" has been on what he calls the "paradox of doxa," namely, "that the established order, with its relations of domination, its rights and prerogatives, privileges and injustices, ultimately perpetuates itself so easily, apart from a few historical accidents, and that the most intolerable conditions of existence can so often be perceived as acceptable and even natural" (2001c, 1).

Yet he also acknowledges that the doxa is not universal, particularly in modern differentiated societies. The doxa is unevenly distributed; it varies by the extent orthodoxy is challenged by heterodoxy, by type of society (degree of heterogeneity), and by one's position held in society. The doxa can be contested in the dialectic of struggle between the challengers (the heterodox), particularly when they come with different kinds of capital from outside a field, and the established order (the orthodox). The doxa in highly differentiated modern societies is far less encompassing than in more traditional homogeneous societies. And heterodox challengers are more likely to contest doxic assumptions than are those defending the status quo. Moreover, Bourdieu admits that he emphasizes the doxic order of social life to register a point, namely, how much order we take for granted and accept as given in spite of our perceptions of freedom from conformity in our highly differentiated and rapidly changing modern societies. But this is a corrective emphasis—another instance of him "twisting the stick in the opposite direction"—not a conceptual foreclosure on the possibility of change (Bourdieu 2000e, 173–74).

The condition for change that Bourdieu mentions most frequently is one of disjuncture between the expectations of habitus and the opportunities of fields. Bourdieu sees practices flowing from the intersection of habitus and field and he understands that intersection dialectically. Reproduction of social structures occurs only when habitus encounters field conditions that are very similar to those in which the habitus was originally formed (Bourdieu 1990c, 63). But for Bourdieu that kind of strict alignment between the individual habitus and particular fields seldom occurs. In most situations there is some degree of mismatch between the opportunities and constraints offered by fields and the expectations of habitus. There is most always a process of adaptation, a condition of some uncertainty since habitus does not possess complete knowledge of all field conditions; habitus addresses present situations in terms of past experience. When the discrepancies between new situations and those in which habitus was formed are slight, only a gradual modification of structures occurs. But when discrepancies are considerable, and the mismatch is large, transformation can ensue. Bourdieu thus sees the possibility that

> the dialectic of mutually self-reproducing objective changes and subjective aspirations may break down. Everything suggests that an abrupt slump in objective relative to subjective aspirations is likely to produce a break in the tacit acceptance which the dominated classes . . . previously granted to the dominant goals, and so to make it possible to invent or impose the goals of a genuine collective action. (Bourdieu and Passeron 1979, 97)

In these kinds of situations, reproduction gives way to either resignation or revolt.[1]

This identifies a set of conditions likely to produce change. However, under what conditions frustrated expectations might lead to self-blame and resignation or hostility and protest are not specified. The outcomes could be quite different. One can imagine different sets of habitus/field disjunctures producing quite different effects. Recall from chapter 7 his own analysis of Algerian peasants where a traditional rural habitus clashed with new economic conditions imposed by French colonialism and associated urbanization. Here a quite different field of constraints and opportunities is imposed upon a traditional habitus. This results in both resignation and armed struggle—two quite different responses. In his analysis of the May 1968 crisis Bourdieu (1988b) speaks of the "temporal transformation of the field itself" where large numbers of middle class students enter the French universities with heightened expectations that the university cannot satisfy and without the requisite cultural skills the traditional university demanded. This disjuncture producing frustrated expectations within the universities conjugates with similar disjunctures in other fields such as the labor market and in the cultural industry in

---

1. Here Bourdieu's thinking about change as one of frustrated expectations of the habitus intersects with relative deprivation theory (Gurr 1970).

particular. This is the case of multiple fields in crisis simultaneously and results in massive protests. One can think of a third kind of situation represented by Bourdieu's own upward mobility into the academic field and then his mobility from philosophy to sociology. Here an individual habitus confronts through social mobility quite different field conditions. These three types of disjuncture can and did produce quite different outcomes. Future research might well examine these and other types of habitus/field disjuncture to develop more a refined picture of the intersection of dispositions and structures in situations of change. Key for a Bourdieusian perspective would be analyses that take into account both dispositions and structures and their complex intersections to understand the reasons for change or the lack thereof. This will call for looking at the more subtle bodily and cultural indicators rather than focusing exclusively on opportunity structures, political ideals, or conscious goals of actors.

Bourdieu does see in political protest some possibility for change. Political protest begins by a break with, or "denunciation" of, the taken-for-granted understanding of the social world (the doxa). Bourdieu writes that "politics begins, strictly speaking, with the denunciation of this tacit contract of adherence to the established order which defines the original doxa; in other words, political subversion presupposes cognitive subversion, a conversion of the vision of the world" (1991b, 127–28).[2] Here he makes a key claim that politics begins when the social order is fundamentally questioned, that is, when the doxa is challenged.[3] This will involve a "conversion of the vision" that will lessen the grip of symbolic violence.

Bourdieu writes that "symbolic violence is that particular form of constraint that can only be implemented with the active complicity—which does not mean that it is conscious and voluntary—of those who submit to it and are determined only insofar as they deprive themselves of the possibility of a freedom founded on the awakening of consciousness" (1996d,

2. He (Bourdieu 1991b, 128) also refers to this as a "heretical break with the established order." It is noteworthy that both the act of science and political action begin by breaking with taken-for-granted assumptions about the social world. As discussed later in the chapter, the scientific field serves as a model that Bourdieu thinks the political field should emulate. How far that might be possible, however, seems limited. Moreover, as noted in chapters 3 and 6, Bourdieu says little about how such a critical perspective can develop beyond the logic of science.

3. I am limiting consideration here to political action that challenges the status quo. Bourdieu (2000e, 187–88) identifies two broad types of political action, one aimed at legitimating the established order and the other that would subvert it.

4). As the latter part of the quote suggests, and in spite of Bourdieu's criticism of Sartre's language of consciousness raising, Bourdieu nonetheless sees the possibility of some effective challenge to the grasp of symbolic violence by increasing awareness of the arbitrary foundations of the status quo. This is precisely the purpose of a critical and reflexive practice of sociology: to produce a partial and temporary measure of freedom from the ongoing process of struggle for symbolic domination (Bourdieu 2000e, 83–84).[4] But not by critical discourse alone. Ever skeptical of overintellectualized claims for the efficacy of discourse for transforming social life, Bourdieu cautions that "it is quite illusory to think that symbolic violence can be overcome solely with the weapons of consciousness and will." In the case of deeply seeded prejudices, he adds that "we know the futility of all actions which seek to use only the weapons of logical or empirical refutation in combating this or that form of racism—whether of ethnicity, class or sex" (180).

He further specifies that a critical break with the established social order "presupposes a *conjuncture* [my emphasis] of critical discourse and an objective crisis, capable of disrupting the close correspondence between the incorporated structures and the objective structures which produce them" (1991b, 128; emphasis added). Political action that challenges the status quo requires, therefore, *both* a "critical discourse" and an "objective crisis." Thus, the possibility for effective political challenge is associated not just with disjuncture between expectations of habitus and demands of a field but with a disjuncture that assumes crisis proportions and a critical discourse that effectively illuminates the crisis. Not critical discourse per se but one that conjugates with situations of crisis. This is precisely what a critical sociology—his socioanalysis—is to do: offer a critically and empirically informed exposure of power conditions that undergird inequalities but go misrecognized.

There are two ways that a critical sociology can aid in bringing about transformation and they point to tensions and complexity in Bourdieu's thinking on the matter. A critical sociology can first of all provide the

---

4. Mauger (2006, 86) draws out a similar implication from this passage, namely that Bourdieu sees his own social scientific work as increasing awareness of the conditions of symbolic violence and thereby offering the possibility of liberating oneself to some extent from its grasp. Indeed, Bourdieu (2000e, 184) suggests that it is only a critical social science—above and beyond political struggle—that is capable of completely unveiling the foundations of symbolic violence (doxa).

cognitive tools and vital information for understanding the crisis. I take this to be what Bourdieu means when he writes that with "the intervention of professional practitioners of the work of making explicit . . . [can bring about] the transfer of cultural capital which enables the dominated to achieve a collective mobilization and subversion action against the established order" (2000e, 188). Here, as noted in chapter 6, he assigns a key role to social scientists in bringing about change. But also noted in chapter 6, this task encounters a fundamental problem of dissemination: how to convey the critical analytical tools and information to those who lack the cultural capital to decode them. As noted in chapter 7, Bourdieu acknowledged this problem in his later years by adopting a writing style, forms of publications, and public interventions in the mass media designed to reach a larger public. But he did not resolve it.

The second way confronts a more fundamental challenge in addressing a deeper problem: the problem of habitus. There needs to be not only transmission of the requisite cultural capital but also a politics of habitus. The transfer of cultural capital to the dominated will fall on deaf ears unless it finds anchorage in fundamental dispositions that are reception to its message. There must be a receptive habitus to the message of critical science or a project of habitus transformation to encourage receptivity. Critical sociological discourse needs to unmask not just the objective structures causing the crisis but also make connections between those structures and the habitus actors bring to the situation. Here the problem is not just one of increasing access to cultural capital. It is a problem of transforming dispositions and this would seem to occur only through processes of re-socialization. One cannot just illuminate oppressive structures and expect habitus to change. Nor can one just transform structures with the expectation that habitus will readily adapt. Such would be tantamount to the kind of rationalist, objectivist illusion that Bourdieu so forcefully argues against. Neither the transmission of knowledge nor a change in structures without a change in habitus makes any sense in Bourdieu's framework. The whole of his sociology shows a more complex relationship between dispositions and structures than such rationalistic visions (illusions from Bourdieu's standpoint) would permit. There needs to be a politics of habitus as well which Bourdieu points to, yet stops short of saying much about how that might take place.

There is therefore an unresolved tension at the heart of Bourdieu's thinking between the strength of the habitus, which carries symbolic violence and operates beyond conscious reach and willful manipulation, and the critical insight of social science that would raise awareness of conditions producing symbolic violence. On the one hand, Bourdieu counts on some degree of consciousness-raising that a critical social science can provide. This will be aided by a crisis situation since consciousness-raising is more likely to fall on receptive ears when traditional expectations are disrupted by crisis. On the other hand, transformation will require a resocializing action at the level of the habitus. On this Bourdieu has little to say about how this might occur. It seems clear that he sees the need for collective undertakings (political labor in political collectivities) that will involve not just public demonstrations but also processes of resocialization to address the inertia of habitus. But just how that political labor is to address the inertia of habitus—particularly in the short run—remains unclear. And in what kind of social relationships is the resocialization to be carried out, by whom, and over what time period? These are fundamental political socialization questions that receive little attention in Bourdieu's writings.

The importance of critical discourse in Bourdieu's thinking for promoting change is frequently overlooked by critics in part because Bourdieu himself stressed the field properties of discourse and the capacity of the bodily dispositions of habitus to escape conscious awareness and manipulation. Bourdieu believed that good social science by its very nature is critical and by challenging the taken-for-granted character of the social order also challenges the basis of power in a way that opens up the possibility for new social arrangements to appear. This reveals an underlying optimism—one might argue naïveté—driving his sociological enterprise given his own emphasis on the embodiment of dispositions characterizing the habitus. His vision for a critical sociology that would help create one of the conditions (that is, loss of legitimation for established power relations) for social transformation stands in tension with this central pillar of social order. As discussed in chapter 7, he would come to see later in his career the need for more direct political engagements using the symbolic capital accumulated through his scientific work. While he warns against the idea of seeing intellectuals as privileged catalysts of significant social change, his vision for a collective intellectual does embody the hope for the power of critical discourse that might lead to some transformative action. However, he stops short of identifying any particular group as a carrier of social change. He clearly sees intellectuals as carriers of universal values and as key players in bringing about change in modern societies. But he never subscribed to a form of new class theory as did, for example,

Alvin Gouldner (1979). More generally, he does not identify historical carriers of social change, such as the industrial working class in capitalism or the Algerian peasantry in decolonization.

While Bourdieu identifies disjunctures between habitus and field as a source of change, he did not theorize changes in field opportunity structures themselves. Here and there he evokes potentially important factors such as the growing division of labor, growth in number of field participants, intrusion of external events into fields, and the dynamics of conflict itself. But these are not assembled into a general theory of change. However, Bourdieu does see a growing set of structural conditions that he believes are increasing the opportunity for progressive change. He (1996d, 382–89) sees the development of new power fields creating a more decentralized distribution of power. Here his thinking follows that of Norbert Elias in seeing the concentration of power of the state extending through lengthening and interweaving chains of interdependent power centers (Bourdieu 2012, 209–10; Elias 1982, 104–16). The field of power is becoming more differentiated as more and more fields emerge becoming more and more autonomous. In modern societies the struggle for power is progressively becoming more differentiated and complex by the increase of the number of fields that influence the struggle for state power (1996d, 389). He suggests that this increasing pluralism in the field of power opens up opportunities for subordinate groups to contest effectively the established order, hence increasing the possibility for progressive politics. Bourdieu sees this change in the distribution of power in modernization as a change, using Durkheim's terminology, from mechanical to organic solidarity. He observes that "as autonomous fields multiply and the field of power diversifies, there is a move away from political indifferentiation and *mechanical solidarity* among interchangeable powers" creating a new kind of power structure that he describes as "an entire set of fields and forms of power united by a genuine *organic solidarity*, and thus both different and interdependent" (386). This organic solidarity in the field of power is facilitated by solidarities provided by family, clubs, commissions, colloquia, and so on, that transcend divisions.[5] This is made possible by the expansion of the education system, particularly elite forms of schooling, which Bourdieu sees as increasingly the principal mediating institution of power relations in modern societies.

---

5. The development of transfield solidarities overlaps to some extent with the circulation of elites Mills (2000) described and forms of ruling elite associations that Domhoff (1978, 1990, 2001) has documented.

This new and growing field pluralism has important implications for democratic politics according to Bourdieu. While the new organic solidarity still creates new and enduring patterns of domination, the task of legitimating power relations is becoming more varied and demanding. The growth in diverse fields that accompanied bureaucratization of the state is lengthening the "chains of legitimation" (Bourdieu 2012, 210). In modern societies the successful exercise of power requires dealing effectively with an increasing number of ostensibly independent sources of legitimation (Bourdieu 1996d, 382–89). This intensifies the need for legitimating powers to meet the growing competition and also makes their effectiveness more precarious because of the increasing claims to define the legitimate view of the social world. Thus the struggle to monopolize symbolic power appears to be increasingly contested. The process has important implications for progressive politics or what Wacquant (2005c, 17) identifies as "strategies of universalization." Bourdieu argues that "we may advance the notion that progress in the differentiation of forms of power is constituted by so many protective acts against tyranny, understood, after the manner of Pascal, as the infringement of one order upon the rights of another, or more precisely, as an intrusion of the forms of power associated with one field in the functioning of another" (1996d, 389).

The growing plurality of powers in the field of power actually enhances the chances for progressive change for two reasons: first, "the dominated can always take advantage of or benefit from conflicts among the powerful" and second, "symbolic universalization of particular interests that, even if its undertaken for the purpose of legitimation or mobilization, inevitably leads to the advancement of the universal" (1996d, 389). Field pluralism and concentration of power are not incompatible forces for Bourdieu but different expressions of the same complex set of power arrangements in modern societies. In this way Bourdieu would sidestep the old elite versus pluralist debate over the distribution of power by seeing key elements in both sets of claims. Power in modern societies is increasingly monopolized by elites in a growing diversity of fields. Yet he sees political struggle among dominant groups as enhancing the cause of the universal. "It is clear that whatever their grounds or motives, these struggles among dominants necessarily add to the field of power a bit of that universal—reason, disinterestedness, civic-mindedness, etc.—that, originating as it does in previous struggles, is always a symbolically effective weapon in the struggles of the moment." Moreover, "symbolic universalization of particular interests that, even if its undertaken for the purpose of legitimation or mobilization, inevitably leads to the advancement of the universal" (389). That is, struggles to show disinterestedness, civic-mindedness though limited by parochial concerns, nonetheless advance those very ideals. This suggests in his thinking both a trend toward increasing elite differentiation within the field of power and considerable optimism in the idea that competing claims to represent universal interests albeit partial somehow advance the ideal of universality. While both ideas are debatable, they nonetheless secure the point that Bourdieu's sociology of symbolic domination and social reproduction is conceptually open to elements of change.

Neither Neutrality nor Advocacy

Bourdieu carves out a distinctive position as a scholar and public intellectual in the current debate over the relationship of sociology to politics—a "scholarship with commitment" position. Four features seem particularly salient. First, Bourdieu brings a critical posture to the study of political life. In the mode of Marx and Enlightenment reason, he employs a "ruthless criticism" of all established powers. Sociology is not a leisure activity, an armchair pursuit, or strictly an academic endeavor. Bourdieu never viewed his sociology as simply knowledge for knowledge's sake, although his call for the autonomy of social scientific work drew inspiration from the "art for art's sake" current in the artistic field. His sociology is critical; it challenges taken-for-granted assumptions and the legitimacy of established powers.

Second, his posture is one of critic, not officeholder, political advisor, or advocate. Bourdieu always took the stance of outside critic of political organizations. He spoke to current political issues without embracing the official position of any of the established political parties or trade unions, including those on the left. While clearly an intellectual on the French left, Bourdieu pursued a strategy of critic of those in power, whether of the French Gaullists, conservatives, liberals, centrists, or socialists and communists. Just as he saw the first step in social scientific analysis as breaking with received views, he debunked the mechanisms of power regardless of political orientation. Thus his political engagements did not lead to the kind of consultant to government that Anthony Giddens adopted in the Blair Labor government in the United Kingdom. And he never pursued an electoral strategy as did Václav Havel in the Czech Republic or Fernando Henrique Cardoso in Brazil. In Bourdieu's view, committed intellectuals "would not rule but, while remaining in their place, they would constitute a very serious control over rules, especially in those domains where they know a great deal, if only by saying that we do not know enough" (Wacquant 1993b, 38).

Yet he was not a critical gadfly speaking publicly to all the issues of the day as in the "total intellectual" tradition established by Jean-Paul Sartre. Part of Bourdieu's criticism of Sartre's "total intellectual" model is that Sartre used intellectual status to speak to political issues outside of his area of expertise. By contrast, Bourdieu confined his public political activities to issues that were connected to his social scientific research. There were exceptions, of course, as when he joined Michel Foucault in organizing a public protest against the silence of the French Socialist government in response to the 1981 military crackdown on Solidarity in Poland. (He was not an expert on eastern European socialist regimes or in international relations.) But his later criticisms of French government measures to reduce welfare-state responsibilities by introducing market mechanisms in the public sector were connected to his research *The Social Structures of the Economy* (2005b) on state housing policy in France and his research *The Weight of the World* (Bourdieu et al. 1999) into the experience of social exclusion. The results from both studies show the French state abdicating its political, indeed moral, role in providing a secure basis for social life. Another notable exception was his criticism of TV journalism that exploded on the public arena with the 1966 publication of *On Television* (Bourdieu 1998e). That work was based on long-standing critical assessments of the media but not on systematic research like he did of the university, the grandes écoles, social exclusion, or housing. But for the most part Bourdieu held to the principle that political voice must come out of solid social scientific research—a third significant feature.

Fourth, his critical posture would also affirm the autonomy of science and the intellectual field more generally. Indeed, defense of the autonomy of intellectual life from political and economic distortions is one of the most enduring themes in Bourdieu's political sociology.[6] In order to be

6. While I argue in this book that Bourdieu's political sociology represents a key window into Bourdieu's sociology and that he became centrally concerned with defending the welfare state against neoliberalism in his later years, it is significant that he chose to publish his final Collège de France lectures on science and reflexivity and not his earlier lectures on the state. In the foreword to *Science of Science and Reflexivity* (Bourdieu 2004b), Bourdieu explains his choice to publish the science lectures because he perceived that the autonomy of science was dangerously threated by impinging economic interests and media seductions. By contrast, the editors of *Sur L'État* (Bourdieu 2012, 594) note that there is no indication that Bourdieu

a credible voice in the public area, sociology needs to establish itself as a legitimate science with considerable symbolic capital—a goal Bourdieu pursued with particular intensity early in his career but maintained in his later years as well.

In sum, Bourdieu's vision for a politically engaged sociology would sidestep the traditional opposition between engagement and autonomy by seeing them as complementary rather than necessarily opposed. Bourdieu's conception of the scientific vocation and political vocation of the sociologist posits a twofold strategic mission: one defensive and the other offensive. On the one hand, the sociologist must defend the autonomy of the intellectual field against all forms of economic and political distortions, particularly the commercialization and politicization of intellectual work. On the other hand, the sociologist must use the methods and findings of research not for advocacy but to critically challenge (debunk) prevailing notions supporting existing power relations in hopes of creating conditions for alternative and more egalitarian social arrangements.

Toward a Normative Vision for Democratic Action

I have argued that Bourdieu views sociology as a tool for enhancing the chances of change toward more equality. Bourdieu does not outline explicitly in any of his writings a political program for progressive politics. But he does have a vision for what democratic political life should look like. Here and there in his writings normative windows appear offering glimpses of Bourdieu's democratic ideals. Bourdieu always viewed his intellectual and public activism as efforts to enhance democratic politics. He was never an apologist for any of the previous or currently existing state socialist societies, despite his sharp criticism of the liberal democracies and his inspiration from Marx. Though clearly on the political left, Bourdieu never became a card-carrying member of one of the French leftist parties (Communist, Socialist, or one of the smaller more radical left groups), unlike several of his contemporary French intellectuals. He staked out a *gauche de gauche* (left that is Left) position that he identified in

---

intended to turn his state lectures into a book despite the rich insights they reveal of his thinking on the topic. Despite the importance of his public political activism in his later years, it is ultimately the defense of the autonomy of science, not the state, that is the more enduring theme throughout Bourdieu's work.

1998 in sharp criticism of the French Socialist Party's policies of reducing welfare-state provision. The expression has become a well-known phrase in French political discourse (Bourdieu 2008e, 296–99). Bourdieu offered a vision of democracy that works to maximize the openness of democratic process and facilitate the participation of all. Indeed, the whole thrust of his work is to attack all instituted practices that form obstacles to that ideal of universal participation. Bourdieu always saw his role as critic in a democratic process—offering a critical sociology oriented toward making existing democracies more open, more genuine, a closer approximation to their ideals.

Neither Markets nor Hierarchies: Democratic Politics as Process

As pointed out in chapter 7, Bourdieu (2005b) rejects the classic liberal vision for political action that rests fundamentally on the autonomy and freedom of individual choice. It is the prevailing form in the liberal democracies where individuals, in the secrecy of the ballot box or with the promise of anonymity in the opinion survey, make their choices. These are aggregated statistically into majority positions that are idealized as the collective will. This utilitarian view of individual freedom is one of choice in isolation from all social influences.[7] But, argues Bourdieu, drawing from Durkheim's (1992) well-known criticism of market egoism (individualism), this outcome is simply the aggregation of individual strategies. It is a statistical artifact rather than a collective process with genuine social significance. It is a usurped identity by those technocratic powers able to mobilize support for artificially construed political views, particularly through opinion polling. To those who see the individual vote and opinion poll as vital safeguards against the conforming pressures of collective mobilization or constraints of ward politics, Bourdieu poses a fundamental question: is there really anything genuinely collective and social about the aggregation of individual votes? His answer is no. The idealized market logic is not fundamentally social. It is but a statistical aggregate, artificial,

---

7. This market view of democratic freedom is idealized by Milton Friedman (2002). Laissez-faire markets may be what Friedman thought of as freedom, but Bourdieu, like Durkheim, thought they were an abomination, tantamount to Hobbes's state of nature where the "icy water of egotistical calculation" reigns supreme and all sense of security and human commitment would bow to the highest bidder (Hobbes 1994 [1668]; Tucker 1978, 475)!

mechanical, and independent of actors themselves since it does not represent the combining of their opinions, or the development of an opinion out of a collective process (Bourdieu 2000b, 85). Moreover, those statistical artifacts are open to manipulation by those with the requisite cultural capital to do so. Like Durkheim before him, Bourdieu does not see the invisible hand of the market as guarantor of democratic life.[8]

Genuine political action does not stand in the final analysis on individual choice as the liberal political philosophy tradition would have it but on the choice of how a collective mode of choice is to be constructed (Bourdieu 2000b, 88). Genuine collective and democratic participation needs to begin with "the choice of the collective mode of construction of choices," by which Bourdieu means that the first task of any group wishing to produce a group opinion must be "to produce an opinion about the way to produce an opinion" (Bourdieu 2005b, 62). This is ostensibly a procedural question but more fundamentally a power issue. His answer focuses on how to make collective political expression more democratic, a genuine collective expression and also one that is not usurped by delegated leadership. To this end,

> one needs to work towards creating the social conditions for the establishment of a mode of fabrication of the "general will" (or of the collective opinion) that is genuinely collective, that is, based on the regulated exchanges of a dialectical confrontation presupposing agreement on the instruments of communication necessary for establishing agreement or disagreement and capable of transforming the contents communicated as well as those who communicate. (62)

Yet, as seen in chapter 4, Bourdieu also points up the problem of delegation in political representation that harbors a tendency to usurp the voice of citizens and to impose hierarchy. The danger with delegation is usurpation—the redirecting away from the collective interest by delegated lead-

8. Near the end of his career Bourdieu became a highly visible critic of neoliberalism, indeed one of the leaders against globalization, as I note in chapter 7. Though not a social movement theorist like Alain Touraine, Bourdieu became a leading voice of the antiglobalization social movement in France and Europe more generally. What this study shows is that Bourdieu's sharp criticism of neoliberal politics was not a recent political move, as some of his critics charged, even if he did adopt more public forms of political expression than he did earlier in his career. Rather, his anti-neoliberal politics were deeply rooted in his political sociology, in the very foundations of how he thought about the social order, reflecting in part the Durkheimian legacy in his thinking. This study has tried to identify those intellectual roots.

ership toward its own vested interest of protecting and accumulating ever more leadership advantage and power. Bourdieu is acutely aware of the dangers of political conformism imposed by social pressures fostered by formal political units such as unions and parties. Indeed his sharp criticism of delegation and dispossession is aimed precisely at that kind of distortion he sees in democratic life. Bourdieu's answer is to work toward conditions that better produce genuinely collective opinion by improving conditions of access and by stressing means of communication that maximize input, discussion, and exchange. His vision for normative democratic action is one where genuine collective decisionmaking occurs—a process where individuals express their intention for how they are to be represented. Thus, the focus of Bourdieu is not fundamentally just to enhance individual autonomy and freedom—though he strongly embraced human rights—but to help create the social conditions for genuine collective decisionmaking. Here, he stands closer to the Durkheimian corporatist tradition than that of utilitarian choice.

Nor does this mean that Bourdieu's vision for genuine political action resides in some idealized democratic state. Rather, it appears in those "subterranean struggles"—everyday actions that are not recognized as explicitly political—where for Bourdieu one indeed finds politics that "profoundly and durably affect the relations of power within the field of power" and also "contain the true principle of stances in political struggles for power over the state" (Bourdieu 1996d, 388). Here Bourdieu stresses the importance of this broader arena of struggles for understanding politics rather than adopting a state-centric view, or a view of political action narrowly focused on the political field. Clearly Bourdieu roots politics first and foremost in civil society. Politics are rooted fundamentally in the formation, maintenance, and enhancement of group existence and identity. However, he does not idealize civil society as a kind of prepolitical state where sociability is devoid of power. Power and politics are at the very basis of group formation and identity itself. Symbolic power is both embedded in the everyday classifications and frames of reference of actors and therefore diffused throughout civil society and also concentrated in state agencies that specialize in expressing and controlling that kind of power. This points up a fundamental tension between his sociology of group formation and identity and his political sociology of state power. Where lies the initiative? In parts of his work the emphasis is on groups and in other parts it is on the state. Of course his criticism of the process of delegation and consequent dispossession shows that democratic processes

of representation are always fraught with distortion. And his critical assessment of the increasing social closure of the French political field and
the monopolizing power of the state over symbolic resources highlight
the challenges facing genuine democratic representation in civil society.
Still, the ongoing dynamics of field struggle and increasing differentiation
and multiplication of forms of capital and fields present here and there
moments of opportunity for dominated groups to gain some measure of
freedom from established hierarchies and a chance to improve their lot
(Bourdieu 1996d, 382–89).

Science as Model for Democratic Process

But if the roots of politics lie in civil society rather than its regulatory bodies of the state, it is the field of science that offers an ideal model of what
the democratic political field should become. Bourdieu sees the scientific
field as a "kind of reasonable utopia of what a political field conforming
to democratic reason might be like." He would extend the "logic of intellectual life, that of arguing and refuting, to public life." By this he has in
mind "the scientific field in its most autonomous forms" that represents "a
regulated competition, which would control itself . . . by its own immanent
logic, through social mechanisms capable of forcing agents to behave 'rationally' and to sublimate their drives" (Bourdieu 2000e, 126). This could
become possible

> by using the ordinary means of political action—creation of associations and
> movements, demonstrations, manifestoes, etc.—the *Realpolitik* of reason aimed
> at setting up or reinforcing, within the political field, the mechanisms capable of
> imposing the sanctions, as far as possible automatic ones, that would tend to dis-
> courage deviations from the democratic norm (such as the corruption of elected
> representatives) and to encourage or impose the appropriate behaviours; aimed
> also at favouring the setting up of non-distorted social structures of communi-
> cation between the holders of power and the citizens, in particularly through a
> constant struggle for the independence of the media. (126)

His ideal, therefore, would be to make of politics a kind of binding normative arena resembling his ideal for the scientific field.

But can a field based on political capital, which is a form of social capital, ever be modeled ultimately on a field based on cultural capital in the

form of science where the ideal is "truth for truth's sake" rather than truth in the greatest numbers, where evaluation is given by professional peers rather than by the masses? Might not the political field, as Max Weber's specific logics of the separate spheres suggest, be fundamentally different if not antagonistic to an intellectual field? Are not the human experiences of searching for truth and organizing the greatest number for some objective fundamentally different experiences that inform human action but do not reduce to the other? Moreover, when the latter has recourse to the means of physical as well as symbolic violence, the struggle for power as an end itself remains distinct from the struggle for knowledge as a form of power. In short, there are limits to which a knowledge field like science can function as a realistic model for the political field.

Still, this idealized vision to improve democratic life by creating more transparent understandings of power relations offers a needed challenge to current political practices. And it is important to recognize that though a sharp critic of existing democracies Bourdieu always saw his efforts as ways of enhancing democratic processes. Indeed, Bourdieu's thinking can be a source of inspiration for the practice of democratic politics (Wacquant 2005b). He invites sociologists to employ social scientific inquiry as a means to debunk taken-for-granted assumptions that seem crucial for maintenance of the established powers that limit political participation. He envisions for the critical sociologist a political vocation that would be politically relevant yet not compromise the science of asking critical questions. Yet there are limits to Bourdieu's vision that is rooted in an excessively strong view of the role of symbolic power in maintaining power relations, a view that seems at odds even with the more direct forms of political activism Bourdieu himself adopted in his later years. Indeed, Bourdieu's own efforts as a public sociologist stand in sharp contrast to aspects of his theory of symbolic power and violence. He saw his sociology as an effort to denaturalize and render less fatalistic the social world, which he tried to communicate to people. But given the powerful force of habitus to operate beyond the reaches of conscious decisionmaking, it is not clear how the debunking force of sociology could be effective against the unconscious force of habitus and the dynamics of misrecognition it reinforces. As noted in chapter 7, Bourdieu's shift in thinking and political practice seems to acknowledge this limitation.

Nonetheless, Bourdieu's perspective challenges the commonly held view that symbolic power is simply "symbolic." Symbolic meanings and classifications are constitutive forces in organizing power relations in stratified social orders. Moreover, the concept of symbolic violence is designed as a critical break with the view that power has become much more benign and less relevant in societies where the most authoritarian and crudest techniques of coercion have been replaced with persuasion, consent, choice, influence, and negotiation. It reminds us that power remains very much an organizing force in modern societies though its forms have changed. And its organizing force can be for change as well as for perpetuating existing power arrangements. Critical sociology, following the example set by Pierre Bourdieu, can play a contributing role for democratic change.

References

Accardo, Alain. 1983. *Initiation à la sociologie de l'illusionnisme social*. Bordeaux: Éditions le Mascaret.

Adams, Julia. 1994. "The Familial State: Elite Family Practices and State-Making in the Early Modern Netherlands." *Theory and Society* 23 (4): 505–39.

Addi, Lahouari. 2002. *Sociologie et anthropologie chez Pierre Bourdieu: La paradigme anthropologique kabyle et ses conséquences théoriques*. Paris: Éditions La Découverte.

Alexander, Jeffrey C. 1995. *Fin de Siècle Social Theory: Relativism, Reduction, and the Problem of Reason*. New York: Verso.

———. 2003. *The Meanings of Social Life*. New York: Oxford University Press.

———. 2006. *The Civil Sphere*. New York: Oxford University Press.

Alford, Robert A., and Roger Friedland. 1985. *Powers of Theory: Capitalism, the State and Democracy*. New York: Cambridge University Press.

Allardt, Erik. 2001. "Political Sociology." Pp. 11701–6 in *International Encyclopedia of the Social and Behavioral Sciences*, edited by Neil J. Smelser and Paul B. Baltes. New York: Elsevier.

Althusser, Louis. 1970. *For Marx*. New York: Vintage Books.

———. 1971. "Ideology and Ideological State Apparatuses." Pp. 127–86 in *Lenin and Philosophy and Other Essays*. New York: Monthly Review Press. Also published in *Education: Structure and Society*, edited by B. R. Cosin, 242–80. Harmondsworth: Penguin Books.

Ancelovici, Marcos. 2010. "Esquisse d'une théorie de la contestation: Bourdieu et le modèle du processus politique." *Sociologie et Sociétés* 41 (2): 39–62.

Ansart, Pierre. 1990. *Les sociologies contemporaines*. Paris: Éditions du Seuil.

Aron, Raymond. 1968. *La Révolution introuvable*. Paris: Julliard.

Aronoff, Myron J. 2000. "Political Culture." Pp. 11640–44 in *Encyclopedia of Sociology*, edited by Edgar F. Borgatta. 2nd ed. Detroit: Macmillan.

Austin, John L. 1962. *How to Do Things with Words*. Oxford: Oxford University Press.

Bachelard, Gaston. 1949. *Le rationalisme appliqué*. Paris: Presses Universitaires de France.

———. 1980. *La Formation de l'esprit scientifique: Contribution à une psychanalyse de la connaissance objective*. 11th ed. Paris: J. Vrin.

———. 1984. *The New Scientific Spirit*. New York: W. W. Norton.

Bachrach, Peter. 1966. *The Theory of Democratic Elitism*. Boston: Little, Brown.

Balandier, Georges. 1970. *Political Anthropology*. New York: Pantheon Books.

———. 1985. *Sociologie des Brazzavilles noires*. 2nd ed. Paris: Armand Colin.

Bang, Henrik P., ed. 2003. *Governance as Social and Political Communication*. New York: Manchester University Press.

Baranger, Denis. 2008. "The Reception of Bourdieu in Latin America and Argentina." *Sociologica* 2:1–20.

Barnes, Barry. 1974. *Scientific Knowledge and Sociological Theory*. London: Routledge and Kegan Paul.

Barnes, Barry, and David Bloor. 1982. "Relativism, Rationalism and Sociology of Knowledge." Pp. 21–47 in *Rationality and Relativism*, edited by Martin Hollis and Steven Lukes. Oxford: Blackwell.

Beauvallet, Willy. 2003. "Institutionnalisation et professionnalisation de l'Europe politique. Le cas des eurodéputés français." *Politique européenne* 9, no. 1 (Winter): 99–122.

Becker, Gary. 1964. *Human Capital*. New York: National Bureau of Economic Research.

———. 1976. *The Economic Approach to Human Behavior*. Chicago: University of Chicago Press.

Benda, Julien. 1927. *La Trahison des clercs*. Paris: Grasset.

Benford, Robert D., and David A. Snow. 2000. "Framing Processes and Social Movements: An Overview and Assessment." *Annual Review of Sociology* 26:611–39.

Benson, Rodney. 1999. "Field Theory in Comparative Context: A New Paradigm for Media Studies." *Theory and Society* 28:463–98.

Benson, Rodney, and Érik Neveu, eds. 2005. *Bourdieu and the Journalistic Field*. Malden, MA: Polity.

Berezin, Mabel. 1997. "Politics and Culture: A Less Fissured Terrain." *Annual Review of Sociology* 23:361–83.

Bernhard, Stefan. 2011. "Beyond Constructivism: The Political Sociology of an EU Policy Field." *International Political Sociology* 5:426–45.

Bernhard, Stefan, and Christian Schmidt-Wellenburg, eds. 2012a. *Feldanalyse als Forschungsprogramm 1: Der programmatische Kern*. Wiesbaden: VS.

———, eds. 2012b. *Feldanalyse als Forschungsprogramm 2: Gegenstandsbezogene Theoriebildung*. Wiesbaden: VS.

Bittlingmayer, Uwe, Rolf Eickelpasch, Jens Kastner, and Claudia Rademacher, eds. 2002. *Theorie als Kampf? Zur politischen Soziologie Pierre Bourdieus*. Opladen: Leske+Budrich.

Blau, Judith, and Keri E. Lyall Smith. 2006. *Public Sociologies Reader*. Lanham, MD: Rowman and Littlefield.

Block, Fred. 1977. "The Ruling Class Does Not Rule: Notes on the Marxist Theory of the State." *Socialist Revolution* 33:6–28.

———. 1987. *Revising State Theory*. Philadelphia, PA: Temple University Press.

Bloemraad, Irene. 2001. "Outsiders and Insiders: Collective Identity and Collective Action in the Quebec Independence Movement, 1995." Pp. 271–305 in Dobratz, Waldner, and Buzzell 2001.

Blondiaux, Loïc. 1998. *La Fabrique de l'opinion. Une histoire sociale des sondages*. Paris: Seuil.

Bloor, David. 1976. *Knowledge and Social Imagery*. London: Routledge and Kegan Paul.

———. 1983. *Wittgenstein: A Social Theory of Knowledge*. New York: Columbia University Press.

Boltanski, Luc. 1973. "L'espace positionnel, multiplicité des positions institutionnelles et habitus de classe." *Revue Française de Sociologie* 14 (1): 3–26.

———. 1974. "How a Social Group Objectified Itself: 'Cadres' in France, 1936–1945." *Social Science Information* 23 (3): 469–92.

Bon, François, and Yves Schemeil. 1980. "La rationalisation de l'inconduite: Comprendre le statut du politique chez Pierre Bourdieu." *Revue Française de Sociologie* 30 (6): 1198–1230.

Boschetti, Anna. 2005. "Des deux Marx aux deux Bourdieu. Critique d'un mythe malveillant." Pp. 121–41 in *Rencontres avec Pierre Bourdieu*, edited by Gérard Mauger. Bellecombe-en-Bauges: Éditions du Croquant.

Bottomore, Tom. 1993. *Political Sociology*. 2nd ed. London: Pluto Press.

Boudon, Raymond. 1969. "La crise universitaire française: essai de diagnostic." *Annales* 24 (May–June): 738–64.

———. 1970. "Mai 68: Crise ou conflit, aliénation ou anomie?" *L'année sociologique* 19:222–42.

Bourdieu, Pierre. 1961. "Révolution dans la révolution." *Esprit* 1 (January): 27–40.

———. 1962a. *The Algerians*. Boston: Beacon Press.

———. 1962b. "Les sous-prolétaires algériens." *Les Temps Modernes* 199: 1030–51.

———. 1963. "Sociologues des mythologies et mythologies de sociologues." *Les Temps Modernes* 211 (December): 998–1021.

———. 1966. "L'école conservatrice, les inégalitiés devant l'école et devant la culture." *Revue Française de Sociologie* 7 (3): 325–47.

———. 1971a. "Genèse et structure du champ religieux." *Revue Française de Sociologie* 12 (3): 295–334.

———. 1971b. "L'opinion publique n'existe pas." *Noroit* 155/156:1–19.

———. 1972a. *Esquisse d'une théorie de la pratique. Précedée de trois études d'ethnologie kabyle*. Geneva: Droz.

———. 1972b. "Les doxosophes." *Minuit* 1 (November): 26–45.

———. 1974. "Avenir de classe et causalité du probable." *Revue Française de Sociologie* 15 (1): 3–42.

———. 1975a. "La lecture de Marx: Quelques remarques critiques à propos de 'Quelques remarques critiques à de *Lire le Capital*.'" *Actes de la Recherche en Sciences Sociales* 5/6:65–79.

———. 1975b. "Méthode scientifique et hierarchie sociale des objects." *Actes de la Recherche en Sciences Sociales* 1 (January): 4–6.

———. 1975c. "The Specificity of the Scientific Field and the Social Conditions of the Progress of Reason." *Social Science Information* 14 (6): 19–47.

———. 1977a. *Outline of a Theory of Practice*. Cambridge: Cambridge University Press.

———. 1977b. "Questions de politique." *Actes de la Recherche en Sciences Sociales* 16 (September): 55–89.

———. 1980a. "Le capital social." *Actes de la Recherche en Sciences Sociales* 31: 2–3.

———. 1980b. "Le mort saisi le vif. Les relations entre l'histoire incorporée et l'histoire réifiée." *Actes de la Recherche en Sciences Sociales* 32/33:3–14.

———. 1980c. *Le sens pratique*. Paris: Editions de Minuit.

———. 1980d. "Sartre." *London Review of Books* 2–20 (October 20): 11–12.

———. 1984a. *Distinction: A Social Critique of the Judgment of Taste*. Cambridge, MA: Harvard University Press.

———. 1984b. "Le champ littéraire: préalables critiques et principes de méthode." *Lendemains* 36:5–20.

———. 1985a. "The Market of Symbolic Goods." *Poetics* 14 (April): 13–44.

———. 1985b. "Social Space and the Genesis of Groups." *Theory and Society* 14 (6): 723–44.

———. 1986. "The Forms of Capital" (1983). Pp. 241–58 in *Handbook of Theory and Research for the Sociology of Education*, edited by John G. Richardson. New York: Greenwood Press.

———. 1987a. *Choses Dites*. Paris: Les Éditions de Minuit.

———. 1987b. "The Force of Law: Toward a Sociology of the Juridical Field." *Hastings Journal of Law* 38:209–48.

———. 1987c. "Legitimation and Structured Interests in Weber's Sociology of Religion." Pp. 119–36 in *Max Weber, Rationality and Irrationality*, edited by Scott Lash and Sam Whimster. Boston: Allen and Unwin.

———. 1987d. "What Makes a Social Class? On the Theoretical and Practical Existence of Groups." *Berkeley Journal of Sociology* 32:1–18.

———. 1988a. "Flaubert's Point of View." *Critical Inquiry* 14 (Spring): 539–62.

———. 1988b. *Homo Academicus*. Stanford, CA: Stanford University Press.

———. 1988c. "Penser la politique." *Actes de la Recherche en Sciences Sociales* 71/72:2–3.

———. 1989a. "The Corporatism of the Universal: The Role of Intellectuals in the Modern World." *Telos* 81:99–110.

———. 1989b. *La noblesse d'État. Grandes corps et grandes écoles*. Paris: Les Édition de Minuit.

———. 1989c. "Le pouvoir n'est plus rue-d'Ulm mais à l'ENA." *Le Nouvel Observateur* 1270 (March 9–15): 80–82.

———. 1989d. "Social Space and Symbolic Power." *Sociological Theory* 7 (1): 14–25. Also published in Bourdieu 1990b, 122–39.

———. 1990a. "Codification" (1986). Pp. 76–86 in Bourdieu 1990b.

———. 1990b. *In Other Words: Essays Toward a Reflexive Sociology*. Stanford, CA: Stanford University Press.

———. 1990c. *The Logic of Practice*. Stanford, CA: Stanford University Press.

———. 1990d. "Opinion Polls: A 'Science' without a Scientist" (1985). Pp. 168–74 in Bourdieu 1990b.

———. 1990e. "The Uses of the 'People.'" Pp. 150–55 in Bourdieu 1990b.

———. 1991a. "Delegation and Political Fetishism" (1984). Pp. 203–19 in Bourdieu 1991e.

———. 1991b. "Description and Prescription: The Conditions of Possibility and the Limits of Political Effectiveness." Pp. 127–36 in Bourdieu 1991e.

———. 1991c. "Genesis and Structure of the Religious Field." *Comparative Social Research* 13:1–43.

———. 1991d. "Identity and Representation: Elements for a Critical Reflection on the Idea of Region." Pp. 220–28 in Bourdieu 1991e.

———. 1991e. *Language and Symbolic Power*. Cambridge, MA: Harvard University Press.

———. 1991f. "Le champ littéraire." *Actes de la Recherche en Sciences Sociales* 89 (September): 4–46.

———. 1991g. "On Symbolic Power" (1977). Pp. 163–70 in Bourdieu 1991e.

———. 1991h. "Political Representation: Elements for a Theory of the Political Field" (1981). Pp. 171–202 in Bourdieu 1991e.

———. 1991i . "Social Space and the Genesis of 'Classes.'" Pp. 229–51 in Bourdieu 1991e.

———. 1992. "Pour une Internationale des intellectuels." *Politis* 1:9–15.

———. 1993a. "Á propos de Sartre." *French Cultural Studies* 4:209–11.

———. 1993b. "Culture and Politics." Pp. 158–67 in Bourdieu 1993i.

———. 1993c. "Esprits d'État: Genèse et structure du champ bureaucratique." *Actes de la Recherche en Sciences Sociales* 96/97:49–62.

———. 1993d. *The Field of Cultural Production: Essays on Art and Literature*. New York: Columbia University Press.

———. 1993e. "Il faudrait réinventer une sorte d'intellectuel collectif sur le modèle de ce qu'ont été les Encyclopédistes." *Le monde*, December 7, 2.

———. 1993f. "L'intellectual dans la cité. Il faut restaurer la tradition de vigilance" *Le monde*, November 5, 29

———. 1993g. "Public Opinion Does Not Exist" (1971). Pp. 124–30 in *Capitalism and Imperialism*, vol. 1. of *Communication and Class Struggle*, edited by

Armand Mattelart and Seth Siegelaub. New York: International General/
IMMRC. Also published in Bourdieu 1993i, 149–57.

———. 1993h. "A Science that Makes Trouble" (1984). Pp. 8–19 in Bourdieu
1993i.

———. 1993i. *Sociology in Question.* Thousand Oaks, CA: Sage Publications.

———. 1993j. "The Sociologist in Question" (1984). Pp. 21–35 in Bourdieu 1993i.

———. 1994a. "L'emprise du journalisme." *Actes de la Recherche en Sciences Sociales* 101/102:3–9.

———. 1994b. "Rethinking the State: Genesis and Structure of the Bureaucratic
Field" (1993). *Sociological Theory* 12 (1): 1–18. Also published in Bourdieu
1998i, 35–63.

———. 1996a. "Champ politique, champ des sciences sociales, champ journalis-
tique." *Cahiers de recherche—GRS, Lyon* 15.

———. 1996b. "For a Corporatism of the Universal" (1992). Pp. 339–48 in Bourdieu
1996c.

———. 1996c. *The Rules of Art: Genesis and Structure of the Literary Field.* Stanford, CA: Stanford University Press.

———. 1996d. *The State Nobility: Elite Schools in the Field of Power.* Stanford, CA:
Stanford University Press.

———. 1997a. "De la maison du roi à la raison d'État: Un modèle de la genèse du
champ bureaucratique." *Actes de la Recherche en Sciences Sociales* 118 (June):
55–68.

———. 1997b. *Méditations pascaliennes.* Paris: Seuil.

———. 1998a. *Acts of Resistance: Against the Tyranny of the Market.* New York:
New Press.

———, ed. 1998b. *Contre-feux: Propos pour servir à la résistance contre l'invasion
néo-libérale.* Paris: Liber-Raisons D'Agir.

———. 1998c. "La pécarité est aujourd'hui partout." Pp. 95–101 in Bourdieu
1998b.

———. 1998d. "Le neo-liberalism, utopie (en voie de realisation) d'une exploitation sans limites." Pp. 108–19 in Bourdieu 1998b.

———. 1998e. *On Television.* New York: New Press.

———. 1998f. "The Protest Movement of the Unemployed, a Social Miracle."
Pp. 88–90 in Bourdieu 1998a.

———. 1998g. "The Left Hand and the Right Hand of the State" (1992). Pp. 1–10
in Bourdieu 1998a.

———. 1998h. *Practical Reason: On the Theory of Action.* Stanford, CA: Stanford
University Press.

———. 1998i. "On the Fundamental Ambivalence of the State." *Polygraph* 10:
21–32.

———. 1999a. "The Abdication of the State" (1993). Pp. 181–88 in Bourdieu et
al. 1999.

————. 1999b. "Scattered Remarks." *European Journal of Social Theory* 2 (3): 334–40.

————. 1999c. "The Social Conditions of the International Circulation of Ideas." Pp. 220–28 in *Bourdieu: A Critical Reader*, edited by Richard Shusterman. Oxford: Blackwell.

————. 2000a. "Conférence: Le Champ Politique." Pp. 49–80 in Bourdieu 2000f.

————. 2000b. "Formes d'action politique et modes d'existence des groups." Pp. 81–88 in Bourdieu 2000f.

————. 2000c. *Les structures sociales de l'économie*. Paris: Édition du Seuil.

————. 2000d. "Monopolisation politique et révolutions symboliques" (1990). Pp. 99–107 in Bourdieu 2000f.

————. 2000e. *Pascalian Meditations*. Stanford, CA: Stanford University Press.

————. 2000f. *Propos sur le Champ Politique*. Lyon: Presses Universitaires de Lyon.

————. 2001a. *Contre-feux 2. Pour un mouvement social européen*. Paris: RAISONS D'AGIR Éditions.

————. 2001b. "L'imposition du modèle américain et ses effets." Pp. 25–31 in Bourdieu 2001a.

————. 2001c. *Masculine Domination*. Stanford, CA: Stanford University Press.

————. 2001d. *Science de la science et réflexivité*. Paris: RAISONS D'AGIR Éditions.

————. 2002a. "Address to the True Masters of the World." *Berkeley Journal of Sociology* 46:170–76.

————. 2002b. "Les conditions sociales de la circulation internationale des idées." *Actes de la Recherche en Sciences Sociales* 145:3–8.

————. 2004a. "From the King's House to the Reason of State: A Model of the Genesis of the Bureaucratic Field." *Constellations* 11 (1): 16–36. Also published in Wacquant 2005b, 29–54.

————. 2004b. *Science of Science and Reflexivity*. Chicago: University of Chicago Press.

————. 2005a. "The Mystery of Ministry: From Particular Wills to the General Will" (2001). Pp. 55–63 in Wacquant 2005b.

————. 2005b. *The Social Structures of the Economy*. Cambridge: Polity.

————. 2005c. "The State and the Construction of the Market" (1990). Pp. 89–125 in Bourdieu 2005b.

————. 2008a. "Appeal for the Organization of a General Assembly of Teaching and Research" (1968). Pp. 41–45 in Bourdieu 2008e.

————. 2008b. "Colonial War and Revolutionary Consciousness." Pp. 3–6 in Bourdieu 2008e.

————. 2008c. "For an International of Intellectuals." Pp. 209–17 in Bourdieu 2008e.

————. 2008d. "The Object of a Writers' Parliament." Pp. 238–41 in Bourdieu 2008e.

———. 2008e. *Political Interventions: Social Science and Political Action*. New York: Verso. Translated from the French edition *Interventions, 1961–2002. Science sociale et action politique*. Marseille: Agone, 2002.

———. 2008f. "Scholars and the Social Movement." Pp. 380–83 in Bourdieu 2008e.

———. 2008g. *Sketch for a Self-Analysis*. Chicago: University of Chicago Press.

———. 2012. *Sur l'État. Cours au Collège de France 1989–1992*. Paris: Raisons d'agir/Seuil.

Bourdieu, Pierre, et al. 1999. *The Weight of the World: Social Suffering in Contemporary Society*. Stanford, CA: Stanford University Press.

Bourdieu, Pierre, Christian Baudelot, Christophe Charle, Jacques Fijalkow, Bernard Lacroix, and Daniel Roche. 1997. "Université: La réforme du trompe-l'oeil." *Le monde*, April 1.

Bourdieu, Pierre, Christian Baudelot, and Catherine Lévy. 1994. "Un questionnaire démagogique." *Le monde*, July 8.

Bourdieu, Pierre, and Luc Boltanski. 1976. "La production de l'idéologie dominante." *Actes de la Recherche en Sciences Sociales* 2–3 (June): 4–73.

Bourdieu, Pierre, Luc Boltanski, Robert Castel, and Jean-Claude Chamboredon. 1965. *Un art moyen: essai sur les usages de la photographie*. Paris: Éditions de Minuit.

Bourdieu, Pierre, Luc Boltanski, and Pascal Maldidier. 1971. "La Défense du Corps." *Social Science Information* 10 (4): 45–86.

Bourdieu, Pierre, and Marie-Claire Bourdieu. 1965. "Le paysan et la photographie." *Revue Française de Sociologie* 6 (2): 164–74.

Bourdieu, Pierre, Jean-Claude Chamboredon, and Jean-Claude Passeron. 1991. *The Craft of Sociology: Epistemological Preliminaries*. 2. Berlin: Walter de Gruyter.

Bourdieu, Pierre, Alain Darbel, Jean-Pierre Rivet, and Claude Seibel. 1963. *Travail et travailleurs en Algérie*. Paris: Mouton.

Bourdieu, Pierre, and Monique de Saint Martin. 1978. "Le patronat." *Actes de la Recherche en Sciences Sociales* 20/21:3–82.

Bourdieu, Pierre, and Jacques Derrida. 1994. "Non-assistance à personne en danger." *Le monde*, December 29.

———. 1995. "M. Pasqua, son conseiller et les étrangers." *Le monde*, January 10.

Bourdieu, Pierre, and Hans Haacke. 1994. *Libre-Échange*. Paris: Seuil/les presses du réel.

Bourdieu, Pierre, and Otto Hahn. 1970. "La théorie." *VH 101* 2 (Summer): 12–21.

Bourdieu, Pierre, and Jean Leca. 1995. "Non à la ghettoïsation de l'Algérie." *Le monde*, March 25.

Bourdieu, Pierre, and Jean-Claude Passeron. 1968. "L'examin d'une illusion." *Revue Française de Sociologie* 9 (special issue): 227–53.

———. 1970. *La reproduction: Éléments pour une théorie du système d'enseignement*. Paris: Les Éditions de Minuit.

————. 1977. *Reproduction in Education, Society, and Culture*. Beverly Hills, CA: Sage.

————. 1979. *The Inheritors: French Students and Their Relation to Culture*. Chicago: University of Chicago Press.

Bourdieu, Pierre, and Abdelmalek Sayad. 1964. *Le déracinement. La crise de l'agriculture traditionnelle en Algérie*. Paris: Éditions de Minuit.

Bourdieu, Pierre, and Loïc J. D. Wacquant. 1989. "For a Socioanalysis of Intellectuals: On 'Homo Academicus.'" *Berkeley Journal of Sociology* 34:1–29.

————. 1992. *An Invitation to Reflexive Sociology*. Chicago: University of Chicago Press.

Braud, Philippe. 2002. *Sociologie Politique*. 6th ed. Paris: Libraire Générale de Droit et de Jurisprudence.

Brubaker, Rogers. 1992. *Citizenship and Nationhood in France and Germany*. Cambridge, MA: Harvard University Press.

Buechler, Steven M. 2002. "Toward A Structural Approach to Social Movements." Pp. 1–45 in Dobratz, Buzzell, and Waldner 2002.

Burawoy, Michael. 2005a. "For Public Sociology." *American Sociological Review* 70 (February): 4–28.

————. 2005b. "Response: Public Sociology: Populist Fad or Path to Renewal?" *British Journal of Sociology* 56 (3): 417–32.

————. 2005c. "The Return of the Repressed: Recovering the Public Face of U.S. Sociology, One Hundred Years On." *Annals of the American Academy*, 1–18.

————. 2005d. "Third-Wave Sociology and the End of Pure Science." *American Sociologist* (Fall/Winter): 152–65.

————. 2010. "Conversations with Pierre Bourdieu: The Johannesburg Moment." University of California Berkeley. http://burawoy.berkeley.edu/Bourdieu.htm

Caillé, Alain. 1981. "La sociologie de l'intérêt est-elle intéressante?" *Sociologie du Travail* 23 (3): 257–74.

————. 1992. "Esquisse d'une critique de l'économie générale de la pratique." *Cahiers du LASA* (12–13): 109–219.

Calhoun, Craig. 1993. "Habitus, Field, and Capital: The Question of Historical Specificity." Pp. 61–88 in *Bourdieu: Critical Perspectives*, edited by Craig Calhoun, Edward LiPuma, and Moishe Postone. Chicago: University of Chicago Press.

————. 2005a. "Centralité du social et possibilité de la politique." In *Bourdieu: Le colloq Cerisy*, edited by J. DuBois, P. Durant, and Y. Winkin. Liège: Éditions de l'Université de Liège.

————. 2005b. "The Promise of Public Sociology." *British Journal of Sociology* 56 (3): 355–63.

————. 2005c. *Roots of Radicalism*. Chicago: University of Chicago Press.

————. 2006. "Pierre Bourdieu and Social Transformation: Lessons from Algeria." *Development and Change* 37 (6): 1403–15.

Camic, Charles. 1986. "The Matter of Habit." *American Journal of Sociology* 91 (5): 1039–87.

Carles, Pierre, dir. 2001. *Sociology Is a Martial Art.* Icarus Films, Brooklyn.

Carlton, Eric. 1996. *The Few and the Many: A Typology of Elites.* Brookfield, VT: Scolar Press.

Carnoy, Martin. 1984. *The State and Political Theory.* Princeton, NJ: Princeton University Press.

Caro, Jean-Yves. 1980. "La sociologie de Pierre Bourdieu: éléments pour une théorie du champ politique." *Revue française de science politique* 6 (December): 1171–97.

Champagne, Patrick. 1979. *Faire l'opinion. Le nouvel espace politique.* Paris: Éditions de Minuit.

———. 1990. *Faire l'opinion: le nouveau jeu politique.* Paris: Éditions de Minuit.

———. 2004. "Sur la 'médiatisation' du champ intellectuel. À propos de *Sur la télévision* de Pierre Bourdieu." Pp. 431–58 in *Pierre Bourdieu, sociologue*, edited by Louis Pinto, Gisèle Sapiro, and Patrick Champagne. Paris: Fayard.

Charle, Christophe. 1987 *Les élites de la République, 1880–1900.* Paris: Éditions de Minuit.

———. 1990. *Naissance des "intellectuels," 1880–1900.* Paris: Éditions de Minuit.

Checa, Sofia, Todd Evans, Sarah Jacobson, Yasser Munif, and Mark Nelson. 2005. "The State of Graduate Political Sociology Training." *Political Sociology: States, Power, and Societies* 11 (3): 10–11.

Clawson, Dan. 2007. *Public Sociology: Fifteen Eminent Sociologists Debate Politics and the Profession in the Twenty-First Century.* Berkeley: University of California Press.

Cohen, Antonin, Bernard Lacroix, and Philippe Riutort, eds. 2009. *Nouveau manuel de science politique.* Paris: La Découverte.

Coleman, James S. 1990. *Foundations of Social Theory.* Cambridge, MA: Harvard University Press.

Coleman, James S., Ernest Q. Campbell, Carol J. Hobson, James McPartland, Alexander M. Mood, Frederic D. Weinfeld, and Robert L. York. 1966. *Equality of Educational Opportunity.* Washington, DC: U.S. Government Printing Office.

Collins, Randall. 1994. *Four Sociological Traditions.* Revised and expanded edition of *Three Sociological Traditions.* Oxford: Oxford University Press.

Corcuff, Philippe. 1998. "Lire Bourdieu autrement." *Magazine Littérarie* 369: 34–36.

Coronil, Fernando. 1997. *The Magical State: Nature, Money and Modernity in Venezuela.* Chicago: University of Chicago Press.

Corrigan, Philip, and Derek Sayer. 1985. *The Great Arch: English State Formation as Cultural Revolution.* New York: Blackwell.

Crossley, Nick. 2001. "The Phenomenological Habitus and Its Construction." *Theory and Society* 30 (1): 81–120.

————. 2002. *Making Sense of Social Movements*. Buckingham: Open University Press.

Crozier, Michel. 1969. *La Société Bloquée*. Paris: Seuil.

Current Research. 1972. Paris: École pratique des hautes études, Maison des sciences de l'homme.

Dahl, Robert A. 1961. *Who Governs? Democracy and Power in an American City*. New Haven, CT: Yale University Press.

————. 1967. *Pluralist Democracy in the United States: Conflict and Consensus*. Chicago: Rand McNally.

————. 1971. *Polyarchy: Participation and Oppression*. New Haven, CT: Yale University Press.

Dean, Mitchell. 2003. "Culture Governance and Individualism." Pp. 117–39 in Bang 2003.

Debray, Régis. 1981. *Teachers, Writers, Celebrities: The Intellectuals of Modern France*. London: Verso.

Dezalay, Yves, and Bryant G. Garth. 2002. *The Internationalization of Palace Wars: Lawyers, Economists, and the Contest to Transform Latin American States*. Chicago: University of Chicago Press.

DiMaggio, Paul, and Walter W. Powell. 1991. "Introduction." Pp. 1–38 in *The New Institutionalism in Organizational Analysis*, edited by Walter W. Powell and Paul DiMaggio. Chicago: University of Chicago Press.

Dobratz, Betty A., Timothy Buzzell, and Lisa K. Waldner, eds. 2002. *Sociological Views on Political Participation in the 21st Century*. New York: JAI.

Dobratz, Betty A., Lisa K. Waldner, and Timothy Buzzell, eds. 2001. *The Politics of Social Inequality*. Amsterdam; New York: JAI.

————, eds. 2003. *Political Sociology for the 21st Century*. Boston: JAI.

Dobry, Michel. 1986. *Sociologie des crises politiques*. Paris: Presses de la Foundation nationale des sciences politiques.

Dogan, Mattei, and John Higley. 1998. *Elites, Crises, and the Origins of Regimes*. Lanham, MD: Rowman and Littlefield.

Domhoff, G. William. 1967. *Who Rules America?* Englewood Cliffs, NJ: Prentice-Hall.

————. 1978. *The Powers That Be: Processes of Ruling Class Domination in America*. New York: Random House.

————. 1983. *Who Rules America Now?* Englewood Cliffs, NJ: Prentice-Hall.

————. 1990. *The Power Elite and the State: How Policy Is Made in America*. Social Institutions and Social Change. New York: Aldine De Gruyter.

————. 2001. *Who Rules America? Power and Politics*. 4th ed. New York: McGraw-Hill.

Du Bois, W. E. B. (1903) 1989. *Souls of Black Folk*. New York: Penguin Books.

Dulong, Delphine. 2010. *La construction du champ politique*. Rennes: Presses universitaires de Rennes.

Durkheim, Emile. 1958. *Professional Ethics and Civic Morality*. Glencoe, IL: Free Press.

———. 1966. *The Rules of Sociological Method*. New York: The Free Press.

———. 1992. *Professional Ethics and Civic Morals*. London: Routledge.

Duval, Julien, Christophe Gaubert, Frédéric Lebaron, Dominique Marchetti, and Fabienne Pavis. 1998. *Le "décembre" des intellectuels français*. Paris: Liber-Raisons D'Agir.

Dye, Thomas R., and L. Harmon Zeigler. 1978. *The Irony of Democracy*. 4th ed. North Scituate, MA: Duxbury.

Dye, Thomas R., Harmon Zeigler, and Louis Schubert. 2012. *The Irony of Democracy: An Uncommon Introduction to American Politics*. Boston: Wadsworth Publishing.

Eldersveld, Samuel J. 1989. *Political Elites in Modern Societies*. Ann Arbor: University of Michigan Press.

Elias, Norbert. 1978. *The History of Manners*. Vol. 1 of *The Civilizing Process*. New York: Pantheon Books.

———. 1982a. *Power and Civility*. Vol. 2 of *The Civilizing Process*. New York: Pantheon Books. Also published as *State Formation and Civilization*. Oxford: Basil Blackwell.

Emirbayer, Mustafa. 1997. "Manifesto for a Relational Sociology." *American Journal of Sociology* 103 (2): 281–317.

———. 2010. "Tilly and Bourdieu." *American Sociologist* 41(4): 400–22.

Emirbayer, Mustafa, and Victoria Johnson. 2008. "Bourdieu and Organizational Analysis." *Theory and Society* 37 (1): 1–44.

Eribon, Didier. 1991. *Michel Foucault*. Cambridge, MA: Harvard University Press.

Evans, Peter B., Dietrich Rueschemeyer, and Theda Skocpol, eds. 1985. *Bringing the State Back In*. New York: Cambridge University Press.

Eyal, Gil. 2000. "Anti-Politics and the Spirit of Capitalism: Dissidents, Monetarists and the Czech Transition to Capitalism." *Theory and Society* 29 (1): 49–92.

———. 2003. *The Origins of Postcommunist Elites: From the Prague Spring and the Breakup of Czechoslovakia*. Minneapolis: University of Minnesota Press.

———. 2005. "The Making and Breaking of the Czechoslovak Political Field." Pp. 151–77 in Wacquant 2005b.

Eyal, Gil, Ivan Szelenyi, and Eleanor Townsley. 1997. "The Theory of Post-Communist Managerialism: Elites and Classes in the Post-Communist Transformation." *New Left Review* 222 (March): 60–92.

———. 1998. *Making Capitalism without Capitalists: Class Formation and Elite Struggles in Post-Communist Central Europe*. New York: Verso.

———. 2001. "The Utopia of Post-socialist Theory and the Ironic View of History of Neo-classical Sociology: Response to Michael Burawoy." *American Journal of Sociology* 106 (4): 1121–28.

Fanon, Frantz. 1965. *A Dying Colonialism*. New York: Grove Press.

————. 1967. *Black Skins, White Masks*. New York: Grove Press.

————. 2004. *The Wretched of the Earth*. New York: Grove Press.

Faulks, Keith. 2000. *Political Sociology: A Critical Introduction*. New York: New York University Press.

Favre, Pierre, ed. 1990. *La Manifestation*. Paris: Presses de la Fondation Nationale des Sciences Politiques.

Feyerabend, Paul. 1978. *Science in a Free Society*. London: New Left Books.

Foucault, Michel. 1972. *The Archeology of Knowledge*. New York: Random House.

————. 1977. *Discipline and Punish: The Birth of the Prison*. New York: Pantheon.

————. 1980a. *Power/Knowledge: Selected Interviews and Other Writings, 1972–1977*, edited by Colin Gordon. New York: Pantheon Books.

————. 1980b. "Two Lectures" (1976). Pp. 78–108 in Foucault 1980a.

————. 1991. "Governmentality." Pp. 87–104 in *The Foucault Effect: Studies in Governmentality*, edited by Graham Burchell, Colin Gordon, and Peter Miller. Chicago: University of Chicago Press.

————. 1997. "Polemics, Politics and Problematization: An Interview." In *Ethics*, vol. 1 of *Essential Works of Foucault*, edited by Paul Rabinow and translated by Lydia Davis. New York: New Press.

Fournier, Marcel, and Lionel Vécin. 2009. "Pierre Bourdieu in Canada." *Sociologica* 1:1–15.

Friedman, Milton. 2002. *Capitalism and Freedom*. 40th anniversary edition. Chicago: University of Chicago Press.

Fritsch, Philippe. 2000. "Introduction." Pp. 7–31 in Bourdieu 2000f.

Gamson, William, with Charlotte Ryan. 2006. "The Art of Reframing Political Debates." *Contexts* 5 (1): 13–18.

Gans, Herbert. 2002. "More of Us Should Become Public Sociologists." *Footnotes* 30 (July/August): 10.

Garcia, Afrânio. 1993. *Droit, politique et espace agraire au Brésil*. Special issue of *Études rurales* 131–132 (July–December).

————. 2003. "Le Déracinement Brésilien." Pp. 305–9 in *Travailler avec Bourdieu*, edited by Pierre Encrevé and Rose-Marie Lagrave. Paris: Falmmarion.

————. 2004. "A dependência da política: Fernando Henrique Cardoso e a sociologia no Brasil." *Tempo Social* 16 (1): 285–300.

Garnham, Nicholas. 1986. "Extended Review: Bourdieu's 'Distinction.'" *Sociological Review* 34 (2): 423–33.

Garrigou, Alain. 1992. *Le Vote et la vertu. Comment les Français sont devenus électeurs*. Paris: Presses de la Fondation Nationale des Sciences Politiques.

Gaxie, Daniel. 1978. *Le Cens caché. Inégalités culturelles et ségrégation politique*. Paris: Seuil.

————. 1990. "Au-delà des apparences . . . , Sur quelques problèmes de mesure des opinions." *Actes de la Recherche en Sciences Sociales* 81 (2): 97–113.

Gemperle, Michael. 2009. "The Double Character of the German 'Bourdieu.'" *Sociologica* 1:1–33.

Giddens, Anthony. 1976. *New Rules of Sociological Method*. New York: Basic Books.

———. 1979. *Central Problems in Social Theory*. Berkeley: University of California Press.

———. 1987. *Social Theory and Modern Sociology*. Stanford, CA: Stanford University Press.

Gieryn, Thomas F. 1983. "Boundary-Work and the Demarcation of Science from Non-science: Strains and Interests in Professional Ideologies of Scientists." *American Sociological Review* 48 (6): 781–95.

Gilbert, G. Nigel, and Michael Mulkay. 1984. *Opening Pandora's Box: A Sociological Analysis of Scientists' Discourse*. Cambridge: Cambridge University Press.

Go, Julian. 2008. "Global Fields and Imperial Forms: Field Theory and the British and American Empires." *Sociological Theory* 26 (3): 201–29.

———. 2011. "Decolonizing Bourdieu: Colonial and Postcolonial Theory in Pierre Bourdieu's Early Work." Department of Sociology, Boston University.

Goffman, Erving. 1959. *The Presentation of Self in Everyday Life*. Garden City, NY: Doubleday Anchor Books.

———. 1986. *Stigma: Notes on the Management of Spoiled Identity*. New York: Touchstone.

Goldberg, Chad Alan. 2003. "Haunted by the Specter of Communism: Collective Identity and Resource Mobilization in the Demise of the Workers Alliance of America." *Theory and Society* 32 (5–6): 725–73.

Goldelier, Maurice. 1972. *Rationality and Irrationality in Economics*. London: NLB.

Goodman, Jane E., and Paul A. Silverstein, eds. 2009. *Bourdieu in Algeria: Colonial Politics, Ethnographic Practices, Theoretical Developments*. Lincoln: University of Nebraska Press.

Goodman, Nelson. 1978. *Ways of Worldmaking*. Indianapolis: Hackett Publishing.

Gorski, Philip S. 2003. *The Disciplinary Revolution: Calvinism and the Rise of the State in Early Modern Europe*. Chicago: University of Chicago Press.

———. Forthcoming. "Nation-ization Struggles: A Bourdieuian Theory of Nationalism." In *Bourdieusian Theory and Historical Analysis*, edited by Philip Gorski. Durham, NC: Duke University Press.

Gouldner, Alvin W. 1979. *The Future of Intellectuals and the Rise of the New Class*. New York: Oxford.

Grenfell, Michael. 2005. *Pierre Bourdieu: Agent Provocateur*. London: Continuum.

Gross, Neil, and Ethan Fosse. 2012. "Why Are Professors Liberal?" *Theory and Society* 2 (March): 127–86.

Gurr, Ted Robert. 1970 *Why Men Rebel*. Princeton, NJ: Princeton University Press.

Habermas, Jürgen. 1962. *The Structural Transformation of the Public Sphere: An Inquiry into a Category of Bourgeois Society*. Cambridge, MA: MIT Press.

———. 1992. "Une union sans valeurs." *Libre*, 16–17.

———. 1996. *Between Facts and Norms*. Cambridge, MA: MIT Press.

Halimi, Serge. 1995. "Les boîte à idées de la droite américaine." In *Le Monde diplomatique*, May.

———. 1997. *Les Nouveaux chiens de garde*. Paris: Raisons D'Agir Éditions.

Hechter, Michael. 1987. *Principles of Group Solidarity*. Berkeley: University of California Press.

Hedström, Peter. 1996. "Review of *Pathologies of Rational Choice Theory: A Critique of Applications in Political Science*." *Contemporary Sociology* 25 (2): 278–79.

Hicks, Alexander M., Thomas Janoski, and Mildred A. Schwartz. 2005. "Political Sociology in the New Millennium." Pp. 1–32 in *The Handbook of Political Sociology*, edited by Alexander M. Hicks, Thomas Janoski, and Mildred A. Schwartz. Cambridge: Cambridge University Press.

Hobbes, Thomas. (1668) 1994. *Leviathan*. Indianapolis: Hackett Publishing.

Honneth, Axel, Hermann Kocyba, and Bernd Schwibs. 1986. "The Struggle for Symbolic Order: An Interview with Pierre Bourdieu." *Theory, Culture, and Society* 3 (3): 35–51.

Hume, David. 1742. *Of the Original Contract*. Library of Economics and Liberty. http://www.econlib.org/library/LFBooks/Hume/hmMPL35.html (accessed May 12, 2012).

———. (1758) 1994. "Of the First Principles of Government." Pp. 16–19 in *Political Essays*, edited by K. Haakonssen. Cambridge: Cambridge University Press.

Inglehart, Ronald. 1997. *Modernization and Postmodernization: Cultural, Economic and Political Change in 43 Countries*. Princeton, NJ: Princeton University Press.

Jacoby, Russell. 1987. *The Last Intellectuals: American Culture in the Age of Academe*. New York: Basic Books.

Jenkins, J. Craig. 2000. "Political Sociology." Pp. 2162–68 in *Encyclopedia of Sociology*, edited by Edgar F. Borgatta, vol. 3. Detroit: Macmillan.

Jenkins, Richard. 1982. "Pierre Bourdieu and the Reproduction of Determinism." *Sociology* 16 (2): 270–81.

———. 2000. *Pierre Bourdieu*. Revised ed. London: Routledge.

Jessop, Bob. 1982. *The Capitalist State*. Oxford: Martin Robertson.

Kahneman, Daniel. 2000. *Choices, Values, and Frames*. New York: Cambridge University Press.

Kahneman, Daniel, and Amos Tversky. 1973. "On the Psychology of Prediction." *Psychological Review* 80:237–51.

Kalberg, Stephen, ed. 2005. *Max Weber: Readings and Commentary on Modernity*. Oxford: Blackwell.

Kauppi, Niilo. 1996. "European Union Institutions and French Political Careers."
    Scandinavian Political Studies 19 (1): 1–24.

———. 1999. "Power or Subjection? French Women Politicians in the European
    Parliament." *European Journal of Women's Studies* 6 (3): 331–42.

———. 2000. "La Construction de l'Europe: Le cas des élections européennes en
    Finlande 1999." *Cultures and Conflicts* 38/39:101–18.

———. 2004. "Bourdieu's Political Sociology and the Politics of European Integra-
    tion." Pp. 317–31 in *After Bourdieu: Influence, Critique, Elaboration*, edited by
    David L. Swartz and Vera Zolberg. Boston: Kluwer Academic Publishers.

Kimmerling, Baruch. 1996. "Changing Meanings and Boundaries of the 'Political.' "
    Current Sociology 44:152–76.

Knorr-Cetina, Karin. 1983. "The Ethnographic Study of Scientific Work: Towards
    a Constructivist Interpretation of Science." Pp. 115–40 in *Science Observed:
    Perspectives in the Social Study of Science*, edited by Karin Knorr-Cetina and
    Michael Mulkay. London: Sage.

Konrád, George. 1984. *Anti-Politics*. New York: Harcourt Brace Jovanovich.

Kornhauser, William. 1959. *The Politics of Mass Society*. New York: The Free
    Press.

Kourvetaris, George A. 1997. *Political Sociology: Structure and Process*. Boston:
    Allyn and Bacon.

Lacroix, Bernard, and Jacques Lagroye, eds. 1992. *Le Président de la République*.
    Paris: Presses de la Fondation Nationale des Sciences Politiques.

Ladd, Everett Carll, Jr., and Seymour Martin Lipset. 1976. *The Divided Academy:
    Professors and Politics*. New York: W. W. Norton.

Lagroye, Jacques. 2002. *Sociologie politique*. 4th ed. Paris: Presses de Sciences Po
    et Dalloz.

Lakoff, George. 2002. *Moral Politics: How Liberals and Conservatives Think*. 2nd
    ed. Chicago: University of Chicago Press.

Lakoff, George, and Mark Johnson. 2003. *Metaphors We Live By*. Chicago: Uni-
    versity of Chicago Press.

Lamont, Michèle. 1992. *Money, Morals, and Manners: The Culture of the French
    and the American Upper-Middle Class*. Chicago: University of Chicago
    Press.

Lamont, Michèle, and Marcel Fournier. 1992. *Cultivating Differences: Symbolic
    Boundaries and the Making of Inequality*. Chicago: University of Chicago
    Press.

Lamont, Michéle, and Vireg Molnar. 2002. "The Study of Boundaries in the Social
    Sciences." *Annual Review of Sociology* 28:167–95.

Lane, Jeremy F. 2000. *Pierre Bourdieu: A Critical Introduction*. Sterling, VA: Pluto
    Press.

———. 2006. *Bourdieu's Politics: Problems and Possibilities*. London: Routledge.

Lareau, Annette, and Elliot B. Weininger. 2004. "Cultural Capital in Educational
    Research: A Critical Assessment." Pp. 105–44 in *After Bourdieu: Influence, Cri-*

tique, Elaboration, edited by David L. Swartz and Vera L. Zolberg. Boston: Kluwer Academic Publishers.

Latour, Bruno. 1987. *Science in Action: How to Follow Scientists and Engineers through Society*. Milton Keynes: Open University Press.

———. 1988. *The Pasteurization of France*. Cambridge, MA: Harvard University Press.

Latour, Bruno, and Steve Woolgar. 1979. *Laboratory Life: The Social Construction of Scientific Facts*. London: Sage.

Laumann, Edwin O., and David Knoke. 1987. *The Organizational State*. Madison: University of Wisconsin Press.

Laurent, Vincent. 1998. "Enquête sur la fondation Saint-Simon. Les architectes du social-libéralisme." *Le Monde diplomatique*, September.

Le Sueur, James D. 2005. *Uncivil War. Intellectuals and Identity Politics during the Decolonization of Algeria*. Lincoln: University of Nebraska Press.

Lebaron, Frédéric. 2004. "Pierre Bourdieu: Economic Models Against Economism." Pp. 87–101 in *After Bourdieu: Influence, Critique, Elaboration*, edited by David L. Swartz and Vera L. Zolberg. Boston: Kluwer Academic Publishers.

Lee, Orville. 1998. "Culture and Democratic Theory: Toward a Theory of Symbolic Democracy." *Constellations* 5 (4): 433–55.

Leite Lopes, José Ségio. 1978. *Vapeur du diable: Le travail des ouvriers du sucre*. Rio de Janeiro: Éditions Paz e terra.

———. 2003. "Pierre Bourdieu et le renouveau des enquêtes ethnologiques et sociologiques au Brésil." *Awal Cahier d'Études Berbères* 27/28:169–78.

Lindblom, Charles E. 1977. *Politics and Markets: The World's Political-Economic Systems*. New York: Basic.

Lindenberg, Daniel. 1975. *Le Marxism Introuvable*. Paris: Calmann-Lévy.

Lipset, Seymour Martin. 1959. *Political Man: The Social Bases of Politics*. Garden City, NY: Doubleday.

Locke, John. (1690) 1980. *Second Treatise of Government*. Indianapolis: Hackett Publishing.

Loveman, Mara. 2005. "The Modern State and the Primitive Accumulation of Symbolic Capital." *American Journal of Sociology* 110 (6): 1651–83.

Loyal, Steven. 2009. "The French in Algeria, Algerians in France: Bourdieu, Colonialism, and Migration." *Sociological Review* 57 (3): 406–27.

Lukes, Steven. 2005. *Power: A Radical View*. 2nd ed. New York: Palgrave Macmillan.

Lynd, Robert S. (1939) 1986. *Knowledge for What? The Place of Social Science in American Culture*. Middletown, CT: Wesleyan University Press.

Mann, Michael. 1986. *The Sources of Social Power: A History of Power from the Beginning to A.D. 1760*. Cambridge: Cambridge University Press.

———. 1993. *The Sources of Social Power: The Rise of Classes and Nation-States, 1760–1914*. Cambridge: Cambridge University Press.

Mannheim, Karl. 1955. *Ideology and Utopia: An Introduction to the Sociology of Knowledge*. New York: Harcourt, Brace and World.

————. 1956. "The Problem of the Intelligentsia: An Enquiry into Its Part and Present Role." Pp. 91–170 in *Essays on the Sociology of Culture*. London: Routledge and Kegan Paul.

McAdam, Doug. 1982. *Political Process and the Development of Black Insurgency, 1930–1970*. Chicago: University of Chicago Press.

McAdam, Doug, Sidney Tarrow, and Charles Tilly. 2001. *Dynamics of Contention*. New York: Cambridge University Press.

Marx, Karl. 1977. *Capital*. New York: Vintage Books.

Mauger, Gérard. 1995. "L'Engagement sociologique." *Critique* 579/80:674–96.

————. 2004. "Résistances à la sociologie de Pierre Bourdieu." Pp. 369–91 in *Pierre Bourdieu, sociologue*, edited by Louis Pinto, Gisèle Sapiro, and Patrick Champagne. Paris: Fayard.

————. 2006. "Sur la violence symbolique." Pp. 84–100 in *Pierre Bourdieu, théorie et pratique. Perspectives franco-allemandes*, edited by Hans-Peter Müller and Yves Sintomer. Paris: La Découverte.

Medvetz, Thomas. 2009. "Les think tanks aux États-Unis: L'émergence d'un sous-espace de production des savoirs." *Actes de la Recherche en Sciences Sociales* 176/177:82–93.

Meillassoux, Claude. 1964. "Essai d'interprétation du phénomène économique dans les sociétés traditionnelles d'autosubsistance." *Cahiers d'études africaines* 4:38–67.

————. 1974. "Reproduction to Production: A Marxist Approach to Economic Anthropology." *Economy and Society* 1 (1): 93–105.

Merrien, François-Xavier. 1998. "Governance and Modern Welfare States." *International Social Science Journal* 50 (1): 57–67.

Meyer, John. 1980. "The World Polity and the Authority of the Nation-State." Pp. 109–37 in *Studies of the Modern World System*, edited by Albert Bergesen. New York: Academic Press.

————. 1999. "The Changing Cultural Content of the Nation-State: A World Society Perspective." Pp. 123–43 in Steinmetz 1999b.

Michels, Robert. 1962. *Political Parties*. New York: Free Press.

Miliband, Ralph. 1969. *The State in Capitalist Society*. New York: Basic.

Mills, C. Wright. 1959. *The Sociological Imagination*. New York: Oxford University Press.

————. 2000. *The Power Elite*. New York: Oxford University Press.

Mitchell, Timothy. 1991a. *Colonizing Egypt*. Berkeley: University of California Press.

————. 1991b. "The Limits of the State: Beyond Statist Approaches and Their Critics." *American Political Science Review* 85 (1): 77–96.

Morgenthau, Hans J. 1978. *Politics Among Nations: The Struggle for Power and Peace*. New York: Alfred A. Knopf.

Mounier, Pierre. 2001. *Pierre Bourdieu, une introduction*. Paris: Pocket/La Découverte.

Nash, Kate. 2000. *Contemporary Political Sociology. Globalization, Politics, and Power*. Oxford: Blackwell.

———. 2010. *Contemporary Political Sociology. Globalization, Politics, and Power*. 2nd ed. Oxford: Blackwell.

Nash, Kate, and Alan Scott, eds. 2004. *The Blackwell Companion to Political Sociology*. Oxford: Blackwell.

Neuman, W. Lawrence. 2005. *Power, State, and Society: An Introduction to Political Sociology*. New York: McGraw-Hill.

Neveu, Érik. 2005. *Sociologie des mouvements sociaux*. Paris: Éditions La Découverte.

Nichols, Lawrence T. 2007. *Public Sociology: The Contemporary Debate*. Piscataway, NJ: Transaction Publishers.

Nordlinger, Eric A. 1981. *On the Autonomy of the Democratic State*. Cambridge, MA: Harvard University Press.

O'Leary, Brendan. 2003. "Political Science." Pp. 749–56 in *The Social Science Encyclopedia*, Adam Kuper and Jessica Kuper. 3rd ed. New York: Routledge.

Offe, Claus. 1984. *Contradictions of the Welfare State*. London: Hutchinson.

Offerlé, Michel. 1987. *Les Partis politiques*. Paris: Presses Universitaires de France.

———. 1999. "Engagement sociologique: Pierre Bourdieu en politique." *Regards sur l'actualité*, 1–14.

Orum, Anthony M. 1989. *Introduction to Political Sociology: The Social Anatomy of the Body Politic*. 3rd ed. Englewood Cliffs, NJ: Prentice-Hall.

———. 1996. "Almost a Half Century of Political Sociology: Trends in the United States." *Current Sociology* 44 (3): 108–31.

Parsons, Talcott. 1960. "The Distribution of Power in American Society." In Parsons, *Structure and Process in Modern Societies*. New York: Free Press.

Pascal, Blaise. 1912. *Pensées et Opuscules*. Paris: Hachette.

Pels, Dick. 1995. "Knowledge Politics and Antipolitics: Toward a Critical Appraisal of Bourdieu's Concept of Intellectual Autonomy." *Theory and Society* 24:79–104.

Pinto, Louis. 1998. *Pierre Bourdieu et la théorie du monde social*. Paris: Albin Michel.

Portes, Alejandro. 1998. "Social Capital: Its Origins and Applications in Modern Sociology." *Annual Review of Sociology* 24:1–24.

Poulantzas, Nicos. 1973. *Political Power and Social Classes*. London: New Left Books.

———. 1975. *Classes in Contemporary Capitalism*. London: Verso.

Poupeau, Franck, and Thierry Discepolo. 2004. "Scholarship with Commitment: On the Political Engagements of Pierre Bourdieu." *Constellations* 11 (1): 76–96.

———. 2005. "Scholarship with Commitment: On the Political Engagements of Pierre Bourdieu" (2004). Pp. 64–90 in Wacquant 2005b.

Power, Michael. 2011. "Foucault and Sociology." *Annual Review of Sociology* 37:35–56.

Przeworski, Adam. 1985. *Capitalism and Social Democracy*. Cambridge: Cambridge University Press.

Pudal, Bernard. 1988. "Les dirigeants communistes. Du 'fils du peuple' à 'l'instituteur des masses.'" *Actes de la Recherche en Sciences Sociales* 71 (2): 46–70.

———. 1989. *Prendre parti. Pour une sociologie historique du PCF*. Paris: Presses de la Fondation Nationale des Sciences Politiques.

Putnam, Robert D. 1976. *The Comparative Study of Political Elites*. Englewood Cliffs, NJ: Prentice-Hall.

———. 1995. "Bowling Alone: America's Declining Social Capital." *Journal of Democracy* 6 (1): 65–78.

———. 2000. *Bowling Alone: The Collapse and Revival of American Community*. New York: Simon and Schuster.

Rey, Pierre-Philippe. 1971. *"Colonialisme, néo-colonialisme et transition au capitalisme," exemple de la Comilog au Congo-Brazzaville*. Paris: Maspero.

Robbins, Derek. 1991. *The Work of Pierre Bourdieu: Recognizing Society*. Boulder, CO: Westview Press.

Robertson, David Brian. 1993. "The Return to History and the New Institutionalism in American Political Science." *Social Science History* 17 (Spring): 1–36.

Rootes, Christopher A. 1996. "Political Sociology in Britain: Survey of the Literature and the Profession." *Current Sociology* 44 (Winter): 108–31.

Ross, George. 1987. "The Decline of the Left Intellectual in Modern France." Pp. 43–65 in *Intellectuals in Liberal Democracies: Political Influence and Social Involvement*, edited by Alain G. Gagnon. New York: Praeger.

Russell, Bertrand. 1938. *Power: A New Social Analysis*. London: Allen and Unwin.

Ryan, William 1971. *Blaming the Victim*. New York: Random House.

Sallaz, Jeffrey J., and Jane Zavisca. 2007. "Bourdieu in American Sociology, 1980–2004." *Annual Review of Sociology* 33:21–41.

Santoro, Marco. 2008a. "Putting Bourdieu in the Global Field: Introduction to the Symposium." *Sociologica* 2:1–32.

———. 2008b. "Symposium/The International Circulation of Sociological Ideas: The Case of Pierre Bourdieu." *Sociologica* 2. http://www.sociologica.mulino .it/journal/issue/index/Issue/Journal:ISSUE:5 (accessed May 12, 2012).

———. 2009a. "Symposium/The International Circulation of Sociological Ideas: The Case of Pierre Bourdieu, 2." *Sociologica* 1. http://www.sociologica.mulino .it/journal/issue/index/Issue/Journal:ISSUE:7 (accessed May 12, 2012).

———. 2009b. "Symposium/The International Circulation of Sociological Ideas: The Case of Pierre Bourdieu, 3." *Sociologica* 2/3. http://www.sociologica .mulino.it/journal/issue/index/Issue/Journal:ISSUE:8 (accessed May 12, 2012).

Sapiro, Gisèle, and Mauricio Bustamante. 2009. "Translation as a Measure of International Consecration. Mapping the World Distribution of Bourdieu's

Books in Translation." Pp. 1–45 in *Sociologica* 2–3:1–45. http://www.sociologica
.mulino.it /journal/article/index /Article /Journal:ARTICLE:340/Item/Journal:
ARTICLE:340 (accessed May 12, 2012).

Sayad, Abdelmalek. 2004. *The Suffering of the Immigrant*. Malden, MA: Polity.

Schultheis, Franz. 2007. *Bourdieus Wege in dee Soziologie. Genese und Dynamik
einer reflexiven Sozialwissenschaft*. Konstanz: UVK.

Schultheis, Franz, and Christine Frisinghelli, eds. 2012. *Picturing Algeria: Pierre
Bourdieu*. New York: Columbia University Press.

Schultz, Theodore W. 1961. "Investment in Human Capital." *American Economic
Review* 51 (March): 1–17.

———. 1963. *The Economic Value of Education*. New York: Columbia University
Press.

Schumpeter, Joseph A. 1975. *Capitalism, Socialism and Democracy*. 3rd ed. New
York: Harper and Row.

Scott, James C. 1985. *Weapons of the Weak: Everyday Forms of Peasant Resistance*.
New Haven, CT: Yale University Press.

———. 1990. *Domination and the Arts of Resistance: Hidden Transcripts*. New Haven, CT: Yale University Press.

Sennett, Richard, and Jonathan Cobb. 1972. *The Hidden Injuries of Class*. New
York: Random House.

Sewell, William H., Jr. 1992. "A Theory of Structure: Duality, Agency, and Transformation." *American Journal of Sociology* 98 (1): 1–29.

Skocpol, Theda. 1979. *States and Social Revolutions: A Comparative Analysis of
France, Russia, and China*. New York: Cambridge University Press.

———. 1981. "Political Response to Capitalist Crisis." *Politics and Society* 10:
155–201.

———. 1985. "Bringing the State Back In: Strategies of Analysis in Current Research." Pp. 3–43 in Evans, Rueschemeyer, and Skocpol 1985.

———. 1992. *Protecting Soldiers and Mothers: The Political Origins of Social Policy
in the United States*. Cambridge, MA: Belknap of Harvard University Press.

Skocpol, Theda, and Edwin Amenta. 1986. "States and Social Policies." *Annual
Review of Sociology* 12:131–57.

Skocpol, Theda, and John L. Campbell, eds. 1995. *American Society and Politics*.
New York: McGraw-Hill.

Somers, Margaret R. 2008. *Genealogies of Citizenship: Markets, Statelessness, and
the Right to Have Rights*. Cambridge: Cambridge University Press.

Stark, David, and László Bruszt. 1998. *Postsocialist Pathways: Transforming Politics
and Property in East Central Europe*. Cambridge: Cambridge University Press.

Steinmetz, George. 1993. *Regulating the Social: The Welfare State and Local Politics in Imperial Germany*. Princeton, NJ: Princeton University Press.

———. 1999a. "Introduction: Culture and the State." Pp. 1–49 in Steinmetz
1999b.

———, ed. 1999b. *State/Culture: State-Formation after the Cultural Turn*. Ithaca, NY: Cornell University Press.

———. 2007. *The Devil's Handwriting: Precoloniality and the German Colonial State in Quingdao, Samoa, and Southwest Africa*. Chicago: University of Chicago Press.

Stoker, Gerry. 1998. "Governance as Theory: Five Propositions." *International Social Science Journal* 50 (1): 17–28.

Swartz, David. 1977. "Pierre Bourdieu: The Cultural Transmission of Social Inequality." *Harvard Educational Review* 47 (November): 545–54.

———. 1986. "French Corporate Leadership: A Class-Based Technocracy." *Research in Political Sociology* 2:49–78.

———. 1997. *Culture and Power: The Sociology of Pierre Bourdieu*. Chicago: University of Chicago Press.

———. 1998. "Universalism and Parochialism: How Gouldner and Bourdieu Understand the Interests of Intellectuals." Presented at the annual meeting of the American Sociological Association, San Francisco.

———. 2002. "The Sociology of Habit: The Perspective of Pierre Bourdieu." *Occupational Therapy Journal of Research* 22 (1): 61S–69S.

———. 2003a. "From Critical Sociology to Public Intellectual: Pierre Bourdieu and Politics." *Theory and Society* 32 (5–6): 791–823.

———. 2003b. "Pierre Bourdieu's Political Sociology and Governance Perspectives." Pp. 140–58 in Bang 2003.

———. 2004. "Le sociologue critique et l'intellectuel public." Pp. 393–411 in *Pierre Bourdieu, sociologue*, edited by Louis Pinto, Gisèle Sapiro, and Patrick Champagne. Paris: Fayard.

———. 2005. "Le capital culturel dans la sociologie de l'éducation américaine." Pp. 453–65 in *Rencontres avec Pierre Bourdieu*, edited by Gérard Mauger. Bellecombe-en-Bauges: Éditions du Croquant.

———. 2006. "Pierre Bourdieu and North American Political Sociology: Why He Doesn't Fit In but Should." *French Politics* 4:84–89.

———. 2010. "Sociologia e politica: Le forme dell'impegno politico di Bourdieu." Pp. 54–82 in *Bourdieu dopo Bourdieu*, edited by Gabriella Paolucci. Novara: UTET.

———. 2012. "Zu einer Bourdieu'schen Analyse der Politik." In *Feldanalyse als Forschungsprogramm 1: Der programmatische Kern*, edited by Stefan Bernhard and Christian Schmidt-Wellenburg. Wiesbaden: VS.

Swidler, Ann. 1986. "Culture in Action: Symbols and Strategies." *American Sociological Review* 51:273–86.

Tarrow, Sidney. 1996. "States and Opportunities: The Political Structuring of Social Movements." Pp. 41–61 in *Comparative Perspectives on Social Movements*, edited by Douglas McAdam. New York: Cambridge University Press.

———. 1998. *Power in Movement: Social Movements and Contentious Politics*. 2nd ed. New York: Cambridge University Press.

Terray, Emmanuel. 1969. *Le marxisme devant les sociétés "primitives": Deux études*. Paris: Éditions Maspero.

———. 1996. "Réflexions sur la violence symbolique." Pp. 11–25 in *Actuel Marx, n° 20, Autour de Bourdieu*. Paris: Presses Universitaires de France.

Therborn, Göran. 1978. *What Does the Ruling Class Do When It Rules? State Apparatuses and State Power under Feudalism, Capitalism and Socialism*. London: NLB.

Thompson, John B. 1984. "Symbolic Violence: Language and Power in the Sociology of Pierre Bourdieu." Pp. 42–72 in *Studies in the Theory of Ideology*. Cambridge: Polity Press.

———. 1991. "Editor's Introduction." Pp. 1–31 in Bourdieu 1991e.

Tiles, Mary. 1984. *Bachelard: Science and Objectivity*. New York: Cambridge University Press.

Tilly, Charles. 1975. *The Formation of National States in Western Europe*. Princeton, NJ: Princeton University Press.

———. 1978. *From Mobalization to Revolution*. Reading, MA: Addison-Wesley.

———. 1991. "Domination, Resistance, Compliance . . . Discourse." *Sociological Forum* 6 (3): 593–602.

———. 1992. *Coercion, Capital, and European States, AD 990–1992*. Cambridge: Blackwell.

———. 1999 "Epilogue: Now Where?" Pp. 407–19 in Steinmetz 1999b.

———. 2008. *Contentious Performances*. New York: Cambridge University Press.

Tilly, Charles, and Sidney Tarrow. 2007. *Contentious Politics*. Boulder, CO: Paradigm Publishers.

Topper, Keith. 2001. "Not So Trifling Nuances: Pierre Bourdieu, Symbolic Violence, and the Perversions of Democracy." *Constellations* 8 (1): 30–56.

Torpey, John. 2000. *The Invention of the Passport: Surveillance, Citizenship and the State*. Cambridge: Cambridge University Press.

Touraine, Alain. 1968. *Le Mouvement de Mai ou le communisme utopique*. Paris: Seuil.

———. 1981 *The Voice and the Eye: An Analysis of Social Movements*. Cambridge: Cambridge University Press.

———. 1985. "An Introduction to the Study of Social Movements." *Social Research* 52 (4): 749–87.

Tucker, Robert C. 1978. *The Marx-Engels Reader*. 2nd ed. New York: W. W. Norton.

Useem, Michael. 1984. *The Inner Circle: Large Corporations and the Rise of Political Activity in the U.S. and U.K.* New York: Oxford University Press.

Van den Berg, Axel, and Thomas Janoski. 2005. "Conflict Theories in Political Sociology." Pp. 72–95 in *The Handbook of Political Sociology*, edited by Alexander M. Hicks, Thomas Janoski, and Mildred A. Schwartz. Cambridge: Cambridge University Press.

Verdès-Leroux, Jeannine. 2001. *Deconstructing Pierre Bourdieu: Against Sociological Terrorism from the Left*. New York: Algora.

Vester, Michael. 2003. "Class and Culture in Germany." *Sociologia, Problemas e Práticas* 42:25–64.

Vester, Michael, Peter Von Oertzen, Heiko Geiling, Thomas Hermann, and Dagmar Mueller. 1993. *Soziale Milieus im Gesellschaftlichen Strukturwandel: Zwischen Integration und Ausgrenzung.* Frankfurt: Aufl.

———. 2001. *Soziale Milieus im Gesellschaftlichen Strukturwandel: Zwishen Integration und Ausgrenzung.* Frankfurt: Aufl.

Vidal-Naquet, Pierre. 1986. "Une fidélité têtue. La résistance Française à la guerre d'Algérie." *Vingtième Siècle: Revue d'histoire* 10:3–18.

Voutat, Bernard. 2002. "L'analyse politique dans la sociologie de Pierre Bourdieu. Quelques aspects introductifs." *Swiss Political Science Review* 8 (2): 101–50.

Wacquant, Loïc. 1992a. "The Structure and Logic of Bourdieu's Sociology." Pp. 2–59 in Bourdieu and Wacquant 1992.

———. 1992b. "Toward a Social Praxeology: The Structure and Logic of Bourdieu's Sociology." Pp. 2–59 in in Bourdieu and Wacquant 1992.

———. 1993a. "Bourdieu in America: Notes on the Transatlantic Importation of Social Theory." Pp. 235–62 in *Bourdieu: Critical Perspectives*, edited by Craig Calhoun, Edward LiPuma, and Moishe Postone. Chicago: University of Chicago Press.

———. 1993b. "From Ruling Class to Field of Power: An Interview with Pierre Bourdieu on *La noblesse d'Etat.*" *Theory, Culture, and Society* 10 (3): 19–44.

———. 2002. "The Sociological Life of Pierre Bourdieu." *International Sociology* 17 (4): 549–56.

———. 2003. *Body and Soul: Notes of an Apprentice Boxer.* New York: Oxford University Press.

———. 2004. "Pointers on Pierre Bourdieu and Democratic Politics." *Constellations* 11 (1): 3–15.

———. 2005a. "Introduction: Symbolic Power and Democratic Practice." Pp. 1–9 in Wacquant 2005b.

———, ed. 2005b. *Pierre Bourdieu and Democratic Politics: The Mystery of Ministry.* Cambridge: Polity.

———. 2005c. "Pointers on Pierre Bourdieu and Democratic Politics." Pp. 10–28 in Wacquant 2005b.

———. 2009a. *Prisons of Poverty.* Minneapolis: University of Minnesota Press.

———. 2009b. *Punishing the Poor: The Neoliberal Government of Social Insecurity.* Durham, NC: Duke University Press.

Waldner, Lisa K, Timothy Buzzell, and Betty A Dobratz. 2002. "Introduction: Theoretical Directions in Political Sociology for the 21st Century." Pp. xiii–xvi in *Theoretical Directions in Political Sociology for the 21st Century*, edited by Betty A. Dobratz, Timothy Buzzell, and Lisa K. Waldner. Research in Political Sociology 11. Oxford: Elsevier Science.

Wallerstein, Immanuel. 2004. *World-System Analysis: An Introduction.* Durham, NC: Duke University Press.

Weber, Max. (1915) 1970. "Religious Rejections of the World and Their Directions." Pp. 323–59 in *From Max Weber*, edited by H. H. Gerth and C. Wright Mills. London: Routledge and Kegan Paul.

———. 1970. "Science as a Vocation." Pp. 129–56 in *From Max Weber*, edited by H. H. Gerth and C. Wright Mills. London: Routledge and Kegan Paul.

———. 1978a. "The Distribution of Power Within the Political Community: Class, Status, Party." Pp. 926–40 in *Economy and Society: An Outline of Interpretative Sociology*, edited by Guenther Roth and Claus Wittich. Berkeley: University of California Press.

———. 1978b. *Economy and Society*. Berkeley: University of California Press.

Wedeen, Lisa. 2002. "Conceptualizing Culture: Possibilities for Political Science." *American Political Science Review* 96 (4): 713–28.

Weir, Margaret, and Theda Skocpol. 1985. "State Structures and the Possibilities for 'Keynesian' Responses to the Great Depression in Sweden, Britain and the United States." Pp. 107–64 in Evans, Rueschemeyer, and Skocpol 1985.

Western, Bruce. 2006. *Punishment and Inequality in America*. New York: Russell Sage Foundation.

Wilkinson, Richard, and Kate Pickett. 2009. *The Spirit Level: Why Greater Equality Makes Societies Stronger*. New York: Bloomsbury Press.

Woolgar, Steve, ed. 1988a. *Knowledge and Reflexivity: New Frontiers in the Sociology of Knowledge*. London: Sage.

———. 1988b. *Science: The Very Idea*. London: Tavistock.

Wrong, Dennis. 1995. *Power: Its Forms, Bases, and Uses*. London: Transaction Publishers.

Yacine, Tassadit. 1993. *Les voleurs de feu. éléments d'une anthropologie sociale et culturelle de l'algérie*. Paris: Éditions La Découverte.

———. 2003. "L'Algérie, matrice d'une œuvre." Pp. 333–45 in *Travailler avec Bourdieu*, edited by Pierre Encrevé and Rose-Marie Lagrave. Paris: Flammarion.

———. 2008a. "Aux origines d'une ethnosociologie singulière." Pp. 21–53 in Yacine 2008b.

———, ed. 2008b. *Pierre Bourdieu. Esquisses algériennes*. Paris: Seuil.

Zeitlin, Maurice. 1974. "Corporate Ownership and Control: The Large Corporation and the Capitalist Class." *American Journal of Sociology* 70:1073–1119.

———. 1980. "On Classes, Class Conflict, and the State: An Introductory Note." In *Classes, Class Conflict and the State: Empirical Studies in Class Analysis*, edited by Maurice Zeitlin. Cambridge, MA: Winthrop.

Zimmermann, Ann, and Adrian Favell. 2011. "Governmentality, Political Field or Public Sphere? Theoretical Alternatives in the Political Sociology of the EU." *European Journal of Social Theory* 14 (4): 489–515.

Name Index

Subject Index